Down on Mahans Creek

Ozarks Studies

EDITED BY BROOKS BLEVINS

Down on Mahans Creek

A History of an Ozarks Neighborhood

Benjamin G. Rader

The University of Arkansas Press
Fayetteville
2017

21   20   19   18   17   5   4   3   2   1

Designed by Liz Lester

⊗ The paper used in this publication meets the minimum requirements
of the American National Standard for Permanence of Paper
for Printed Library Materials Z39.48-1984.

Library of Congress Control Number: 2016954397

CONTENTS

SERIES EDITOR'S PREFACE

What politician wouldn't die for Benjamin G. Rader's origin story? Born in one of the most remote places in a region renowned for its remoteness. First ten years of life lived in a log cabin. It may have been better served for someone in the public's eye, but being raised in a log cabin wasn't totally wasted on a historian, as this book proves. Retirement's another thing Ben has had no interest in wasting. Some people prune rose bushes, others go RV'ing. Esteemed historians sometimes craft unique studies that deepen our understanding of family, region, and the human condition.

I can think of no better work to launch our Ozarks Studies series than *Down on Mahans Creek*. Placing the Ozarks within the broader context of the Upland South, it is at once a meticulously researched community study, a model for crafting scholarly yet accessible family history, and an insightful examination of popularly held assumptions about the people who called the rural Ozarks home in the nineteenth and early twentieth centuries. It is a book that places region and the perception of region front and center, without becoming too esoteric and without ignoring the larger questions that any good topic always poses.

My institution and Ben's alma mater, Missouri State University, has long carried a torch for Shannon County, Missouri, the location of Mahans Creek. A collaborative project in the late 1970s and early 1980s produced two documentary films based almost exclusively on footage recorded in the county, one of the poorest in the state and perhaps the most remote and undeveloped. The same project spawned historical studies, oral histories, and multimedia presentations, such as *Sassafras: An Ozarks Odyssey*. The documentaries—especially the beautiful, stirring, and award-winning first one, *Shannon County: Home*—

manage to evoke the spirit of a preindustrial, Arcadian existence even as they deal with a heritage that includes a massive logging and lumber boom in the early 1900s. Shannon County is the kind of place that tends to heighten our sense of nostalgia. It's the kind of place that comes nearer to satisfying our preconceptions of the Ozarks than just about any other place you can visit.

Thus, *Down on Mahans Creek* serves as the perfect antidote to the brain-altering substances that generate nostalgia—or are generated by it. Which is not to suggest that Ben Rader, or any historian for that matter, is immune to the powerful drug of sepia-toned memory. As a child of Mahans Creek, whose family left for better opportunities and greener pastures elsewhere, Ben's attachment to the idea of the place is undoubtedly strong and influenced his understanding of his family's and his region's past throughout his lifetime. But, as both an insider and outsider (someone who grew up both in and out of the community) and a professional historian, he is able to dig beneath the surface of the story, to separate folklore from fact and image from reality. Leveling the clear-eyed gaze of the historian on his family's history and community, Ben Rader shows us a people and place shorn of romanticism but not stripped of vitality and occasional peculiarity. If all you know about Shannon County and the rest of the rural Ozarks is what you've seen on *Shannon County: Home* or what you've read in glossy travel magazines and books of tall tales, then you may be surprised at the lives and times revealed in these pages. Not bad for a little retirement project.

Brooks Blevins

PREFACE

My Journey into Ozarks History

In 1933, my grandfather Edward Martin "Sam" Rader let family members unfamiliar with his ways know who he was. "I live in the backwoods, and I love the women," he wrote in the family's monthly newsletter.[1] He loved women, in general, but he had a favorite, Ada May Pummill, whom he had married in 1896. Ada enthralled him with her long, black hair, her haunting eyes, her wit, and her good humor. And he loved the backwoods of the Missouri Ozarks, especially Mahans Creek with its spawning yellow suckers and its swimming holes of cold, clear water. Sam relished the cornbread that Ada baked to a golden brown in a greased cast-iron skillet. And he loved his hounds, in particular, Caruso, whose voice when echoing up and down the hollows reminded him of the great Italian tenor whom he had heard sing on the family's Victrola. Sam may have lived in what he described as the backwoods, but he was not unfamiliar with ways of the outside world.

For seventeen years, Sam had the good fortune of enjoying all of his loves at once, but in 1913 Ada died. He not only lost his mate but suddenly faced the prospect of rearing seven children alone. He sank into a deep "melancholia." He needed a new wife and, after an appropriate period of mourning, set about looking for one. He learned of a winsome widow who lived in the nearby town of Winona. They seemed a good match since Sam offered her a home—he owned a pretty good farm on Mahans Creek—and she even liked Sam's rambunctious children. But when Sam proposed marriage, she made an unexpected demand. She told him he had either to choose her or his hounds. Sam chose the hounds.

Fundamentally, *Down on Mahans Creek* is an effort to understand why Sam elected to keep his hounds rather than wed the Winona widow. Of course, it may be that his decision sprang from specifics regarding him or the widow (whose name has been lost to history) that have not survived, but a full understanding of his choice requires a scrutiny into the history of the ways of his neighborhood and his family. Hence, in this book I try to reconstruct the fundamental customs, beliefs, and behaviors that governed the lives of the families residing on the Mahans Creek watershed of the Missouri Ozarks from its settlement in the nineteenth century to the mid-twentieth century. Families are of key importance to the story. In 1931, the *Current Wave*, the weekly published in Eminence, Missouri, a town near Sam's farm, put the point this way: "Family life is a powerful force in the hills and has a great influence in shaping the morals and manners and customs of a people who have their feet deeply set in the soil."[2]

I began this enquiry with an excess of confidence. While I had had no formal training in Ozarks history, I had done some reading in the subject, and, above all else, I counted on the knowledge that I had garnered from my firsthand experience. After all, I had been born on Mahans Creek and had lived there in a log cabin for the first ten years of my life. Plowing ahead with unrestrained hubris, I early on embraced the conclusion that the families resident in the Mahans Creek neighborhood were latter-day representatives of the Scots Irish (usually called Scotch Irish in America) who had migrated to America mostly in the eighteenth century. Put slightly differently, my central idea—alas, not an original one—was that modern Ozarks folkways had direct origins in Northern Ireland and Scotland and had changed little over the centuries since then.[3] Bluntly speaking, then, Sam's decision reflected the continuity of his family culture from the mists of eighteenth-century British history to the early twentieth-century Ozarks.

I also thought I knew why the traditional folkways displayed such an astonishing persistence. It was the physical habitat of the settlers, I reasoned. For more than a century, the deep hollows and the dense woods had shielded the settlers from outside influences. Given this predisposition, imagine my delight when shortly after beginning research for this book I ran across the following phrase in an obscure Missouri county directory compiled in 1915. Due to their unique terrain, the settlers in Osage County, Missouri, wrote C. J. Vaughn, "were jealous of any invasion that threatened established custom."[4]

But, as I dug into the subject, nagging doubts began to surface. Partly, it was a matter of thinking more deeply. For example, I soon recognized that there was not much in my own experience that confirmed the importance of Scots Irish ethnicity to Ozarks folkways. I never remembered any of my kinfolk talking about being Scots Irish. Indeed, much later—not to mention that the Rader surname is of German origin—it dawned on me that the singular instance of a recollection of the possible significance of ethnicity in the family's history was not Scots Irish but Irish! On occasion, my father regaled us children with the oddity that our great-great-grandmother—Mary Hare—was of Irish Catholic origins. Unlike more recent immigrants in the United States, as far as I knew, no long-term residents of the Ozarks saw their identities cloaked primarily in their ethnic origins. I also eventually learned that there was probably more English ancestry in my own family than there was Scots Irish.

And partly my reassessment was a matter of discovering the recent findings of other students of Ozarks' history and culture. In particular, Brooks Blevins, the Noel Boyd Professor of Ozark Studies at Missouri State University, contributed to my rethinking.[5] (I also owe Brooks an enormous debt for his careful readings and critiques of this entire manuscript as well as for the title for this book.) From him and other scholars, I learned that much of my conceptual baggage about the Ozarks arose from stereotypes, especially the idea of the hillbilly. In short, I had accepted too uncritically the notions of the region developed by the popular culture and not infrequently fostered by the Ozarks people themselves.

Research in the primary sources contributed equally to my reconsideration. I soon found evidence that family cultures in the Ozarks were far more complex than the stereotype offered by the Clampetts in *The Beverly Hillbillies* or that prevalent among some scholars.[6] For example, I had long known that we Raders admired the Pummill side of our family, which suggested nothing so much as the elemental fact that not all families shared the same folkways. Research into the history of the two families offered me some vital clues as to why we esteemed the Pummills. Both families had lived for several generations in the cultural region that may be labeled as the Upland South, but only one of them was a product of the heartland of this region.[7] That was the Rader and Childress side of the family. The Raders and the Childresses had migrated from Philadelphia down into Virginia, across the mountains, eventually to Hart County, Kentucky, and then in 1878 to the Mahans Creek neighborhood of Shannon County, Missouri. Still, while most of the menfolk in the family held broadly shared attitudes toward work, leisure, and society, I found that the Raders' and the Childresses' ways were far from simple; they actually consisted of a weaving together of three distinctive strands of family cultures found in nineteenth-century Hart County.

Neither were the ways of the Pummills and the Matthewses side of the family homogeneous. The Pummills lived for several generations on the periphery or the "borderlands" of the Upland South—in Highland County, Ohio, and Osage County, Missouri—before arriving in Shannon County in 1892. As with the Childresses and the Raders, the Matthewses too migrated across the heartland of the Upland South, but, unlike them, their family tree is replete with preachers and teachers. Both the Matthews and Pummill families were ambitious, hard-working, civic-minded, and lovers of learning. In key respects, their ways were closer to those of the Yankees to the North than were those of the Raders and the Childresses. If the issue was one of trading two dogs for two pigs, my uncle Gilbert Rader once quipped, the Raders would opt to keep the dogs while the Pummills would choose the pigs.[8]

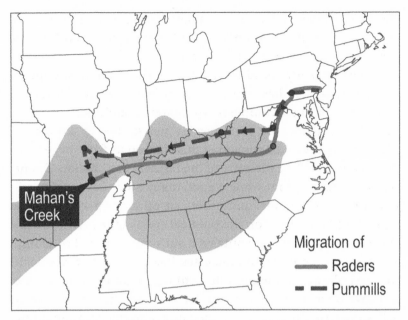

Migration of Rader and Pummill Families across the Upland South to Mahans Creek, Missouri. The shaded area represents the approximate boundaries of the Upland South. *Courtesy of Katie Nieland.*

By way of another confession, I learned during my journey into Ozarks history that I needed to reexamine the premise that men were the main if not the sole agents in determining the history of the peoples in the Upland South.[9] Not only did I discover a growing scholarship on the role of women in the region and that the Rader-Pummill women frequently contributed to and made specific decisions critical to the welfare of their families, but also that, while participants in a broadly common culture, values and behaviors within families often divided along gender lines. Most obviously, for example, men and women rarely shared the same enthusiasm for hunting and fishing. For the most part women were more concerned than men with order and stability within both the family and the neighborhood. No single documentation of differences in gender ways is clearer than the fact that women tended to participate in the religious life of the hollow neighborhoods with far more alacrity than did the men. Finally, I found that many Ozarks women welcomed modern ways of consumption and leisure with an enthusiasm that frequently exceeded that of the men.

I changed my mind about yet another common conception of these families: that, comparatively speaking, they led isolated lives unencumbered by material ambition. In 1895 the *Current Wave,* the local weekly newspaper of Eminence, Missouri, expressed a version of this view on its front page when it declared that "the majority of the farmers in Shannon County do not farm for profit while a good many more farm with a rifle and a pack of hounds, and others sit on a dry goods box and whittle and comment on the political status of the day."[10] While this sweeping assertion contains a substantial kernel of truth, I learned that, contrary to much that has been written about the lives of hollows families, few of them were without some drive to improve their material lots and that they were never completely self-sufficient. They sold or traded furs, ginseng, and sometimes farm animals for necessities such as salt, condiments, and farm equipment. The local merchants who usually provided these goods frequently obtained them from distant points.

Furthermore, the physical isolation of the settlers did not necessarily equate with them having little to do with "outsiders" or with one another. Not only did locals themselves frequently move back and forth from the creek to other places, large numbers of newcomers (sometimes more than 70 percent within a single decade) regularly arrived on the creek. Despite imposing physical barriers, from the earliest times they visited one another regularly, formed kinship networks, developed a local folk culture, and eventually founded schools and churches.

✦ ✦ ✦

Still, while the families on Mahans Creek were not infused with distinctive qualities springing from their origins in the British Isles, nor were they, strictly speaking, bastions of premodern folkways, they were residents of a specific subregion within the Ozarks, a region in which the rugged terrain did affect many

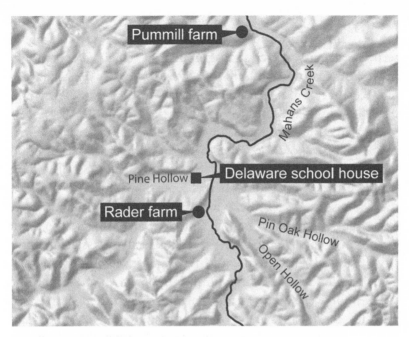

Relief map of Mahans Creek waterway. *Courtesy of Katie Nieland.*

aspects of their daily existence.[11] No mountains as imposing
as the Blue Ridge exist there, but, as my elderly cousin Arch
Pummill reminded me in 2014, the part of Shannon County
in which the creek is located is an area of exceptionally "deep
hollers." Shannon County has 329 places officially called hollows, more than any other single county in the United States.
Something of the significance of terrain to the early settlers can
be gathered from their inclination to give every stream, knob,
hollow, cave, spring, and set of hills a name; in short, as one
student of Ozark life has put it, "Every nook and cranny had its
name."[12] As a generic term to describe the inhabitants of this
rough terrain, I frequently employ the words "hollers people."

At the center of much of this story is the Mahans Creek basin
itself. Because of its relative isolation and physical ruggedness,
settlers arrived there later and in fewer numbers than in other
parts of the Ozarks. Shannon did not officially become a county
until 1841, twenty years after Missouri had joined the Union as

a state. Until the arrival of the timber boom in the 1890s, thousands of the county's acreage remained in the public domain. In terms of density, the county's population remained sparse. For most of its history, high rates of poverty were also a stark fact of life. Except for an interlude during the timber boom, few counties in the United States were poorer than Shannon.[13]

Yet, in addition to its clear, cold water and its annual bounty of spawning yellow suckers, the surrounding hillsides and hollows of the Mahans Creek waterway furnished an abundant supply of wood for cabins, barns, fences, and fuel. All of these, the early settlers assumed, were indicators of a place highly favorable to human habitation. But, alas, the trees and the water were something like the bare-breasted sirens of classical mythology that lured sailors to their deaths by their seeming availability and their seductive singing. Only small patches of land on the creek floor were suitable for growing corn, the all-important crop for the local farmers. And even that soil was sandy and porous. For a good yield it required steady rains throughout the growing season.

Differences in the terrain within the creek waterway, I discovered, frequently served as an indicator of a family's material circumstances. While none of the settlers became wealthy by national standards, soon a few of the families acquired considerably more wealth than their neighbors. Those living on the better bottomland along Mahans Creek, I term "creek-bottom" families, though they constituted a tiny minority of all of those living near the banks of the creek. Most of those living on the waterway itself were of modest means, and, indeed, some were impoverished.

At the other end of the social spectrum were those that I have labeled as the "branch-water" families.[14] They lived up the narrow hollows alongside spring branches. At best they had only a tiny patch of ground for a garden and perhaps a few acres for a corn patch. The upshot was that for decade after decade, faced with utter ruin, many branch-water families, along with the poorer families on the creek itself, had no choice but to leave the Mahans Creek basin in quest of opportunities elsewhere.

But almost always other families heard of the bountiful woods and the clear water streams and came in to take their places. While recognizing the gross disparities of wealth among families within the Mahans Creek neighborhood throughout its history, I use the term "hollers people" broadly to describe all those residents on the waterway.

As an agency propelling the creek families into modern life, nothing quite equaled the arrival of the railroad in 1893 at the Jim Rader farm on Mahans Creek. The railroad figuratively flattened the otherwise rugged terrain and brought with it the timber boom, which entailed the harvesting of the area's abundant short-leaf, yellow pine. With the railroad and the timber industry's introduction of a predominately cash-centered economy, self-sufficiency and bartering shrank in importance. Growing numbers of the local residents participated in the nation's new consumer bonanza. In their houses and their home furnishings, in their courtships, and in their celebration of holidays, the better-off families began to imitate more closely their middle-class counterparts elsewhere in the United States. Finally, the timber boom helped to trigger a great religious awakening in the Mahans Creek neighborhood. Perhaps no single fact suggests the neighborhood's surge into modernity more than that my great uncle, Elva Pummill, who as a machine operator in the hub mill plant in West Eminence received in 1912 a majority of the votes in the neighborhood (the Delaware Township) as the Socialist candidate for the Missouri assembly.[15] Even Mahans Creek was not immune to the great changes transforming America.

Beginning in the mid-1910s, with the end of the timber boom and falling farm prices, Shannon County and the Mahans Creek neighborhood fell into a protracted economic contraction. In coping with a return to hard times, most of those families remaining on the creek waterway selectively seized on both the old and the new. They kept intact as long as they could their three one-room schools and their two churches, and they even found emotional comfort, as Sam Rader put it, in their identity as a "backwoods" people. Along the same lines, writing this history brought back a memory that is suggestive. While students at Southwest Missouri State College in the late 1950s, I and a group of other Shannon County boys formed an intramural basketball team that we named "The Ridge Runners." Still, even in the midst of the depression, families on Mahans Creek purchased cars, radios, and, even later, television sets and cell phones. Indeed, with the closing of their local schools and churches and with many of them taking jobs in nearby towns, most of the families experienced an increasing reorientation of their daily lives from the countryside to Eminence, Winona, and Birch Tree. In key respects, their lives continued to resemble Americans, especially those living in rural areas, everywhere.

As for Sam Rader, until the very end, he loved Mahans Creek, women, watermelons, cornbread, and his hounds. In 1950, at the age of seventy-six, before dawn, he rode out alone with his hounds to coon hunt. While picking his way down an exceptionally steep ridge into Al Honeycutt Hollow, "Old Rock," his normally reliable saddle horse, either stumbled or bucked, throwing him to the ground and breaking his hip. Old Rock proceeded home without him. Despite excruciating pain, Sam somehow managed to blow his cow horn. Hearing its lonely wail far down the creek, his son, Hulbert, eventually found him. Rushed first in the back of a neighbor's pickup truck to a hospital forty miles away in West Plains, Missouri, and then later taken by ambulance a hundred miles away to Springfield, Missouri, Sam somehow survived the painful ordeal. After what seemed to be a partial recovery, he accepted an invitation to fly for the first time in his life—from Kansas City to far-off San Francisco— where he was to visit his youngest son, daughter-in-law, and grandson. Less than two days after his arrival in California, a heart attack killed him.

This book begins with a prologue describing the magic of Mahans Creek. It seeks to provide a picture of the creek basin's power in shaping the lives of its inhabitants. What follows is four parts. The first two, entitled "Their Kentucky Homeland" and "Settling on Mahans Creek," treat the origins of the Rader and Pummill families and their experience in living in the fun-

damentally agricultural societies found in nineteenth-century
Hart County, Kentucky, Highland County, Ohio, and Osage
and Shannon Counties in Missouri. These parts seek to sort
out and explain differences in family cultures within the Upland
South. The third and fourth parts, entitled "'The Scream of
the Sawmill'" and "When in Places Even the Creek Went Dry,"
begin in the 1890s and conclude in the 1950s. These parts tell of
the impact of the timber boom and its aftermath on the Mahans
Creek neighborhood. *Down on Mahans Creek* closes with the
epilogue. "The Creek Has Changed a Lot since Then" seeks to
sum up what has happened to the Mahans Creek neighborhood
since World War II.

✦   ✦   ✦

During my journey into Ozarks history I soon discovered that
there are limits on the quantity and quality of sources for this
kind of inquiry. Unlike New Englanders and their descendants,
the peoples of the Ozarks were not inclined to keep diaries or
personal correspondence. In the absence of written primary
sources of this sort, I have had in many instances to rely on my
own knowledge. Indeed, on occasion the reader may be jarred by
my use of the first person in the narrative, but I concluded that
this was the most honest way I could write this history. Another
limit flows from my extensive reliance on the memories of others.
Fortunately, people from down in the hollows are talkers and
storytellers. Hence, I have repeatedly interviewed by phone, face-
to-face, by correspondence, and by email dozens of people, many
but not all of whom are kinfolk. I remain to this day not only
awed by their memories but in appreciation of their candor.

Heading the list are two cousins, Arch Pummill and
Gloria Dene (Rader) Fry. Gloria Dene, a longtime resident of
Eminence, Missouri, organizes and hosts the annual Rader-
Pummill reunion that is held at Alley Spring, Missouri, and is
the keeper of a large body of family memorabilia. I have been the
beneficiary of her extensive knowledge of family and Shannon
County history and also of her introductions to numerous

kinfolk and non-family local residents. By way of another helpful cousin, Jerome Rader, I made the acquaintance of 101-year-old (as of 2015) Arch Pummill, a genial man of twinkling eyes and a contagious sense of humor who lives in Springfield, Missouri. I have repeatedly called upon my cousin Arch's peerless memory for stories and information about kinfolk as well as for the history of the Mahans Creek neighborhood. If anyone deserves credit as the joint author of this book, it is Arch.

How to understand the proper role of legends in the history of the Mahans Creek neighborhood and its families presented me with ever-present problems of interpretation. As often as not subsequent generations explained critical turning points in the family and the neighborhood's past by resorting to dramatic stories that were unverifiable from other sources. Almost always the stories featured individual decision-making and behavior as the major determinants of the course of events. For example, elders in the Rader family loved to thrill their descendants with the tale of "Uncle Mike" "gutting" a neighboring man in a no-holds-barred fight; fear of retaliation or that Mike might be charged with murder, they said, led the Rader family to flee their Kentucky homeland for the hollows of Shannon County. Apart from the absence of corroborating evidence, I learned that a large body of "facts" from other sources indicates that it was far more likely that hard times rather than Mike's fight drove the Raders to migrate from Kentucky to Missouri.

Still, legends, though usually embellishments of fact, remain important. They are a part of the collective memory of a particular people. As such, while recognizing that they might offer a wildly inaccurate explanation of a particular episode in a family's or the neighborhood's past, they aided me in comprehending how the people themselves understood their history and how that understanding—perhaps more than the "realities" of their past—shaped their own responses to later contingencies in their day-to-day lives. In addition, the legends sometimes revealed more about the fundamental beliefs, customs, and behaviors of the hollers people than did the "hard" data found in the census, land records, or other documentary sources.

Nonetheless, this study rests for the most part on more conventional sources. Supremely important among these is a massive document on the Rader family's history, assembled and in part written by a cousin, Jayne Rader. Jayne's manuscript contains a potpourri of facts, legends, invaluable genealogical information, copies of government documents, and a few personal letters. Especially helpful in this endeavor was her father and my uncle, Hulbert Rader (now deceased), who was for many years the most knowledgeable person of the family's history. On occasion over the years he bent my ear with stories of the past, but, alas, I paid him far less attention than I should have. His sons, Jerome and Jon Maxwell Rader, loaned to me a cache of useful family memorabilia that included legal documents extending back to the 1880s, newspaper clippings, and even copies of loans made to various Raders. An additional document of some significance to the Rader family's history is a round-robin series of letters written between 1945 and 1950 by Sam Rader and his adult children (as well as one letter by my mother, Lydia).

The richest written single source on both the Rader and Pummill family is *The Passerby*. Beginning in 1932 and continuing into 1939, each month members of the extended Pummill family were urged to send letters telling "what they were doing" to James Everett Pummill, the superintendent of schools at Eureka, Missouri. Everett then distilled the contents of their letters into his own words and frequently added commentary of his own. For Everett the newsletter was a labor of love; he spent countless hours on weekends editing, writing, and typing (single-spaced) the usually one-page (back and front) mimeographed newsletter and then mailed it himself. To an uninvolved reader, much of its contents seem trivial at best. It frequently includes accounts of weather, family visits, achievements of family members, how gardens are faring, sicknesses, and even, in one instance, the plight of a family dog, but it also contains an abundance of remembrances of life on Mahans Creek. Via *The Passerby*, contributors who still resided in the neighborhood kept those that had dispersed up to date on the latest happenings in their homeland. With reference to the Pummills, I am also indebted to Virginia (Pummill) Dailey and her husband, Don, for providing me with copies of a spirited, handwritten memoir composed by Virginia's mother, Crystal, as well as other Pummill family memorabilia.

I was delighted to find that Shannon County's weekly newspapers were far richer in content for this kind of study than I had expected. I perused every extant issue of the *Birch Tree Record* from 1893 through 1907, the (Birch Tree) *Shannon Herald* from 1907 through 1948, the (Winona) *Shannon County Democrat* from 1903 to 1947, and the (Eminence) *Current Wave* from 1876 through 1951, all of which are on microfilm at the State Historical Society of Missouri at Columbia. Especially helpful was the *Current Wave*, named after the nearby river. The *Wave* frequently recounted local history and folklore, and even more importantly it irregularly published columns—written by residents—that summed up the news in the Mahans Creek neighborhood. From them I gleaned information on subjects ranging from pie suppers at the schoolhouse and church services to which families visited whom and reports of who was planting corn or putting up hay. Above all, I was kept abreast of neighborhood fishing and hunting exploits. When Sam Rader bought a cream separator in 1916, the news appeared, of course, in the *Current Wave*.

Government documents are another important source for this study. Laurel Muff carefully and cheerfully recorded US Census population data onto spreadsheets, and Vanessa Huang did statistical analyses of them. In addition, for the nineteenth century, I turned to the manuscript agricultural censuses, which provide detailed data on the farming operations of many of my ancestors as well as their neighbors. Officials in both Osage and Shannon Counties gave me access to land records and sometimes court records, though, alas, some of these for Shannon and Hart Counties have been lost in courthouse fires. I also obtained an array of documents from the State Historical Society of Missouri at Columbia, the Missouri State Archives in Jefferson City, the Center for Ozark Studies Collection in the Special Collections of Missouri State University in Springfield, the State Historical Society of Missouri Rolla Research Center in Rolla, the Kentucky Department of Libraries and Archives in Frankfort, the Arizona State Library Archives and Public Records in Phoenix, and the National Archives at College Park, Maryland.

Visiting scattered archives with local history collections was one of the more pleasurable aspects of my journey into Ozarks history. These include historical societies in Hart County, Kentucky, Highland County, Ohio, Marion County, Tennessee, and in Osage, Shannon, Texas, Douglas, and Wright Counties in Missouri, as well as the Sharlot Hall Museum in Prescott, Arizona. I shall never forget the graciousness and helpfulness of the mostly volunteer personnel at these depositories. Perhaps most memorably was my witnessing with my sister Ada an elderly, somewhat frail volunteer climbing an extension ladder to retrieve a source located on a shelf near the ceiling of a former bank building that now serves as the quarters for the Wright County Historical Society in Hartville, Missouri. Equally unforgettable was Carolyn Short, who introduced me to Calvin Childress. A distant cousin, Calvin escorted my wife, Barbara, my daughter-in-law, Vicki Tobias, and me around the stomping grounds of the Rader homeland in Hart County, Kentucky. Mary Anne Schulte not only aided my wife and me by "googling" the subject of bedbugs but introduced me to another distant cousin, Diane (Matthews) Franken. Diane escorted me around the stomping grounds of the Pummill and Matthews families' homeland in Osage County, Missouri.

Closer to home in Lincoln, Nebraska, was the assistance offered by colleagues at the University of Nebraska–Lincoln, especially John Comer, Vanessa Gorman, Wendy Katz, Timothy Mahoney, William Thomas III, and Kenneth Winkle. At the university's library, I am indebted to Brian O'Grady and Charles Bernholz. For the maps and drawings in this book, I thank Katie Nieland. Financial help for the extensive traveling required by this project came from two grants by the Maude F. Wisherd Fund of the University of Nebraska–Lincoln Faculty Alumni Association. At home, Barbara Rader probably read at least once every page of this manuscript, heard endless monologues about its contents, and usually accompanied me as I jaunted about the country. Nearly four hundred miles away, in Fayetteville, Arkansas, the always encouraging Larry Malley offered an especially useful reading of the entire manuscript. Even farther away in Madison, Wisconsin, Vicki Tobias provided me with indispensable genealogical information.

Lest this acknowledgement become intolerably long, I offer a list of others who extended help. I am grateful to each of them: Tom Akers, Craig Albin, Shelia Allen, Anne Baker, David Benac, Daniel Borstelmann, Phyllis Boyse, John Bradbury Jr., John Brenner, Betty Bresnick, Nancy Brewer, Robyn Burnett, James Chilton, Ada (Rader) Cochran, Michael Cochran, Marty Cochran, Paul Conkin, Robert Cunningham, Robert Diffendal, Douglas Dowden, Martha Gammons, Ken Gatter, Kimberly Harper, Lavon Harrison, Carl Herren, Champion Herren, Cline Herren, James Huffman, Genevieve Kyle, Kelly Loyd, Miles Loyd, Phillip Loyd, Jorene McCubbins, Kitty (Pummill) McFee, Kathleen Morrison, Carolyn Olney, Lucille (Pummill) Orchard, Joe Pickett, Donald Pummill, Anne Rader, Mike Rader, Nicholas and Sondra Raper, Edibeth (French) Ross, Linda Ross, Judy Scharpes, Danny Searcy, Nancy (Rhinehart) Sevy, Iva (Eddings) Shumate, Alice (Rader) Smith, Barbara Ellen Smith, Melany Williams, and Lesley Yates. For those whose names I have misplaced or forgotten, I beg forgiveness.

The Magic of Mahans Creek

DEEP IN THE hollows of the Missouri Ozarks, the days warmed and the dogwoods began to bloom. Word came from downstream. "The yeller suckers are here!" Up and down the creek, the farmers, including my grandfather Edward Martin "Sam" Rader and his brother-in-law and my great uncle, Arthur Pummill, took down their gigs from resting places, sharpened the barbed prongs, and tested the lines attached to the long gig handles. Normally, they were in no hurry when they strolled about their farms, accompanied by their hounds and perhaps counting their cows, but they now stepped out quickly and purposefully. At one of the deepest holes in the creek, perhaps it was one of the creek's historic holes—the Blue, Baptisin', Pummill, or Rowlett—Sam positioned himself on a log that bridged the lower end of the hole while Arthur stood on a gravel bar at the upper end of the hole.

The suckers darted first to one end of the hole and then to the other. Sam and Arthur repeatedly hurled their gigs at the elusive fish. Each time that one of them successfully gigged a fish, he, in one continuous motion, pulled the sucker out of the water and flung it onto the creek bank and there, with a jerk, dislodged his catch. Soon the banks were alive with flopping fish. According to family lore, Grandpa Sam and Uncle Arthur gigged more than one hundred suckers that day. They shattered forever the Mahans Creek record for a single outing.[1]

Sam Rader and Arthur Pummill were neither the first nor the last of the residents on Mahans Creek to gig spawning suckers. It is likely that even the Osage Indians, who had hunted along the creek more than a century earlier, had also speared the suckers. And as early as the 1880s Sam Rader and his brothers probably participated in the annual spring kill. In the 1930s, a decade after Sam and Arthur had enjoyed so much success, I remember my father, Lowell Leslie Rader, continuing the practice of his forebears. After "Pap," as I called him, had scaled and gutted his bounty, Lydia, my mother would fry a huge mess of them for supper, our evening meal. We ate fried suckers again for breakfast. My mother, like the women in other creek families, may have canned the remainder for future consumption. Gigging suckers not only put food on the table, but for the men was an exciting escape from the tedium of farm work. As with their ancestors back in Kentucky, Tennessee, Virginia, and the Carolinas, the men on Mahans Creek rarely permitted an opportunity to hunt or fish to pass them by.

The magic of Mahans Creek extended beyond the annual bounty of fish. There was the uniqueness of the creek itself. By flowing from south to north, it seemed to defy the logic of the Mississippi River drainage system. Fed by cold, clear springs, the creek rushed from one side of the narrow, steep-sided, tree-covered hollow to the other, in some places carving out limestone bluffs and caves along the way. Dense stands of willows and towering sycamore trees grew along its banks. Oak and pine flourished on the hillsides of the creek's hollows. Pools usually no more than three feet deep emptied into stretches of faster-running water that ran no more than a few inches above the yellow gravel and sand that comprised its bottom. It was in these stretches less accessible to predators that the yellow suckers spawned.

Watercress grew in the stillness of the pool's shallower parts. My family claimed—doubtless with exaggeration—that they lived on watercress gathered from the creek during the Great Depression of the 1930s. The creek itself was alive with animals, not just yellow suckers in the spring but countless varieties of minnows, bass, hog suckers, crawdads, muskrats, mink, and water snakes. In the drought years of the 1930s, the Raders even dammed the creek and pumped water out of it to irrigate their nearby parched corn fields. While the exact date is unknown, Sam discovered that watermelons could be grown in the sandy soil along its banks. Eventually, he achieved some local renown for the wagonloads of luscious melons that he sold in nearby Eminence and West Eminence. In the summers, my father, his clothes soaked heavy with sweat from farm work, would finish his day by stripping off his overalls and underclothes and taking a dip in the always-cold creek.

The creek was a source of endless diversion, especially for children. In the summers, whenever we could, we boys (my brother Mike and I) lollygagged naked in the creek. Some experiences were not so exhilarating; when my brothers Leslie (in 1942) and Howard (in 1943) were born, my mother sometimes insisted that we had to rinse out their soiled diapers in the creek before we could go swimming. "There was always something to do on the creek," explained my first cousin Jerome, who lived with his family on the creek until he went away to college. Indeed, Jerome remembers as a child that he had no desire to accompany his family on trips to the nearby towns of Eminence, Birch Tree, or Winona. Except for an occasional attendance at a cowboy movie, the lure of town life could never compete successfully with the attractions of the creek. Another cousin, Arch Pummill, who like me spent his first years on the creek, recalled almost ninety years later (in 2010) that he "bitterly resented leaving the creek" and to this day has never forgiven his parents for moving the family to Pittsburgh, Kansas, in the early 1920s.[2] For many years afterwards, long after I had accompanied our family on a permanent move to a dry-land farm near West Plains, Missouri, in 1944, memories of life on the creek flooded me with nostalgia. They still do.

PART I

THEIR KENTUCKY HOMELAND

Not all details of the wedding have survived in family legends or in documentary sources, but we do know that George Washington Rader married Nancy Jane Childress on June 23, 1852, at the home of Nancy's parents, John W. and Mary "Polly" Hare Childress. To witness the occasion, the Childresses may have welcomed kinfolk and neighbors to their newly built dogtrot log house. The house nestled in a hollow not far from the Nolin River on the far west side of Hart County, Kentucky. No one present dreamed that some twenty-six years later the newly created family would leave their homeland and eventually settle on Mahans Creek in the heart of the Missouri Ozarks.

For his day, the groom was a big man, six feet tall, fully bearded, and broad-faced. while the thin-lipped bride was

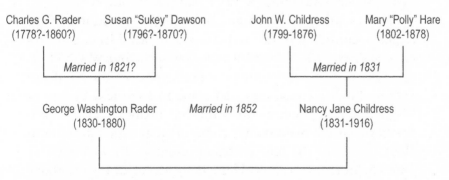

The Rader-Dawson and Childress-Hare families in nineteenth-century Kentucky. *Courtesy of Katie Nieland.*

slight in build, blue-eyed, and wan in appearance. Among the guests, we can surmise, were George's father and mother, Charles and Susan "Sukey" Rader, and perhaps Sukey's mother, Nancy Dawson. Likely to have also been present were Nancy Childress's six siblings and all seven of George Rader's brothers and sisters, as well as Polly's "half-witted" brother, Bartholomew Hare. Each newly arrived guest may have been treated to an enthusiastic greeting from John Childress's dogs.

The Childress-Rader wedding entailed more than a simple bonding of two Kentucky families. It brought together peoples representing three distinctive strands of a newly developing Upland South folk culture. The smallest and least consequential of these was represented in the person of George's father, Charles Rader. Charles was the only German-born person of his generation in the entirety of Hart County. While Charles, or Karl, as he was known as a youth, never fully shed his German ancestry, he eagerly embraced the ways of his central Kentucky neighbors. Charles's wife and George Rader's mother, Sukey, on the other hand, was a Dawson. Residents of the expansive Green River valley where it flowed near the county seat of Munfordville, the Dawsons traced their ancestry back to central Virginia, Tidewater Maryland, and, ultimately, the British Isles. While not approximating the wealth and splendor enjoyed by the Coastal South's cotton nabobs, several Dawson family members employed slave labor to grow tobacco on what they called their "plantations." They lived not in log houses but in well-appointed structures of brick and sawed lumber.[1]

Representing the third and most influential strand of the region's culture was the self-described "Childress clan" of George's new wife, Nancy. Like the Dawsons, John W. Childress and his ancestors were militant Protestants of mostly if not entirely English stock; they had come to Kentucky by way of Virginia and Tennessee. But with that many of the similarities between the two families ended. Perhaps the most anomalous person of the four parents present at the wedding was John Childress's wife, Polly Hare. Polly was of an Irish Catholic family by way of Maryland. While viewed with suspicion by her anti-Catholic neighbors, Polly Hare could not be ignored. She was a spirited woman of good cheer who was proud of her Irish origins. The Childress clan, a product of the union between Polly and John, evolved into quintessential hollers people who clung tenaciously to their old ways. They built log cabins near the springs or creeks in the hollows of western Hart County and, as one of their descendants put it, "lived by growing what [they] ate, kept a few chickens, hogs, mild [milk] cows, rasied [sic] some sheep."[2] The Childresses, more than either the Dawsons or the Raders, would stamp on Nancy Childress and George Rader's family and their descendants a way of life that in many of its essentials persisted for a century or more.

CHAPTER 1

The Childress Clan

DESPITE THEIR SHARPLY divergent origins, in time John and Polly Childress formed a blended family culture of their own. Of the two opposing strands, Polly's heritage may have been the more significant. Perhaps it was her influence and not John's that enabled the family's descendants to confront the hardest of times with a striking degree of composure and good cheer. From their experiences and those of their neighbors in western Hart County, John and Polly also learned how to seize upon the immediately available resources of their physical habitat for basic sustenance. Over time, they and their descendants forged a clan-like relationship with one another. Membership in "the Childress clan," as they described themselves, provided family members with not only a more secure sense of their own identities, but also a wide array of resources otherwise unavailable for responding to the vicissitudes of life in western Hart County, Kentucky.

John W. Childress enjoyed few comforts in his final years. Painful rheumatism made physical work impossible. "His limbs were drawn up, and his legs so drawn up that they could not be straightened," reported a friend.[1] His material possessions remained modest. Upon the occasion of his death in 1876, he owned only eighty acres, of which perhaps only forty were "cultivable." Age had also caught up with Polly. She died in 1878.

Both were buried in the family's little cemetery next to the Old Maple Methodist Church, located across the hollow from the family's dogtrot cabin. Today, by moving aside some tall grass and a few day lilies, one can see their tombstones and visit their final resting place.

In his declining years, John's religious faith offered him some consolation. In 1844, at the age of forty-five, he received a license as an exhorter from the Methodist Episcopal Church. For a time he preached at small gatherings, but growing infirmity left him incapable of standing and holding forth. Yet he still loved nothing more than religious discussions. On these occasions, a friend reported, John forgot his pains. In 1873 he bequeathed an enduring religious legacy to his neighborhood when he deeded two acres of his farm to the Methodist Church South. There, the local settlers built a log church house, known variously as the "Old Maple Church," "Old Maple Chapel," or "Old Methodist Church." Until well into the twentieth century, the old church house also served the Roseburg neighborhood as a schoolhouse.[2]

John surely found some comfort in his family as well. He and Polly successfully created a large, extended family. Of John's thirteen or possibly fourteen children to reach adulthood, all but two or perhaps three of them settled on farms within a Sunday-afternoon-visiting-distance of the original Childress homestead. By 1876, the pair had thirty-eight blood-related descendants clustered in a dense network of neighboring farms. The Childresses were of modest means, but, according to a descendant, they were "family-loving citizens" who enjoyed a positive reputation among their neighbors."[3] When delivering a baby, erecting a cabin, or getting hay stacked before a thunderstorm, a Childress could always count on help from kinfolk. On occasion, a clan member sought to improve his or her fortune outside of western Hart County. But almost always, when they came face-to-face with the uncomfortable, sometimes frightening world beyond, like a rabbit seeking its hiding place, they scurried back to the warm comfort offered by their kinfolk in Hart County.

"The woods [remain] . . . full of" Childresses to this day.

So reported a cousin, Hulbert Rader, from Missouri, who visited the Roseburg neighborhood more than one hundred years later (in 1978).[4] Apart from the many female descendants, who by virtue of marriage gave up the Childress name but continued to reside in Hart County, the local area's 2010 phonebook listed forty-four Childress surnames.[5] As one of them, Calvin Childress, explained to me, it was difficult for an unmarried person of the Childress bloodline to find a spouse who was not a blood relative. Family intermarriages have been so common over the years that ascertaining the exact kinship of one person with another is difficult and sometimes impossible.

✦ ✦ ✦

In 1831, twenty-one years before the marriage of his daughter Nancy to George Rader, thirty-two-year-old John W. Childress badly needed a wife. His first wife, Sarah, had suddenly taken ill and died, probably from childbirth complications. While such deaths were not uncommon for his day, her death was especially untimely for John since it left him without a soul mate and with the task of rearing six small children. Not infrequently on such occasions, a sister or a cousin of the deceased wife stepped forward to fill the void, but none of the female relatives of Sarah lived in Kentucky. They were all back in Virginia. Neither did the idea of marrying a stranger, raising someone else's children, and taking up a life on a primitive farm deep in the hollows of western Hart County appeal to local women eligible for such an assignment. In spite of these drawbacks, and in what was surely a jaw-dropping surprise to those who knew him, John found himself a new wife and his children a new mother when he married Mary "Polly" Hare in 1831.

Within the Childress clan, there are several versions of how this unusual marriage came about. According to one, John first learned of Polly by way of her brothers, Thomas and Bartholomew Hare. John met the Hare brothers while the three men were erecting a stone wall together at a Catholic convent, possibly Bardstown, where Polly was said to have been a nun, a novice, or perhaps a servant. Upon learning of John's plight, her brothers suggested a solution; John should marry their sister. In pressing this suggestion, perhaps the Hare brothers had more in mind than simply solving John's need for a new wife. They may have reasoned that Polly, at the advanced age of twenty-nine or perhaps thirty, was surely otherwise destined to become an "old maid." After all, as long as Polly remained single, given the customs and the laws of the day, the Hare brothers had a duty to look after her. Or perhaps the Hare brothers simply liked John (even though he was a Protestant of mostly English origins). It may be that the Hare brothers and John worked out all the details of the prospective union in advance.

Polly was strong-minded in her own right. She did not at once acquiesce to the plan hatched by John and her brothers. After all, marrying a Protestant was a big step, and, in addition, she may have taken vows of celibacy and poverty. Before abandoning her religious life and sacrificing her identity to her prospective husband, she sought an unmistakable sign from God. Accordingly, she put God to the test. At the convent where she was said to have been an inmate, "one night she left a candle burning on an altar in a closed room and told herself that if the candle were still lit the next morning she would continue her life in the Order—but if it were not lit she would marry John."[6] Upon awakening the next morning, she discovered that the flame of the candle had flickered and then gone out.

John and the Hare brothers quickly put into motion a scheme for consummating the marriage. On a wet, wintry day, January 8, 1831, Bartholomew Hare met the nuns at the convent and told them a bald-faced lie! Polly must accompany him home at once, he explained, so that she could comfort their sick mother. (The Hares' mother was already dead.) Sympathetic to Bartholomew's plea, the sisters agreed to let Polly go. In the meantime, some miles away, and after an all-day ride in the saddle, John Childress and Thomas Hare appeared before the clerk of the Hardin County court in Elizabethtown, Kentucky. John requested a marriage license. Thomas signed a bond as surety and swore under oath that both John and Polly were twenty-one-years of age or older. Later, that same day at the cabin of Robert Bryan, a Protestant preacher, Polly joined hands with John in matrimony.[7]

It appears to have been a good marriage for John and Polly. John not only gained a new wife and a mother for his tiny children, but Polly's strange thirty-five-year-old brother, Bartholomew, or "Uncle Bartley," as he was known in the family and in the neighborhood, joined the Childress household as well. For more than thirty years, Uncle Bartley assisted John with his heavy-duty farm and stonework. With a crop of unruly red hair, a face disfigured from having fallen off a steep bluff while coon hunting, and unable to talk clearly—if at all—Uncle Bartley's very appearance terrified local children. Adults, too, were afraid of him. Not only was he possibly dangerous, they concluded, but people in the neighborhood also believed that he was "half-witted."[8]

✦   ✦   ✦

John and Polly came from sharply opposing backgrounds. A diminutive, ebullient woman with dazzling red hair, Polly was a compelling storyteller. She liked to regale her children and grandchildren with memories of Ireland and of her life before her marriage to John. One of her favorites concerned an incident from her childhood. The story went this way. As with countless other impoverished Irish families, her family decided to leave the Old Country and seek their fortunes in America. At the pier, the family boarded a jig that was to take them out to an American-bound ship that was anchored in the harbor. As little Polly was about to step into the jig, she slipped and fell overboard. Sinking quickly into the cold, turbulent water and with only "her brilliant red hair floating on the surface," a fellow passenger reached down and "grabbed [her hair] . . . and pulled her to the jig and safety."[9]

This tale gave substance to the fiction that Polly's birthplace was Ireland. She "often told [others] of being born in Ireland," it was said. No one seems to have doubted her. So accepted did the legend become within the Childress clan that many years later one of her sons, William Childress, scribbled in his family Bible the word "Ireland" as his mother's birthplace. Yet, a careful perusal of the US censuses in both 1850 and 1860 challenge the accuracy of Polly's claim. Someone, perhaps Polly herself or perhaps it was her husband, John, told the census takers that both Polly and Uncle Bartley had been born in the United States, more specifically, in the state of Maryland. Born in 1802, she apparently accompanied her brothers when they migrated from Maryland to central Kentucky.[10] Why they made this move is uncertain, but likely it entailed a hope that greater opportunities lay ahead for them in the Bluegrass State. While Polly never learned to read or write, sometime after the family's arrival, she may have entered the convent of the Sisters of Charity of Nazareth, located near Bardstown, Kentucky.

Still, even if she was not born in Ireland and had never lived in a Catholic convent, these family legends throw into sharp relief her importance to the Childress family's history. To everyone who knew her, nothing impressed them more about Polly than her characteristically Irish behavior. She spoke with a lilting accent, was exceptionally good-humored, and was warmly supportive of her new family. Both her own children and her stepchildren loved her. While impossible to verify, she may have passed on to her progeny an invaluable asset—her unabashed enthusiasm for life. For even when Childress clan members suffered under the most adverse of circumstances, neighbors marveled at the family's equanimity. The clan possessed what J. Anderson Childress later was to describe as an unusual "devil-may-care" attitude toward life.[11]

In some respects John Childress remains a bigger mystery than Polly Hare. We do not even know with certainty his middle name. He always appears in public records as "John W. Childress," so subsequent family members assumed that he had been named after the founder of Methodism, John Wesley. No photographs or physical descriptions of him survive. By inferences from the physical features of his descendants, it may be safe to say that he was slightly above average in height and physically slim, perhaps even gaunt in appearance. We also know little about his personality. Unlike his sprightly, expressive wife, it is likely that John, as with most upcountry southerners, was reserved in his relationships with others, including even Polly and his own children. He probably masked his strongest feelings, including his loves and hates, with a nervous laugh or with teasing and bantering—or even with utter silence. Such was a personality trait commonly found among his descendants.

Arriving in North America in the late seventeenth or the early eighteenth century, the Childress or Childers (the spelling varied) family appear to have originated in England though there is no hard, surviving evidence of their exact European origins.[12] John's first ancestor in America may have been indentured to a member of the Virginia gentry. Even if he had the good fortune of being a "freeman," he necessarily deferred to those above him in the social order. Upon approaching a "gentleman" or a "lady," he acknowledged their social superiority by bowing and doffing his cap. It would be a century later, during the Revolutionary era, before the ordinary people of Virginia began to question their subordination to the "wellborn."

Virginia records tell us something of John's father. In the late eighteenth century, a Phillip Childers or Childress (1750–1812) lived on a small farm near the tiny village of Manakin in Virginia's Goochland County. Many years later the village merged into greater Richmond, and to this day a substantial number of persons with the Childress surname continue to reside in the vicinity. Philip in time acquired a small acreage, though his land for many years seems to have been encumbered by debt. Primary to the family's survival, as with so many other early American settlers, was probably an annual corn crop, some of which was fed to chickens, to two or three hogs, and perhaps to a milk cow while the remainder was ground into meal for use as bread and a cereal by the family or perhaps made into whiskey. If Phillip planted any tobacco, given the intensive labor required in bringing it to market, we can presume it was a small patch of less than an acre. Apart from subsistence farming, Phillip did stonework, an important skill that he passed on to several of his sons. At the conclusion of their lives, Phillip and his wife, Mary, could point to one unalloyed success; they had managed to accumulate enough land so that they could pass on a small inheritance to each of their eight children.[13]

One of these was John W. Childress, their youngest son. Given descendants' theories regarding John's middle name, it is quite likely that Phillip and Mary were Methodists; perhaps they had been converted to that persuasion during one of the revivals that burned through the Virginia countryside during the late eighteenth century. Many of John's descendants were also Methodists, though by the late nineteenth century, there may have been an equal number of Baptists in the Hart County Childress clan. John exhibited a streak of independence. A few years after his marriage in 1817 to Sarah Jordan, John sold his tiny plot of Virginia farmland and sought to improve his fortunes by striking out with his newly formed family across the mountains to Tennessee.

Said by his descendants to have been an "indifferent farmer" and perhaps victimized by land speculators, John soon dissipated his small inheritance. Of equal importance, John and his family may have been influenced by what geographer Terry Jordan-Bychkov has termed "the Tennessee hearth" of the Upland South's emerging folk culture.[14] If Jordan-Bychkov is correct, the Childresses encountered in Tennessee a new regional culture in the making, one that brought together folkways from peoples who had migrated across the mountains from mostly Virginia and the Carolinas. The largest number in the Tennessee cohort probably traced their European ancestry back to Northern Ireland, though substantial numbers also came from England, Wales, Scotland, and even Germany. Blended together in Tennessee and influenced by the state's rugged terrain, according to Jordan-Bychkov, they were pioneers in the evolution of a major regional culture within the United States.

It may be, however, that John remained in Tennessee for only four or five years before heading out again—this time for central Kentucky. The 1830 census reports a "John W. Childers" and family living in Washington County, Kentucky. Since this census did not disclose the names of other family members, it is impossible to know with certainty that this is the John W. Childress family, though the size of the family and the ages of family members indicate that it probably was. In the meantime, John's wife, Sarah, died, and in 1831 John married Polly Hare. Soon thereafter, if not at once, the new couple settled in Hart County, Kentucky.

✦ ✦ ✦

John W. Childress may have first looked into possibilities for farming on the wide, fertile expanses of the Green River Valley or on the Bacon Creek waterway, but, if he did so, he soon abandoned that quest. The best farmland in these places had already been taken up. In the end, he chose to settle deep in the hollows west of Munfordville, the Hart County seat. Here, the hillsides were steeper and the hollows narrower. It was a remote place where land titles were in dispute and settlers simply squatted, hoping someday in the future to obtain a clear title to the land that they occupied. Because of its nearness to the Nolin (pronounced as two words, "no lin") River and its tributaries, local people referred to the area as "the Forks." It was also known as "Cave Country," because of its numerous underground caverns, including Mammoth Cave, which, as the crow flies, is only twelve miles away. Some thirty miles to the northeast was Hodgenville, the birthplace of Abraham Lincoln. The nearest post office was the Cross Roads (renamed Cub Run in 1876); later on there would be a post office, country store, and blacksmith at a place called Roseburg, which was across the hollow from John's farm. John's farm itself was less than a half mile from the Nolin River.

When the Childresses first arrived at the site of their new home in the Forks, there were no cleared fields, roads, or nearby inhabitants, and for a time the family may have lived in a tent or a lean-to. Of the site's features, the family prized above all else the clear, cold water that gurgled out of a spring in a small cave about a hundred yards away. From its mouth flowed a year-around tiny stream, or what locals called a "branch." While lugging water up the branch's steep bank was an onerous task, it not only furnished fresh water for drinking and cooking, but also cooled the family's milk, butter, and other foodstuffs. From this site, John and his family could look down into the hollow and out across to the other side. Beyond their farm were miles and miles of dense woods. In time, others, including John and Polly's descendants, would squat and try to eke out a living from farms in these same woods.

At first John and Uncle Bartley erected a simple four-sided structure of round, un-hewed logs cut from nearby poplar or oak.[15] Perhaps aided by neighbors, they lifted the heavy green logs into place. They chinked the cracks between the logs with rocks, clay, and small sticks. Split shingles or shakes probably comprised the roof. Some twenty years later, the family built a far more substantial "dogtrot" log house. It featured two pens with full-dovetail notching at the corners and with an open breezeway or dogtrot between the pens.[16] An ingeniously versatile structure, during the hot, humid summers of central Kentucky, the breezeway helped to moderate temperatures in both sides of the house. The breezeway was a favorite spot for the family's dogs, but it was also a fine place for family members to sit, chat, eat, smoke, and sleep during hot weather. Each pen in John's house had separate functions. Standing outside the end of one pen, a large, stone, wood-burning fireplace provided heat for cooking and warmth in the wintertime. (Today, several flat, worn stones, presumably left over from a chimney, remain at the site of the cabin.) Metal pots and one or more heavy frying pans hung over the fireplace on metal racks or tripods. At first, Polly may have had one exceptionally large pan in which she carried water, mixed bread, fed one or more cows, milked into, and carried woodchips for the fireplace.

The house was a workplace; it contained a spinning wheel and a loom. In time John probably made several chairs bottomed with white-oak splints. In the wintertime, the entire family may have eaten and slept in the same room. During warmer times, family members—typically ten or more—spread out to the loft and perhaps the second pen, where they slept on blankets or perhaps ticks filled with dried leaves or straw. In time, feathers or cotton may have become the ticking of choice and the beds may have been covered with pieced and quilted comforts. In such close quarters, strict personal privacy was impossible. Perhaps it was little wonder that the immodesty of backcountry women frequently shocked visitors from other regions of the country.

✦   ✦   ✦

As satisfying as John Childress may have found his large progeny, the behaviors of his descendants, and the certainties of his religious faith, he could take little consolation from his material circumstances. Wealth accumulation, the singular measure of success for most of his fellow Americans in the nineteenth century, always eluded him. During his lifetime, he rarely offered his offspring anything more than the barest of necessities. Neither did he meet another goal of those residing in agricultural societies. They were unsuccessful in building up a patrimony in land that could be passed on to their sons.

The story of the Childresses in Hart County was one of interminable struggle. When he first surfaced on the county's tax rolls in 1833, (for tax purposes) John owned only one horse and *no* land. Even a decade later, his situation had not improved much.[17] How the family managed to survive during these early years requires conjecture. Apart from food that they obtained via farming, we can guess that wild game, fish, berries, nuts, and roots must have helped to fill the empty stomachs of the growing family.[18] Even with the sharp decline in deer, wild turkey, and raccoon populations in central Kentucky, wild game may have remained a component of the Childress family diet. There were always plenty of rabbits and squirrels. Indeed, as the predators of these animals were systematically wiped out by the local settlers, their numbers actually proliferated. Settlers even began complaining about the armies of squirrels that invaded their cornfields, and visitors frequently reported finding a squirrel or two simmering in a pot over the fireplace in the log houses of the local farmers.

Ultimately, however, hunting and gathering was not enough. To feed, clothe, and shelter themselves, the Childress family, as with their neighbors, had to wrestle a livelihood from the land. In time, John did acquire land of his own, indeed, in terms of sheer acreage, lots of land. By 1849, according to tax records, John had amassed a whopping 370 acres, of which, reportedly, fifty acres were "improved," that is, cleared of trees and brush, though not necessarily suitable for row crops. The Hart County assessor valued it at a mere $115 for tax purposes; little of his vast acreage could have been worth much.[19]

The US decennial agricultural manuscript censuses offer a more complete picture of the Childress's household economy.[20] Three "milch" cows in 1850 provided the ten-member family with an ample supply of milk and butter. While John owned four additional head of cattle, the Childress family, like their neighbors, rarely if ever ate beef. John's seven sheep may have produced enough wool for Polly and their daughters to clothe the family. Polly apparently planted a tiny garden as well. Still, in 1850, the family reported growing only one bushel of peas and beans as well as only fifteen bushels of Irish potatoes. For feeding such a large household, the family's potato crop seems inadequate, though upland southerners were less enthusiastic about eating potatoes for their starch (they preferred corn) than were their Yankee counterparts.[21] Local maple trees furnished the family with ten pounds of sugar. They likely stored some of these items in a root cellar for winter consumption.

These dietary items paled in importance when compared to corn and pork. If cotton was the king of the Deep or Coastal South, corn was the king of the Upland South.[22] Easily grown, stored, and ground into meal when needed, and rich in carbohydrates, corn was the foundation of the region's diet. The Childresses and their neighbors ate corn in some form at virtually every meal of the day. Some families distilled the grain into whiskey and poorer people used the shucks for mattresses. All families fed corn, if they produced enough, to their hogs, chickens, and cattle. If typical in their diets, the Childress family probably needed to produce nearly 200 bushels of shelled corn annually for their own consumption.

If the agricultural censuses are accurate, John and his family grew a relatively small quantity of corn. In 1850, for example, John reported harvesting only 150 bushels, a full 100 bushels less than a majority of his nearby neighbors and far below the average of farmers living north of the Ohio River. In the Sugar Creek Township of Sangamon County, Illinois, for example, each farm family produced an average of 1,100 bushels of corn in 1850.[23] A decade later, in a household continuing to sustain ten persons, John's yield grew to 250 bushels, but in the following years it again shrank sharply. In 1870, in a household of four persons, he reported harvesting a mere 50 bushels.

An all-important source of protein and fat, hogs were the king of Upland South's livestock. They reproduced prolifically and, provided there was an ample acorn crop, could survive in the woods with little or no human aid. Their flesh could be preserved easily by curing, salting, or canning. John Childress reported owning only twelve hogs in 1850, eight less than the average of his nearby neighbors. The number fell to four in 1860, and none in 1870. Even if we presume that John underreported the number of his hogs, perhaps because they were foraging in the woods or he was worried about having them assessed for taxes, they seem to have been far less important to the Childress family diet than they were for most of their neighbors.

As farmers, other members of the Childress clan appear to have been no more—indeed, in some instances even less— successful farmers than John. While in 1874 John reported possessing a "pleasure carriage" and one horse, of his sons, only Elijah owned a horse. By this time, however, because of disabilities accompanying age, John did little farming. Elijah was the only family member who had *any* hogs more than six months old, but he owned only seven of them. Of John's sons, only Elijah was required to pay any local taxes.[24] If anything, several of the family's next generation appear to have been even worse off than their ancestors.

In assessing the farm economy of the Childress family, it appears that on at least one occasion in the post–Civil War era, the family sought to improve its cash flow by plunging into the unpredictable market for burley tobacco. In 1874, John and all except one of his sons and sons-in-law harvested between 400 and 1,000 pounds of tobacco each—not insubstantial sums for single households.[25] The experiment must have failed. For there is no evidence that the family ever again grew more tobacco than they themselves consumed. Tobacco did not grow particularly well in the western part of Hart County, required intensive labor, was expensive to transport to Munfordville and beyond, and tobacco prices were sometimes below the costs of production.

TABLE 1.
Farms of the John Wesley Childress Clan in 1874

NAME	RELATIONSHIP TO JOHN W. CHILDRESS	AGE	TOTAL ACRES OWNED	VALUE	CORN (BUSHELS)	TOBACCO (POUNDS)
John W.		75	80	$240	50	400
John S.	Son	49	65	$200	NA	NA
Elijah	Son	38	50	$150	150	500
Thomas M.	Son	35	10	$50	50	600
Benjamin F.	Son	29	113	$350	20	800
Henry T.	Son	27	NA	NA	100	1,600
George Rader	Son-in-law	41	NA	NA	50	1,000
Jacob West	Son-in-law	55	39	$107	100	1000

Source: J. Anderson Childress, ed., *Beyond the Cross Roads: A Genealogy, History, and Traditional Folkways of Western Hart County, Kentucky* (Utica, KY: McDowell Pubs., 1981), 86–86. Transcribed by J. Anderson Childress from the Hart County Tax List in the Kentucky Historical Society.

A conclusion is inescapable. If limited to their agricultural endeavors, the Childress clan's material standing was usually slightly below the median when compared with their nearby neighbors. Contrary to the presumption that an abundance of cheap land, wood, and water had a leveling effect on the accumulation of wealth by individual settlers, the social structure of John Childress's neighborhood quickly became stratified. A few wealthy farmers soon monopolized the best land and stood atop of the neighborhood's economic pyramid; by 1850, the top five of 172 neighborhood settlers owned farms worth more than ten times as much as John W. Childress's farm. His farm, which was assessed for tax purposes at $300, was close to the median of all farms. The top five likewise owned vastly more acreage than their neighbors; four of them possessed more than one thousand acres each. By 1850, obtaining enough acreage to join the ranks of these more prosperous farmers, indeed, even joining the middling-income ranks in the neighborhood, must have been extraordinarily difficult even for the most shrewd and hard-working family. To have achieved this feat in Hart County required a substantial amount of capital, something that the Childress family and more than 90 percent of their neighbors simply did not have and could not obtain. In terms of farming, they were left for the most part with an unbreakable ceiling to their material aspirations.[26]

However, income from non-agricultural sources was important to the welfare of the Childress clan. The extended family became well known in western Hart County for their stonework, which entailed a set of artisan skills that had been passed down from their ancestors. Near the family homestead, John erected a small horse-powered grindstone "factory," one that cut sandstone into grindstones for the sharpening of tools. For neighbors, the family also built stone chimneys, stone-lined wells and cisterns, and, sometimes, stone walls. In exchange for their work, money rarely changed hands; instead, the Childresses usually bartered for foodstuffs and other goods or services. A surviving document indicates that in 1874, Thomas M. Childress, "the Chimney Builder," agreed to construct "the chimney, and two fireplaces [for John Wilson's new house] for the price of a milk cow and maybe a little money."[27] Apparently, at least some of the Childresses considered stonemasonry rather than farming their primary occupation.

Other part-time or wintertime jobs eased the material hardships of the Childresses. Several of John's sons did some carpentry. One of them for a time operated a small gristmill on Little Dog Creek, another taught school, one owned a saloon at the

Cross Roads (Cub Run), and yet another owned a country store and ran the post office in Roseburg. In the late nineteenth century and continuing into the twentieth century, several family members, including both men and women, took up the laborious task of making baskets from strips of white oak. The quality of their workmanship eventually won some renown, even beyond the confines of Hart County. At first they peddled their baskets in central Kentucky and in southern Indiana. Later on, they sold them during trading days in the Cub Run and Mammoth Cave vicinity.[28] As their engagement in stonework and basket making and basket selling makes clear, the Childress family's lives were not strictly limited to the rugged hollows of western Hart County.

Yet, for decade after decade most aspects of the day-to-day life of the Childresses changed little, even as they entered into the twentieth century. Indeed, there is reason to believe that the clan's material circumstances actually declined in the post–Civil War era, a period in which most of the residents of western Hart County sank into a deep economic depression.[29] It was in this era that Nancy Jane, her husband, and her children fled their homeland for Shannon County, Missouri.

The relative "backwardness" of the clan was a matter of wonder to five-year-old Lilly May Rader, a granddaughter of John and Polly Childress, who, along with her Mahans Creek, Missouri, family, returned for a visit with Hart County kinfolk in 1908.[30] Lilly May, whose perceptions may have reflected the material success of her own family and her youth more than an accurate assessment of the circumstances of her Kentucky kinfolk, reported that her great uncle, Henry Childress, proudly displayed to his Missouri relatives his newly built log cabin made of "small saplings" that were "still unchinked." The house had a packed dirt floor. Henry's cabin was even more primitive than the dogtrot house that John and Uncle Bartley had built before the Civil War. By contrast, Lilly May's family back in Missouri lived in a two-story house of cast cement blocks with pressed tin ceilings and floors of sawed lumber. Another family in the Childress clan—she observed with surprise but with admiration for the family's ingenuity—kept their newborn infant in a crib consisting of a hollowed-out log. To little Lilly May, the Kentucky Childress clan seemed frozen in time.

✦ ✦ ✦

In 1978, J. Anderson Childress, one of John's great grandsons and a perceptive chronicler of the family's history, confessed to the dilatory inclinations of the Childress men. "They have always been referred to in their community, as not overly ambitious or industrious and I jokingly refer to the[m] as lazy," he wrote in letter to a Missouri cousin. He added, "If the brothers of Aunt Nancy [referring to John Childress's daughter and my great grandmother] had any significant trait, it was their happy-go-lucky attitude towards life. I never heard of them worrying about anything, even when they didn't know where the next meal was coming from."[31]

On the face of it, Anderson Childress's characterization of the family resembled the popular stereotype of the southern highlands "hillbilly."[32] According to this image, the hillbilly was typically an unshaven, bare-footed, shiftless, violent, moonshine-drinker, who sat for countless hours on his cabin porch in a rocking chair smoking a corncob pipe, perhaps whittling sticks with a pocket knife, while propped up against his cabin wall was his rifle and nearby his jug of corn liquor and his lolling hounds. The hillbilly clearly subordinated work to leisure. But he was also frequently depicted as an ambiguous figure, for he possessed a fearless individualism. He was said to be free of the demands that society frequently sought to impose on him.

Still, as much as the Childress men and most of the neighboring men valued leisure, their ways of work and play were much more complicated than that suggested by the popular image. In the first place, there is (with perhaps one exception) no evidence of their inclinations to resort to violence to settle disputes.[33] Neither did they engage in any long-standing feuds with their neighbors or neighboring clans. Indeed, Anderson Childress himself observed that they were recognized among their neighbors as "a good family." "Almost without exception," he wrote, the reputation of the "family has been an honorable one, taking pride in their unselfish devotion to Family-God-and Country."[34]

In the second place, the brute realities of their existence served to limit their material aspirations. Not only were opportunities for material advancement sharply circumscribed by the quality and growing costs of agricultural land in Hart County, but experience also taught the men living in the hollows that additional toil rarely resulted in a proportionate amount of material rewards. Indeed, typically, each unit of work beyond that necessary to sustain a family's existence resulted at some point in what economists describe as "diminishing returns." Beyond keeping their farms in working order, the men intuited, additional work was an unnecessary vanity that paid few benefits.

By no means did such thinking exempt the men from exhausting toil. In planting and harvesting seasons, they necessarily engaged in great bursts of work, which left them laboring from daybreak to dark. Even in wintertime, wood had to be cut, fires made, corn shucked, animals fed, and fences fixed. But otherwise, except when engaged in stonework or basket making, and in singular instances of store and saloon keeping, for much of the year the Childress men were free of pressing work demands. They were less inclined to seize on these "free" times, as did farmers more involved in the marketplace, to clean fence rows, clear more land, fix farm equipment, or repair their barns or their homes.

Unlike many of their contemporaries, neither was the Childress clan driven to hard work by strong religious or moral convictions. Although nearly all professed some kind of religious faith, they did not share the Puritan belief that God had commanded all humans to commit themselves unsparingly to the pursuit of a this-worldly calling, be it as a merchant, a farmer, or a lowly servant. Neither did they share the Puritan belief that time was sacred and hence never to be wasted. They remained mostly immune to such thinking, even when in the nineteenth century the religious foundations of a strong work and time ethic gave way to the popular secular idea that diligence in work and the full use of time enhanced the individual's likelihood of material success.

Given the value that the Childress men placed on premodern work and leisure ways, we can easily imagine their distaste with the prospect of working in the nation's fast-growing factories. Even the possibility of becoming a professional person held a negligible appeal to them. From their engagement in stonework and basket-weaving, tasks over which they enjoyed a measure of control over their work experience, they also may have gained some understanding of the psychic costs of work that was dictated by the clock and the machine rather than by themselves, the daylight hours, or the seasons.

Yet, it is a serious mistake to conclude that the Childress men experienced *no* rewards from work. It is likely that they found the artisanal skills required in stonework and basket-weaving rewarding. And they, as indeed did farm people in general, took pride in their acquisition of the multiple skills essential to farming. At a tender age boys learned how to shoe and break horses, how to castrate a pig without it bleeding to death, and how to plant, cultivate, and harvest corn. To be sure, much of their work was hurried, makeshift, and lacking in quality; but nearly all the Childress boys developed at least rudimentary skills in making handles for axes and hoes, repairing wagons and plows, carpentering, mixing mortar, and laying rocks. They all learned how to handle an ax, a crosscut saw, and a mall and wedges. And, unlike the workingmen on the assembly lines, who may have been responsible for repeatedly performing a single, simple task, the Childress men and their neighbors could take satisfaction from participation in work projects from the beginning to the end. They could experience firsthand the exhilaration of clearing a patch of ground of sprouts, plowing it, planting corn in it, watching it grow, cultivating it, and harvesting it.[35] While women's work tended to be more repetitive and unrelenting than that of the men, they too found some fulfillment in such tasks as spinning wool, fabricating cloth on the family loom, and sewing the cloth into clothing. They also might take pride in their skills in making soap, baking bread, drying fruit, and preserving pork.

✦   ✦   ✦

Nothing divided the experience of work and play among the Childresses and other hollers people more than gender. The cyclical demands of men's labor simply offered them far more time free of work than the women ever had. A separate leisure pathway for men began to develop in childhood. Boys found endless sources of diversion outside the home. Nothing quite equaled the experience of traipsing through the woods, of wet sand on bare feet, of catching a toad or a tortoise, or of beating a snake to death with rocks and sticks. The physical environment with all its surprises and variations held an equal fascination for grown men. It was there that they hunted, trapped, fished, and communed directly with the vagaries of nature. Unlike the women, the men could with far more ease simply mount their horses and ride away from the farm. In the instance of the Childresses, they could ride to the farm of a nearby relative or go to the general store and post office at the Cross Roads or later at Roseburg. At these sites, they picked up the mail and purchased family necessities. They could deliver corn at the local gristmill, where it would be slowly ground into meal. At these essentially all-male sites, they swapped stories and perhaps goods, smoked, and whittled.

The Childress women, as well as farm women elsewhere, took on duties executed almost exclusively within the home. These included child birthing and rearing, cooking, churning butter, spinning wool, cleaning, washing, sewing, tending garden, milking a cow or two, and caring for farm animals. "A man works from sunup to sundown, but a woman's work is never done," went a country saying. Men rarely crossed over the gender boundary to do routine household chores or care for children; the most to be expected from them was occasional aid in carrying in wood and water.

From predawn to after dark, nearly all of the waking hours of the Childress family's female members revolved around household chores. This included Nancy Jane, the oldest daughter and my great grandmother. As a child, Nancy assisted her mother, Polly, in caring for her six younger brothers and in doing other chores assigned to women. Perhaps for this reason, Nancy apparently never attended the nearby one-room school. At least we know that upon two occasions she signed her name to official documents with an "X," indicating her illiteracy, though my father, Lowell Rader, insisted to me that "Granny could read and write." Reports in at least two US censuses support my father's claim. However, there are no surviving letters or other documents written by her.

Gender was also at the center of the family's religious life. Attendance at and participation in religious services offered women a singular but important opportunity to escape at least temporarily the home. While most evangelical groups insisted that the Bible prohibited women from preaching, women did find opportunities in church services for teaching Sunday schools and sometimes for offering public testimonies of their religious experiences. Evangelical Protestantism aided the women in transforming the home itself into a sacred place. It was there that mothers taught the virtues of self-restraint, moderation, and sobriety. Nancy Childress is again a case in point. She was said to have professed Christ at the age of fifteen and thereupon joined the Methodist Church South.[36] When she reached adulthood, in recognition of perhaps both her father and the founder of Methodism, Nancy named one of her sons John Wesley Rader. And, after marriage, within her own household, she insisted on rigorous self-restraint, propriety, and moderation. She permitted no card playing, no dancing, and no drinking in her home.

Even though the Childress men may have been just as dedicated to evangelical beliefs as their wives, they early on found themselves confronted with the lure of a traditional male subculture that conflicted with the neighborhood's evangelical culture.[37] In its most brazen forms, the male culture deposited status and honor on those men who bested other men in competitive activities. These could include feats of drinking, gambling, tall-tale telling, fighting, hunting, and swearing. While the Childress men eschewed the more outrageous behaviors associated with the Upland South's male culture, they enthusiastically participated in such less controversial all-male activities as hunting, loafing, swapping, and storytelling.

No activity of the Childress men threatened family security or conflicted with evangelical culture more deeply than their enthusiasm for swapping. For them, trading possessions was a fun-filled, albeit serious, sport. No form of recognition by other men in the neighborhood for one's shrewdness and status exceeded that of "skinning" another man in a trade. The item to be traded was itself of small consequence; the excitement was in the process and results of bargaining. Before goods changed hands, parlaying might go on for three or four hours or even for days. No possession was held back as a potential good for trade. Swapping included even farms. While John Childress himself apparently never traded away any land, J. Anderson Childress reported that John's "sons and grandsons generally were constantly trading farms and moving from place to place."[38] But, of course, in nearly all cases this was in the immediate vicinity of Roseburg. Because goods and, in rare instances, money changed hands, men were usually able to sustain the illusion that swapping was not a form of gambling. Yet bad judgment in determining the age of a horse, the fertility of a plot of land, or the condition of a carriage could have disastrous consequences for one's family.

Why was it, J. Anderson Childress further queried, that "there were never kept within the [Childress] clan heirlooms or keepsakes such as other families were likely to keep?"[39] Of course, poverty was part of the answer, but Anderson Childress identified another culprit—the "obsession" of the men in the family with seizing on every opportunity they could to swap goods. Yet, the alacrity with which the Childress men bartered away what was considered in other circles as family's treasures had a deeper significance than that suggested by Anderson Childress. It brought into sharp relief fundamental differences between the Childresses and many other American families of their day. While the American upper class had always exhibited an inclination to preserve heirlooms, the emerging middle class of the nineteenth century also began to bolster their claims to permanency and importance by investing certain of their material objects with profound meanings. Furniture, silver, and quilts that formerly had had only economic significance now became treasured family heirlooms. So did photograph albums, diaries, letters, and other memorabilia. Creative engagement with consumption seemed to assist middle-class families and their members in refashioning their identities. More elegant housing, smart clothing, and more lavish consumer goods signaled a family's economic success and higher social standing.[40]

The Childress clan, on the other hand, was for the most part indifferent to these markers of gentility. Family members rarely if ever exhibited inclinations to acquire status by building fine homes of brick or lumber, by preserving heirlooms as evidence of the family's existence as a historic entity, or by publicly displaying their refinement by dressing more fashionably than their neighbors. Partly, it may have been a matter of their continuing adherence to a Methodism that condemned ostentation and, partly, it was doubtlessly due to an absence of wealth among family members. Comfortable with the security and identity offered by membership in their clan, they also experienced little or no need to employ material objects as evidence of who they were. In time, everyone locally knew who the Childress family was. Identity was firmly grounded in the family's kinship network; family members could proudly explain in detail their relationship to other members of the clan. No one could challenge their claim that they were "natives," not "furrinners" or "strangers" of Hart County.[41] Hart County was their homeland.

✦   ✦   ✦

It was in this clan and this milieu that Nancy Jane Childress came of age, a young woman with a wry sense of humor, seasoned in coping with the trials of rural poverty in the Upland South. We do not know when and under what circumstances

Nancy met her future husband, George Washington Rader.[42] When first encountering one another, we can imagine that both were painfully shy. Typical of upcountry young people, they only gradually and slowly lost their awe of each other. Perhaps they were never completely comfortable in one another's presence. What we do know with far greater certainty is that despite their commonalities as upland southerners, George Rader came from a different kind of family than his future bride. It is to his family ways that we now turn.

✦ CHAPTER 2 ✦

The German Hat Maker's Family

IF WE CLOSE our eyes for a moment, we can then imagine a four-year-old boy, Karl Rader, or Raeder, as his parents probably spelled their surname, walking down the gangplank of a recently arrived sailing ship in the bustling port city of New York, or perhaps it was in Philadelphia. The year was said to have been 1782, one year before the official end of the American Revolution.[1] Alongside the lad would have trudged his father, Erich H. Rader, and his mother, a brother, and perhaps a sister. Their backs strained from the heavy bags of personal belongings that they had slung over their shoulders. Other kin or acquaintances may have accompanied the Raders, but, if they did, no documentary evidence about them survives. According to an oral account passed down through the centuries by the Rader family, Karl's brother later lived in Tennessee, but we otherwise know nothing about him.

As the Raders disembarked, they found themselves in a strange land where they at once encountered the babble of an unfamiliar tongue. Since they were from Prussia, which later became a part of modern Germany, none of the Raders spoke or understood English. Their native language was German. In German, the word *rad* means "wheel"; hence, the last name of Rader or Raeder suggests that at one time the family made wheels for carts and wagons. Insofar as we know, none of the Raders had been farmers in Germany.

An unsubstantiated family legend holds that the Raders lived for a time in Pennsylvania. The presence of fellow Germans may have lured them there. Indeed, a local German could have paid their passage to America in exchange for their becoming "redemptioners," in other words, indentured servants for a term of five to seven years. Except for the legal obligation of eventual freedom, this popular work system bore similarities to black slavery. While in Pennsylvania, or perhaps elsewhere, Karl learned an unusual trade, that of a "hatter." We can guess that he began acquiring hat-making skills as a ten- or twelve-year-old apprentice to a master craftsman in Philadelphia. He may have lived with the hat maker's family and may have remained legally bound to the senior craftsman until he reached his twenty-first birthday. Making hats was no simple task. Since hats represented something of a fashion statement by the gentlemen of the day, buyers could be difficult to please. Karl may have taken several years to learn the intricacies of forming the tough felt of animal skins or wool into a particular style and to shape it to the specifications of its would-be owners. Yet, it could be a profitable skill, especially for a young man on the frontier.[2]

Indicative of Karl's adventurous and ambitious spirit was his decision (probably in the 1810s) to seek his fortune across the mountains in far-off Kentucky. He passed up possibilities of settling either in the Cumberland Mountains or the famed Blue Grass region of Kentucky; he chose instead to stake his future farther west in or near the tiny town of Munfordville in Hart County. Unlike most migrants of the day, especially those of German descent, Karl apparently made the trek alone. For several decades he was the sole German-born person residing in Hart County. Employing his hat-making skills, he may have at first lived in Munfordville. Perhaps it was there that he courted, proposed, and married Susan "Sukey" Dawson. Inasmuch as Sukey gave birth to their first child, Alfred, on November 21, 1822, we can guess that the couple married in 1821 or 1822, though there is no documentary evidence to support this assertion. In 1824, he acquired one hundred acres on Bacon Creek.

✦   ✦   ✦

While we know far less about Sukey Dawson herself than we do about the women in the Childress clan, it is clear that Sukey came from a different background than either her husband or the Childress family. Of English and Scots Irish origins, the Dawsons were to become one of Hart County's more prominent families. Unlike the Childresses, the Dawsons never evolved into a clan. Jeremiah, Sukey's father, and his descendants settled on the more fertile and flatter lands near the Green River in central Hart County. There, they farmed on terrain similar to what they had left behind in eastern Maryland and Virginia. Members of the Dawson family never made Hart County their permanent homeland. While the Childresses looked mostly inward to their kinfolk for not only economic assistance but also emotional support, the Dawsons' fundamental orientation was outward toward Munfordville and beyond, where they sold their tobacco, bought and sold slaves, purchased goods for their homes, and cultivated friendships. They were decidedly not a hollers people.

In the seventeenth century, a John Dawson, one of many with the same forename in the family, migrated from York, England, to Maryland.[3] A direct descendant also named John, apparently seeking to improve his lot, sometime in the mid-eighteenth century left Maryland for Bedford County, Virginia. There, John tilled land said to have been only a "stone's throw" from the present-day Appalachian Trail. In 1760, he married a Susannah Wood, believed to have been born in Decent, England. As a child Susannah may have lived for a time in Connecticut, which suggests the possibility that she passed on some New England traits to the Dawson family. In any case, John and Susannah had eight known children, among them Jeremiah, their firstborn son.[4]

As a young man, Jeremiah cut an imposing figure. He was said to have been a "muscular" man of "great physical" strength.

At six feet and two inches in height, he towered over most of his contemporaries. Reportedly, "a sober man with excellent habits, simple tastes and high moral character," he allegedly "cared little for the acquisition of wealth." Instead, he devoted "his early years to the manly sports of bear and deer hunting, only giving that attention to his farm required for the maintenance of his family, and the education of his children."[5] Such a characterization, perhaps absent the commitment to the education of children, was apt for countless other men in the southern upcountry; and it may be, though we have no direct proof to support this contention, that Jeremiah Dawson's love of hunting influenced the ways of his descendants, including the Raders who were later to settle on Mahans Creek in southern Missouri.

In 1788, soon after the American Revolution, Jeremiah married a Virginian, Nancy Agnes Dollard. Virtually nothing is known about her except that she reportedly was of Scots Irish and Welsh origins. At the time of her marriage, her family lived near New London, a crossroads inn about fifteen miles from Fredericksburg. Inasmuch as the Virginia militia deployed armaments in New London during the Revolution, it may have been there that Jeremiah first met and courted Nancy. That a Baptist preacher, one Jeremy Hatcher, conducted their marriage ceremony suggests that the Dawson family may have been Baptists in their religious affiliation. Perhaps in 1792 or 1793, Jeremiah and his wife, with two babies in tow and possibly accompanied by his sister, Nancy, and his brother-in-law, Peter Fitzhugh, first crossed the mountains from Virginia to Madison County, Kentucky.

Claiming land granted to him by Virginia for his Revolutionary War service, in 1819 Jeremiah took up acreage in what is sometimes described as the "bends and knobs part" of the Green River basin in the eastern part of what became Hart County. The river flowed through steep banks about fifty feet below the surrounding tablelands, which, because of the absence of trees, were sometimes described as "the Barrens." The soil was not especially rich, but it did have enough fertility to produce bountiful crops of burley tobacco. Even today, under proper management, it can produce more than one hundred bushels of corn or three thousand pounds of tobacco per acre.[6]

The decennial agricultural censuses of 1850 through 1880 offer details about the farming operations of Jeremiah Dawson's sons. Prior to 1850, Jeremiah (who died in 1846) and his sons appear to have been much like their neighbors, essentially self-sufficient farmers who sold and bought little in the marketplace, though they did own more and better acreage than the typical Hart County farmer. It was during this time that Sukey Dawson met and married Karl "Charles" Rader. Perhaps Jeremiah was not "overly ambitious," as the author of his obituary claimed, but by the 1850s, evidence suggests that his casual work attitudes, if they were indeed such, must not have been shared by his sons. By 1860, Jeremiah's second son, Thomas, owned, by central Kentucky's standards, a substantial farm of more than 200 acres, 70 of which were cultivatable. Thomas had six slaves. According to family lore, Thomas and his family "lived in a large brick house, the best in the neighborhood."[7] Ransom Amos Dawson, a younger son, owned an even larger place. In 1860, it consisted of 125 acres of cultivatable land, which was valued at $2,750. Ransom and his three sons between them owned twenty-one slaves.[8]

Both the value of their farms and their ownership of slaves (fewer than one in five farmers in Hart County possessed slaves) indicate the depth of involvement of the Dawsons in the expanding market economy of the day. By the 1850s the Dawson sons began to live well. Unlike many of their neighbors and nearly all of the residents in the western part of Hart County, the Dawsons built for themselves two-story houses (called Plantation Plain style locally but in national terms better known as I style) of sawed lumber and sometimes brick with a central hallway. They owned horse-drawn carriages, purchased expensive furniture, ate with imported silverware, wore fine clothes, and employed African American slaves as both household servants and field hands.

In the post–Civil War era, most of the Dawsons apparently found life and opportunities in Hart County too constrictive.

The war's abolition of slavery undermined the foundations of the tobacco-growing plantation system, and, after the war, tobacco prices fell so drastically that even the most hard-working planter had trouble making a profit. Unlike most of their upland Southern counterparts, many of the Dawsons also had skills and experience in commercial farming that eased their transition from a slave-based economic system into new career paths opened up by the wider economy of late nineteenth-century America.

In short, opportunity beckoned them elsewhere. Towns and cities drew the younger Dawsons, especially the men, away from their kinfolk and the place of their origins. In the late nineteenth century, they dispersed to such far away spots as Louisville, Kentucky, and Denver, Colorado, and to rural Iowa, where they became newspaper editors and publishers, lawyers, merchants, and farmers.[9] By 1900, few traces of the family remained in Hart County. In 2010, there was not a single Dawson surname listed in the local Munfordville phone book and the descendants of the George and Sukey Rader family have completely lost track of their Dawson kinfolk.

✦   ✦   ✦

A startling fact about the Rader family remains: Charles, as he had anglicized his name, was probably sixteen or perhaps seventeen years older than his new wife, Sukie Dawson. Why Sukey agreed to marry a much older man in his early forties who spoke with an accent and exhibited strange ways is unclear. Perhaps Charles's sheer exoticism excited her, but in addition he may have been able to promise her more security than other potential suitors. After all, he was a hat maker and a would-be farmer. Not only that, German Americans had a positive reputation in the southern uplands for their exceptional strong work habits. There was also the matter of Sukey's own "advanced" age; upon their marriage she was at least twenty-three years old, perhaps even twenty-five. By the standards of the day, she was virtually an "old maid." The Dawsons may have also taken some comfort from the fact that Charles was not a Yankee (from a New England family) and apparently not a Catholic. Whatever doubts the Dawsons may have had about their new son-in-law appear to have dissipated over time. Nancy Dawson, Sukey's mother, upon becoming a widower in 1846, actually lived in the Charles Rader household until her death seven years later.

Despite a yawning gap in their ages and ethnic origins, Charles and Sukey Rader did not deny themselves in the marriage bed. They had lots of children—perhaps eight—seven of whom we know with certainty. Among them was their fourth child and the future husband of Nancy Childress, George Washington Rader, who was in time to lead his own family into the Missouri Ozarks. Sukey's children came with clockwork predictability. Her first recorded childbirth was in 1822, when she was some twenty-six years old, some five or six years older than when women in nineteenth-century rural America typically birthed their first child. After about two years of lactation, Sukey probably became pregnant again. The same scenario repeated itself through the remainder of her pregnancies. In other words, from 1822 until about 1842, a rigorous cycle of pregnancies, childbirth, nursing, and childcare dominated her life.

Few hard facts about the ways of the Rader family survive, but it is reasonable to surmise that the family evolved a set of blended customs, beliefs, and behaviors that owed something to both their mother and their father. The parents concluded that their sons, though not their daughters, should acquire at least elementary skills in reading and writing. These skills they probably developed while attending the "Rader School," said to have been located in Rader Hollow. While there are no surviving letters written by family members for this era, one tantalizing scrap of evidence that surfaced many years later indicates that at least one of their sons, Alfred, was a serious reader. Lillie May Rader Raper recalled hearing that, upon the death of her great uncle Alfred in 1887, her father, Jim, received from him not only a "small sum of money" but also a "box of big thick old books."[10] That George, my great grandfather, left no known books, not even a lone Bible, to his descendants suggests that he had little or no interest in books. Neither did any of his children exhibit an unusual interest in formal learning. However, all of them were literate, provided that the term is defined generously.[11]

We can presume that the men in the family normally dressed in high-waisted trousers, homespun shirts, and boots and wore the large-brimmed hats of the day. Suspenders rather than belts (belts belong to the twentieth century) held up their trousers. Women's dresses nearly always consisted of home-spun linsey-woolsey (a coarse, woven fabric of wool from sheep and linen processed from flax) but, as family circumstances improved, cotton may have become the fabric of choice. The faces of family members can exist only in our imaginations. The only extant photo we have is of a son, George, which was taken several years after the Civil War. Probably male family members resembled George, whose most striking feature was his unusual height of six feet. We also know from Confederate army records that his brother, Jeremiah, grew to six feet and one inch. Jeremiah and George may have inherited their unusual height from their maternal grandfather, six-feet-and-two-inch Jeremiah Dawson.

✦   ✦   ✦

If not at once, in time the Charles and Sukey Rader family enjoyed more material success than the Childress clan. Part of the reason may have been Charles's propensity for hard work and returns from his hat-making skills.[12] But the family also had the good fortune of owning a farm that was on a busy wagon road. The road provided the Raders with an easy route for the marketing of surplus corn, flax, hogs, cattle, or tobacco in Munfordville. Their land, the "cultivatable" part of which was likely to have been in patches scattered on the Rader Hollow or Bacon Creek floor, was also more fertile than that farmed by the Childress clan. The thirty acres of which were "cultivatable" in 1850 yielded 750 bushels of corn, a not insignificant number for that day. Indeed, the total was more than any of Charles's nearest neighbors.

Charles and Sukey may have passed on a strong work ethic to

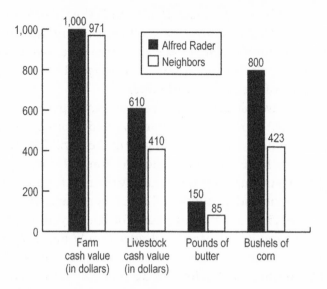

Alfred Rader's farm compared with the average of his neighbors' farms in Hart County, Kentucky, 1860. *Source:* US Bureau of the Census, "Non-Population Census of Fifteen Southern States, Agricultural" (Hart County, Kentucky, 1860), microfilm copy in Kentucky Department of Libraries and Archives, Frankfort, Kentucky.

their sons, in particular, to their eldest son, Alfred. Said to have had a "sweetheart" as a young man, Alfred never married. He was probably the beneficiary of a common practice in rural societies; in return for agreeing to care for his aging parents, he would inherit the family farm. Apparently, none of the Rader's other children inherited any land. In any event, in the 1850s Alfred took over operation of the farm and apparently integrated the farm's productivity more fully into a growing regional market that was occasioned in part by the completion through Munfordville of the Louisville and Nashville Turnpike in 1849 and the Louisville and Nashville Railroad a decade later. By 1855, Alfred had added two hundred acres to the original family homestead, and by 1857 his total landholding had jumped to four hundred acres, only eighty of which was reported as cultivatable.

Alfred, unlike the Dawsons, eschewed slave labor. Instead, he apparently relied mainly on adult kinfolk: his brother, George, at least one of his brothers-in-law (Benjamin Taylor), and a nephew (Samuel Taylor). Alfred may have entered tenant agreements with these adult male relatives as well as with other families. His family network also included several teen-aged boys who were probably part of the farm's workforce.

The extensive military operations in and around Munfordville during the Civil War may have offered Alfred additional opportunities to profit. In 1865, the final year of the Civil War, Alfred's earnings were large enough to require him, as one of only a handful of Hart County residents, to pay the new federal income tax. By 1875, he had accumulated a 638-acre farm, which was assessed at $1,538, a substantial sum for that day. Reflective of Alfred's growing wealth was the Rader family home. Built of logs, it consisted of two stories with seven rooms as well as a basement. In short, well before his death in 1887, by local standards, Alfred had become a moderately wealthy man.[13] Alfred's story of material success as a bachelor suggests that the conventional wisdom holding that children were economic assets in agricultural societies may be open to question.

✦ ✦ ✦

The Raders differed from the Childresses in other respects. Whereas the Raders had the material wherewithal to enjoy a higher position in Hart County's nineteenth-century social hierarchy than did the Childresses, it is unclear to what degree they were accepted among the local people as "natives." It may be that not only Charles's German origins but also the family's apparent absence of enthusiasm for evangelical Protestantism prevented the family's complete integration into Hart County society. The family was never swept up by the revivals and camp meetings that were regularly held on Bacon Creek at the nearby town of Bonnieville.[14]

On the other hand, since Charles Rader's wife, Sukey, was a Dawson, we can surmise that the Raders had an ongoing relationship with at least some members of the disparate Dawson family. Furthermore, the marriages in the 1840s of their three daughters—Elizabeth, Martha, and Mary—to John Taylor, John Logsdon, and Benjamin Taylor, respectively, tied the Raders to local families whose claims to being natives were indisputable. The senior Raders seem to have been particularly close to their daughter and son-in-law, Mary and Ben Taylor, who lived on an adjacent farm. Sukey Rader may have lived in the Taylor household during her declining years, and Alfred for a time employed Samuel Taylor, a nephew, as a hired hand. The Rader family cemetery, in which Charles, Sukey, and Alfred were buried, was on property apparently first owned by Alfred and then later by Ben Taylor. The three Rader sisters had twenty-two surviving children.[15] Many of whose descendants live in Hart County to this day.

But even if his neighbors never fully accepted Charles as a native, he rapidly assimilated much of their culture. While Charles spoke with a deep accent throughout his life, nothing survives in the family's history of anything that could be considered conspicuously "German"—no words or phrases, no special German foods, no distinctively German clothing. He never insisted upon bestowing an explicitly German forename on any of his children. Instead, he and Sukey chose names familiar to their neighbors. Upon three of their five male children they even assigned names associated with the early history of the American republic, suggesting perhaps a rejection by Charles of a German identity. The forenames of their children in descending birth order were Alfred (named after an early Anglo-Saxon monarch?), Elizabeth (biblical and former queen of England), Martha Jane (biblical), George Washington, Mary Magdalene (biblical), Jeremiah Dawson (probably named after Sukey's father), Thomas Jefferson, and Andrew Jackson.[16]

That they named their youngest sons Thomas Jefferson Rader and Andrew Jackson Rader, respectively, suggests that the family members were Jacksonian Democrats in their political leanings, as were most of their neighbors. While neither Charles nor any of his sons ever actively engaged in politics, one of Sukey's uncles, a James A. Dawson, was elected clerk of Hart County twice as a Democrat, voted for Stephen A. Douglas in 1860, and after the war won election as the state land officer twice as a candidate of the Union Democracy Party.[17] We also know that later all four sons of George Washington Rader, Lewis, James, Jeremiah, and Martin Edward (known as Edward Martin "Sam"), who settled on Mahans Creek in Missouri, at one time or another publicly supported the Democratic Party. Their allegiance to the party of Jackson can be plausibly traced back to their grandparents, but it is equally plausible that they obtained their party allegiance from their mother's family, the Childresses, who, according to family lore, were also mostly Democrats.[18]

✦   ✦   ✦

In the meantime, the newly married (as of 1852) George and Nancy (Childress) Raders enjoyed far less material success than the more senior Raders. According to the Hart County tax rolls in 1851, George owned no land and had no taxable farm property. One year after his marriage, he had acquired a horse, two cows, and three hogs, but still no land. Neither did he report the production of any corn, wheat, or tobacco. He surely grew corn but it is likely that his contribution was reported as part of his brother Alfred's farming operation. That George did not even appear in the 1860 agricultural census, one that required an annual production of commodities worth at least $100 in order to be counted, suggests that George was making virtually no headway toward becoming a successful farmer.[19] Everything that he produced probably went to the sustenance of his rapidly growing family or as payments-in-kind to his brother for the use of his sibling's land.

George did succeed in siring a large family. During the first twenty-four years of their marriage, Nancy had thirteen children, at least two of whom died during infancy. Nancy, as with perhaps most hollers women and perhaps reflecting the influence of her Irish American mother, probably approached the on-coming pregnancies with mixed feelings or perhaps fatalistic resignation.[20] Even if and when she wanted to avoid pregnancies by practicing abstinence, the close quarters of cabins crowded with children may have encouraged her to acquiesce quietly to the sexual advances of her husband. In addition, in her family culture, it appears to have been expected that women would have many children. Children, Nancy and George may have reasoned, could provide additional help in their log home or on the farm and, as the children reached adulthood, offspring could offer security to their aging parents. Given the drudgery and seclusion of much of her life, Nancy may have even welcomed the addition of children for their companionship, and they may have given a larger meaning to her otherwise bleak existence. As one mother in Appalachia put it many years later, "If I didn't have my children, I wouldn't have nothin'."[21]

In the choice of forenames for their children, Nancy and George acknowledged their ancestors and extended family. Their first five children all bore ancestral first names: Mary (the forename of Nancy's mother, Mary Hare), Charles (George's father), John Wesley (Nancy's father), and Jeremiah (George's maternal grandfather). Some of the siblings of Nancy (Robert and James) and George (Martha, and Mary) may have also had family names. While seven of the names can be traced back to the Bible, all of these except Keziah (one of Job's three daughters) and Rose were the names of close relatives as well.[22]

Despite the family's modest circumstances, for their time and place the children received a reasonably good education. All of them were literate, though Robert "Mike" was an indifferent speller. Lewis, on the other hand, was described in his later years as a "very brilliant" man; for many years he assisted Shannon County, Missouri, officers in carrying out their duties. And my grandfather, E. M. "Sam," possessed good spelling and handwriting skills, was an avid reader of popular periodicals, and authored crude poetry. James "Jim" and Keziah were also known for their quick minds; and Jeremiah "Jerry," for his storytelling abilities. All of the children apparently attended one-room schools, either in Roseburg, Kentucky, or (the younger ones) in Delaware, Missouri.

Despite good intentions, a gulf, one that may have widened over time, appears to have separated the lives of Nancy and

George. Nancy's life experiences, as with nearly all farm wives of her day, were more physically circumscribed; they consisted of dwelling and working almost exclusively in the close confines of the family's home or nearby on the farm. Other women and children comprised her primary associations. As with nearly all farm women, Nancy's life entailed unremitting sacrifice, first on behalf of her husband, followed by her sons, then her daughters, and lastly on behalf of herself. With perhaps a dim awareness, she may have experienced some consolation by looking upon her lot as a calling arising from her sex, one of service on behalf of others and of suffering to be borne meekly and without complaint.

George probably shared little of Nancy's day-to-day life. Apart from eating and sleeping in the same cabin with his wife and children, he spent much of his time with other males and outdoors, where he toiled on the farm and during seasonal lulls was for the most part foot-loose and fancy free. He trekked through the woods, visited the local country store and post office, and did nearly all of the family's buying and selling.[23] Something of the daring and recklessness of youth remained with him and most other upcountry men throughout their lives. For them, there was always the excitement of conquering a bit of the wilderness, of hunting, fishing, and trading.

There is other evidence that, despite their daily interdependence and their sexual union, a chasm may have existed between the couple. An important one was religion. Unlike her husband, Nancy not only came from a strict evangelical family but also was known for her religiosity. At the age of fifteen, she had had a searing conversion experience that shaped her entire life. Unlike the family of her in-laws, she apparently attended religious (Methodist) services regularly, both before and after her marriage to George. From her feminine-dominated world of home and church, conflict may have arisen over her efforts to restrain the more freewheeling behavioral universe of her husband and her male children.[24]

As thoroughly Protestant as Nancy was, she admired no one more than her Irish American mother (Mary Hare Childress) and exhibited in much of her life a singular boldness and determination in the face of adversity similar to that of her Irish ancestors. The 1874 Hart County tax roll revealed that Nancy even owned taxable property of her own—a horse and three head of cattle![25] For their time and place, this was unusual. It may have even meant that the couple's relationship had festered into open hostility. That they may have resolved their differences in this singular respect can be inferred from the absence of reports of separate property ownership after 1874, but their presumed resolution of this issue does not allay the possibility that, sadly, in an important psychological sense, they remained forever apart.

✦ CHAPTER 3 ✦

Hard Times in Hart County

IN THE WAKE of the firing on Fort Sumter, South Carolina, on April 12 and 13 of 1861, nothing at first changed very much in Hart County. But then, in the fall and early winter, alarming reports began to spread up and down the hollows and across the barrens of the county. The whole area became "a sort of no-man's land with a great deal of scouting activity and numerous skirmishes," a Civil War historian later wrote.[1] Finally, on the chilly morning of December 5, 1861, the realities of warfare struck close to home, indeed, almost at the back doors of the Rader families. Only four miles away, up Bacon Creek toward Bonnieville, the family learned that John Hunt Morgan and his Confederate cavalry unit had set fire to the Louisville and Nashville railroad trestle. Afterward, Alfred and George Rader may have ridden up the creek to survey the damage. Morgan quickly moved on to other targets, and Union forces rebuilt the bridge, but, determined to slow the shipment of Northern troops and supplies into Kentucky and Tennessee, thirty days later "Morgan's Raiders" returned. After heaping stubble and wood on the trestle, they set fire to it again.

With Morgan's daring raids and with hundreds of Union troops now guarding the nearby Louisville and Nashville Railroad, the Raders no longer enjoyed the luxury of ignoring the war. As with most Kentuckians, the older folks may have initially pined for a compromise between North and South, or, barring that, they may have hoped that Kentucky could somehow remain neutral. But men began to choose sides. In late 1862, both Alfred and George, the older boys in the Charles Rader family, joined the Kentucky Volunteers of the Union army. In the meantime, in far-off San Antonio, Texas, their younger brother, Jeremiah "Jerry" Dawson Rader, signed with the Confederacy's Second Texas Cavalry. For the Charles and Sukey Rader family, the Civil War was not just symbolically a familial conflict; it had become, in fact, a deadly "brother's war."

✦ ✦ ✦

The war was not a happy occasion for Jeremiah Rader. He had had hopes of becoming a successful Hart County farmer like his brother Alfred; in 1854 he had purchased one hundred acres from the public domain.[2] At that date he was twenty years old. Probably the same piece of land (in Jeremiah's name) appeared on the tax rolls of Hart County in 1859. From that date, the land continues to be listed regularly on the tax rolls until 1867, when Jeremiah, as a landholder, disappears from the public record. Seeking adventure or better economic circumstances, sometime in the 1850s Jerry left Hart County; he may have accompanied a branch of his mother's family (the Childresses) who settled in Texas during the late 1850s.[3]

In the meantime, the Civil War began, and, perhaps induced by a $50 signing bonus, Jerry enlisted as a private with Company E of the Second Texas Cavalry regiment in San Antonio, Texas. According to Confederate war records, he had grey eyes, light brown hair, and stood six feet and one inch tall. In 1861 and 1862, he saw military action in what later became the territories of New Mexico and Arizona. Perhaps it was then that he contracted syphilis from a prostitute who accompanied his unit; in any event, on May 2, 1863, the General Hospital in Houston, Texas, admitted him as a patient suffering from an acute case of "syphilitic rheumatism." Except for brief furloughs, he remained hospitalized in Houston until the surrender of his unit to Union forces on June 2, 1865. At the bottom of his parole document, which bears his signature, is written "Munfordville, Ky."[4]

Whether Jerry made it back to Munfordville, however, is a mystery. A legend persists in Hart County that he did, but that he then died shortly after his return. At the least, the Hart County tax rolls continued to report him as the owner of one hundred acres. Finally, in 1868 not only does his name disappear from the tax rolls but Alfred's landholding increased by one hundred acres, suggesting that Alfred may have inherited or assumed ownership of his land. During this entire time frame in which Jeremiah owned the land, the tax rolls indicate that no one actively farmed the acreage. It seems likely that Alfred paid the taxes that accrued on the property.

✦ ✦ ✦

While neither Alfred nor George Rader immediately volunteered for service—not even in the wake of Morgan's raids in 1861 and 1862—a more concerted effort by the Confederacy to invade Kentucky, where it was believed that there were thousands of Southern sympathizers, may have precipitated their decisions. Surviving Union records indicate that a "George Rader," precisely six feet tall and with gray eyes, joined Company B of the Thirty-third Kentucky Infantry for a three-year hitch on August 14, 1862, one day after his first cousin, James A. Dawson, had been granted permission to organize the unit. On September 2, an "Alfred Rador" enrolled under the same terms in the same company. That Alfred's age was listed as forty years (and therefore conforms to his age as given in the census) is evidence that his name should have been recorded as "Alfred Rader" and that he was, in fact, the older brother of George Rader. Yet mystery surrounds Alfred's Civil War record. While he appeared on Company B's "Muster-in Roll" on September 13, 1862, as well as on the roll of Company B on December 23, 1862, it appears that he never actually mustered for active duty. It could be that, given Alfred's advanced age and the need to have someone stay on the farm to care for the family's aging parents and perhaps George's wife and children as well, that George, and perhaps even James Dawson, his cousin, who was commander of the infantry unit, advised him to simply ignore calls to active service. In any case, a cryptic note in his file indicates that he was absent from the company's muster roll of December 31, 1862, and that he was "not bourne [carried or present?] on subt [subsequent?] rolls for Co [B?]."[5] No other evidence exists of Alfred's service.

Questions remain. Why did George volunteer? After all, he was thirty-two years old, almost ten years older than the typical volunteer, married, and had six children. And why did he side with the Union? His younger brother was already in service for the Confederacy, and, according to family legend, George's wife, Nancy, or perhaps it was his mother, Sukey, was pro-Southern. On one occasion, according to family lore, Sukey would not let him in the house until he shed his Yankee uniform.[6] It is easy to imagine that, since Sukey had at least one son fighting for the Confederacy, she might have made such a demand. However, her extended family (the Dawsons) was pro-Union. According to the memory of Nancy (Rader) Priddy, her father, Mike Rader, told her that "grandmother would not let him [George] in the house until he got rid of his dirty uniform and donned clean clothes."[7] Reportedly, Sukey feared that his uniform might have been infested with lice.

In any case, George's decision to bear arms for the Union seems to have been in harmony with the extended Rader family. While several of the Dawsons owned slaves, it appears that most, perhaps all of them, remained loyal to the Union. Indeed, not only did James A. Dawson, a son of Ransom, help form the Twenty-sixth Infantry Regiment of the Kentucky Volunteers, he also served as the adjutant general of the regiment. (Later on, James pursued a successful career as an official in Kentucky state government.) Only one Childress—Elijah—seems to have joined the Union army; he, like George, volunteered for the Twenty-sixth Infantry Regiment commanded by Dawson. There are no Childresses from Hart County listed on the rosters of the Confederate army.

Still, given that his brother joined a Rebel cavalry unit in Texas, that he was of an advanced age, that he had a large family, and that, insofar as we can tell, the family had been adherents of the Democratic Party invites speculation about why George volunteered for service.[8] Perhaps it had something to do with his namesake, George Washington, who had been immortalized as the Father of the Country and symbolized more than any other single American the construction of the new union that became the United States. As with many in the Upland South, it may also have been that, while George Rader regarded blacks with contempt, he simultaneously opposed slavery. Most compellingly of all, George, as with countless other volunteers, was swept up by the excitement of the moment. Several of his friends and kinfolk leapt to the colors. Three of his friends—his future son-in-law Lewis Perkins and Lewis's brother, James, along with George's brother-in-law, Benjamin Franklin Taylor—all volunteered in the same regimental unit.[9] A cash enlistment bonus, said to have totaled $350, and the prospect of receiving $13 a month in pay as a private surely contributed most of all to George's decision. With that much money, he could purchase a small tract of unimproved farmland, which he apparently did in 1865. In short, he may have seen the enlistment bonus as an opportunity to become an independent yeoman farmer.

Apparently, neither George nor any of his local friends participated in one of the most important military engagements in Kentucky, the Battle of Munfordville, or the Battle of the Bridge, as it is sometimes called. (George was not mustered into service until three months after the battle.) Both North and South recognized the strategic importance of the Louisville and Nashville Railroad, which crossed the Green River near Munfordville. A widely recognized technological marvel when it was completed in 1859, the 1,000-foot-long bridge consisted of five massive spans of steel that towered 115 feet above the river. Union troops, who were mostly from Indiana and, incidentally, of German descent, fortified the bridge against a possible Confederate assault.

On September 14, the Rebels struck; they launched an

unsuccessful attack on the fortification that left 35 of their men dead and 253 wounded. The next day additional Confederate troops arrived; they surrounded and laid siege to the Union forces. On September 17, the Union commander, John T. Wilder, after having been allowed to tour Confederate ranks firsthand, concluded that he and his men confronted overwhelmingly adverse odds. He surrendered nearly 5,000 men to the Rebels. The Southern commander, Braxton Bragg, proceeded to burn the bridge and parole the captured Union troops.

In terms of Rader family history, there is a curious footnote to the Battle of Munfordville. On September 20 and 21, the third and fourth days after Wilder's surrender, Alfred Rader sold in total sixty bushels of corn and five hundred pounds of hay for $50 to the Confederate army![10] Bragg's army, which was about to embark on a march northward out of Munfordville, was in desperate need of supplies. Perhaps Alfred was coerced into selling the goods or perhaps his sympathies had shifted in favor of the Rebels, but, given his history of successful entrepreneurship, it is possible that he seized on the opportunity to profit by trading with the Rebels.

As with countless other Civil War soldiers, George Rader's most serious problem while in the army was sickness rather than wounds or death from combat. Only three months after the Battle of Munfordville, on December 23, 1862, his commanding officer reported him as absent with leave because of an unnamed illness.[11] While seeking to recover, Nancy probably cared for him at their nearby home. But on February 13, 1863, only a little more than a month later, he was convalescing in the Munfordville military hospital (housed in the local Presbyterian Church) with a high fever. He remained hospitalized for sixty-one days. According to the post surgeon, C. D. Moren, George had a "long spell of Typhoid Fever, of about 3 months duration, locating in the left leg, once affected [infected?] by 'white swelling' atrophy of the leg & in consequence of which he is unfit for duty. Said disability occurring in the line of duty."[12] On April 2, 1863, less than seven months into his enlistment, the army granted Rader an honorable discharge based on his physical disability.

During the subsequent years of the war, thousands of troops

either encamped or passed through Hart County. A substantial number of Union solders, many of whom were former slaves, garrisoned at Munfordville itself. In order to suppress widespread Confederate guerilla activity and Southern sympathizers, on July 5, 1864, President Abraham Lincoln imposed martial law and suspended the writ of habeas corpus throughout the state of Kentucky. The military governor of Kentucky, General Stephen Burbridge, savagely enforced the measures, including an order for the execution of four captured Confederate guerillas whenever any "unarmed Union citizen" was "murdered." Burbridge also used his extensive powers to try to control Kentucky's state and presidential election in 1864.[13] Although there is no concrete evidence that the Rader family opposed Burbridge's actions or that any family members joined the local Ku Klux Klan after the war, it is conceivable that these repressive measures ensured that the Rader family would emerge from the war as Democrats.

George Rader never fully recovered from the effects of his Civil War illness. In an application (in 1874) for a pension, he claimed that he was "totally disabled from obtaining his subsistence by his physical labor." Although he could hardly walk, let alone do heavy farm work, on his atrophied left leg, the US government, based on the technicality that it could not locate the records of his unit at the time of his illness, refused to extend to him any benefits.[14] In the meantime, he and his wife, Nancy, confronted another emotionally wrenching experience; their twins—Martha and Frank—died in infancy in 1865. That year the tax list reported that he had three horses, thirteen head of cattle, and six hogs, but George grew only seventy-five bushels of corn on what was probably his newly acquired farm.[15] Little did the family anticipate additional setbacks, which eventually drove them to flee their Kentucky homeland.

✦   ✦   ✦

How much was legend and how much was fact can never be determined. One version of the story insists that it happened in 1878, somewhere in Hart County, Kentucky, when Robert

George Washington Rader, about 1878. While in
formal attire he appears to be prosperous, other evidence indicates that the family was not well off, even
by the standards of Hart County, Kentucky, in his
day. *Courtesy of the author.*

Michael "Mike" Pitch Patrick Napoleon Calhoun Rader, a son
of George and Nancy Rader, brawled with a neighboring man,
Alonzo "Lon" Stewart. Too much drink, an argument over cards,
or a dispute over the affections of a young woman may have
precipitated their no-holds-barred fight. Perhaps it was a matter
of honor, a subject about which upland Southern men were
extraordinarily sensitive.[16] Eighteen-year-old Mike may have

taken offense to something twenty-year-old Stewart had said about the Rader family or Mike may have questioned Stewart's paternity. Perhaps it was Mike's hot temper. He was known locally as "the Fighting Irishman," a sobriquet that he apparently acquired because his grandmother, Polly Hare Childress, was of Irish origins. Years later, Mike's daughter acknowledged that her father was "as ready with his fists as he was with his wits" to put right a perceived wrong.[17]

According to oral accounts passed down by the Raders, the stout young men grappled with one another before Stewart, baring his teeth, tried to rip Mike's upper lip from his face. With his dangling lip bleeding profusely, Mike retaliated by pulling a knife out of his pocket and shoving it deep into Lon Stewart's belly. Thinking that he had surely killed his antagonist, Mike then fled the scene. Upon arriving at the Rader family home, Mike borrowed a mirror, a needle, and some thread, and sewed his own lip back into place. But, alas, his mother, Nancy, told him that the "black dye [in the thread] would poison him, [so] he removed [the thread] . . . and re-sewed it with white [thread] occasionally whistling with pain [as he did so]."[18]

Fearful that the local authorities might press murder charges against their son and that the incident might touch off a bloody feud with the Stewart family, George and Nancy Rader panicked. Or at least this is one version of the story. Quickly gathering up their children and what possessions they could, they fled Kentucky for the Missouri Ozarks. But, later on, upon learning that Lon Stewart had somehow survived the knifing (apparently, Mike had not actually "gutted" his victim as he believed he had done), Mike returned to Kentucky to finish the job. He never got a chance, for in the meantime, according to family legend, Stewart had disappeared. Yet, cold fact suggests that the legend was in error; for the 1880 census reported that Stewart was still living near Cub Run, not far from where the Rader family had lived before they had departed for the Ozarks. By this time, Mike, who was a part-time farmer, stonemason, builder, and general roustabout, may have returned to Missouri, or perhaps for reasons unknown the feud between the two men had abated.

Whatever had happened, we can presume that in the telling

and retelling of this story, facts may have been lost or distorted. What it did do was offer subsequent generations of the Rader family a mythical hero of epic proportions. Recounting of this dramatic fight by Mike's later kinfolk also strengthened a sense of their identity as a historic family.

Still, there are good reasons to doubt that the brawl had much, or anything, to do with the final decision of the Rader family to flee their small farm near Roseburg, Kentucky, where they lived in the midst of the Childress clan.[19] Indeed, the tussle between Mike Rader and Lon Stewart might have occurred *after* the remainder of the Rader family had departed for Missouri. In any case, behind the family's decision to leave Kentucky was a more elemental reality. From their marriage in 1852 to their departure to Missouri in 1878, George and Nancy had been unable to secure a firm place in Hart County's agricultural society. The story of their hard times in Hart County sheds light not only on the George Rader family's ways but also on the extraordinarily difficult circumstances—growing family size, rising land prices, warfare, and falling farm prices—that they and countless other upland southern farmers encountered in mid-nineteenth-century America.

✦ ✦ ✦

In coping with grinding poverty, the Rader family was not alone in Hart County. The years following the Civil War, J. Anderson Childress wrote many years later, "were lean times for the Hill People." The soil on the hillsides had never been as fertile as the bottomland along the creeks and the rivers. And "after the first hill land had been cleared," explained Childress, "the top soil began to be quickly leached into the creeks and rivers."[20] Soil exhaustion was not the only problem. "The some 15 years after the Civil War," added Childress, "the [hill] country was in the grip of a deep recession; the price of tobacco and other products of the farm were at rock bottom. The people were, with very few exceptions, in a dire state of poverty."[21] In desperation, many of them abandoned their farms for points westward.

In the wake of the war, the Raders themselves experienced a series of setbacks. The leg injury that George had sustained in the CivilWar made hard, manual labor difficult if not impossible for him. In March or April of 1865, Nancy was pregnant yet again. That dry summer their farm produced a mere seventy-five bushels of corn. Only aid from George's brother, Alfred, and the Childress clan may have kept starvation at bay in the Rader household. But the family did have one consolation; finally, after thirteen years of marriage, they acquired some land of their own.[22] Because a fire destroyed Hart County's land records, the location of this farm is uncertain, though it appears that it was near Roseburg on Cane Creek in the vicinity of the Childress clan.[23]

It must not have been a very good farm. The tax rolls suggest that nearly all of the land was unsuitable for growing corn, wheat, or tobacco. For the years from 1865 through 1869, assessors placed its value between $100 and $250, figures that were near the bottom quartile for Hart County. Even more revelatory of the farm's inadequacy and the family's dire straits was the size of George's annual corn crop. He typically grew between one hundred and two hundred bushels per year (a piddling figure—less than a third as much as Alfred Rader). George owned only five or six hogs, a couple of horses or mules, and four to six head of cattle.

As the family continued to grow in size, the tax rolls from 1870 through 1874 show George as suddenly owning no land. Neither did his sons. Perhaps George either sold the original one hundred acres or forfeited it because of his inability to pay taxes or to pay off a loan that he had on the land. It is also possible that the one hundred acres reverted to Alfred Rader. In any case, he and his immediate family completely disappear from the tax rolls of 1870 and 1871.[24] It may be that during this time George took up farming as a tenant on some of the land owned by John W. Childress, his father-in-law, or land owned by another family member.

In 1875, the family's condition improved, but at best only slightly. George again reportedly owned one hundred acres, which was assessed at $400. George now owned two horses or mules, eight cows, and five hogs. It is, of course, possible that George underreported the size of his farm's operation. In particular, we can suspect that he might not have told the assessor about hogs he had that were living on the open range. Unfortunately, surviving tax assessment records for Hart County end in 1875, but we can surmise that the family's economic circumstance remained unchanged or worsened in 1876, 1877, and 1878. These were years of a nationwide depression triggered by the Panic of 1873.

✦   ✦   ✦

In the midst of these hard times, the Rader family began to toy with taking a life-altering step: why not pull up stakes and seek a better life elsewhere? Still, the argument against leaving the family homeland must have been a strong one. In 1878, George was forty-eight and Nancy forty-seven years old. They had deep emotional ties to western Hart County. It was a familiar physical habitat, one that had offered them the only way of life that they knew. And above all there were the family ties, especially to the Childress clan. "A son is a son until he takes a wife," went an Irish saying. "A daughter is a daughter all her life." We can imagine that the generous Childresses, as best as they could, provided the Raders with temporary jobs and emergency food and clothing. George and Nancy also had at least some continuing ties with George's siblings, both his brother Alfred and his married sisters.[25]

The arguments for abandoning their poor, hillside farm on the Cane Creek waterway were equally compelling. Not only had they experienced year after year of hardship, but George and Nancy had failed to fulfill a customary obligation of rural families. They had been unable to make any headway in providing their male children with an adequate start in life. In exchange for land, it was understood that their sons would care for them in their declining years. In 1878, with only one hundred acres, most of which was unimproved, George and Nancy Rader had virtually no land to will to their offspring. (It may be that one of their sons, Mike Rader, did later acquire this land.) The future prospects for George and Nancy and their sons acquiring additional quality farmland land in Hart County were next to non-existent. Since 1850, the county's population had nearly doubled; and improved land, even the poor ground on the hillsides, could cost as much as ten dollars per acre.[26]

Family deaths may have tipped the balance in favor of the family's departure. In 1876, Nancy's father and the patriarch of the clan died, and two years later, Polly Hare Childress, her mother, passed away. No longer was Nancy obligated to care for her parents. Her strongest ties to Hart County had been forever severed.

✦ ✦ ✦

That the George Washington Rader family chose to begin their lives anew in a particular place, Shannon County, Missouri, should occasion little surprise. True, being without a railroad or a turnpike, it was a far more isolated place than Hart County, but its ruggedness was similar to the family's homeland, and, above all else, it was there that they could find cheap land. It was a center of bushwhacking during the Civil War and Reconstruction era; thus, dozens of families had fled the county, leaving behind their log houses and small farms. The Raders eventually settled on one of these abandoned farms. According to the 1880 census, only 3,341 people resided in the entirety of Shannon County, even though in land area the county was the second largest in the state of Missouri. While Hart County boasted 41 persons per square mile in 1880, Shannon County had only 3.5 persons per square mile. My mother, Lydia (Eddings) Rader, had it right when she wrote several years ago that in Shannon County, the Raders found "more elbow room" and more opportunities for "hunting and fishing" than they had enjoyed back in Kentucky.[27]

The Raders may have already had some concrete knowledge of the Ozarks. Among their sources could have been their very own daughter, Mary, and her husband, Lewis Perkins. The census of 1870 reported that Mary and her family resided in

Pocahontas, Randolph County, Arkansas, which is some fifty miles south of Shannon County. It could be that the Perkins family traveled through the county while on their way to or from Kentucky; it is even possible that they lived in the county for a brief time.[28] The two oldest Rader sons also may have visited the county more than once prior to 1878. Another relative may have been Benjamin Franklin Childress, a brother of Nancy's, whom, it was said, resided for a time in Shannon County in the 1870s. He returned to Hart County but later on moved back to Mahans Creek, "where the fishin' was awful good," he explained.[29] So, it is possible that Ben Childress, the Perkins family, and perhaps others regaled the Raders with the wonders of south central Missouri. In the hills and hollows of Shannon County, they may have told an attentive family, one could still find a place to farm, hunt, fish, and live largely undisturbed by the outside world.

✦   ✦   ✦

The Rader trip to Missouri in 1878 bore only a faint resemblance to the popular image of a pioneer family making their way westward in covered wagons pulled by oxen through the vast spaces of the Great Plains and the Rocky Mountain West. Neither did it correspond to a more contemporary image of traveling westward by steamboat or rail. Instead, the Rader party set out in mule- or horse-drawn wagons on muddy or, conversely, dusty, deeply rutted roads. They encountered no Native Americans. For most of their trip across Kentucky, Indiana, Illinois, and Missouri, they passed through settled areas of framed farmhouses, cultivated fields, fences, and numerous small towns. They even crossed several railroad tracks.

At least twenty-one persons, perhaps several more than this, made the trip. They included George and Nancy Rader and all their living children. They loaded their wagons with essentials —clothing, cooking utensils, axes, and perhaps a few chickens. A non-essential item included a heavy stalagmite from the Childress Cave in Kentucky that Nancy insisted on bringing along for future use as her gravestone. To their wagons they may have tethered a cow or two. When not chasing rabbits, a couple of dogs trotted alongside the wagons. Riding in the wagons were probably the older folk—George, Nancy, Lewis, and Mary—while the others either rode horseback or walked. At evening time, they gathered around a campfire to eat. Provided that it was not raining, most of the family slept on the ground in the open air. It was a long, slow, and sometimes tortuous, sometimes fun (at least for the children) journey. It could have taken them at least a month, perhaps two, to traverse more than four hundred miles.[30] Wherever they went, the local people must have stared at the slow-moving entourage of poor Kentuckians with some surprise, perhaps even some misgivings.

Their route is uncertain. The first segment may have taken them from Roseburg, Kentucky, down the nearby Green River Valley toward the Ohio River. Supportive of this contention is an episode probably first told by Mike Rader. Mike claimed that the Rader sons got into a "pitched battle" with a "gang of Negro boys" at Owensboro, Kentucky. Why is uncertain. Neither side incurred deaths or serious injuries. According to Nancy (Rader) Priddy, the daughter of Fighting Mike, it was "not racial prejudice" that led to the melee but "just two gangs of boys itching for a fight."[31] Nonetheless, the boys never told their father, George, about the incident for fear that he might punish them severely. And Nancy Priddy's interpretation notwithstanding, we can suspect, if indeed this fight occurred, that it could have been reflective of the deepening racial hostilities of the day.

Presumably, the Rader caravan crossed the Ohio River near or at Evansville, Indiana, and then proceeded westward across the southern part of Indiana and Illinois. They then ferried across the Mississippi River at Greer's Ferry near Cape Girardeau, Missouri, a popular river crossing point of the day. From there, they apparently journeyed southwestwardly to Van Buren, Missouri, or they may have floated down the Ohio River to near Cairo, Illinois, where they may have ferried across the Mississippi. They then proceeded westward to Poplar Bluff and from there to Van Buren. At Poplar Bluff, they first encountered the Ozarks, where the land was poorer, settlement was thinner, the trees were much denser, the hills were steeper, and the roads were unimproved except for the removal of bigger tree stumps and rocks, either of which, by the breakage of wagon wheels, tongues, or axles, could cause long delays.

After having ferried across the Current River or forded it upstream where the water was shallower, they continued westward on a rough road that paralleled modern US Highway 60—known at the time as the Springfield Road—to a general area called Woodland. Woodland was some two miles east of Birch Prairie (later known as Birch Tree) in Shannon County. A fellow Kentuckian, John Weaver, who had been living there for several years, may have recommended this spot to them. There, the Raders took up tenant farming.

✦   ✦   ✦

Upon arrival at Woodland, the Rader family surely had some misgivings about leaving their Kentucky homeland. By fleeing to Shannon County, Missouri, they in effect stepped back in time. There was not a single graveled toll road in the entire county, while Munfordville was on a busy all-weather toll road that connected Louisville, Kentucky, to the north, and Nashville, Tennessee, to the south. Neither was there a single mile of railroad track in Shannon County; the nearest railroad head in 1880 was Salem, which was some forty-five miles from the county seat of Eminence. Even before the Civil War, people could board a train in Munfordville and find themselves in Louisville or Nashville in less than two hours. Downtown Munfordville featured brick stores and churches as well as several elegant private homes, while Eminence, the biggest town in Shannon County, had less than 150 residents, nearly all of whom lived in log houses. In 1885, the local weekly proudly announced that mail now arrived from Salem three days rather than one day a week.[32]

Woodland was a temporary stop for the Raders. The Raders, as a neighbor later observed, "were comparatively late comers [to the area and] the best of the land had been settled" earlier.[33] The terrain was unfamiliar; the Woodland area was flatter and more

open than western Hart County. Since it only faintly resembled
their homeland, we can surmise that the family almost at once
began to scout nearby areas for a location more to their liking.
Regardless, the agricultural census reported that at Woodland
in 1879 the family produced 250 pounds of butter, 500 bushels
of corn (on 16 acres), more than 100 bushels of wheat (on 20
acres), and 75 gallons of molasses.[34] For that neighborhood,
none of these were insignificant sums and exceeded considerably what the family had been producing on their farm back in
Kentucky. At last, or so it seemed, the family had received an
omen of better times ahead.

PART II

SETTLING ON
MAHANS CREEK

The Rader family's good fortunes failed to hold. In 1880, two years after George and Nancy Rader had settled in the Woodland area, George died. According to one account, a log that he was hewing or splitting got away from him and ripped a patch of skin from his leg. Blood poisoning set in, and after a painful, albeit short time, as the family watched helplessly, George passed away on March 18, 1880.[1] A formal appeal by Nancy for a pension arising from George's service in the Civil War offers a different version of George's death. In this document, Nancy claimed, George died from a relapse of the measles that he had acquired during the Civil War. The disease, Nancy explained, had "settled in his lungs."[2] While this is the first mention of measles as the source of George's Civil War disability, Nancy may have confused it with the typhus fever that George had contracted (according to a military physician) while serving in the war. In any case, she makes no mention of the logging accident. She may have had good reason to remain silent. Perhaps the accident never happened or perhaps she justifiably feared that acknowledgement of it would keep her from collecting a pension from George's service in the Civil War.

If legend is to be believed, the family lost more than its patriarch. In a story similar to that found in many family legends, George was said to have possessed a hidden fortune, a cache of gold coins that he had wrapped in a red bandana and kept in a pot which he buried somewhere on the family's Woodland farm. On occasion, George brought out from hiding the glittering gold pieces and showed them to his astonished family. According to one account, Sam Rader, the youngest of George's children, "learned how to count while sitting on Grandpa'[s] lap and counting gold pieces; all 3,196 of them!"[3] If this story were true, it meant that the Rader family was well off indeed.

But, there is ample reason for doubting the accuracy if not the gist of this story. A neighbor, Oscar Harper, remembered local people, or perhaps it was Rader family members themselves, claiming that George had "some gold coins"; and Wayne Rader, George's great grandson, recalled having heard that the value of the coins was $300.[4] While it is plausible that George owned and kept a *few* gold coins in hiding, all extenuating evidence—as we have seen in previous chapters—points in one direction. The family was without any substantial financial resources. Supporting this contention is also a report by Harper that the family, while living in the Woodland neighborhood, did not even own a single gun and that the adult Rader sons were forced to hunt with the aid of a shepherd rather than a hound dog. In order to kill the squirrels and opossums that they had shaken out of the low-lying scrub oaks, Harper claimed, the sons had to beat the animals to death with rocks or clubs.[5] It was said that on his deathbed George tried to tell the family where he had buried his pot of gold, but, alas, he could mutter only one word, "money." The coins, presuming they ever existed, were never found. What the legend potentially did, as such tales did for other poor families, was to offer the Raders an enhanced sense of their own importance as a historical entity.

Apparently, George's death triggered the family's relocation. Despite their success in farming in the Birch Prairie area, the family members appear to have yearned for the familiarity of the Upland South's hollows. In any case, soon after George's demise, according to one source, two of his sons, Jeremiah "Jerry" and Charles Rader, set out in search of a place for the family to resettle. They hitched up a wagon and drove north down into Pine Hollow on a road that followed a mostly dry creek bed for some eight miles. The terrain through which they rode was rough, much more like their homeland in western Hart County, Kentucky, than the plateau-like land around Birch Prairie. They finally came upon "a clear stream [Mahans Creek] and a [abandoned?] log house," presumably what later became known as "Granny's house" (Nancy's). It was near the hillside at the juncture of Mahans Creek and Open Hollow in the Delaware Township. They liked what they saw. Jerry told Charley, "Take the wagon and get Ma and the kids and I will start clearing the land."[6]

✦ CHAPTER 4 ✦

Like Coming Home Again

WHEN FORTY-NINE-YEAR-OLD Nancy (Childress) Rader first rode up Mahans Creek on a buckboard wagon sometime between March 18 and June 7 of 1880 to see the new home site discovered by her sons, she had a good reason to worry. Having passed away only a month or so earlier, George had left Nancy with an awesome set of responsibilities. She had little or no money and owned no farmland, but was burdened with a household of eleven plus an orphaned child of a family friend, fourteen-year-old Malinda Weaver. Since her own daughters were only fourteen, twelve, and ten years old, Nancy may have taken Malinda into her own family as "help" in doing house-keeping and other chores. Conceivably, the Shannon County Court might have extended to Nancy a small stipend—the usual method of dealing with orphans in that time—to care for the juvenile. Not all was grim for Nancy. Six of her seven sons were old enough to do heavy farm work. And, compared to Hart County, farmland in Shannon County was cheap; scattered through the Mahans Creek drainage system were at least a dozen farms with small patches of bottomland that had been abandoned during the Civil War and Reconstruction era. Even as late as 1880, such land could be had for virtually nothing. But, perhaps superseding all else was what she saw when she looked out across the horizon: Mahans Creek. The spring-fed, year-round, fresh-water creek and the surrounding steep, heavily wooded hills reminded Nancy of nothing so much as the Childress neighborhood back in Hart County, Kentucky. If she had been less stoical, she would have cried. It was almost like coming home again.

✦   ✦   ✦

Few places in the Ozarks were more rugged and isolated than what the Raders chose as their new physical habitat. The clear creeks and rivers, the springs, the caves, the hollows, and the hills set it apart, indeed, so much so that much later, in 1964, Congress enacted into law measures designed to protect its uniqueness. A corridor along the Current and Jacks Fork Rivers (Mahans Creek drains into the Jacks Fork) officially became the Ozark National Scenic Riverways, a belt in which private development was limited. It was the first of its kind in the nation.[1] The creeks and rivers within the riverways area are fast moving; Shannon County's elevation drops nearly a thousand feet from its northern boundary near where the Current River begins to the river's exit into Carter County in the south. Over several million years, unnavigable (except by johnboats or canoes) streams eroded intricate mazes of deep, narrow hollows.

The difficulties that residents had in reaching the county seat of Eminence mirrored the area's relative isolation. News of the outside world trickled in like rain dropping from the leaves of a tree, a drop here and a sprinkle there. In the 1880s a stage line began to offer daily service from Salem to the north, a distance of some forty-five miles from Eminence, but the road from Eminence was at times simply impassable. Heavy rains and rising water on the Current and Jacks Fork Rivers could completely isolate Eminence—sometimes for days at a time.[2] In June of 1873, or perhaps it was in 1874—the source for the story was uncertain—rain fell in the area for twenty-two consecutive days. Fortunately, a gristmill on Mahans Creek supplied Eminence with enough cornmeal and the local deer hunters provided residents with fresh venison. "So we got along about as well as usual," Rufus Kenamore recalled many years later.[3]

In a possibly apocryphal story that likely reveals more about the local sense of humor than fact, all was well except in one key respect, at least according to "Big" Hugh Ware, a town leader. He called upon Eminence's residents to organize a "council of defense." "Gentlemen," he announced at a public meeting at the county courthouse, "we are cut off from the world and have been for nearly a month. . . . This is not particularly worrisome as [is] a fact that has just come to my knowledge—something that demands immediate attention. I have just been over to Marion's [an Eminence general store] and ran a ramrod down in the last barrel of whiskey [in town], and there is not more than six inches in the barrel." Rufus Kenamore agreed with Big Hugh: "Now this was a bad situation, especially in a rainy spell of weather."[4] Fortunately, the rains soon stopped and Marion's was able to restock its short supply of whiskey.

Mahans Creek's weather reminded the Nancy Rader family of their Kentucky homeland. The summers were hot and humid. Heavy thunderstorms frequently rolled in from the Southwest during the spring and summer months; the area averaged more than forty inches of rainfall annually. The river and creek bottoms in which the farmers planted nearly all their row crops were subject to disastrous floods. Rains were uneven; during critical times in the growing season, especially July and August, rainfalls might be painfully light. Droughts, such as those in 1881, 1901, 1911–1914, 1933–1936, and 1939–1943, devastated local farmers. The droughts were particularly disastrous for corn, a crop upon which the local farmers were so dependent. The winters were normally temperate, though sometimes temperatures plunged below freezing and remained there for several days at a time. The area enjoyed an average growing season between 190 and 200 days, a season long enough to see a large number of field crops reach maturity. Although the weather forced the residents to have some form of shelter, they could get by, as nearly all of the first settlers did, with temporary, hastily constructed log houses or simple single-wall "sawmill houses." The latter were built with unseasoned and unpainted lumber sawed by a water-powered sawmill.

For the settlers, the appeal of a temperate climate could

trump other adversities. In 1884, a writer for the local weekly newspaper, the *Current Wave*, published in Eminence, reported that a farmer from Illinois, Andrew Phelps, had had his fill of life on Mahans Creek. He "concluded to return to Illinois, and accordingly took a 'straight skoot' for that state of doubtful politics [i.e., Republican] and horizontal reduction [i.e., flatlands], going down Shawnee [Creek] and [it] became cooler, an ominous soughing of the wind in the surrounding pines was heard, and, remember[ing] with a shiver, the rigor of Illinois winters, he lost heart. He hitched his team to the rear end of the wagon and came backwards to Mahan's Creek. There is no place like Shannon."[5]

The Mahans Creek area supported a striking diversity of plant and animal life. As in the past, settlers frequently relied on "gathering" from the woods and streams as a part of their subsistence. One old-timer claimed that "there was an abundance of wild strawberries, grapes, plums, crab apples, huckleberries, blackberries, dewberries, pawpaws, persimmons, black walnuts, butternuts, hickory nuts, and hazelnuts. Plenty of game and fish for meat. . . . Honey could be had by coursing wild bees to their trees."[6] Also in the woods, some of the early settlers harvested ginseng (a prized weed that allegedly enhanced male sexual prowess), goldenseal, and wahoo in the spring and summer months. They sold or traded these medicinal herbs in Eminence or shipped them to St. Louis. In the twentieth century, both my maternal grandfather, Alford A. Eddings, and my great aunt, Mayme (Perkins) Pummill, collected and sold these herbal medicines.[7] But without any regard for conservation, the supply of the plants soon diminished so much that the effort and time needed to collect them was no longer worthwhile.

As late as 1875, explained an old-timer, "you could ride for miles and never see the stump of a tree. It was one boundless unbroken forest of pine and oak."[8] Then a person could see a "long ways," according to my great uncle, Lewis Perkins. Oldtimers remembered that nothing quite equaled the awe-inspiring grandeur of the stately short-leaf, yellow pine that grew on the south side of the hills. On the north side of the ridges, oak predominated. Apart from the use of trees in housing and fencing, settlers called the resin-filled pine knots "trading wood" or "a widow's offering"; highly prized, the knots could be exchanged, it was said, for the attention of a widow or another unmarried woman. For many years, settlers also used the knots as fuel for light in gigging fish at night. In those days, more grass, especially little bluestem, grew on the forest floor. Along the creeks and in the narrow hollows, settlers encountered an array of ash, hickory, box elder, birch, willow, sycamore, elm, and maple trees. "The dense forests of Shannon County present the most pleasing appearance of this season of the year," reported the *Current Wave* in the fall of 1885, "variegated as they are with every hue of the rainbow."[9]

Yet, contrary to the popular beliefs of the hollers people, the abundance of oak and yellow pine was not an indicator of good soil. Everywhere—not just on the hillsides but in the hollow floors as well—the topsoil was thin, especially when compared with that of the Upper Midwest. It was also frequently porous. Water seeped through it quickly. To grow bountiful row crops required unusually generous rainfalls in July and August. Except along some of the river and creek bottoms, wrestling a living exclusively from the soil was virtually impossible. The best that all but a few could hope for was a subsistence based on a small corn crop, a garden, running some pigs and cattle on the open range, gathering nuts and berries from the woods, and fishing and hunting.

Hunting and fishing helped to offset low yields from farming. Bison or elk no longer roamed the area, but a few black bear remained. White-tailed deer, wild turkey, raccoons, opossums, groundhogs, rabbits, and squirrels were in far greater supply; though, mainly in response to the amount of rainfall, their populations fluctuated from season to season. One early Shannon County settler claimed that he had seen "a thousand turkeys fly up from a field at one time, and . . . [had] killed many of them while driving them away from [his] . . . corn shocks and other grain"[10] A few turkey continued to inhabit the hills and hollows until the 1930s, when drought and over-hunting nearly wiped them out.

Huge flocks of passenger pigeons "would darken the earth

similar to the way a heavy cloud does when it passes between the earth and the sun," reported a Mahans Creek old-timer.[11] Unthinkingly, local settlers went about indiscriminately slaughtering the pigeons just as they did other game. On one occasion, two neighborhood hunters "went shooting on a moonlight night, each taking a sack along to carry them [the killed pigeons] in. After they had shot what they thought would be needed to fill the sacks, they started gathering more. They had more than enough to fill them. Then, what to do with the rest of them? So, they pulled off their red flannels, tied knots in the legs and filled them too."[12] By the end of the 1880s the county's pigeon population had been decimated.

Killing sprees by Shannon County hunting parties sharply reduced other animal populations. For example, a fall hunting party in 1887 proudly reported killing thirty deer and countless turkeys.[13] How much of this carnage found its way onto the plates of local residents is unknown, but it is safe to guess that much of the killing was for sport rather than food. Indeed, from time to time there was a negative reaction in the county to the indiscriminate killing of deer and fish. In 1887 in a mostly vain effort to restrict the carnage, farmers in the Round Spring area even organized a short-lived Shannon County Gun Club.[14]

More important than anything else was the water, the cold clear water from the springs, creeks, and rivers. And then there was all about them the abundant woodlands that provided potential building materials for homes, barns, and fences, fuel for fireplaces, a habitat for feral animals, and also "open ranges" for grazing domestic animals. About them as well were also peoples with similar origins and customs. The Raders had found a place congenial to the retention of the family's traditional ways. However, had they known more about the past that hung over the creek, they might have been far less sanguine about their choice of a new homeland.

✦   ✦   ✦

A few scattered artifacts, documents, and place names remain to this day. They confirm the belief that Native Americans once lived or at the least hunted on the Mahans Creek watershed. Local Euro-American occupants sometimes referred to Mahans Creek itself as "Indian" or "Delaware Creek." Other nearby streams bore the names of Shawnee Creek and Little Shawnee Creek. And there is Delaware itself, the name of the township in which the creek is located. On occasion, the pupils of the one-room school at Delaware referred to their sports' teams as the "Indians." In dispatches to the local *Current Wave*, the students even went so far as to contribute to prevailing stereotypes of Native Americans by describing themselves as "hostile" and "blood thirsty savages."[15]

The name served as a reminder that in 1820 and 1821 a band of Delaware hunted and farmed on either the creek or on the nearby Jacks Fork of the Current River, into which the creek drained. In exchange for vacating their land claims in Pennsylvania, Ohio, and Indiana, the Delaware had received promises of land in Missouri (the location unspecified), annual annuities, as well as financial aid for transportation, language interpreters, and the services of a blacksmith. In the spring of 1821, they planted corn at their new site, "but a heavy frost killed the young crop," and, according to neighborhood lore, local whites stole some of their horses. In the meantime, the band received assurances that they could settle on land set aside for them as a permanent home on the James Fork of the White River in southwestern Missouri. The Delaware moved there in September of 1822.[16]

If native peoples found the Jacks Fork and Current Rivers area uncongenial to permanent settlement, so initially did potential Euro-American settlers. So few white families trickled into the area that Shannon County itself was not created until 1841, twenty years after Missouri had achieved statehood. And even then settlement was sparse; the county contained no towns, and as late as 1850 its population totaled only 1,190 people. At least half of them, according to censuses, came from Tennessee or Kentucky. Most of the remainder migrated there from other places in Missouri.

Without a single town of any consequence in the entire county, a commission appointed in 1841 had a problem of where to locate the county seat. Eventually, they settled upon a remote spot on a hillside overlooking the Current River near Round Spring. Naming it "Eminence" because of its lofty perspective, they built there a log courthouse and eventually a jail.[17] While crude roads connected the site to other parts of the county, nobody lived there permanently. Officials carried out the county's business, such as it was, from their own homes. On several occasions the county did not even bother to hold local elections. For a half dozen years or more, the same man served as both the county's tax collector and treasurer. He allegedly rode from cabin to cabin accepting as tax payment furs, tobacco, honey, meat, almost anything he could wheedle from the impoverished settlers. Opened in 1848, the Eminence Post Office was in the cabin of Alfred Deatherage, a farmer who operated a country store a short distance downriver from the courthouse.[18]

The 1850s represented something of a watershed in the county's history. In that decade the county's population nearly doubled, from 1,190 to 2,284 people. By 1850, much of the land surrounding the Ozarks as well as the plateaus of the Ozarks themselves had been settled. Only isolated pockets in Missouri, such as Shannon County, contained substantial quantities of unclaimed public land. The area attracted rural people in quest of cheap land and a familiar physical and cultural habitat; many of them came in kinship groups.[19] A whopping 64 percent of Delaware Township's twenty-one and older population in 1860 came from Tennessee and from other parts of Missouri. All of the remainder except one person (from Massachusetts) had been born in the South or portions of states that may have been part of the Upland South. According to the census, not a single foreign-born person, Native American, or African American resided in the township.

The new migrants usually arrived via ox carts or tar-pole wagons drawn by a yoke of oxen or a team of horses. Since the axles and hubs were molded from wood (usually oak), they had to be regularly greased with tar melted out of fat pine. Smearing the resin on the axle ends minimized the friction of the turning hubs. So that the tar could be applied when needed, the settlers frequently hung an oaken bucket of tar on a pole on the back of their wagons, hence the descriptor, "tar-pole wagon." Early settlers also used pine tar to caulk the windows and doors of their log houses.

Most of the first settlers squatted on unoccupied land. Since they had few possessions and were always on the lookout for a better farm site, they moved with startling frequency. One family moved so often, according to the pioneering grandmother of Shannon County resident David Lewis, that "every time they hitched up the horses, the chickens automatically crossed their legs to be tied."[20] The Graduation Act of 1854 encouraged the influx of new settlers. Initially offering public lands to settlers for one dollar per acre, it provided that if the lands went unsold, the price would gradually be reduced until after thirty years it could be purchased for twelve-and-a-half cents per acre.

No indicator of the continuity of the Shannon County settlers' material culture was more conspicuous than their loyalty to the vernacular architecture found in other parts of the Upland South. While no buildings from the early days survive today, contemporary descriptions and later structures confirm the conclusion that nearly all of them consisted of hewed, horizontally laid logs, joined at the corners by V or half dovetail notching. At first nearly all of the houses were a single story with a single pen, that is, a single log exterior. Later on, as the settlers' families grew in numbers, they frequently appended a shed to the side or rear of their dwelling, or more rarely built a new log structure with a second floor. Log barns and other outbuildings also resembled those found in the places from which the settlers had come.[21]

Terrain, more than anything else, served as an index to settlement patterns and social divisions in the Delaware Township.[22] The first settlers sought out the bottomlands along the fresh-water stream of Mahans Creek itself. There they built log houses, usually of pine. They cut or girdled a few nearby trees in order to plant some corn, Irish potatoes, sweet potatoes, beans, sorghum, and perhaps a little bit of cotton and tobacco for personal use. They frequently turned their hogs and their cattle loose in the woods to forage and fend for themselves.

✦   ✦   ✦

By 1860, the Delaware Township's population, which at that time included not only the Mahans Creek neighborhood but also most of the lower Jacks Fork River waterway, had reached 244, more than triple the figure for 1850. Settlement was sufficient by 1855 for William "Billy" Mahan to dam up the creek and install a small gristmill made of stone burrs fastened to a wooden shaft. With a capacity of milling fifty bushels a day, Mahan reported that his mill ground $1,100 worth of cornmeal in 1859. Apart from grinding grain, the mill served as a "gathering place" at which neighbors "swapped yarns and gossip for pastimes and sometimes made horse trades." In 1855, Billy Mahan also received an appointment as the neighborhood's first postmaster and began to operate a small country store on his farm.[23]

The 1860 census, taken by a thirty-five-year-old Virginian, James M. L. Jamieson, who taught at a one-room "subscription" school on the creek, offered a snapshot of the township. It had one schoolteacher, though Jamieson actually lived in the Current River Township, and had no lawyers or doctors. In addition to Billy Mahan, the township had one other "merchant" as well as a "wagon maker" and a "carpenter." The census listed all other heads of households as "farmers." The Delaware Township was slow to support organized religion. In 1860, there was not a single preacher or church edifice in the entire township. However, it is safe to presume that Methodist circuit riders and visiting Baptist exhorters held irregular services in private homes.[24]

Even as early as 1860, it was already clear that Delaware failed to correspond to a Jeffersonian vision of a township comprised of yeoman farmers of nearly equal wealth. At the top of the social hierarchy were the better-off or leading families, those who were sometimes described by locals as the "creek-bottom folk." They had taken up land first on the banks of Mahans Creek. The most eminent of these was the extended family of the first settler, a William Mahan. In 1860, the four Mahan families owned between them farms valued at a whopping $10,380. On the average, each Mahan family owned $2,595 worth of real and personal property, produced six hundred bushels of corn annually, and had six horses, twenty-four head of cattle, and seventeen hogs.

Below the four Mahan families was a group of ten farmers or so who comprised what might be called a "middling sort." Still lower on the wealth pyramid was a set of poor farmers—about half of the township—who occupied some of the smaller farms along the creek bottom but mostly farms up the narrow hollows leading away from the creek. Local people later referred to the poorest of these as the "branch-water folk" because many of them lived on the small seasonal streams that drained the hollows and, instead of digging wells, often obtained their water, including drinking water, from branches that ran near their homes. Latecomers to the township found that eking out a living on Pine and Open Hollows, the two major tributaries branching out from the creek, was more difficult than on the lower reaches of Mahans Creek hollow. From the outset of settlement, the farm families in these branch-water hollows began to develop traits that were in some respects distinctive from their better-off neighbors living along the creek itself.[25]

In 1860 half of the farm families in Delaware Township owned real and personal property worth $500 or less, produced an average of three hundred or less bushels of corn, and owned two or less horses, fewer than seven head of cattle, and fewer than six hogs. Sometimes these families were even too poor to own hounds; instead, they may have had one or two yellow-haired mongrels. According to one description, the typical branch-water family owned a weather-beaten wagon, perhaps pulled by a mismatched horse and a mule, "both old, feeble and thin in flesh." The families seldom remained long in one place. When ready to move on, the branch-water man put "all his household effects" including "his wife and children into the creaky old wagon [and] whistl[ed] to his dog."[26]

By 1860 the settlers on the Mahans Creek waterway had taken on most of the trappings of a permanent neighborhood. They had a gristmill, a store, and a school. A crude road ran along the creek from the Jacks Fork River southward until it reached the mouth of Pine Hollow. From there it proceeded up Pine Hollow to Birch Prairie (Birch Tree). Missing from the neighborhood was any form of regularly organized religious service. And what no one foresaw as the new decade opened was the sheer terror that soon wracked the neighborhood.

✦   ✦   ✦

"On [a] . . . damp dark night in 1865 [my] family fled in terror, away from the bushwhackers who had [already] taken one life that night and would not hesitate to take . . . father's because he lived as a 'Federalist' [i.e., a Union man]," thirteen-year-old James Edgar Canavit remembered. In a ploy to escape the detection of the pro-Southern, armed bushwhackers, his father had disguised himself by donning women's clothes. Before departing their cabin, James's mother sobbed as "she turned for one last look at the homestead where her three children were born. . . . She [then] spent a quiet minute at a cherished bubbling spring behind the house" and said a "small prayer" for the safety of her "lovely" handmade dishes that had been hidden in a nearby cave. The Canavits were more fortunate than many pro-Unionists in their Shannon County neighborhood. They were able to elude the pro-Southern guerillas and make their way safely to Illinois, where they lived for the remainder of their lives. They looked back fondly to the time that they had lived in Shannon County, but they never returned.[27]

From the outbreak of the war in 1861 until the mid-1870s, Shannon County was virtually without civil authority. Rule by law all but collapsed, and social norms weakened. Since neither the Union nor the Confederacy saw the rugged, isolated, and thinly populated area as of much strategic importance, neither side maintained a permanent military presence in the county. A motley array of armed groups stepped into the vacuum: Union (usually state militia) patrols, bands of mostly irregular Confederate gorillas, and outright bushwhackers, some of whom had no ties to either side. Each group plundered the local farm families. They commandeered horses, cattle, hogs, and corn, and sometimes they burned houses and barns and even summarily killed those whom they thought were aiding their enemies.

The war unleashed smoldering but previously suppressed personal animosities. Neighboring families seized on the opportunities offered by the war to settle old quarrels. Pro-Southerners, who were in the majority, embarked on a more-or-less organized campaign of cleansing the county of Union families, even though some of the Unionists had been long-time neighbors and friends. Pro-Unionists retaliated by calling upon the assistance of Northern military forces stationed at nearby Rolla, Houston, or Salem, Missouri, to rid the county of pro-Southerners. The war's terrors even continued after the formal peace in 1865. While civil authorities re-imposed a modicum of order in the county, even then the war's dark legacy continued to linger long afterward.[28]

✦ ✦ ✦

If not at the outset, in time the overwhelming majority of Shannon County's residents supported the Southern cause. Unlike many of the counties in the Missouri Ozarks, Shannon County had always been a Democratic stronghold. Even though the county grew almost no cotton and had only three slaveholders (who owned a total of thirteen slaves), it cast only two votes for the Republican presidential nominee, Abraham Lincoln, in 1860![29]

In an attempt to understand Shannon County's deep attachment to the South and the Democratic Party, a local historian, Robert Lee, working under the common misperception that the highlands people of the South were overwhelmingly Unionists, speculated that the county's early settlers had been followers of the party of Andrew Jackson from the outset and that nearly all of them had come from the lowlands of western Tennessee and Kentucky, rather than from the hills farther to the east. While Lee's generalization about the origins of the settlers by *states* is true, the censuses did not distinguish the birthplaces of settlers by *regions within the states*.[30] As historians have found for other

parts of the Upland South, a more plausible explanation of political preferences of the county can be found by examining the
allegiances of local elites. No elite family was more important
in the history of Shannon County than the Chilton family. As
one local observer put it many years later, the "notions" of the
"wilderness-loving Chilton Clan . . . [in Shannon and Carter
Counties] were the law of the land."[31] The Chiltons, in effect,
"governed" Shannon County single-handedly, and, in the end,
they sided with the Confederacy.

The Chiltons were Shannon County pioneers. In 1818,
Thomas Boggs Chilton arrived on the Current River with his
family from the Great Smoky Mountains of eastern Tennessee.
He hacked out a farm on Owl Bend, some eight miles below
the mouth of the Jacks Fork River. Soon more Chiltons came
and established farms up and down the Current and Jacks Fork
Rivers. By 1860, fifteen separate families with 94 members bore
the Chilton surname, and countless others were either blood
relatives or related by marriage to the Chiltons. In addition,
fifteen clan members with the Chilton surname lived downriver
in adjacent Carter County.[32]

Not just in numbers or in the degree of family cohesion did
the Chilton clan occupy a conspicuous place on the Current
and Jacks Fork waterways. More successful materially than
most of their neighbors and enjoying the warm esteem of the
local residents, the Chiltons soon, if not at once, stood atop the
area's social hierarchy. At the head of the clan was swashbuck-
ling Joshua Chilton, known locally as the "King" or "Boss" of
Shannon County. The county's voters repeatedly elected him to
the Missouri state assembly and to the state senate in 1861. In
addition, in the antebellum era, several other Chiltons, one of
whom (Shadrach) was said to have killed a bear with his bare
hands, held county offices. Shadrach also later served as a captain in the Second Missouri Infantry of the Confederate army
that fought in the Battle of Wilson's Creek near Springfield,
Missouri.[33]

According to Chilton family folklore, when war first broke
out, Joshua Chilton was "neutral," and, in fact, he did pass up an

opportunity to attend the pro-Confederate rump session of the Missouri legislature in 1861, a session that voted for Missouri's secession from the Union. Yet evidence suggests that, as the war unfolded, Joshua began to assist Confederate recruiters. A Union officer, Lieutenant Colonel J. Wedemeyer, asserted that Chilton "did more to induce men to join the southern army than perhaps any other man in this state." One of Chilton's personal rivals, John Worthington, a Current River farmer living upstream from Joshua, apparently convinced Federal authorities in Salem that Chilton was a "very Dangerous rebel." In late August of 1862 a company of Union cavalrymen surprised and captured Chilton near his farm home. On the way to headquarters in Rolla for questioning, the troops apparently murdered Chilton along with two of his captive neighbors in cold blood. Officially, the unit commander claimed that the prisoners had been shot while trying to escape.[34]

Chilton's "execution" not only enraged the huge and powerful Chilton clan but also activated many of the county's previously neutral residents. This may have been the case of the Mahan clan on the Mahans Creek and Jacks Fork River waterways. Even though their roots extended back to Pennsylvania, Ohio, and Illinois, and they owned no slaves, like the Chiltons, the Mahans stood atop of their neighborhood's social hierarchy. Indeed, William "Billy" Mahan was the wealthiest farmer in the Delaware Township and was a judge-elect of the county's three-man administrative body when the war began. In any event, the Mahans became ardent supporters of the Southern cause; four of the nine men known to have seen military service in the Delaware Township were Mahans. At least two Mahans lost their lives in the conflict.[35] Not a single man from Delaware, insofar as I have been able to determine, joined a Northern military force.

Apart from those who enlisted in the regular Confederate army, several men in the Mahans Creek neighborhood at one time or another served in bands of pro-Southern guerillas. Most were part-time warriors who fought only after their corn crops had been put in and during other "slack" times when they were not needed on the farm. While situated outside of the limited perimeters of towns such as Salem, Rolla, Houston, and West Plains that were garrisoned by Northern troops, they usually (but not always) enjoyed the support of local partisans who offered them provisions and informed them of the whereabouts of Union patrols. On horseback and comprised of small bands of ten or fewer men, their main activity was to harass Union supply trains and patrols. Typically, they fired a volley or two into enemy ranks and then promptly fled by horseback, scattering into the wooded hills. Later they reconnoitered at a pre-designated spot. While they suffered minimal or no losses from these "skirmishes," this tactic forced the Union to add extra troops for the protection of its supply lines and to try to bring the guerillas to heel by increasing the number of forays by cavalry patrols into the wild Shannon County countryside.

Under these circumstances, neither Shannon County nor the Mahans Creek neighborhood failed to escape four years of intermittent warfare. Even before the assassination of Chilton, the Fifth Kansas Cavalry of the Union army had ridden through the county on its way south to Arkansas. In Eminence, the county seat, it had skirmished with some of the men of Colonel William O. Coleman, a Confederate recruiter from Rolla. Then, in late August, a patrol of the Union's Third Missouri Cavalry from Salem captured and killed Joshua Chilton. In January of 1863 General John Davidson marched a huge force of nearly ten thousand bedraggled Union soldiers from West Plains north to Eminence; they apparently marched through the Mahans Creek neighborhood, foraging and destroying food supplies as they went.[36]

When in 1863 the Union began enrolling all young men for the draft in Shannon County, Federal authorities not surprisingly encountered armed resistance. On October 14, 1863, while escorting and protecting the enrollment officer, a squad of forty men under the command of Lieutenant Michael S. Eddlemen of the Fifth Missouri Cavalry skirmished for about ten minutes with "about twenty to thirty" guerillas near "Man's [Mahans?] Creek." Before the enemy "took to the brush," Edelman reported, his men succeeded in killing two and wounding two others. The cavalrymen then severed the heads of the two dead guerillas, one of whom was a "boy," and tied them to their saddles as trophies and as warnings to the locals of the dangers in resisting Federal authority.[37]

Under such circumstances, county government came to a halt. In 1863, allegedly either Union soldiers or militias burned the Shannon County courthouse and jail at the original town of Eminence, perhaps in retaliation for Rebels in the county having earlier burned an adjacent county's courthouse, the Texas County courthouse in Houston. In any event, with its destruction, Shannon County officials abandoned Eminence. For the duration of the war, the county collected no taxes, it held no elections in 1862 or 1864, and the county court, the county's governing body, did not meet from the December term in 1861 until the October term in 1866. In 1866 and 1867, it appears that county officials operated from their homes and a log house located on the Billy Mahan farm. Prompted by a donation of forty acres of land by Thomas J. Chilton, in 1868, the court relocated the county seat to its present site on Prospect Hill on the south side of the Jacks Fork River. The town that then slowly grew up around the courthouse also became known as Eminence.[38]

According to legend, probably apocryphal since variations of it exist in other counties as well, in order to safeguard the county's funds from the Union militia and bushwhackers, the treasurer, one Alexander Deatherage, secretly buried the money on his Spring Valley farm. Deatherage then went off to war on behalf of the Confederacy. He fought at the Battles of Wilson's Creek and Lexington in Missouri. At the end of the war, Deatherage returned the $2,000—or $4,000, according to another account—in gold and silver to surprised county officials.[39] Whether the unlikely story is true of not, Deatherage and his descendants made the most of it. In gratitude "for this noble act of honesty," Shannon County repeatedly elected Deatherages to countywide public offices.

✦   ✦   ✦

In terms of sheer terror, no raid into the Mahans Creek neighborhood equaled that of the "notorious" Lieutenant John W. Boyd in November of 1863. At the outbreak of the war, Boyd was a farmer on the nearby Jacks Fork waterway.[40] Because of his Union sympathies, neighboring farmers, including Henry Mahan, made life uncomfortable for him. According to Boyd's own account, though he offered no specifics, "[My neighbors] have hunted me like a wild beast and tried to kill me for my principles."[41] The war provided Boyd with an opportunity to retaliate. Perhaps he asked for—at least he received—orders in 1863 to lead twenty-five cavalrymen of the Sixth Provisional Regiment of the Missouri Militia stationed in Rolla on a patrol deep into the Jacks Fork and Mahans Creek area where his former neighbors lived.

From Houston, Boyd's cavalry first rode down the Jacks Fork River east toward the Current River. Along the way, they burned two houses to the ground. Boyd reported that in the Delaware Township they "camped at Widow [Anne] McCormicks. Had positive evidence that the widow kept a general rendezvous for [Thomas R.] Freeman's and [William O.] Coleman's [Confederate] guerillas. On the morning of the 6th burned the buildings [of Widow McCormick but did not kill her. She had eight children in her household]. Learned from the widow's son, a young lad, that on the previous evening James Mahan had got him to give news of our approach.[42] Sent back and took Mahan prisoner." Having lived on a farm adjacent to Henry Mahan's farm, Boyd probably knew James, a cousin of Henry's, personally.

Then, Boyd's unit turned from the Jacks Fork up Mahans Creek southward on the "Thomasville Road." While James Mahan was allegedly trying to escape, Boyd's men shot and killed him. They then camped at Billy Mahan's farm on the evening of November 8. "On the morning of the 9th, [we] marched up Mahan's Creek," Boyd continued in his report. "About 9 o'clock [we] discovered about 20 of the enemy on the bluff above us; fired a few shots at them, when they fell back. I took 20 men up the hill and reconnoitered, expecting to find them in force to give us battle, but they had all fled into the rocky ravines and hills, where it was impossible to pursue to advantage."

About a mile farther up the road in Pine Hollow, Boyd's unit encountered three other men whom they presumed to be Confederate guerillas; the militiamen killed two of them while the third escaped. About two additional miles up the road "we captured William Story on a United States horse [which presumably he had stolen]. . . . He was recognized and well known as a notorious horse thief. He attempted to escape, and was killed."[43] (Story had earlier been a hired hand of none other than Joshua Chilton and was allegedly a Confederate deserter.) A few days later, "at the house of a John Nicholson, a known rebel and bushwhacker," Boyd, or his men, shot and killed three men, including Jesse Story, William's fifteen-year-old cousin. Boyd's force then returned to Houston. Boyd proudly toted up the results: he reported to his superiors that on the six-day, 145-mile march through Shannon County, his unit had "killed 10 men, returned 1 prisoner [a boy], burned 23 houses, recaptured 9 horses . . . and took 6 contraband horses and mules." How many barns he had ordered burned and how much livestock and grain he had confiscated went unreported.

Boyd's scorched earth march through the Mahans Creek neighborhood did not go unnoticed by his superiors. On November 20, 1863, a "Captain [John] Lovell" was sent to Houston "to investigate the conduct of Lieutenant Boyd . . . [and to] ascertain by what authority twenty-three houses were burned" and whether the last five victims had been killed while prisoners at Boyd's order. In his response, Boyd elaborated on his earlier report by claiming that the victims were shot while trying to escape. He then went ahead to write that most of the houses that he had burned were vacant and had been used as quarters for Rebel bushwhackers. Boyd offered no direct justification for some of his actions, such as, for example, his burning of the home and barn of Widow Anne McCormick. Nonetheless, Lovell concluded that "Lieutenant Boyd acted correctly, and for the good of the service." While escaping both censure and punishment for his acts, Boyd would forever live in the infamy of Mahans Creek folk history. Local residents considered him nothing less than a murderous bushwhacker hiding behind the authority of a Yankee uniform.

Neither did Boyd's expedition end conflict in the county. Responding to a report that there were "some 89 bushwhackers" camped on the Jacks Fork River, on January 5, 1865, Captain Levi E. Whybark led forty-five men of the Missouri State Militia Calvary into the river area. They found several small camps and killed at least ten men, some of whom may have been in or from the Mahans Creek neighborhood. While Whybark's report lacked the specificity of Boyd's earlier account, it is possible that some of Whybark's victims were buried in unmarked graves at the site that later became the Rader Cemetery.

✦ ✦ ✦

For Mahans Creek residents, the war had been extraordinarily brutal. In the 1860s nearly eight out of every ten heads of households either died or fled the neighborhood. Also, in the 1870 township census a strikingly large number of women (five)— at least four of whom were widows of the Civil War—headed farm households. The war nearly wiped out the male side of the Mahan family. Never again would the clan occupy a prominent place on the creek. "We . . . were *milked dry* and *bled white*," complained an old-timer some fifty years later.[44] During the 1860s Delaware Township's corn yields fell 32 percent and the total number of cattle dropped by 45 percent. Indeed, every measure of farm productivity fell except for hogs.[45] Difficult for the wartime looters to catch, prone to rapid reproduction, and adept at fending for themselves in the woods, hogs surely saved a few of the township's farm families from even worse disasters.

Imbibing from the "bucketful of home-made whiskey and a tin cup that always sat on the principal pine stump on the public square" in Eminence may have provided temporary relief to some of the locals, but poverty in the postwar era continued to grip nearly everyone.[46] Asked in 1868 if he was the wisest man in Shannon County, David C. Reed, the county's newly elected state representative quipped, "No but I am the only man there that has shoes to wear."[47] In the summers of 1872 and 1873, the situation worsened; a grasshopper plague wiped out the county's corn crop.[48] In 1874, nearly ten years after the war, the county had only three sawmills and two operating gristmills.[49] Only one-third of those who lived in Delaware in 1870 continued to reside there in 1880. The county's population stagnated; in 1880, only 89 people lived in the county seat of Eminence.

Neither did the county settle into a new era of political tranquility. In the wake of the war, Missouri's Radical Republicans sought to exclude former Rebels from power and enfranchise African American men. In response, defenders of the old order in Shannon County organized a secret society, "The Sons of Liberty"; exactly what this society did, if anything, is unclear. But in an 1867 special election, Missouri's secretary of state voided Shannon County's vote for a Conservative (pro-Southern) state senator. In the same year, to suppress opposition to Radical rule in Shannon and Oregon Counties, the governor created a special militia company under the command of the "notorious" William Monks, who lived in nearby West Plains. Although Monks and his men marched through Shannon County, he apparently encountered no resistance.[50] In the meantime, popular support for Missouri's Radical Republican government waned; and, in 1870, the Radicals agreed to restore all the rights of those who had rebelled against the Union.

The 1870 election signaled the return in Shannon County of the prewar political order. Led by the Chilton clan, the Democrats resumed complete control of county politics. Not a single Republican garnered more than twenty votes in 1870, and those elected to countywide offices resembled nothing so much as a gallery of the county's most prominent, surviving ex-Confederate soldiers. Apart from George F. Chilton Sr., who was elected as the county's representative to the Missouri legislature, the voters selected for countywide office three men from the Delaware Township who had served the Confederacy: John M. Daugherty (clerk of the county court), Jesse Orchard (sheriff), and Henry Bayne Catlett (assessor).[51] Suggestive of the complex, interlocking membership of the county's pro-Confederacy elite, Catlett's wife was Margaret Mahan, a daughter of Billy Mahan.

The war and the brief reign of Missouri's Radical Republicans continued to resonate in Shannon County's political history until far into the twentieth century. Reflective of the county's abiding political allegiance was a poem in which a Shannon County wife explained that her foxhunter husband named his new pup "Republican," but when three weeks later the pup opened its eyes, he renamed it "Democrat."[52] The weekly *Current Wave*, which labeled itself as "A Democratic Newspaper"—no doubt, in part, in order to ensure that it received the county's printing business—invariably reported favorably on a candidate's service to the Confederacy or his support otherwise of the Southern cause. As late as 1897, Confederate veterans held an annual reunion in the country.[53] A known Union supporter in the war simply could not be elected to a countywide office. At least up to World War I, an equally effective political tactic was for the weekly to associate the Republican Party with African Americans.

✦ ✦ ✦

Long afterwards, the legacy of the Civil War and Reconstruction remained important to the creek neighborhood. Participation in a common cause and cleansing the basin of Yankee sympathizers led the residents to increasingly see themselves in terms of their commonalities and their differences with the outside world. It encouraged the development of a shared folk culture based largely on oral traditions, an already deeply entrenched wariness of strangers, and an equally deep reluctance to join one another on behalf of neighborhood-wide enterprises. From experience, the creek's residents looked inward to themselves and their kinfolk for the resources needed to cope with the trials of everyday living, many opted for the old ways over what they described as new-fangled ways, they prized family ties over other connections with neighbors, and they usually sided with individual over any form of group action.

✦ CHAPTER 5 ✦

Granny and Her Family

NANCY JANE (CHILDRESS) RADER was not simply a product of the hollows of Hart County, Kentucky. In the parlance of the hollers people, she was a "head strong" woman who repeatedly exhibited the spiritedness of her Irish American mother, Nancy (Hare) Childress. In Hart County, by owning some property of her own, even though her husband was alive, she had defied conventional upcountry attitudes toward the proper role of women. When the family decided to move from Kentucky to Missouri, she had insisted that they bring along a two-hundred-pound stalagmite taken from the Childress Cave. It was to serve as her tombstone, she told the family. While upon the death of her husband, George, in 1880, it was Nancy, and Nancy alone, who provided the family with a sense of direction. Her stalagmite tombstone stands today in the Rader Cemetery on a hillside overlooking Mahans Creek as a monument to her determination and resourcefulness.[1]

✦　✦　✦

Arriving in the wake of Reconstruction and before the timber boom in Shannon County, Nancy and her family appear to have chosen a good time to settle on the creek. The joint owners of the land upon which they squatted no longer lived in the county and had been unable or unwilling to pay their local taxes. Perhaps they had been Union men and had fled the neighborhood for fear of their lives. In any event, the 1880 census reported Nancy (age forty nine) and ten of her eleven children (five of whom were eighteen years of age or older) plus a fourteen-year-old female boarder living on a farm that they "sharecropped" in the Delaware Township. According to the agricultural census of 1880, the farm consisted of eighty acres, of which twenty were "cultivatable." The land plus the buildings on it were reported as worth $300.[2]

The estimated value of the farm in 1880 may have been an exaggeration, for five years later, in 1885, Nancy purchased sixty of these acres at a sheriff's sale for a mere $32 in unpaid back taxes and costs. In 1886, she bought the twenty remaining acres for $154.[3] How much land clearing and fence building the family did is unknown. Given the family's size, it seems likely that the older boys may have at once begun building an addition to the abandoned log house that they had found upon their arrival. They may also have added a corncrib, a root cellar, and a rail fence to protect the family's cornfield and garden from roaming livestock.

With ready cash extraordinarily difficult to come by, for the first decade or so the family depended for sustenance on whatever food they could produce themselves (mainly a garden, corn, hogs, and chickens) and on hunting, fishing, and gathering. Nearly all of their protein came from chickens and pork; in 1880 the family owned thirty hogs and thirty chickens—both substantial numbers—but they had only one milk cow.[4] That the family had six horses suggests that each of the older Rader boys may have owned his own horse. After all, ownership of a horse, even if the horse was essentially a plow rather than a saddle animal, may have been seen as a precondition for manhood.

As back in Hart County, corn was the starting point for the family's survival. Each spring the Rader family planted as much corn as they could cultivate; given the number of adult males initially in the family during the 1880s, this could have been as much as thirty acres. They grew corn not for the marketplace but for feeding livestock and for home consumption. When there was adequate rainfall and moderate seasonal temperatures, the bottomland next to the creek may have occasionally yielded more than thirty bushels of corn to the acre.[5] But, even in the best of years, obtaining enough food for the large Rader household of the early 1880s was not an easy matter.

In the worst of times intermittent droughts drove down corn yields. Such was the case in the summer of 1881, only the second summer after the Raders arrived on the creek. Day after day that summer the creek's farmers faced soaring temperatures and virtually no rainfall. In long stretches, a rare thing occurred; in places the creek itself went dry. As their corn wilted, we can also imagine that the Rader boys went out to the cornfield only to discover an invasion of chinch bugs. In dry seasons the bugs pierced the young corn stalks and sucked out the sap, leaving the stalks wilted, stunted, and yellowed. Corn productivity plummeted in 1881. The Rader farm probably harvested less than ten bushels to the acre that summer and possibly much less. "Nothing was raised that year," according to an account passed down to the next generation. Conditions were so bad that "the people stripped leaves from mulberry, elm and sassafras [trees], cured and stored them for livestock feed."[6]

For the Raders, the winter following the dismal 1881 corn crop was almost a disaster. It was probably to the winter of 1881–1882 to which Sam referred when he told his son Hulbert: "Before Granny [Nancy] got her Civil War pension . . . [the family] just about starved one winter and would have too if the bigger boys hadn't gone to a place near Salem [Missouri] to cut and sell cordwood."[7] (The cordwood was probably shipped by rail to St. Louis, where it could be sold as fuel for the steamboats that plied the Mississippi and Missouri Rivers).

A hog cholera epidemic added to the family's woes. In 1884, Granny and the boys probably heard some of their hogs screaming in agony. Upon closer examination, the boys found that the skin of the affected hogs had turned a brilliant red. Tumors soon covered the bodies of the diseased animals; in the next stage the hogs became convulsive; and death usually followed. As quickly as they could, the boys separated the diseased animals from the flock, shot them, and then burned their carcasses on a nearby brush pile. The family, along with the majority of the county's farmers, could have lost half or more of their hogs to the cholera epidemic of 1884.[8]

After a one-year reprieve, 1886 and 1887 were also bad years for the family. In 1886, the local newspaper reported that "crops are light, no employment of any kind for laborers; even politics is running low."[9] Perhaps desperate, thieves—the newspapers reported—were catching and butchering hogs that had been put out on the open range. The next year another hog cholera epidemic erupted. Added to these woes were ever-lurking forest fires. A fire in 1887 on Mahans Creek damaged some one thousand wooden rails on the J. Ben Searcy farm.[10] And did untold damage to the rail fences on the nearby Rader farm. In 1887, corn yields in the county fell again. That year the *Current Wave* had its own problems; it reported with droll humor that the "fish are biting; so are ticks; flowers are blooming; turkeys are gobbling; farmers are plowing; forest fires are raging; and printers are suffering from a want of cash."[11]

As if forest fires, hog cholera, drought, and a want of cash were not enough burdens, in 1892 and 1895, huge floods wreaked havoc on the neighborhood. Rain commenced on Saturday morning of April 2 and continued unrelentingly until Monday afternoon, April 4, 1892. Along the creek, water licked up to the front steps of McCaskill's general store, swept away U. M. Randolph's barn, and sent Ben Searcy's gristmill hurtling down the creek. The flood washed out rail fences up and down Mahans Creek and its tributaries. Still, time remained that summer for the farmers to get in their crops; and, indeed, with more than normal rainfall in the late summer of 1892, many of them were the beneficiaries of unusually good yields.[12]

Such was not the case in 1895 when the creek's residents became the victims of a second, far more disastrous flood. A great cloudburst on July 5 filled the creek's hollow with water from hillside to hillside; ten to twelve feet of water stood over some of the lower spots. The flood washed away much of the fencing and the corn crop; estimates placed the prospective yield at less than half of normal. Up Pine Hollow, the flood destroyed several miles of the Cordz-Fisher tramline and carried away several log camp houses. Rising waters "lifted" the schoolhouse from its foundations and carried it some sixty yards downstream where it lodged against a grove of trees. For days afterward, a great stench hung over the hollows from the carcasses of hogs, horses, cattle, and other drowned animals. With the proposed site for relocating the county seat from Eminence to Delaware suddenly three to four feet under water, the flood dashed all hopes of Delaware becoming a town of any consequence. But, unlike in nearby Winona, where eleven people drowned, somehow not a single person in the Mahans Creek neighborhood perished in the Great Flood of 1895.[13]

✦   ✦   ✦

Neither natural disasters nor hard times dispirited Granny Rader. Her firm religious faith, her self-deprecating Irish humor, and her odd beliefs and behaviors brought some relief from the distress that the family suffered in the 1880s. The family laughed with and at her. Granny claimed, for example, that she could not sleep while it was raining. However, one night she slept soundly through a downpour. Awakening the next morning to discover it had rained during the night, she exclaimed: "Why didn't you wake me? You know I can't sleep when it's raining."[14] In her later years, she loved to have her grandchildren—at least Hulbert and Lowell—cross Mahans Creek from the house in which they lived and visit her. As youngsters, we would "run horse races, on our hands and feet," Hub recalled, "the length of her broad porch and aggravate her." Frequently, she invited them to stay the night with her, which they enthusiastically did. For doing her this favor, she sometimes rewarded them with a nickel each.

Her insistence on the preservation of old ways also served as a counterweight to the ravages imposed on the family. As with many other hollers people, Granny hung on to the old ways. While she owned a wood-fueled cook stove in later life, she still

Nancy Jayne Childress Rader. *Drawing courtesy of Katie Nieland.*

preferred to do fireplace cooking. "One time when I was there," remembered Oscar Harper, a neighboring boy, "she was drying pumpkin rings on a pole by the fire place. She prepared apples and dried them on the porch roof, just as it had been done for over a hundred years."[15]

A devout Methodist, Granny stoutly opposed drinking and gambling.[16] When her sons once brought home a deck of cards, she angrily hurled them into the fireplace. Yet, she had difficulty imposing her will on her grown sons, who all may have engaged in some of the less offensive activities of the local male culture. In particular, Lewis, who, from her perspective, had strayed away the most from the family's strict ways, must have upset her. Until they reached adulthood, neither did she have much success in converting her children to her religious beliefs and practices. Only her daughter, Keziah, fulfilled her dreams of becoming an active Methodist. Perhaps because there was not a Methodist church in the Delaware Township, she may have in her final years joined the Holiness Church (the Holiness movement frequently grew out of Methodism) in Open Hollow; at any rate, she chose a Holiness exhorter to conduct her funeral. On her deathbed in 1912 she testified to her faith by quietly singing, "Lord, I Am Coming Nearer to Thee."[17]

✦ ✦ ✦

Economic circumstances for Nancy may not have improved much until the late 1890s. In 1892, we know that, apart from her farm, she owned two horses valued at $125 and a mule worth $50.[18] Three years later the county assessed her farm at $300, a modest figure, and valued her personal property at $195. In July of 1897, after she had apparently sold twenty acres to her youngest son, Edward Martin "Sam," who had married a year earlier, she reported that she owned only forty acres of land worth $250, two young horses worth $30, one cow and one calf worth $15, ten hogs worth $30, and household items valued at $10. Her neighbor, John Hezekiah Pummill, the father of two of her daughter-in-laws (Rebecca and Ada), supported her contention that she was virtually impoverished. She derived her entire living, Pummill wrote in a statement in support of her Civil War pension claim, from a forty-acre farm worth only $200. "We estimate," he reported in an affidavit signed on July 30, 1897, "that her entire income from all sources does not exceed $25.00 per year and that she is dependent upon her own exertions for a living outside of the amount she derives from her property as above."[19]

As tough as times were, John Pummill's claim appears to have exaggerated her impoverishment. Unreported was her receipt of farm produce from Sam as payments for land that he had purchased from her. In addition, Sam, Jerry, and, sometimes, neighbors sharecropped some of her acreage. In the summer of 1898, for example, the local paper reported that a neighbor, George Mahan, "will make a crop with the widow Rader this summer."[20]

The eventual receipt of a Civil War pension from the federal government not only relieved most of her financial distress but may have also have had important consequences for her extended family. While in 1862 Congress had enacted legislation that extended pensions to those who had suffered disabilities from the war, for unknown reasons, perhaps ignorance of the law, George took no steps to receive compensation arising from his physical impairment until twelve years later. He then failed; an examining physician claimed that George's physical disabilities, which included an atrophied leg, were *not* due to his Civil War service.[21] In 1890 Congress enacted a new law that paid pensions to *any* Union veteran (or widow of a veteran) of the Civil War who had served for at least ninety days, was honorably discharged, and suffered from a disability, even if not war-related. Perhaps because of ignorance, Nancy did not press a claim for compensation under its provisions until 1897. This time, her application won approval.[22]

With pay of $8 a month extending back to July of 1890, Nancy suddenly found herself the unexpected beneficiary of a lump sum of some $640 plus a monthly stipend for the remainder of her life. By the time of her death on March 26, 1916, the monthly benefit had risen to $36. Few other residents of the creek equaled her annual net cash income of $432. A part of the money she plowed back into the joint farming operations of Sam and herself. For example, according to a recollection by Hulbert of a story told to him by Sam, she sent Sam with a $20 gold piece to Winona to buy a new Springfield wagon, allegedly the best one made. (In fact, she must have given Sam more than twenty dollars as a new wagon cost at least three times this figure).[23] From her new largesse, it seems likely that she extended some financial aid to several other family members as well. In short, "the pension," Hub reported, "made her one of the well-to-do in the community."[24]

✦   ✦   ✦

In the meantime, Nancy Rader's family had dispersed. "Some went up the holler; some went down the holler; and some went catawampus," explained Hub Rader, in a ditty composed many years later. Nancy's four oldest sons (John Wesley, Charles, Lewis, and Mike) not only soon left the home place but also eventually married and left the neighborhood as well. Two (Mattie and Rosa) of the four daughters did the same. Nancy's other five children (Mary, James "Jim," Jeremiah "Jerry," Keziah, and Edward "Sam") all remained in the creek neighborhood. Those who stayed behind married, had numerous children, and evolved into the largest single-family network in Delaware Township. There, with the important exception of those family members who moved out of the neighborhood, Nancy's family came to resemble the Childress clan of Hart County, Kentucky.

TABLE 2.

Estimated size of the Nancy Jane Childress Rader Household, selected years, 1880–1916

Number in household	12*	9	8	6	5	4	2	2	1
Year	1880	1883	1884	1886	1889	1890	1891	1896	1896-1916

*Includes a boarder, Malinda Weaver.

That three of the four oldest sons went "catawampus" in the early 1880s reflected a larger trend in the neighborhood's history—an exceptionally high rate of geographic mobility among the local residents. By the middle of the decade all of the better farmland along the creek bottom was occupied, leaving behind only small patches of flatter ground up the hollows that drained into Mahans Creek. Indeed, of the Raders who remained on the creek, all of them except Sam and eventually Jim obtained farms up the hollows fed by the spring branches. For them, survival itself was always an ever-present struggle.

At least one of the oldest boys (Charles) who went catawampus may have had no choice, except perhaps at gunpoint. In 1883, he got Amanda Mills, a fourteen-year-old girl from the nearby neighborhood of Bartlett, pregnant. At a shotgun wedding before Amanda's father and a local justice of the peace, Charles married Amanda. Three years after this inauspicious beginning, the couple divorced, and apparently Charles embarked on a quest across southern Missouri in search of opportunity. In 1890 he married Flora King from Mt. Vernon, Missouri. Charles and Flora eventually settled some fifty miles away in Wright County, Missouri, where they had five children.[25]

In a newspaper item of October 22, 1884, we learn something of the second son, John. "Not long ago John [Wesley] Rader, formerly of this county, married Ann Woods of Douglas County," reported the *Current Wave*. As a gag wedding gift, his "brother Lewis Rader of Eminence sent him 330 deer tracks (fresh), two dozens of nothings and three bushels of wheelbarrow seed."[26] The new couple took up permanent residence in Christian County, Missouri, but five years later, after the death of his first wife, John Wesley joined the Oklahoma land rush; he rode a mule into the Cherokee Strip, where he claimed one hundred acres of the public domain. Upon becoming an Oklahoma cotton farmer, he, with his third wife, Dolly Rector, eventually had twelve children. As with the other Rader boys, he loved to hunt. That he named his newborn son William Jennings Bryan in 1896 suggests that he, like his brothers Lewis, Jim, and Sam, was a Democrat and an advocate of free silver.[27]

None of the Rader boys was more footloose than Mike, the fourth son. It was "Fighting Mike" who had knifed a neighbor back in Kentucky. Purchasing jointly with his younger brother,

Jim, forty acres of rough woodland up Turner Hollow in 1887, Mike apparently considered making the Mahans Creek waterway his permanent home. But not for long. In quest of adventure and opportunity, in the 1890s he wandered into northern Arkansas, into southeastern Missouri (where in 1895 he married sixteen-year-old Irene Eastman, who died from typhoid three months later), and finally back at least briefly to Mahans Creek. In 1896 he built his newly married younger brother, Sam, a house and a barn on the Mahans Creek Rader farm. Eventually, Mike settled down on a tiny farm near the Rader's old home place in Roseburg, Kentucky. There, he married a local woman, Mary Waddle, by whom he had two children. Eventually divorced, he married yet again.

Virtually no information survives about the Rader girls who left the Mahans Creek neighborhood. In 1885 Mattie married William Oliver Cheney, with whom she had eight or perhaps nine children. For a time the family farmed in nearby Douglas County, but the 1910 census found them in Carthage, Missouri, where William worked as an engineer for a powder company. In 1890, Rosa married George P. Crandell, the son of an Eminence physician. In 1896, after birthing three children, Rosa apparently died from childbirth complications in Alton, Missouri.

✦   ✦   ✦

Perhaps none of the Rader boys had a more colorful life than Lewis, the fifth son, who went catawampus in more ways than simply relocating geographically. He was even a protagonist in one of the many rural legends involving interactions with the notorious James brothers. Reportedly, as an Eminence barber, he cut the hair of Frank James when Frank, along with his brother, Jesse, lodged there in 1881 while the brothers were said to be returning to Jackson County from their train robbery in Blue Cut, Missouri. Described by a county leader as "a very brilliant man," Lewis quickly made his mark in the tiny town. For example, in 1884 he served on a four-person committee that staged a "grand ball and supper at the Eminence Hotel" on Christmas Eve. Two years later he became something of a local hero when he helped save the lives of seven persons by bravely rushing from room to room announcing that the hotel in which they were sleeping was afire. In 1886, he married a local woman, Adeline Boyd, whose family for many years owned a hotel in Eminence.[28] Elected to the Eminence school board in 1892, he was active in local Democratic politics and in 1896 was an enthusiastic supporter of William Jennings Bryan for the presidency. That year he chaired the Eminence Free Silver Club and led a parade—said to be the largest political gathering in the history of the county—of more than a thousand persons, all sporting badges proclaiming "Death to the Goldbug" down the main street of the county seat.[29]

Living at various times in Eminence, Summersville, and West Eminence, Lewis was something of a jack of all trades. In 1884, the *Current Wave* reported, "L. A. Rader & Co. are prepared to appease the appetite of those who 'love licker.' Call on them at Graham's old stand."[30] Besides saloon keeping, he worked off and on as a barber, carpenter, surveyor's aide, fishing guide, farmer, pool hall operator, storekeeper, landlord, and aide to county officials (in a range of tasks including bookkeeping and serving as a deputy sheriff). He was said to be a physically "powerful man." As a deputy sheriff in 1899, he escorted Oscar Baker up the scaffold for his execution by hanging, the only legal hanging ever to take place in the history of Shannon County. Reportedly, there were more than 2,500 people crowded into the courthouse square to witness the event.[31] Playing for the Eminence "picked nine" in 1896, Lewis was also the first known of the Rader sons to have played baseball.

During the heyday of West Eminence, Lewis owned and sold a few lots in what was sometimes referred to as "Rader Town." There, he brooked no compromise with would-be thieves. In 1920, he warned in the newspaper: "NOTICE: I keep my bulldog at the barn or feed house to protect my property at night and anyone bit by him on my premises must stand the loss."[32] To this day, "Rader Street," in what has become almost a ghost town, serves as a reminder of his life there. The couple had five children, two of whom passed away before reaching adulthood.

Lewis's siblings and perhaps his mother, Nancy, considered Lewis as something of a "black sheep" in the family. Of Nancy's children, only Lewis is recorded as having been involved in any public disturbances. During a "serious shooting affray" at a dance in 1886 near Summersville, a town just across the Shannon County border in Texas County, one of the disputants drew a pistol and fired a shot into Lewis's left leg. The un-extracted bullet continued to bother Lewis for the remainder of his life, but his friends at the dance fared even worse: someone shot Jerry Orchard in the back and left hip, and Riley Martin received shots in the right arm, the left chest, and his shoulder. Martin died from his wounds.[33] On another occasion, authorities arrested Lewis, along with several other Eminence men, for playing the card game of pitch; but, when no one stepped forward to testify against the card players, the charges were dropped. Alone among Granny's sons, Lewis was not averse to drinking or selling alcoholic beverages, at least not in his younger years.[34] In two separate time periods he owned or managed a bar in Eminence. On one occasion Lewis and one his cousins (a Perkins) got into a drunken brawl. Exhausted after nearly an hour of combat, they were said to have fallen asleep in one another's arms under the front porch of Lewis's house.

However, for the most part, Lewis enjoyed a reputation in Eminence and West Eminence as a solid citizen. His list of public service activities was a long one, including an appointment in 1895 to a committee to draw up plans for a new courthouse, and in the following year he was the marshal for Eminence's Fourth of July celebration. When the Democratic candidates were doing their speaking tours during election campaigns, they routinely turned the keys to their courthouse offices over to Lewis. On these occasions Lewis managed the entire courthouse single-handedly. Although he failed in a bid to become the Democratic candidate for county treasurer in 1894, he was a stalwart in the party and on several occasions the beneficiary of patronage. In 1912, Eminence elected his son, Ruel, as the town's constable. As he grew older, Lewis seems to have become more settled. In 1911, characteristically like his brothers, of whom several publicly announced their faith at an advanced age, Lewis "professed a hope in Christ." In addition, Lewis won the esteem of locals for

the tender care that he extended to his wife, who was invalided
in her declining years.[35]

It may be that one of the Rader brothers for a time practiced
medicine in Eminence. The October 8, 1884, issue of the *Current
Wave* reported, "Drs. Bailey and Rader are attending the case
of Ira Carr. They fill the bill, but there is talk of having Rader
indicted for practicing surgery without a license." Carr had shot
himself between the toes of his right foot with a Winchester rifle
and was expected to recover in two or three weeks. Another item
in the *Current Wave* of October 15, 1884, declared, "Doctors
Bailey and Rader splintered Ira Carr's toe yesterday. Dr. Rader
will soon become one of the foremost in his profession in the
county." Apparently the wound became infected. A third item
in the *Current Wave*, December 3, 1884, reported, "Yesterday Ira
Carr had one of his toes amputated by Drs. Bailey and Rader."
The weekly never mentioned a Dr. Rader again.[36] Only Lewis
Rader is known with certainty to have lived in Eminence in
1884, though it is possible that Charles Henry Rader resided
there as well. But there is no evidence from the family's oral history that either of the brothers practiced medicine. The mystery
of the identity of this particular Rader remains unsolved.

✦   ✦   ✦

As Hub claimed in his poem about several of the Raders going
catawampus, the remainder of Nancy's grown children all
took up farming up or down the hollows of the Mahans Creek
waterway itself. The families of both Mary (Rader) Perkins and
Keziah (Rader) Klepzig acquired small farms in Open Hollow.
Between them, Mary and Keziah had twenty-one children.
Farming a hillside place of only fifty-six acres, Jeremiah "Jerry"
Benjamin Rader married Sarah Jane Honeycutt in 1896 and had
six children. Unusually diminutive, while his wife was equally
impressive for her largeness, Jerry was known far and wide as a
consummate storyteller who frequently interrupted his narra-
tives with uncontrollable fits of laughter.

The descendants of Nancy Rader soon became by far the

largest extended family in the Delaware Township. Encouraged to remain in the Mahans Creek waterway by the arrival of the timber boom, by 1910 their numbers had grown to seventy-one. By then, one of every three persons in the township was related to Granny Rader. So conspicuous were they in the local school, the newspapers sometimes referred to it as the "Rader" school, rather than by its proper name of "Delaware." Likewise, they were just as likely to refer to the local train stop on the Jim Rader farm as the "Rader" flag station as they were to call it by its proper name, the "Delaware" station.

The Mahans Creek Raders bore some striking resemblances to their Childress kinfolk back in Hart County, Kentucky. While the Raders settled into a dense cluster of farms nearly a half century after the Childresses, both clans traced their origins back to specific pairings—to that of John W. Childress and Mary "Polly" Hare, in the instance of the Childresses, and to George Washington Rader and Nancy Jane Childress, in the case of the Raders. Like their Childress ancestors, the Raders offered all their kinfolk—no matter how impoverished—a sense of identity and something of a "last resort" safety net. As with the Childress clan, several of the Raders developed a local reputation of "not being overly ambitious." Still, as little Lilly May Rader observed in 1908 when her family visited the Kentucky Childressses, her own family (that of Jim Rader), as well as perhaps two or three of her uncles, enjoyed more material prosperity than her Kentucky kinfolk. Neither, to her, did the Raders seem quite as adverse to the forces of "modernity" as did the Childresses.[37]

Had Lilly May Rader thought a little more deeply about the matter, she might have concluded that the differences that she detected between the Rader and the Childress clans sprang from something more than the greater material success that a few of the Raders came to enjoy. She might have considered the importance of her mother in shaping the values and behaviors of her own family. While her father, Jim, was the son of Nancy (Childress) Rader, her mother, Rebecca "Beckie," was a Pummill. The Pummills, who bought a farm on the creek in 1892, were unlike any other family in the neighborhood.

✦ CHAPTER 6 ✦

That Old Red Should Be Killed

NOTHING PROVIDED A more vivid example of the unusual qualities of the Pummill family than a debate over the fate of Old Red. Early in the first decade of the twentieth century, Lydia Pummill, her six sons, and one of her three daughters gathered around the fireplace of their log house on Mahans Creek. With Lydia, who was "knitting or just holding her hand before her eyes to shade them from the light, and smiling at the nonsense of her wonderful (in her eyes) family," acting as the judge, the debate began. "Subject of debate—Resolved that Old Red should be killed and thus relieved of his misery."[1] One of the sons, Arthur, took the affirmative side. As an act of mercy, Arthur contended, the old hound should be put away.

For the negative, his younger brother, Everett, insisted that Old Red should live on. "Old Red's voice—though old and weak . . . should continue to be heard far away in the head of Bascom and Waterfall [Hollows]," he intoned. Everett ended his oration with an effort to imitate Patrick Henry: "I know not what course others may take . . . but as for me, I say let him amble about over the old farm, bark in the sunshine, or rest in the shade of the old cedar tree—I say Hon. Judge, let him live until the Greater Powers than man can avail calls him, and then let him lie down and die in peace and contempt (Of course, this speaker meant contentment)." Needless to say, Everett remembered that, "considering the subject and the judge of the debate, who would *not* have decided in favor of the affirmative under any circumstances, the negative won. Of course, I was proud of this, for believe me; A[rthur] L. could 'spill out' some oratory in those days."[2]

Aspects of the scene described by Everett Pummill could have been found almost anywhere within the Upland South families, including the families of Everett's older sisters, Beckie and Ada. Married, respectively, to Jim and Sam Rader, they lived up the creek from the Pummills. As with the Raders, the material circumstances of the Pummills were modest, but they were better off than their branch-water neighbors. The Pummills depended mostly on a 160-acre farm that had only some 40 acres of bottomland. Apart from a team of horses, several hogs, and a few cows and calves, the family owned three hounds. In the fall and winter the boys hunted; they used their hounds to track raccoons, opossums, foxes, and wolves in the nearby woods. When the dogwoods began to bloom in the springtime, the boys gigged the spawning yellow suckers that swam upstream in the clear-water creek that ran through their farm. For their entire lives, the Pummills treasured the dilatory, traditional way of life of their childhoods.

Still, the existence of the mock debate over the fate of Old Red introduces a complication to this otherwise familiar setting. The children of Lydia and John Pummill "were talkers," remembered a nephew many years later.[3] The Pummills adored words, and words not just for the sake of elementary communication, but also for their power to persuade and to evoke memories. True, other upland families liked to tell stories that gave meaning to their lives, but their respect for formal learning was minimal. Few upland families would have referenced a speech by Patrick Henry, as Everett Pummill had done in his oration. Nor did other families imbibe as deeply as the Pummills in the literary culture of their day. In particular, they loved to read, recite, and compose poetry. The typical hollers family, on the other hand, rarely saw any need to develop anything more than the most rudimentary skills of "readin', 'ritin', and 'rithmatic."

For them, common or horse sense nearly always trumped formal learning. Rather than those adept at speculation or abstract analysis, they admired most those given to practicality.

In short, the imaginations of the Pummills extended far beyond their farm and their neighborhood. While they never abandoned their love of hunting, fishing, visiting, and whiling away the time, Everett Pummill remembered that during the fireside scenes of their youth, there were "yearnings in the hearts of all the boys for great things."[4] In the ink-smudged document in which Everett made this statement, it appears he scratched out "and the girls." More than Everett recognized or at the least acknowledged, the Pummill girls also dreamed of great things.

✦ ✦ ✦

The uniqueness of the Pummills arose principally from the experiences and customs of their ancestors. The family's direct paternal lineage extended back to seventeenth-century eastern England, specifically, to the tiny village of Sidestrand, a hotbed of English Puritanism.[5] While evidence from contemporary sources is absent, possibly remnants of Puritan piety, a strong work ethic, and a respect for formal learning could have been passed down from one Pummill family to the next. But what is unmistakable is that the Pummills' migratory history in America differed from that of the typical Upland South family. More than anything else, it was the experience of the Pummills and the Matthewses in making their way across America that shaped the distinctive Pummill family culture on Mahans Creek.

The first Pummill ancestor in North America disembarked sometime in the late seventeenth century at the Quaker city of Philadelphia. From there, Henry Pummill, or maybe his surname was spelled "Pummel" or "Pumel," eventually made his way inland to nearby Chester County, Pennsylvania, where in 1694, according to one version of the family's history, he was "christened" (into what faith is unknown) in the neighborhood of Nantmeal. Perhaps there he was a cooper by trade and influenced in his ways by the local Quakers.

A direct descendant of Henry, Adam Pummill, fought in the American Revolution and for his service received a grant of forty acres. He chose, as the site for his acreage, land that was nestled in Virginia's beautiful Shenandoah Valley. Living with his family amidst independent yeoman farmers of Scots Irish, German, and English ancestry, his neighborhood of a mixed ethnicity may have left an imprint on him and his descendants. Not all members of the family were above moral reproach, however, for on October 12, 1807, Shenandoah County's authorities charged one of Adam's sons, Hezekiah, with financial support of "a base born child of Cath. Gets."[6] Hezekiah did not marry Catherine Gets, but he did later marry a Barbara Knisley, by whom he had eleven children.

In 1799, the direct ancestor of the Mahans Creek Pummills migrated from Virginia to another part of the Upland South, to Highland County, in southern Ohio.[7] But, while a majority of the local settlers had come from Virginia and Kentucky, the area straddled two great cultural regions: the Upland South and the Midlands/Yankee culture of northern Ohio. Unlike in Virginia and Kentucky, several antislavery Quaker families from Pennsylvania lived in the Pummill neighborhood. Enthusiasm for public schools was far more pronounced there than on the southern side of the Ohio River; the Land Ordinance of 1785 had set aside public lands to build and support schools. Slavery did not exist in Ohio either; the Northwest Ordinance of 1787 prohibited slavery north of the river.[8] Here, in southern Ohio, a whole generation of Pummills grew up in a regional culture unlike that of their future Rader kinfolk in Kentucky.

✦ ✦ ✦

Seeking opportunity elsewhere, one of the Pummills, twenty-six-year-old Sampson Pummill, struck out from Ohio in 1829 for Osage County, Missouri. That same year he purchased eighty acres from the public domain in the Deer Creek watershed, where Sampson became a farmer and a Baptist preacher. Apparently, he enjoyed only moderate success as a preacher, but we do know that he held services regularly on Deer Creek and performed several marriage ceremonies in that neighborhood. While, like Charles Rader in Kentucky, he was bereft of an extended family network in Osage County, his overt religiosity may have eased the way for his early acceptance by his neighbors as a "native" settler.

Over time Sampson improved his material lot. Since the Baptists did not pay their preachers a regular stipend, Sampson and his family's livelihood depended almost entirely on farming. Initially, times were "very hard" and money was "scarce," complained a nearby Missourian, George F. Terry, in 1841.[9] But within nine years Sampson told the federal census taker that he owned thirty acres of "improved land" and fifty acres of "unimproved land." His acreage, the estimated cash value of his farm, the cash value of his livestock, and the quantity of corn, oats, and butter that he produced were almost identical with the averages of his neighbors (as revealed in graph 2). However, Sampson did own more milk cows (a total of 5 to an average of 3.6 for his neighbors) than his fellow Osage County farmers, and he produced almost twice the amount of butter as they did.

Three surviving orders made by Sampson Pummill to the St. Louis merchants James and Chapman in the late 1840s provide additional clues about the life of his family. On January 27, 1847, Sampson requested, "Sirs pleas[e] Send me by the Barer [bearer] 1 Bushel of Salt 1 pare [pair] of Boots 1 pare of Shoes" and eleven yards of various kinds of fabric. That he purchased fabric indicates that his family probably no longer depended completely on linsey-woolsey cloth that they had manufactured for themselves. On December 16, 1848, he ordered from the same merchants two "pare of Boots," coffee, sugar, and "1 lbs of Salaratus [saleratus, a baking soda]." A little over a month later, Sampson asked James and Chapman to pay John Burt ten dollars on his behalf and purchased two dollars' worth of coffee plus one pair of "Woman Shoes no. 6."[10] From these orders, we know that Sampson and his family were involved in the marketplace. Situated near the Missouri River, the Osage County settlers had relatively easy access to the St. Louis market. What

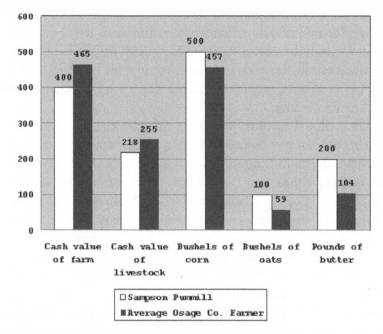

Farm of Sampson Pummill compared with average Osage County farms,
1850). *Source:* US Bureau of the Census, "Non-Population Census,
Agricultural" (Osage County, Missouri, 1850), microfilm copy in State
Historical Society of Missouri, Columbia, Missouri.

Sampson sold to obtain cash for the purchase of leather foot-
wear, salt, sugar, coffee, fabrics, and baking soda is unclear. It
could have been tobacco, hemp, wheat or corn, livestock, trees
for lumber, or perhaps donations that he received for his services
as a preacher.

Sampson Pummill's religiosity surely affected the values of
his family. As a Baptist exhorter, nothing probably concerned
him more than the fate of his children's souls. He implored
them to accept Jesus as their savior, conducted bible readings,
and probably led long dissertations on theological issues. Each
Sunday, family members heard Sampson or another preacher
deliver impassioned sermons. Unlike the Childresses or Raders
of Hart County, Sampson was likely to have attributed to work
itself a special moral value. The requirements of an intense

piety meant not only using one's time according to God's will, but also taking ideas seriously. In the end, not all—perhaps none—of his children were quite as religiously demanding as their father, including his son, John, the future patriarch of the Pummills on Mahans Creek; but still, his offspring never forgot his admonitions.

Since Sampson died in 1852, when John was but eight years old, John always described himself in later years as an orphan, though, strictly speaking, he always lived within a kinship network. According to his obituary many years later, John developed "at a very tender age the principle of self-reliance."[11] While John eventually received an inheritance of $55.61 from his father's estate, perhaps indicative of a belief in greater gender equality than was typical of the time, Sampson's unmarried daughter, Rebecca, received the same inheritance as each of the unmarried sons.[12] Apparently, John attended a local one-room, rural school long enough to achieve a degree of literacy that far exceeded most of his neighbors.

When the Civil War began in 1861, sixteen-year-old John was working and living with his brother-in-law and sister. Roughly a year later, on August 4, 1862, he, along with his older brother Joseph, volunteered in Company D of the Twenty-eighth Regiment of the Enrolled Missouri Militia (EMM). In terms of relative risk to life and limb, John probably made a wise decision. Created by the state's Unionist government, the EMM's main role was not to actively engage with Confederate forces but to guard local supply depots and railroad bridges and to track down families accused or suspected of disloyalty to the Union. Except when needed in Osage County, the enrollees pursued their civilian lives. Indeed, John's company did not organize until April 27, 1864. Between April 27 and November 9, 1864, John saw forty-three days of active duty. He had the rank of a corporal. Apparently, none of his service included actual combat but probably consisted of sporadic guard duty.[13]

On January 7, 1869, twenty-four-year-old John married a neighboring young woman, nineteen-year-old Elisa Lydia Matthews. From the outset to John's death thirty-one years later, the couple seemed to have been exceptionally compatible. It was probably a good match for the young man, who, insofar as we can tell, brought little to the union except an ambitious disposition and an inquisitive mind. On the other hand, his wife's extended family—the Matthewses—were already, or soon-to-be, a firmly ensconced family of some prominence in Osage County's Mint Hill neighborhood. The Matthewses influenced the ways of the family on Mahans Creek as much or perhaps more than did the Pummills.

✦ ✦ ✦

The Matthews side of the family got off to a better start than many immigrants. John Mathews (spelled with one "t"), a yeoman from Strabane, County Tyrone, Northern Ireland, was the beneficiary of a land grant that had been made by the royal governor of colonial Virginia to a Benjamin Borden. To lure Mathews to his holdings, Borden in 1741 granted Mathews "297 acres, 2 roods, and 10 poles." On this site near the Natural Bridge in the headwaters of the James River, John, with his wife, Anne Archer, who was also from Northern Ireland, reared eleven children. They prospered. One of their sons, a Sampson Mathews, according to a family history, rose to become a "prominent figure." In both 1780 and 1791, Rockingham County elected him to the Virginia state senate.[14] From this auspicious beginning, descendants of Sampson Matthews developed a set of family folkways broadly different from those of either the Raders or the Pummills.

One of Sampson's sons, a Samuel John Matthews, sought to improve his fortunes elsewhere. Shortly after his marriage in about 1800 to Mary Green, an alleged Native American, the couple apparently lived for a time on a farm on Pitman Creek in Pulaski County, Kentucky. Perhaps they remained there until sometime in the 1810s, when they moved again, this time to Marion County, Tennessee, a mountainous area near the present-day city of Chattanooga. While several of family members achieved some prominence in Marion County, apparently, in

1834, some members of the Samuel Matthews (he was dead) family and the John Arthur Boyse family packed their most important belongings onto one-horse or perhaps oxen-driven carts and made the long trek across Tennessee to central Missouri, to what was to become Osage County. Among the possessions of the Matthews brothers were three large cast-iron pots, at least one of which survives and is today in the possession of a direct descendant, Diana (Matthews) Franken.[15]

Two of the sons, Alexander Quincy and Samuel Jerome Matthews, settled in the Mint Hill neighborhood of Osage County. There, they established an important alliance with the Boyses, who had taken up farming near the Byron post office. In 1848, Alexander and Samuel married sisters Beditha and Ruth Boyse, respectively. Shortly after his marriage to Beditha, Alexander (in 1856) purchased 120 acres from the public domain in the Mint Hill neighborhood.[16] Alexander was a religious man; in his final years before his premature death at the age of thirty-six in 1859, he was a Primitive Baptist preacher. By 1880, Mint Hill was the center of a large network of more than one hundred persons of Boyse and Matthewses ancestry.

✦ ✦ ✦

Located about nine miles northeast of Linn, the Osage County seat, Mint Hill, acquired its name from the wild mint that grew in abundance on the surrounding hillsides. The hills were not as steep or the valleys as deep as the hills and hollows of Tennessee or those of the Mahans Creek waterway.[17] Yet the early settlers encountered many pure and wholesome springs as well as creeks; the bottomland was extremely fertile, while the hillsides were not without topsoil. In both the valleys and hillsides, the first families grew tobacco, corn, and some wheat, much as they had done back in Appalachia.

Unlike in Shannon County, Osage County's farmers had relatively easy access to markets. Whatever meager surpluses they managed to produce they could send by barge down the Missouri River to St. Louis, where they might exchange receipts from their

sales for essential household items, clothing, and farm imple-
ments. Later on, in 1856, the Missouri Pacific Railroad completed the construction of tracks along the Missouri River that
connected the Osage County towns of St. Aubert and Chamois
to St. Louis. By the middle of the nineteenth century, the bustling little village of Mint Hill included a general merchandise
store, a blacksmith shop, a post office, and a non-denominational
church.

In some respects Mint Hill was strikingly similar to other
parts of the Upland South. Two out of three of the adult settlers
in 1860 had been born in Virginia, North Carolina, Tennessee,
Kentucky, or Missouri. While not indolent, according to a local
historian writing in 1915, most of the earliest settlers in the area
did "take life easy." The men spent much of their time hunting
and fishing. And, like their ancestors, the local farmers were
said to have been culturally conservative. "They were jealous of
any invasion [of outside influences] that threatened established
customs," as the editor of a local directory put it.[18]

The experience of the Civil War and Reconstruction for the
Mint Hill neighborhood was quite different from that of Hart
County, Kentucky, and Shannon County, Missouri. Despite
the existence of a slave population of less than 5 percent and
the predominance of the Democratic Party prior to the war,
the presence of large numbers of German Americans contributed to a strong Unionist sentiment in the county. Indeed, with
258 votes, Abraham Lincoln received only 50 fewer votes than
John C. Breckenridge in the 1860 presidential election. The
Confederacy recruited few troops in the county and no important military battles were fought there. Radical Republicans even
controlled the county government for a few years during the
Reconstruction era, but the county experienced none of the violence that wracked Shannon County during these years.

Perhaps this was because Osage County was far more culturally diverse than either Hart or Shannon Counties. Located
geographically on the periphery of the Upland South, in what
might be called a "borderlands" between the Upland South and
Yankee culture to the North, nearly one in four of Crawford

Township's—the home township of the Matthews family—adult population in 1860 was foreign-born. The township included 132 German-born plus 33 French-born adults. Unlike in either Hart or Shannon Counties, perhaps one in four of the township's population was also Catholic. In addition, the township contained 93 slaves. Until sometime near the end of the nineteenth century, a few black families continued to live in the Mint Hill neighborhood. While we have little specific knowledge of the interaction of family members with their black, foreign-born, or Catholic neighbors, it may be safe to infer that their close physical proximity broadened the horizons of the Matthews, the Boyse, and the Pummill families. We know, for example, that one of Lydia's brothers taught in a "colored" school after the Civil War, that blacks attended Mint Hill's Union Church after the war, and that the Pummill boys who settled on Mahans Creek themselves held advanced opinions regarding immigrants, blacks, and women.

When joined with their pronounced religiosity, the cultural diversity of their neighborhood may have also encouraged their greater civic engagement and community awareness. While the Boyse, Matthews, and Pummill families were not immune to the relaxed, individualistic lifestyle characteristic of many of their fellow settlers, they also earned a reputation for their strong work ethic. The substantial granite and marble tombstones of the family members found today in the Summers, Mint Hill (Shirley), and Harris cemeteries of Osage County—nearly all far more impressive than those of the Raders and the Childress families of Hart County—bear mute testimony to their success in achieving a permanency and prominence in their neighborhood.

✦   ✦   ✦

Lydia Matthews, the future wife of John Pummill, came of age and for most of her early years lived on a farm overlooking a tributary of Bailey's Creek in the Mint Hill neighborhood. None of the farm had what could be called real bottomland, but the hillsides sloped gently away and up from the branch. While the land was good for pasture, corn was another matter. Clay based, with a thin layer of topsoil, the land rarely yielded more than twenty-five bushels to the acre. Sometime between 1856 and 1859, Lydia's parents, Alexander and Beditha "Biddy" (Boyse) Matthews, built a log house. Based upon the alignment of its foundation stones today, its outside walls measured twenty-six by twenty-eight feet. The family needed a big place; at one time six surviving children, Alexander, possibly his mother, Mary, and Biddy all lived there at once. Below the knoll on which the cabin was perched, some one hundred yards away, the Matthews family had access to a year-round fresh-water spring. During dry spells the spring furnished their neighbors with fresh water as well.

No one influenced Lydia's upbringing more than her mother. Only thirty-one years of age when Alexander died in 1859, Beditha, known locally as "Aunt Biddy," emerged as a "tower of strength" both within her family and in the Mint Hill neighborhood. When reports—in retrospect, obviously false—circulated through the area during the Civil War that local Indians were on the warpath, neighbors automatically gathered at Aunt Biddy's cabin. She had more "sense than any of the" other people in the neighborhood, one of her sons reported.[19] She was extraordinarily self-sufficient.

With six children under the age of eleven in her care when her husband died, she did not despair. She took charge of the farm. She kept a milk cow and took it upon herself to raise fruits, vegetables, chickens, and sheep. She sheared the sheep herself, carded the wool, spun it, and converted the yarn into cloth on her "little" loom before cutting and sewing the cloth into homemade woolen garments for her family. She had "a warm loving personality" and cared for other family members beyond her own children. Perhaps most remarkable of all, but indicative of a heritage she may have passed on to her Pummill descendants, was her insistence that her children—both boys and girls—attend school.[20]

Biddy was staunchly religious. Rather than the Cumberland Presbyterian Church of her family, she first united with the Methodist Church, but after her arrival in Missouri, she joined the "Regular Primitive Baptist church and lived a devout

Christian life."[21] Unlike the Missionary Baptist Church, the Primitive Church embraced the strict Calvinistic doctrine of predestination. She not only heard the sermons of her young husband before his untimely death, but possibly heard Sampson Pummill preach as well. Her children and most of her grand-children were also religiously active, pious, and strict in their personal behavior. They for the most part worked hard, took life seriously, renounced spirituous drink, and did not dance or play cards. The appraisal of the family many years later by a descendant, Arch Pummill, seems equally appropriate for the extended Matthews family of the nineteenth century; he then described them as "a straitlaced bunch."[22]

The Biddy Matthews family was unusual in other respects. Lydia's older brother, John Franklin, became a locally well-known Regular Primitive Baptist preacher. The family prized education. Said by family members to have been an indifferent farmer, Claiborne Lenox, a brother two years younger than Lydia, taught in Osage County one-room schools for twenty-three years, including a short tenure teaching black children during the Reconstruction era. Voters in the Benton and Crawford Townships elected Samuel Jerome, another brother, to the Osage County Court for the 1892–1894 term; shortly thereafter Samuel joined the Mint Hill Baptist Church and received a license to preach. Gilbert Dodd, the youngest brother, became a successful farmer and veterinarian. At least two, perhaps all, of the brothers were active Masons, and all were said to be "Republicans with a capital R."[23]

Arguably, then, it was this maternal ancestry rather than the paternal ancestry that most directly fed the aspirations of the Pummill boys on Mahans Creek, although the heritages of the families were more complementary than antagonistic. John Pummill and his immediate descendants recognized the importance of the Matthews-Boyse families when they chose the first names for their offspring. In examining the first and middle names of the children of John and Lydia Pummill and, in turn, their children, and their children's children, we find a striking number of somewhat unusual first names and middle names passed on by the Matthews family to the Pummills. These include Ada, Arthur, Theodosia, Lydia, Delbert, Hulbert, Lenox, Gilbert (several family members), Eugene, Donald, Jerome, and Maxwell. Even after the settlement on Mahans Creek the Pummills continued until the late twentieth century to correspond with and visit the Matthewses in Osage County with some regularity.[24]

✦   ✦   ✦

Marriage to John Pummill in 1869 initially distanced Lydia Matthews from her kinfolk in Mint Hill. The young couple first farmed 80 acres near Deer, the home place of John's family. According to both the population and the agricultural censuses of 1870, the cash value of their farm was $800. They owned two milk cows, six sheep, and ten swine, and the farm produced 240 bushels of corn plus 100 bushels of wheat and 1,200 pounds of tobacco.[25] The family and farm animals probably consumed all of the corn and wheat themselves, but John likely sold much or all of the tobacco.

Three years later, in 1873, Lydia's brother, Claiborne, apparently sold 160 acres of the Matthews homestead in the Mint Hill neighborhood to John and Lydia Pummills for $150.[26] Since this price was far below its market value, it must have been some kind of "sweetheart" deal, one in which perhaps Biddy Matthews played a part. Here, on a farm with two major fields of some 30 acres, the John Pummill family lived in the Matthews family's original log house until 1884.[27] (Today one of the Matthews' descendants, William Matthews, and his wife, Paula, live on part of the same land.) For reasons that are not completely clear, in the 1880s John and Lydia began to dispose of part of the farm.[28] There is documentary evidence to suggest that in 1882 or shortly thereafter Lydia Pummill may have inherited some money from the estate of Lydia's uncle, Burgess Matthews, of Marion County, Tennessee.[29] These sources appear to have provided a nest egg with which Lydia and John were later to buy the Billy Mahan farm on Mahans Creek.

The records of Mint Hill's one-room Liberty School offer a clear harbinger of the developing connections between the Pummill family and education. The Matthews and Boyse families founded the school in 1875, and relatives Newton D. Boyse, S. W. Agee, and Claiborne L. Matthews were early teachers at the school. In 1881, the district elected John Pummill as one of three "directors" of the school, and all of his children, when they were of age, attended the school. But what is most intriguing is that John and Lydia Pummill's twenty-two-year-old daughter, Ada May Pummill, my grandmother, taught the school year of 1893–94 at Liberty. For a six-month term, Liberty paid her $150.[30] No one then realized that six of her eight siblings would at one time or another teach school. Of these, three would become career Missouri educators.

✦ ✦ ✦

"Push and pull" considerations similar to those that had caused the Raders to leave Hart County led the John and Lydia Pummill family to pull up stakes in Osage County. As with the Raders, living among kinfolk may have kept the Pummills from moving earlier than they did. While the Pummills were better off than the Raders had been when they left the Childress neighborhood in 1878, the decade of the 1880s had not been kind to the Pummills or other Osage County farmers. Declining farm prices and a severe drought in 1881 may have discouraged John and Lydia Pummill. They too had a large family; in 1888, they had six children, four of whom were boys, ranging from two to eighteen years old. Future prospects for the boys in Osage County were not particularly bright; the population per square mile in Osage County was twice that of Shannon County and an influx of German American immigrants into the county had driven up the price of farmland. As one of the county's historians observed, many of the "children of the pioneer settlers were glad to sell their land [to mostly German immigrants] and move farther west."[31]

Both documentary and oral evidence reveals that in the

1880s the John Pummill family began a multi-year, complicated quest in search of a new place to settle. In 1881 the Pummills transferred sixty acres of their farm at Mint Hill to Lydia's younger brother Gilbert Matthews, and in 1884 they sold the remaining one hundred acres of their farm to one of Lydia's uncles, Hugh Matthews. Between 1884 and 1889, the family totally disappears from surviving documentary sources; it may be that in these years they remained on the farm that they once owned at Mint Hill or that they rented another farm in either Osage or Maries County. In 1889, with the reappearance of John Pummill on the tax roll in Osage County, they finally surfaced again, but on March 22 of the same year the census indicates that one of their sons, Elva, was born in Dent County, which was some seventy-five miles south of Osage County and next to Shannon County's northern border.[32]

In the spring of 1890, they rented a farm in Shannon County, one later owned by Jim Rader, at the juncture of Pine Hollow and Mahans Creek.[33] The farm was adjacent to the Granny Rader farm, and it was doubtlessly then that their oldest daughter, Rebecca, "Beckie," first met Jim Rader, whom she married in 1891. How long the Pummills remained on the rented farm is uncertain. It could be that they returned to Osage, Dent, or both counties in 1891, but that same year it appears that they moved back onto the Mahans Creek waterway. Many years later Crystal Pummill, daughter-in-law of John and Lydia, described their trek. The family loaded their household goods into two wagons and brought along "all the stock, cows, horses, and chickens [that] they owned." Apart from winter weather, they encountered "rough," primitive roads and the necessity of crossing several "treacherous" streams.[34] When they neared Round Spring, on September 19, 1891, their baby boy, Frank, less than a year old, passed away. They buried him in a homemade coffin in Rader Cemetery in their newly adopted county.

What specifically pulled them to this particular spot is unclear. Nearly a century later, Crystal Pummill offered one perspective: "The beautiful rolling hills . . . were covered with virgin pine trees, and underneath grew sturdy grasses." Years later, one of John's sons, Arthur, told his children that when they first arrived "you could see through the [pine] timber and could ride a horse anywhere without your clothes being torn by thorns and bushes."[35] In addition, "Shannon County was especially noted for its swift flowing streams and rivers and for its large and small springs," wrote Crystal Pummill. According to her, it seemed to promise a less strenuous life than Osage County. "The streams were teeming with fish and the woods were full of wild game such as deer, fox, turkey." That "some big lumber companies decided to move in and cut off the virgin pine forests . . . gave promise of jobs to those who chose to work." (In fact, the systematic cutting of the pine timber in the Delaware Township of Shannon County got underway *after* the Pummills had arrived there.) She confessed that the farms were small and without much tillable land, but she observed that the "water was pure and plentiful" and that "there was free range for all [domestic farm] animals [to forage and graze]."[36]

The farm that they purchased in 1893, known locally as the Billy Mahan farm, was one of the oldest and largest in the Mahans Creek waterway. Accompanying the land was a large log house once owned by the Mahans. Later, the logs of the structure were used to build a cabin in the Winona, Missouri, town square, which for many years served as the town's library. A breezeway or dogtrot connected the main house to a smaller log structure that the Pummill women used as a kitchen. A nearby spring furnished fresh water and a place for cooling milk, butter, watermelons, and other edibles. Soon after their arrival, John Pummill began to make a mark in the family's new neighborhood. In August of 1892, the Shannon County Court appointed him as an election judge for the Delaware Township.[37]

✦ CHAPTER 7 ✦

The Neighborhood

IN A POEM written almost a century later, Hulbert Rader offered a humorous retrospective of life on Mahans Creek in the 1880s and early 1890s.[1] While his ode lacked literary merit and offered an exaggerated picture of the Rader family's contributions to the neighborhood's welfare, Hub made some salient observations. Above all, he recognized the continuing importance of the hollows to those living on the creek. There, as in the past, the Raders and their neighbors sought to squeeze out an existence by raising corn, putting their hogs out on the open range, making hay, and planting "taters." Hub might have added that the hollers people nearly always had a flock of chickens, planted a garden, owned a few cows, perhaps made some molasses, set out a few fruit trees, searched for honey bee trees, hunted, and fished. As elsewhere in the southern upcountry, the men usually did the fieldwork while the womenfolk cared for the home, the garden, and the chickens and milked the cows.

What is conspicuously absent from Hub's brief historical saga is an accounting of the neighborhood's associational life. If we had only his document as a source, we might be tempted to conclude that the neighborhood was essentially a collection of autonomous families whose connections with one another and the outside world were weak or nonexistent. Certainly, the Civil War and its aftermath did leave behind smoldering animosities and a local economy in disarray. Not only did the economy not fully recover until the late 1890s, but it relied as much on subsistence farming as it had in the past, perhaps even more. While the 1890 manuscript census was destroyed by fire, making it impossible to calculate the rate of residential persistence for the final decades of the nineteenth century, it is noteworthy that of the heads of households of forty-four families living in Delaware Township in 1880 only eight remained there in 1900. Compare this figure with New England, in which during the nineteenth century more than half the families typically remained in the neighborhood from one census to the next.[2] An exceptionally high rate of residential flux surely contributed to an abrasion of the neighborhood's social connectedness.

Still, such data is misleading. In the first place, in overwhelming numbers, the newcomers came from other parts of the Upland South and hence shared a wide array of customs with the farm families on Mahans Creek. In the second place, a negative assessment of the neighborhood associational life overlooks the development in the 1880s and early 1890s of a complex set of less formal but nonetheless strong ties that connected families to one another and to nearby towns.

✦   ✦   ✦

No single indicator of an impoverishment in the neighborhood's formal ties was more conspicuous than the absence of a single church or sustained support for churches in the creek waterway. To the recently arrived Raders, who were familiar with the many churches and camp meetings in rural Hart County, Kentucky, the relative absence of organized religious life in the county and in their neighborhood must have been something of a surprise. In the 1890 religious census, only 8 percent of Shannon County's residents acknowledged that they were "active communicants" of any church, and there were only eight exclusively religious edifices in the entire county.[3] Eminence, in particular, acquired a reputation for its alleged hostility to organized religion. The Birch Tree *Herald*, on June 23, 1899, sneeringly observed that evangelist D. R. Walker "even had enough nerve" to try to hold a revival there in 1897. While this may have been a tongue-in-cheek assessment of the county seat's hostility to churches, the town did not have a permanent church until the mid-1880s. By 1900, a nondenominational church, the Union Church, hosted Baptist and Methodist ministers on alternating Sundays. Even then, attendance at Sunday morning services seldom exceeded 10 percent of the town's population.[4]

While not a single organized church or congregation existed in the entirety of the Delaware Township during the 1880s and 1890s, groups of worshippers did meet irregularly in private homes, where they sometimes heard sermons by Methodist circuit riders. In the late 1880s, an "M. E. Society" (Methodist Episcopal Society) met occasionally in the schoolhouse and sometimes hosted preachers who led services there on Saturday nights and Sunday mornings. Frequently sharing food and conversation as well as listening to sermons together, these "meetin'" days were both spiritual and social occasions. It seems likely that Nancy Rader attended at least some of these gatherings. We do know that one of her daughters, Keziah (Klepzig), was active in local Methodist meetings.[5] Nonetheless, until the twentieth century, none of Nancy's sons apparently joined a church.

✦   ✦   ✦

When considered solely in terms of newspaper reports and legends, the alleged incidence of disorderly conduct in the towns and hollows of Shannon County in the 1880s and 1890s suggests a society weak in social connectivity. Not only did two saloons prosper in Eminence, the *Current Wave* reported in 1882, but also public drunkenness was rampant. Almost every day or night of the week, one could hear or witness in the county seat public brawling, "the rattling of the dice, [and] fierce oaths." A decade later, at least according to Joshua Sholar, the editor and publisher of the *Wave*, the situation was equally bad. "Surely there are more idlers around Eminence than any other place of its size in the known world," he wrote. Sholar recommended that those men "who fill up with whiskey and parade bravely by bulldozing peaceable well-meaning citizens by threatening them with a pistol or otherwise . . . should be shot down like a dog" and those who killed the offender "should be set scot free." [6] Furthermore, the Winona newspaper editor asserted, "Our little town has [a reputation] abroad for gamblers, sneak thieves, loafers and dead-beats."[7]

On Mahans Creek reports of violence against persons occasionally surfaced in the local weeklies, though mostly the neighborhood was either peaceful or such acts went unreported. In 1886 one or more would-be villains allegedly tried to poison the meat of an entire creek household, that of J. Ben Searcy, his wife, his children, and his [share] "cropper." Fortunately, only "Doc" Bolin, the sharecropper, ate some of the poisoned meat and, as a result, according to the *Current Wave*, "came near to being killed."[8] Searcy posted a $500 reward for any information leading to the arrest of the culprit; perhaps Searcy suspected someone in the neighborhood. Apparently, no one stepped forward to claim the reward. Plausibly, the meat had not been poisoned in the first place, but had otherwise been contaminated with bacteria.

"We are informed that last Saturday evening a fight occurred on Mahan's Creek between Peter and Lloyd Buffington on the one side and James Alexander Hill, son of [James] 'Bear Hunter' Hill," on the other, read the *Current Wave* in 1887.[9] The *Wave* offered no explanation for the fight, but it did report that the Buffington brothers hurled rocks at Hill and pummeled him with their fists. Somehow—the details are unclear—Hill was able to get his hands on his revolver and fire two or three shots at his assailants before they escaped by leaping over a rail fence and fleeing into the woods. Presumably considering the fight a private matter, local authorities filed no charges. Neither did the combatants. Both the Buffington and Hill families were longtime, albeit antagonistic, residents of the neighborhood. Hill may have been predisposed to employ violence. In any case, twenty-six years later the county attorney charged him with a "common assault," but in this instance the newspaper did not name the victim. A few months later, Hill allegedly assaulted yet another man.[10]

Still, caution should be exercised in accepting the widespread reports of social disorder at face value. While it is plausible that the per capita rate of crimes against person was higher in Shannon County than for the Upland South or the nation generally, the publishers of the local weeklies were both town boosters and from the "respectable class" of the towns.[11] As champions of law and order, they appear to have exaggerated the incidence of drunkenness, yelling in the streets at nights, the firing pistols in public places, and instances of violence. (Because of courthouse fires, there are only a few public records to verify the number of arrests, assaults, thefts, armed robberies, or even general disturbances.) Furthermore, the accuracy of the oral legends of violence is suspect. After all, how better could the old timers enthrall their younger listeners than to embellish their stories with lurid accounts of past violence?

In fact, according to oral legend, virtually no one in the 1880s locked their doors, and farmers frequently turned out their hogs and cattle onto the open range without branding them adequately or knowing of their precise whereabouts for days at a time. Farm animals whose owners were unknown regularly wandered onto the farms of neighbors; the *Wave* carried descriptions of such animals and requests by local farmers for their owners to retrieve them. A typical example: "Taken up at my farm on Delaware Creek one black sow about 225 pounds with both ears off the head. Owner please call and pay expenses and get same."[12] Crimes against property were said to have been rare. No one worried about theft during the 1880s, claimed an old timer, G. R. Kenamore. Among the items that he first stocked in his general store in Eminence, he remembered many years later, were twelve padlocks. It was a mistake, he said. "When I sold out ten years later, I had 11 of them on hand—somebody had bought one through curiosity."[13]

✦ ✦ ✦

Despite a general lack of material prosperity, the absence of
formal voluntary associations, and the difficulties of travel, the
neighborhood's history in the wake of the Civil War is replete with
evidence of less formal forms of social connectedness. One falls
under the general rubric of "neighborliness." No reputation—
not for wealth or longevity on the creek—was prized as much as
being a good neighbor. Good neighbors were known not only for
their friendliness, but also for their concern and helpfulness to
others, including non-kinfolk. Even a wandering stranger, once
he had established himself as no threat to the family, would
usually be welcomed to share the family's "supper" and to stay
overnight.[14]

One good neighbor, James "Bear Hunter" Hill, became a
legendary figure in local creek folklore. Born in Alabama and
said to have been a veteran of the Black Hawk War of 1832, Hill
arrived in Shannon County during the 1840s, where he quickly
gained a reputation for his hunting exploits and story-telling
talents. After a hunting expedition, "he sometimes came in with
four [bears] in an ox wagon," reported one of his descendants.
His "smokehouse bulged with all kinds of game being smoked to
preserve it. . . . He was very generous at heart."[15] Whenever Bear
Hunter heard of a new settler family in need, he immediately
saddled his horse and rode over to their place to offer them help.
One of these could have been the newly arrived Nancy Rader
family in 1880. In any event, Nancy's youngest son, Sam, and
Bear Hunter's son, James Alexander Hill, as well as their respective families, became lifelong friends.[16]

Although the township's post office had been closed in 1873,
the schoolhouse, a country store, at least two gristmills, and,
above all else, family homes comprised sites for a shared neighborhood life. Despite the barriers on travel imposed by the steep
ridges and the swift-running creeks, visiting among members of
the same extended family occurred with striking frequency. But
other residents also dropped in on non-kinfolk neighbors—as
often as not without forewarning—and they might stay for the
night or the weekend. Indeed, many, if not most, of the families
formed visiting networks, which included an informal cycle of

visiting between a set of families. Dancing was a popular pastime. For example, the local newspaper at Eminence reported that Charles Klepzig, a German-born immigrant by way of Illinois, scheduled a Christmas dinner and dance on Christmas Day, 1884, at his home in Delaware. He charged each couple fifty cents.[17] It may have been then that Keziah Rader first danced with her soon-to-be husband, Thomas Archibald Klepzig, a son of Charles Klepzig.

Young and old alike found entertainment in the nearby towns. No event regularly excited more interest than circuit court sessions in Eminence. The attendees spent hours debating the performances of some eleven attorneys who regularly worked out of the county seat. For many years Frank Stringer entertained the aficionados of the court with his banjo playing outside the courthouse. The county's residents turned the occasion into a vacation; they packed into the local hotels in Eminence and camped out along the banks of the nearby Jacks Fork River. Fourth of July celebrations held in Eminence, Winona, Birch Tree, and, later, Alley Spring were also well attended. They usually included a wide variety of contests and dancing, though the newspaper sometimes lamented that excessive drinking and wrangling spoiled the occasions.[18]

The *Current Wave* regularly carried stories of dancing on weekends until the wee hours of the morning. In 1884, the newspaper reported that a "leap year kissing bee" of "young men and maidens" was sweeping through the county.[19] While generally approving of these diversions, the newspaper condemned the drunkenness and the carrying of pistols by the young men that sometimes accompanied the dances. Given the potentially explosive combination of alcohol and firearms apparently present at such occasions, the paucity of reported cases of personal violence is somewhat surprising.

In the summer of 1886, young men in the county became infected with a "base ball craze." Delaware fielded a local team. The editor of the Eminence paper had no sympathy for the obsession. Disgusted with the young men hanging around his office endlessly discussing baseball, he finally wrote: "We want it distinctively understood that the WAVE office is not base ball headquarters."[20] The Reverend John T. Boyd, owner of the local hotel, was equally upset with the sport of another group of young men—that of horseshoe pitching. He would be gratified, the *Wave* reported, if "Eminence sports would cease pitching horseshoes near to the foot of the shade tree in front of his hotel."[21]

Much of the neighborhood's more formal social life revolved around the Delaware schoolhouse, a log structure apparently erected in 1870 upon the occasion of the formation of the township.[22] It was centrally located near the intersection of where the Pine Hollow branch, a seasonal creek, dumped into Mahan's Creek; students ranging in ages from about five to fifteen or so initially gathered for four or five months of instruction by one teacher. The house itself contained desks of hewed logs and a fireplace at one end of the single room. A majority of the children of school age rarely or never attended school.[23]

Still, the schoolhouse served as a community center. Not only did it host the neighborhood's primary school and religious services, it also served as a site for burial ceremonies. While weddings usually entailed the bride and groom simply seeking out a justice of the peace, who married them with little or no fanfare, the entire neighborhood turned out for funerals. Meeting at the schoolhouse in 1884, for example, George Martz, the local Methodist circuit rider, preached the funeral services for a member of the Hill family. No one reportedly preached when "Uncle Joe" Buffington, who, weighing a whopping 347 pounds, was interred on July 15, 1886, at the schoolhouse.[24] Perhaps the absence of a funeral sermon arose from an on-going feud between the Buffington and Hill families. During election campaigns, the schoolhouse was a regular stop for stump speeches by candidates seeking countywide offices. People walked and came by horseback, mules, and wagon. With no hitching racks, local families tied their animals to nearby trees. Much to the irritation of the neighborhood's baseball-playing fraternity, by gnawing on the bark, mules killed a "favorite tree near 'home base.'"[25]

In the 1880s, the neighborhood hosted a general store run by Polly Lancaster, the wife of farmer John Lancaster, and two gristmills, one owned by Aaron Lloyd on Mahans Creek and another owned by John Alley at Alley Spring on the Jacks Fork River. (Until 1909 the Alley area was part of the Delaware Township.) For several years, the Lloyd mill ground most of the corn and wheat for the residents of nearby Eminence. Farmers carried corn to the mills, where they had it ground into meal; they then paid the miller with a portion of the meal or, on rare occasions, with cash or other goods. The mill also served as a gathering place; men met there, frequently out under the shade of the trees, to talk about the weather, their crops, politics, and, above all else, their hunting or fishing exploits. Seeking voters, candidates for public office made the mills a regular part of their rounds.[26]

Some ninety years after the event (in 2010) Arch Pummill remembered as a boy of six that his German American grandfather, August Henry Drewel, placed him on "Old Hattie," an aging mare, with two sacks of white corn and sent him to Alley Spring to have the corn ground into meal. Upon arrival, the miller helped Arch down from his horse and unloaded his corn. To what seemed to Arch to be several hours later, the miller approached him: "Do you want something, boy?" he growled. "I want my meal," answered Arch. "Boy," the miller responded, "I don't have any of your corn." Worried lest he return to his grandfather's empty-handed, tears began to well in Arch's eyes. The miller finally relented and loaded Arch's portion of the newly ground meal on Old Hattie. Though the experience may be seen as a rite of initiation for boys into adulthood, Arch to this day has never forgiven the miller.[27]

Compensating in part for the low level of formal associational life in the neighborhood was also an emerging indigenous folk culture. A fundamental foundation of the culture was a shared knowledge by the residents of the surrounding physical geography. No spot—no hollow or farm (occupied or not)—was too small for a name. Another foundation of the local folk culture was an intimate knowledge by the residents of one another's families. Dead or alive, everyone seemed to know who was related to whom. Thirdly, the neighborhood shared a common history. Local residents remembered in staggering detail instances of past misbehavior, of hunting and fishing feats, of suffering and sorrow. While none of these cruxes were exclusive to the creek, they provided a common frame of reference for those living there; they strengthened the bonds of the neighborhood, helped to socialize the local children, and frequently offered a source of entertainment.[28]

✦   ✦   ✦

As the decade of the 1880s closed, the Mahans Creek inhabitants took comfort in two facts. One was in the familiarity of the surrounding hills and hollows; for many, the terrain resembled the places from which they had come. Another was in the fact that their neighbors were in fundamental respects much like themselves.

"The Colored Lunatic
of Jackson Township"

CAMP JACKSON, AN African American born in 1868, came by his name in an unusual way. Perhaps on a whimsy, his father, Cyrus Jackson, decided to call him "Camp" in recognition of an army camp, Camp Jackson, which was near St. Louis, Missouri. In 1861, shortly after the Civil War had begun, Captain Nathaniel Lyon had led a newly organized Union volunteer unit in the capture of Camp Jackson, then under the control of the Missouri Volunteer Militia, a unit sympathetic to the Confederacy. Thereby, Lyon early in the war established Union control of St. Louis and its vicinity. The Union victory may have also released Cyrus Jackson from slavery. Perhaps he was confiscated as "contraband" by the Union army. Later on, he may have joined the Third Regiment of the United States Colored Army Artillery. At least the regimental roll includes a "Cyrus Jackson."[1]

While nothing is known about Camp's mother, sometime later in the century, probably in the late 1890s, father and son moved from the St. Louis area to Shannon County. At first they may have worked together in the timber industry, and, perhaps aglow with the prospect of finally becoming self-sufficient, Cyrus bought a farm in Jackson Township. But all was not well for the two black men. An ominous item appeared in the February 8, 1900, issue of the *Current Wave*. Referring to thirty-two-year-old Camp, the weekly asserted, "The colored lunatic of Jackson township [is] reported on a rampage again."[2]

How are we to understand this report? Was Camp Jackson given to spells of insanity or drunkenness? Did he destroy property or physically harm others? Apart from the newspaper's assertion, there is no surviving evidence that he had ever been arrested, nor are there any surviving oral legends in the county of his depredations. One possibility is that the newspaper deliberately printed a falsehood or at the least a wildly exaggerated account of his behavior. That the newspaper employed such words as "the colored lunatic" and "rampage" suggested that it was playing on white fears of out-of-control black men. The timing was right for this interpretation, for it coincided both within the county and nationwide with a rising tide of racism. Within six years after Camp Jackson's purported lunacy, a series of riots and lynchings accompanied the expulsion of blacks from several Ozarks towns.[3]

Given the racial climate of the day and that Camp Jackson had been described as a "colored lunatic" by the local weekly *Wave*, the Jacksons may have been forced to leave their farm by their Shannon County neighbors. At least, according to the *Wave*, no blacks resided in the county in 1902.[4] Neither did either of the Jacksons surface again in the public record until 1910, when the census reported that Camp Jackson (single) lived on a farm in Bonhomme Township of St. Louis County, Missouri. In 1918, his father died, apparently a pauper, and was buried in a St. Louis potters grave.[5] Until his death in 1952 at the age of eighty-four, Camp Jackson himself continued to toil within a white household (the Frank Dennis family) as a "farm laborer" and "caretaker" in St. Louis County. While unwelcome in Shannon County, Jackson was buried next to a white family (Dennis) in Resurrection Cemetery, a Catholic cemetery at Afton, Missouri, in St. Louis County.[6]

Unknown to all but a few local people, another African American resided in Shannon County as well. In 1900, she lived with a white family on an isolated farm in the Casto Township adjacent to the Texas County border. Apparently born a slave in 1835, she was first listed in the census of 1870 as Fannie Smith, but otherwise was known as "Fanny Janes," "Fanny J. Garrison," or "Black Fan." She had accompanied her owner, Nathan Lowder, and his wife, Mildred, when they moved in the 1850s from Arkansas to a farm in Shannon County. Nathan died in 1871, but Fannie remained in the various households in which Mildred resided. According to the Lowder family's oral history, Fannie helped rear Mildred's children, and she was said to have "loved the kids like a nanny."[7] Sometime in the 1880s or the 1890s Fanny and Mildred joined the household of Mildred's son-in-law, Robert G. Morris, a farmer in Shannon County's Casto Township. The 1900 census listed Fannie as "Fanny J. Garrison," "colored," and as a "pauper/boarder." Both she and Mildred disappear from the public record after 1900.

✦   ✦   ✦

Until the 1970s, no black ever resided permanently in Shannon County again. Still, race long occupied a conspicuous place in the county's public discourse. If printed sources are to be credited, much or most of the concern stemmed from politics rather than economic issues. In particular, memories and reminders of the brief reign of the Radical Republicans in Missouri during the Reconstruction era continued to resonate among Shannon County residents. In election after election, despite abundant evidence to the contrary, the Democratic *Current Wave* in the county seat at Eminence sought to rouse fears that Missouri's Republican Party was determined to extend full equality to African Americans.

If this was successful, then the Republicans threatened the security that many white voters enjoyed in identifying themselves as whites. For example, the following newspaper reports must have reinforced "whiteness" as a source of identity among many of the county's white residents. "'Look at that coon,' was the remark frequently made on the streets [of Eminence] Monday, as a big fleshy negro passed through town" in 1887.[8] "A very dark specimen of the descent of Ham was a curiosity to the little folk of this place this week," observed the *Wave* a decade later. "There is one negro in the county [Fannie Smith?], and right here let it be said that 'one's a plenty.'"[9] Upon reading such stories, no matter how poor or miserable they may have been otherwise, many local whites probably took some comfort from not being black themselves and from living in a county bereft, or almost bereft, of blacks.

As in much of the remainder of the nation, racism and racial anxiety in Shannon County seems to have reached a peak during the first decade of the twentieth century. That in 1901 President Theodore Roosevelt invited a black leader, Booker T. Washington, to dine with him and his family at the White House confirmed suspicions in the county that the Republican Party was continuing to foster an alliance with black Americans.[10] In 1902, just weeks before a countywide election, the *Wave* published an incendiary cartoon, which it had apparently lifted from another Missouri newspaper, entitled "Links of Republican Sausage."[11] The caricature included an ostentatiously dressed black man with a diamond stickpin, one Giles Bell, a black politician from Fulton, Missouri, who was of some prominence in state Republican circles, and Jonathan D. Young, a white Republican politician, negotiating for the state's black vote. The white politician reassures the black man that "we Republicans love our colored brothers and they will not be forgotten." To add to white anxieties, the cartoon asserts that the black man then touches a knife that he has secretly stowed in his pocket.

As suggested by the printing of the cartoon, the *Current Wave*, which was published and edited by the county's longtime representative to the Missouri legislature, Pleas L. Lyles, contributed to the foregrounding of race into Shannon County's politics at the turn of the century. In 1904, Lyles observed that Theodore Roosevelt's nomination for the presidency at the Republican National Convention had been seconded by a black Maryland delegate. He warned, "With a new epoch of Negro influence in National Politics, with negro equality preached in high places and miscegenation practiced and tolerated among the cultivated citizens of the north . . . , it may not be many moons before the term 'American' ceases to designate a Caucasian, but refers to a nation of little brown men."[12] On April 19, 1906, Lyles even backhandedly endorsed the lynching of three African Americans by a huge white mob in Springfield, Missouri. "Springfield must be a white man's town," Lyles opined.[13]

But it may be that not everyone—in particular, some of the county's Republican voters—shared Lyles's extreme views. At least my great uncle Joseph Pummill, a local one-room school teacher whose family had roots in central Missouri's Radical Republicanism of the Reconstruction era, took the negative side in a 1903 public debate held in Eminence: "Resolved that all people now in the United States who possess any negro blood should be sent to Africa."[14] (Perhaps incidentally, in 1912, Joe's brother, Elva Pummill, a Socialist, ran unsuccessfully against Lyles, a Democrat, for the county's representative to the Missouri legislature.)

Neither did the *Birch Tree Record* or Winona's *Shannon County Democrat*, the county's other weeklies, print patently negative opinions of blacks. Their only references to African Americans consisted of scattered reports of black minstrel performances in their towns and the temporary importation of black laborers into Winona to do the heavy and dangerous work of loading ties onto railroad cars. On at least one occasion in Winona the tie workers played a baseball game against a local white team, the results of which were apparently not deemed important enough to be published in the local newspaper. In 1902, the *Birch Tree Record* informed its readers that attendance at "Uncle Tom's Cabin," a play performed by a traveling troupe, was "well worth the money."[15] Still, until 1928, the *Current Wave* continued to take notice of and commend the county for its exclusion of African Americans. In 1921, in a characteristic refrain, the *Wave* reported, "We are pleased to announce that Shannon County has no negroes and we will no doubt be just as well off to continue without them."[16] Such anti-black commentary only ended in the 1930s when William French acquired the paper.

Unlike in surrounding areas, there was apparently no Ku Klux Klan activity in Shannon County during the 1920s. While the *Wave* neither endorsed nor condemned the Klan, it did on occasion, but without editorial comment, print short reports on Klan activity in nearby counties; and in 1923 Winona's *Shannon County Democrat* republished without commentary a statement of Klan principles originally published by a Klan sheet in Wichita, Kansas.[17] The apparent absence of enthusiasm for the Klan may have indicated a declining racism, anti-Semitism, and anti-Catholicism, but more likely it reflected the county's overwhelmingly rural character. The revived Klan tended to recruit most successfully among lower-middle-class whites in the smaller towns. Except for perhaps a half dozen or so Catholics and one Jew (a resident of Eminence, who became a Christian convert and married a local woman), everyone in the county was either a Protestant or a non-believer of Protestant descent. Given that Al Smith, a Catholic, carried Shannon County in the presidential election of 1928 by a much closer margin (343 votes) than any previous Democrat suggests, however, that the county was not exempt from anti-Catholicism.[18]

In the meantime, almost annually one or more groups of itinerant African Americans entertained Shannon County whites. Exotica appear to have been a central characteristic of all of these performances. In 1922, for example, two black musicians performed on Eminence's street corners on a Saturday afternoon and "put on a show" that night at the opera house before a "large crowd" without incident. On Monday night, they repeated their performance at West Eminence before an enthusiastic audience. One of those in attendance was my seven-year-old cousin, Arch Pummill, who watched in wide-eyed amazement as the musicians performed a medley of songs, including "Dem Bones." In the following year, 1923, as a money-raising venture, the white members of Winona's High School basketball team put on a black-faced minstrel show.[19]

An advertisement for a 1923 vaudeville show in Eminence left nothing to chance in instructing white audiences on the meaning of a sparring match between a "Professor George N.

White" and "the Hindor negro Wamego." Before the bout began, the black man "crowed muchly and loudly about his strength and prowess as an exemplary exponent of the manly art"; but, at the conclusion of the bout, "those present, numbering over 400 people, were eloquent and vociferous in acclaiming White the victor." Referencing black champion Jack Johnson's defeat of former white champion James Jeffries in 1910, in a bout weighed by the public with racial significance, the ad claimed that the exhibition "sure did cure Wamego of that complaint or ailment now so common and popular among the colored populace . . . known as Jacksonitis." After the bout, Wamego "was very meek and humble." The white pugilist had relegated "the black man to his proper sphere," the ad concluded.[20]

Equally popular in the late 1920s and the 1930s were the appearances of black baseball teams from West Plains, Missouri, at public events in Eminence and Winona. Two "sons of Ham" teams from West Plains played against local white teams at the Old Settlers Reunion held at Eminence in 1927. One was integrated to the extent of having two white players in its lineup. The *Wave* assured its readers that the black teams had been "given a square deal." If newspaper reports are correct, the teams frequently advertised themselves in frankly racial terms. For example, the "Southern Coons," a team comprised of African Americans from West Plains and northern Arkansas, played a local white Eminence team at the Fourth of July picnic in 1931.[21]

Apart from the excitement generated from sheer exoticism, the sporadic appearance locally of itinerant African American entertainers served as a reminder to Shannon County whites of their own racial identity. The entertainers apparently made no effort to counter prevailing stereotypes of blacks; indeed, they seem to have employed common white perceptions of blacks as a means of attracting white audiences to their venues. In these same years, Shannon County residents, along with other Americans, witnessed the display of behaviors said to have been intrinsic to blacks in local opera and movie houses. In the 1930s, radio, with such enormously popular shows as "Amos and Andy," also began to contribute to the construction of race as a major source of identity for Shannon County whites as well as whites nationwide.

Suffice it to add that while the local people's views of race may have differed little from those prevalent across the nation, there was also a striking example in the World War II era of the region's involvement in international current events; and at least a few of its residents were concerned about the fate of European Jews. At a meeting in 1943 of the N.T.W. Club, a literary organization of Eminence women, Pauline Knight, made a presentation on Ben Hecht's revelation of "the Nazi treatment of the Jews," which, she informed the *Current Wave*, "was very realistic and informative."[22]

✦ PART III ✦

"THE SCREAM
OF THE SAW MILL"

A few days before Christmas in 1892, the John Hezekiah Pummill family had moved into adjacent log cabins on what was once the old Billy Mahan farm on Mahans Creek. On the evening of their arrival, or perhaps it was shortly thereafter, the newly arrived Pummills from Osage County, Missouri, had visitors—their oldest daughter, Rebecca "Beckie," and her husband, James "Jim" Rader. Beckie and Jim lived on a farm some two and a half miles up the creek. The newlyweds warmly welcomed the Pummills to their new home. As was the wont of hollers families on such occasions, the Pummills invited Beckie and Jim to stay for the night. The next morning, Jim and one of Beckie's younger brothers, twelve-year-old Arthur Pummill, arose before daybreak and set out to hunt. In the nearby woods, "they caught a possum, a coon and a squirrel."[1] Their success thrilled everyone. How could there be a more positive omen of the Pummill family's future on Mahans Creek?

Still, no one on this occasion anticipated that the Pummill and Rader families were about to launch a much larger and more intricate set of familial ties, ties that long affected the history of the neighborhood. More than anything else, marriages knotted the Pummills and the Raders together. Two of the Pummill daughters—Beckie in 1891 and Ada in 1896—married Rader boys Jim and Edward Martin "Sam," respectively. Figuring out the precise relationship of kinfolk became even more complicated when, in 1905, Arthur Pummill wed Mary May "Mayme"

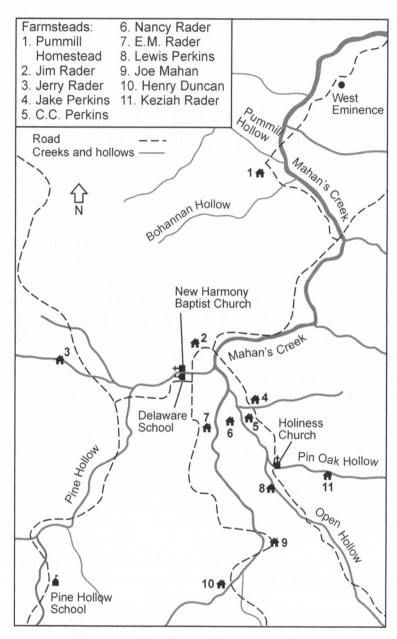

The Rader-Pummill family farmsteads of Mahans Creek, Missouri, 1910.
Courtesy of Katie Nieland.

Perkins, the daughter of Mary (Rader) Perkins, an older sister of Jim and Sam Rader. For a time, members of these families functioned as something similar to a clan. Their children and grandchildren attended school together at Delaware; the families frequently visited and aided one another in times of need.

When Jim Rader and Arthur Pummill returned from their morning hunt in 1892, neither the Raders nor the Pummills foresaw another, even more momentous change in the neighborhood—the arrival of the timber boom era. Until then, virtually all of the Mahans Creek, Jacks Fork River, and Current River waterways remained under a canopy of an ancient virgin forest, much of which was comprised of short-leafed, yellow pine. That soon changed. Everywhere, according to the *Current Wave,* one heard "the constant whack of the hammer, . . . the scream of the saw mill, and the exhortation of the evangelists."[2] The timber boom shattered the region's physical isolation. Before it mostly spent itself in the late 1910s, it unleashed previously circumscribed material aspirations and introduced the creek's farm families to a fast-growing cornucopia of consumer delights as well as a new world of commercially driven recreation.[3] The boom likewise touched off a new era of religiosity, contributed to the growth of a new middle-class sensibility, and encouraged a thickening of the neighborhood's associational life. No longer was the neighborhood an isolated outpost. The hollers people of Mahans Creek finally fell into step, or so it seemed, with the historical trajectory of the nation as a whole.

Not all families greeted the new age in the same way. Indeed, a few continued to live much as they had in the past. My grandfather, Sam Rader, for instance, remained throughout his life essentially a subsistence farmer; and, as with his Childress ancestors, hunting and fishing occupied a major part of his life. Still, he and his family did buy some of the newly available consumer goods and engage more actively than before in the life of the neighborhood, including helping with the founding of the New Harmony Baptist Church in 1905. His older brother, Jim, also loved the dilatory ways of the family's ancestors; and, though he resisted the blandishments of the evangelists, he, even more

enthusiastically than Sam, joined in the neighborhood's political
and educational life. Unlike Sam, Jim also enthusiastically seized
on the opportunities introduced by the timber boom to become
one of the biggest agricultural entrepreneurs in Shannon County.
Most members of the Pummill family responded to the boom
in yet a third way. While they, too, retained an abiding affection for the creek and the old ways, upon reaching adulthood,
all six of the boys and the youngest daughter eventually ven-
tured away from the family farm. Instead of striving to become
future farmers and accumulate agricultural land as a patrimony
for their descendants, five of the boys at one time or another
taught school, and three of them sought to secure their futures
by becoming lifelong educators. The adult lives of these three,
along with their immediate families, were spent in Ozark towns.
These families subsequently became "town people," a term
that rural people used to describe those whom they frequently
saw as adopting the ways of the nation's newly emerging urban,
middle class.

✦ CHAPTER 8 ✦

The Coming of Euphemia

THE RUMOR HAD been circulating for more than a year.
Many of the creek farmers did not believe it, but finally a brief
item that was buried deeply in the pages of the *Current Wave*'s
"Local Happenings" column of February 1, 1893, confirmed
the rumor. Without fanfare, the *Wave* announced that the Cordz-
Fisher Mining and Lumber Company of Birch Tree was about
to build a tramline connecting its lumber mill to the pine forests
north of town. Construction proceeded quickly, initially using
white oak rather than steel as rails. The new tramway plunged
northward down Pine Hollow to Mahans Creek. To provide a
more gently curved roadbed at the sharpest turns in the narrow
hollow, the workers had to blast their way through rock outcrop-
pings with dynamite.

In time, Cordz-Fisher added makeshift spurs up the tributaries of Pine Hollow. When the harvesting of the timber was completed in one hollow, the workers then picked up the rails and
laid them out a new location where they began cutting again. By
1897, Cordz-Fisher's main line extended from Birch Tree to the
Jim Rader farm near the Delaware schoolhouse. To pull the cars
laden with heavy logs up the hollow to Birch Tree, Cordz-Fisher
contracted with a well-known firm in Lima, Ohio, to build a tiny
but powerful locomotive that became known affectionately in
Shannon County as *Euphemia*.

Nothing since the Civil War excited so much interest in the neighborhood as the coming of *Euphemia*. When operating the little steam engine, its engineer, an Irishman, Hugh Sullivan, ignored caution. It was said that he pulled the throttle out "at the beginning of each trip as far as it would go and let it stay there until the run was finished."[1] When *Euphemia* crossed Pine Hollow Creek near the Delaware schoolhouse, the teacher had no choice but to call a halt to all formal learning. She permitted the giddy children to stand on top of their desks and stare out the windows at the noisy, new marvel. They had seen nothing like it before. One of the students, a little boy named Oscar Harper, remembered "seeing great ricks of pine knots [stacked] along the track . . . where the trainmen refueled."[2] Filled with sticky resins, the burning knots generated the steam that drove the log train along its tracks.

Birch Tree became a boom town. Cordz-Fisher eventually employed more than four hundred men, set up two large company stores, built an entire system of waterworks, and installed an electric power plant and telephone system. The local weekly reported that with the mill operating twenty-four hours a day, in 1899 the company shipped from Birch Tree more than 16 million feet of pine lumber and 125,000 railroad ties.[3] For a time the mill's prefabricated "Fisher Homes" competed in popularity with the prefabricated Sears and Roebuck bungalows of the day.

To harvest the pine forest, outsiders—or "furriners," as the creek people called the workers from Wisconsin and other lumbering regions—flocked into the neighborhood. Some at first lived in tents, but in time, the company built them "shotgun" shacks that could be loaded on flatbed rail cars and moved by train from one campsite to another. Camps bearing such monikers as Log, Dry, Nine Row, Puerto Rico and Cuba (reflecting the current news concerning the Spanish-American War in 1898), Store, Spring, Oklahoma, Pine Hollow, and Delaware sprang up in the logging area.[4] Eventually, Delaware, the largest of the Cordz-Fisher camps, featured a boardinghouse, a company store, a baseball team, and a company doctor.

While cutting the pine was the first order of business for Cordz-Fisher, the hewing and transporting of railroad ties, mostly from oak, ranked a close second. In 1897, N. C. Honeycutt, a local resident, reported that the Cordz-Fisher Tramway was shipping "40 car loads a day from the big tie works in Delaware township."[5] In the 1910s, Buckhart, a stop on the Salem, Winona, and Southern Railroad farther up Mahans Creek, was the site of an equally large tie works. Elsewhere in the county, the Smalley Company floated flotillas of tie logs that sometimes extended as many as fifteen miles down the Current River to a site near Van Buren, Missouri. There, they were loaded onto railcars.[6]

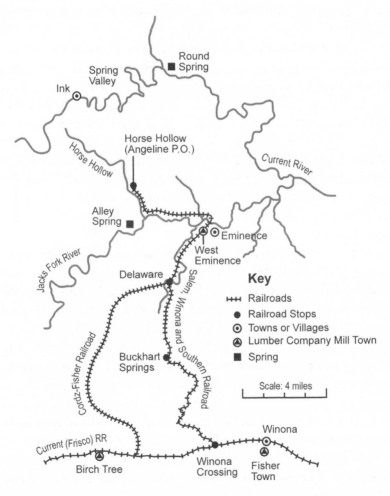

The Shannon County railroad and lumber boom era, 1890–1920. *Courtesy of Katie Nieland.*

The completion of the Cordz-Fisher Tramway into the Delaware Township was only the first, albeit an important step in harvesting the area's pine forest. In order to cut the pine in the most isolated part of Shannon County—the area along the Jacks Fork River and the northern Current River drainage basin—the giant Missouri Lumber and Mining Company created a subsidiary corporation, the Salem, Winona, and Southern Railroad (SW&S). In 1907, the SW&S Railroad completed a standard-gauge rail line from the Current River line at a point about two and one-half miles west of Winona (called Winona Junction) northward down Mahans Creek to its mouth at the Jacks Fork River.

After crossing the Jacks Fork, the tracks swung westward along the river bottom to the mouth of Horse Hollow, where they turned sharply northward and climbed up to the Horse Hollow log camp (or, as the post office there was known, Angeline).[7] Eventually, the company added more than seventy miles of tram track that reached up the narrow hollows and steep ridges north of the Jacks Fork River. In its heyday, the Horse Hollow camp, the largest of about a dozen camps scattered along the tram lines north of the Jacks Fork, included more than two hundred families, a weekly visit from the company doctor, and a company store.

The construction of the rail line from Winona Crossing north to the Jacks Fork River permitted the Missouri Lumber and Mining Company to move its huge lumber mill from Grandin, Missouri, some sixty-four miles away in Carter County, to a new location in the Mahans Creek basin. Only two miles north of the Pummill farm, the site became known as West Eminence. By the end of 1910 the West Eminence mill was sawing seventy thousand feet of lumber a day; to keep the mill running at full capacity required the daily arrival of thirty-six trains, its cars loaded with logs from the outlying camps. To its lumber-milling operations, the company added mills for producing shingles and wagon hubs. The ordinary millworker received $1.50 for a ten-hour day. Foreman, sawyers, and other skilled workers earned slightly more.

Logging in the steep-sided hollows was a scary enterprise.

"We have had a good many drivers quit . . . afraid to bring their loads off the hills," explained C. C. Shepard in a letter to the company president in 1907.[8] Still, within two decades of the railroad's arrival, thousands of acres of pine fell before the two-man crosscut saws of the timber men. Every pine tree of twelve or more inches diameter at the stump became a potential source of lumber. After cutting the pine logs into twelve-feet lengths, the workers skidded them (or carried them in oxen, horse, or mule-drawn wagons) to the nearest tramway, where they were then loaded by hand onto log cars and transported to the mill in West Eminence. On one single July day in 1907, the *Current Wave* reported, sixty trains, each with its cars loaded with logs, arrived at the mill. The logs were sawn into lumber, dried, and shipped by rail to their final destinations.[9] Claiming to operate the largest lumber sawmill in the world, the company within a decade stripped northern Shannon County of more than 150,000 acres of short-leaf yellow pine.

Partly in an effort to resist the blandishments of labor unions, the Missouri Lumber and Mining Company built a classic company town at West Eminence.[10] Almost at once, three hundred homes went up, consisting mostly of three-room, single-walled houses of unpainted pine boards. The company charged the workers $1.50 a month for rent. Nearly every house featured running water and a private privy, improvements unfamiliar to most of the nearby hollers people. A steam-driven generator provided power for streetlights. In addition to houses for the married workers, the company built a boardinghouse for unmarried workers and a huge variety store. Each morning storekeepers walked about the town soliciting orders for groceries, which they then delivered in the afternoons. The company also provided a post office, a doctor's office, a train depot, an icehouse, two hotels, an ice-cream parlor, a community hall, a gymnasium, a new schoolhouse (shared with nearby Eminence and still in use today), a house for vaudeville and movies, a baseball diamond, and a public library (open three nights a week). The company required that each worker carry a health insurance policy costing $1.50 monthly.

Unbeknownst to the public and the workers, the company

routinely placed local ministers on regular retainers. Presumably in exchange, the preachers then aided the company by encouraging among the workers self-restraint, sobriety, and resistance to labor organizers. Rather than paying wages, the company paid its employees in "scrip," which could be used in turn to pay for rent, food, and other services provided by the company. That the scrip soon began to circulate locally as money encouraged the development of a more thoroughgoing money-centered economy in Shannon County.[11]

✦   ✦   ✦

With the arrival of the railroad, the Mahans Creek people suddenly found themselves the beneficiaries of a nationwide transportation grid. Before the railroads, transporting livestock in or out of the waterway could be prohibitively expensive. Until the completion of the Current River (later Frisco) Railroad through Birch Tree and Winona in 1889, livestock had to be driven overland to such distant rail heads as Salem, Missouri, a trip over exceptionally rugged terrain of more than fifty miles. Local transportation costs fell when the Salem, Winona, and Southern Railroad built a loading chute and pens as well as a flag station on the Jim Rader farm at Delaware in 1909. Subsequently, the creek farmers were able to ship livestock to and receive goods directly from Springfield, St. Louis, Kansas City, or other distant points.[12]

The railroads also offered passenger service. Even before the laying of tracks by the Salem, Winona, and Southern into the Delaware Township, on special occasions the Cordz-Fisher Tramway added to its logging train a car for passengers. For example, in 1899 the *Euphemia* carried a carload of people from Birch Tree to Delaware. From there, the crowd slogged by foot, horseback, or buggy on a muddy road from Delaware to Eminence so that they could witness the hanging of Oscar Baker.[13] With the building of the Salem, Winona, and Southern through Delaware after 1907, creek families had available once-a-day round-trip passenger service from Horse Hollow to Winona and a once-a-day round-trip service from West Eminence to Winona.

On occasion, worshippers even used the railroad to travel to religious services. For example, in order to attend a Sunday service at the New Harmony Baptist Church in Delaware in 1910, "a number of Eminence and West Eminence people, principally of the juvenile class," took the train. Passengers could flag down or stop the train to get off anywhere along the route. In 1912, the *Current Wave* observed that the Salem, Winona, and Southern was the "most accommodating railroad in the state. It runs [special] excursions to our fairs, ball games and speakings . . . and in every way serves the public."[14]

The tracks could be used for other purposes. Elva Pummill purchased his own handcar, which he used to get back and forth from the family farm on Mahans Creek to work in the

Local railroad timetable from the *Current Wave*, December 11, 1908.

Martin hub mill in West Eminence. His son, Arch, remembers riding in the car and hearing the weeds and tall grass that grew in the middle of the tracks whack against the handcar's underside. Even more vividly, he recalled the terror of hearing the whistle of an approaching train. To avoid a fatal collision, he and his father had to instantly leap off the handcar and manhandle it off the tracks.[15]

In other respects, the coming of the railroad was a mixed blessing. The 1909 fare of $1.20 for a round trip to Winona and sixty cents for a round trip from the Rader flag station to West Eminence equaled or exceeded a day's prevailing wages in the local sawmills and lumber camps. Indeed, the Salem, Winona, and Southern averaged carrying only eight passengers per train mile in 1913, which may have been a banner year for traffic service by the railroad.[16] In short, almost no one in the county could afford to make daily use of the train for travel. While train travel was increasingly popular, particularly for long distances, until the mid-1920s, when better-off families bought cars, local travel continued to depend almost entirely on walking, riding horseback, or taking wagons or buggies.

Locals had other objections to the railroad. Riding the train was none too comfortable. Rather than SW&S standing as an acronym for the Salem, Winona, and Southern Railroad, a local wag joked, it should stand for the "Start, Wobble and Stop" railroad.[17] Sometimes the sparks from the locomotives set fire to the dry grass and brush along the right-of-way, triggering raging fires that destroyed rail fences and did untold damage to the nearby forests. Sam Rader was unhappy about a locomotive running over and killing two of his hounds, and Jim Rader sued the railroad for killing one of his mares and tried (and eventually succeeded) to get the company to pay for some right-of-way fencing. By presumptuously laying track on a part of the public road running up Mahans Creek, the railroad forced the local residents to rebuild the road; the freeholders petitioned the county court for damages, but to no avail. Despite these woes, DeForest Rhinehart, owner of the largest ranch in the county, was the only landholder known to have refused to sell a right-of-way for the construction of a tramline or a standard-gauge railroad through his properties. Railroad work was also dangerous. *Euphemia* jumped the tracks three times in 1899 alone, and a collision involving *Euphemia* and several log cars in 1904 killed Mark Honeycutt and cut off one of Billy Boston's legs.[18]

✦ ✦ ✦

In the wee hours of a summer morning, before the eastern sun rose over the ridges, the Pummills on Mahans Creek could have been awakened by the bawl of a hungry calf sequestered from its mother, the gentle mooing of cows, pigs squealing in a nearby pen, or by their hounds suddenly alerted to intruders by rustlings in the leaves or the pungent smell of a nearby possum or a coon. But, even more likely to have interrupted their sleep was the shrill blast of the mill whistle in West Eminence. To awaken the slumbering mill workers, it sounded at 5:30 a.m. every morning except Sunday. At 7:00 a.m. the whistle blew again, reminding the workers that they should be at their posts, and that afternoon at 6:00 p.m. the whistle blew a third time, announcing the end of the workday.[19] The whistle signified more than points on the clock governing the routines of the West Eminence lumber mill. It served as a daily reminder of the change that had been wrought on the creek by the railroad and the timber industry.

The harvesting of the yellow pine suddenly dumped thousands of new dollars into the local economy, though by no means was the largesse distributed equally among the Mahans Creek farmers. The biggest beneficiaries were the local landholders who happened to own stands of yellow pine on acreage for which they may have paid virtually nothing; they suddenly found company agents at their doors offering them several hundred dollars for the rights to cut their timber. For example, Jim Rader, one of Delaware's largest timber holders, received more than $1,500 for timber rights on his land, a very large sum for that day. This nest egg, more than anything else, helped to jump-start Jim's career as a successful farmer-trader.

Yet ignorance and pressure from the big companies led

many of the timber holders to sell their rights at below market value. When in 1906 a group of landowners on the creek tried to hold out for higher prices for their pine, the Missouri Lumber and Mining Company sent two men into the area who "spent a couple of days," as a company official put it, visiting local landholders "to a good effect." "The farmers on Delaware [Mahans] Creek," he added, "displayed considerable anxiety" but in the end capitulated. "Some of them reduced their prices by as much as $100," he proudly reported to the company president.[20]

Payrolls, albeit on a smaller scale, provided another, more continuous transfusion of cash into the local economy. Men from families of longtime residents joined the ranks of itinerant timber workers in providing the labor force for the railroads, the camps in the woods, and the mill at West Eminence. The demand for local farm produce increased. Jim Rader regularly sold pork to the company store in West Eminence, and, in season, his brother Sam hawked wagonloads of watermelons to families in Eminence and West Eminence. In the neighborhood of Ink in northern Shannon County, my great aunt Minnie "Minta" Cox, unladylike, rode astride her mule from camp to camp, where she sold home-produced eggs, milk, and garden vegetables to housewives.

In the Mahans Creek neighborhood, Mary Randolph, the wife of prosperous farmer Ulysses M. Randolph, did the same. After the Randolphs moved to the mouth of Pine Hollow in 1893, Mary, who formerly had owned and operated a millinery shop in Winona, began selling farm produce to local timber-working families. In 1900, she used the proceeds that she had saved— said to have been $800 that she had buried in a fruit jar in the corner of her garden—to help build the family the finest house in the neighborhood. Mabel L. Cooper remembered years later that when she was a little girl Arthur and Mayme Pummill brought "vegetables and other farm produce, in a wagon, to the big sawmill town of West Eminence." "My mother bought produce from them on several occasions," she said.[21]

The boom induced an explosion in the creek neighborhood's population. In only one decade, that of the 1890s, the Delaware

Township's numbers grew by almost 70 percent; by 1900, nearly every forty-acre plot along the creek bottom and up the nearby hollows sported a sawmill house, a small corn patch, and perhaps a garden. Between 1890 and 1910 the sheer number of farms in the township nearly doubled; more than a thousand additional acres, much of it on the hillsides and hitherto considered marginal in terms of productivity, were put to the plow. The average number of so-called improved acres per farm increased from fifty-two in 1890 to sixty-eight in 1910. The total bushels of corn produced more than doubled while the cash value of farms in the neighborhood more than tripled.[22]

Rising prosperity touched off a building spree in the neighborhood. The log house, long a mainstay of hollers people, all but disappeared. With cheap pine lumber immediately at hand, one family after another built themselves a structure sometimes called a "sawmill house." Hastily built and without stud-wall framing, a sawmill house usually consisted of vertical planks of pine. The builders nailed the planks to a sill at the bottom and a two-by-four at the top. They then added battens to cover the seams between the boards. In a frequently vain effort to keep out the cold or retain the heat, the residents of such houses pasted newspapers to the inner walls. Crudely built fireplaces of uncut stone invited the possibility of a house-destroying fire, an omnipresent danger in the neighborhood. Newly constructed barns also accompanied the housing boom. The barns were often little more than sheds, though the better-off farmers built structures that included a central passageway, stalls for animals on both sides, and perhaps a hay mow on a second floor. In the early twentieth century, the farm of U. M. Randolph, probably the neighborhood's most successful farmer, sported two barns and two concrete silos.

Nothing confirmed the neighborhood's pell-mell lurch into modernity more than a growing enthusiasm for the latest mass-manufactured consumer goods. Even the branch-water families gazed longingly at the goods displayed in the annual Sears and Roebuck catalogs. Surviving photos indicate that the younger, better-off women in the neighborhood were bobbing their hair and suddenly buying and wearing more fashionable clothing. More and more families furnished their new homes with lace curtains, rugs, and easy chairs. They bought more exotic food from local stores. For the most affluent, it meant the preservation of family heirlooms and perhaps purchasing, above everything else, a pump organ or even a piano. Better-off families hired instructors to teach their daughters the proper way of playing the new instruments. Apparently, Gettie Randolph became so adept at the keyboard that Birch Tree school officials invited her to play at the school commencement exercises in 1914.[23]

Families patronized commercial amusements in the nearby towns as never before. With the railroad easing travel, each of the local towns soon sported an opera house that provided space to traveling troupes offering a medley of music, dance, and skits, showed silent movies, and hosted dances and basketball games. The Fourth of July attracted even larger crowds to Alley Spring and Riverside Park on the Jacks Fork River at Eminence.

✦ ✦ ✦

Of the creek farmers who seized on the opportunities offered by the timber boom to improve their material lots, none welcomed the new era with more alacrity than Jim and Beckie Rader. Jim's nephew, Arch Pummill, loved to reveal Jim's hard-driving personality with a story. In 1910 or so, Jim agreed to furnish an order of fresh pork to the Missouri Lumber and Mining Company's store in West Eminence. But, alas, before Jim could butcher, the weather turned unseasonably hot. Afraid that the meat might spoil, the store manager tried to back out of the agreement. But Jim brooked no compromise. Everything was in place to butcher. Indeed, he had already employed the wives of local farmers to process the meat. Despite protests from the store manager, Jim announced, "Tomorrow we butcher!"[24] Jim's defiance was perfectly in character. No one, not even the store manager of what was acclaimed as the world's largest sawmill, crossed Jim Rader without a fight.

This heated incident, only one of several in a long and

tangled legacy of conflict, spilled over into the courts. Parties to his lawsuits included the corporate giants: the Missouri Lumber and Mining Company (twice), the Cordz-Fisher Lumber and Mining Company, and the Frisco Railroad. He sued Shannon County's prosecuting attorney as well as U. M. Randolph, the wealthiest farmer in the neighborhood. On at least one occasion, his neighbors turned against him. John A. Creagar, "a hustling young farmer and trader," joined several of his fellow Mahans Creek farmers in a filing a suit against Jim over a disputed road right-of-way.[25]

Jim Rader was unlike Nancy Rader's other six boys. Except perhaps for his "Irish" temperament, he "took after" his uncle Alfred Rader more than he did the Childress side of the family. He was nothing if not a fighter. He hated to lose, even if it was at a game of marbles. "Man alive! That man could stand at 'home tau' [outside the circle drawn in the dirt] and fudge half way to 'old middler'" before releasing the marble, Everett Pummill remembered years later.[26] Dapper in appearance, with penetratingly clear blue eyes and nearly six feet tall, he cut a more imposing figure than any of his brothers. Above all, "he was a goer and a blower," Arch Pummill marveled.

Lean and with sharply chiseled features, Jim's wife, Sarah Rebecca "Beckie" Pummill Rader, the oldest child of John and Lydia Pummill, was equally impressive. In no uncertain terms, she let everyone, including Jim, know exactly what she thought. As with her Pummill siblings, she possessed a self-deprecating sense of humor. Her lifetime ambition, she once said, was to learn how to swim and to dance, but, when she tried to swim, "her feet came up for air and her head went under" the water. When she tried to dance, her feet tangled awkwardly and were suddenly and unaccountably heavy.[27]

✦　✦　✦

Jim's early life offered few hints that one day he would become a local agricultural entrepreneur of consequence. Until he reached twenty-four years of age, along with at least two sisters and two brothers, Jim lived in the log house with his widowed mother, Nancy. In 1887, Jim was the beneficiary of a small inheritance from his recently deceased Hart County, Kentucky, uncle, Alfred Rader. Jim then joined his brother, Mike, "the Fighting Irishman," in purchasing forty acres of rough, mostly timbered land in Turner Hollow, a tributary of Mahans Creek, for $115. At first, the young bachelor may have remained at home while cultivating a tiny patch of corn on his new acreage and running a few hogs on the nearby open range, but in 1890 Jim bought Mike's half-interest in the farm for $500. The next year, he married Beckie Pummill.[28]

Perhaps equally important, during the late 1890s Jim formed a friendship with William Marion Freeman, who was the son of Thomas Roe Freeman, a Shannon County folk hero. One of the county's most renowned residents, Thomas Roe had been a Confederate colonel in the Civil War. Marion, as his son was known locally, was well connected by marriage; he had married Anna Chilton, a daughter of Joshua "Boss" Chilton, who the local people continued to revere as a martyr of the Southern cause. On separate occasions, the county elected Freeman, a Democrat, as their tax collector and sheriff. Freeman also farmed, surveyed, and speculated in timber in Shannon, Dent, and Crawford Counties.

Marion Freeman helped tutor and finance Jim in the fast-paced business world that accompanied the county's timber boom. In 1898, Beckie and Jim bought the old Catlett place of 360 acres from Freeman for $1,500. It is also possible that Freeman aided the Raders in obtaining a whopping reduction in their tax burden. In 1899, the county court reduced the assessment of their property from $4,500 to $3,100. What is known with more certainty is that Jim and Marion jointly filed a $1,000 damage suit against the Cordz-Fisher Lumber Company in 1898 for trespassing on some of their jointly held land while harvesting the pine of one of their neighbors.[29] In subsequent years, Jim continued acquiring and selling land, sometimes in his name alone, on one occasion with Freeman, and at other times jointly with Beckie. By 1914, the couple owned in excess of 400 acres, including a farm east of Eminence.[30]

In terms of advancing their fortunes, the Raders could hardly have chosen a better spot. The steep hillsides of their farm included large groves of virgin pine. Until the arrival of the Cordz-Fisher Lumber and Mining Company Tramway into the creek's waterway in 1893, the local pine had been virtually worthless, but, with the building of the tramway, all of a sudden, Jim and Beckie found themselves the owners of valuable timber. While the records of Jim's timber transactions are incomplete, there is documentation of Cordz-Fisher paying him $708 and $550 in 1898 for "all the Pine Timber" on a 40-acre plot that he owned and of a substantial sale of timber rights in 1914.[31]

Location was serendipitous for the couple in other respects. Straddling the juncture of Pine, Open, and Mahans Creek hollows and adjacent to the Delaware schoolhouse, the Jim Rader farm site had long been important to the creek neighborhood.[32] While without a post office in Jim's day, it was at Delaware that the first settlers built their schoolhouses and, later in 1905, the New Harmony Baptist Church. Before the great floods of 1892 and 1895—despite the absence of a real town—the county's residents had even considered moving the county seat from Eminence to Delaware. Given its central location and the hollows leading into it, Delaware was more accessible than Eminence to a majority of the county's residents. With the arrival of the railroad down the creek from Winona in 1907, Jim Rader dreamed of putting in a store and a post office and was even imagining the possibility "of starting a town" on his farm at Delaware.[33]

While incomplete, the irregular reports in the *Current Wave* offer insights into Jim Rader's livestock business. As early as 1893, the *Wave* announced that Jim had sold ninety hogs to a James A. Jadwin. Jim hired a local farmer, Daniel Mahan, to drive the hogs to Jadwin's farm in Spring Valley near the Current River.[34] After "feeding out" the animals, Jadwin then apparently drove them overland to Salem, where they were loaded onto boxcars and shipped to St. Louis. This transaction may have been the beginning of Jim's career as a livestock dealer. Two years later, according to the *Wave*, Louis H. DePriest, a local stock trader, and Jim together purchased a "drove of cattle for the St. Louis market." But in this instance, the market was unkind to them. "The boys returned, [after] suffering heavy losses on the sale of their cattle," the *Wave* reported.[35]

Such setbacks failed to deter Jim Rader. Indeed, with farm prices rising after 1896, Jim expanded his operations. In the fall of 1897, he bought two hundred (a huge number by local standards) head of cattle from a fellow livestock dealer and, in order to fatten them over the winter, he not only fed them corn from his own cribs but also purchased additional corn from his neighbors.[36] Indicative of the growing size of Jim's operation was a report in the Winona *Shannon County Democrat* in 1903: "James P. Rader, a prominent farmer and a Folk Democrat, was in [Winona] from Delaware township Saturday to deliver 60 head of hogs to Mr. Osborn."[37] By that date, he employed local, hired hands according to need and had one or more tenant farmers who lived in cabins that he owned in the hollows off the main creek valley.[38]

Jim recognized the importance of having ready access to cash and credit. He needed cash to pay the farmers directly for their livestock but also to pay taxes, hauling fees, and hired hands and for the purchase of additional feed for his livestock. To obtain money for these transactions, Jim turned to a source unfamiliar to readers today. While banks and individuals were reluctant to incur the risks associated stock trading, Jim repeatedly went to the Shannon County Court (the county's administrative body) and requested loans from the township's school funds.[39] These were funds accumulated from school land sales and general school tax levies. In order to borrow from this fund, Jim had to mortgage one-half the value of a piece of "first class real estate."[40] So, for example, if he wished to borrow $100, he had to mortgage acreage valued at $200 or more. Between 1896 and 1915, Jim received at least $3,136 (worth more than $70,000 in today's dollars) from the fund. While profits from his livestock operations were never predictable and the totals are unknown, he used the cash from his sales to pay the annual interest on school loans and the principal when it came due ten years later.

Jim soon emerged as among the biggest operators in the county. One large, almost comprehensive, reassessment of property for tax purposes in Shannon County, that of 1913, offers insight into Jim's relative financial position (see table 3). In terms of land ownership, the reassessment reveals that the disparity between the neighborhood's wealthiest farmers and those at the bottom was huge. For example, at the bottom of the pyramid, Jim's nephews, Jake and Columbus Perkins, owned farms up Open Hollow of only 40 acres, with each valued at a mere $150, while his brother-in-law, Lewis Perkins, owned 60 acres assessed at $400. The wealthiest landholders owned more acreage than their fellow farmers, and a greater percentage of their acreage consisted of bottomland better suited for row-crop farming. If the valuations represent a reasonable approximation of the value per acre, then each acre of Jim Rader's 258 acres was worth more than twice as much as the median value per acre for all farmers in the Delaware Township. Based on the sale of his farm in 1915, it appears that the actual market price for Jim's farm in 1913 was nearly $10,000, a large sum for that day.

TABLE 3.
Four wealthiest land-holding farmers in Delaware Township, 1913

NAME	ACRES	ASSESSED VALUE	VALUE PER ACRE
U. M. Randolph	360	$2,400	$6.67
J. P. Rader	258	$2,000	$7.75
J. W. Creager	235	$1,500	$6.38
E. M. "Sam" Rader	131	$1,000	$7.63
Median of all farmers	120	$400	$3.33

Source: Board of Equalization, Shannon County, 1913. According to a report of the Missouri Board of Labor Statistics, *Missouri, 1912–1913–1914: Resources, Advantages, and Opportunities in a Thriving Commonwealth* ([Jefferson City, MO, 1914], 480), Shannon County assessments ranged from one-half to one-fifth of actual value.

Another marker of Jim's apparent success sprang from his family's engagement in the turn-of-the-century's nationwide consumer revolution. Despite his impoverished origins, among his kinfolk, Jim had a reputation for "putting on airs." For example, he could afford and did take his family out to eat at the local hotel in Eminence. He bought the family a fancy white carriage. He dressed more fashionably and travelled more than his kinfolk. In 1907, he escorted an extended family group that included not only his own family but also his sister-in-law, Ada (Pummill) Rader, back to Osage County, Missouri, where they visited relatives and friends. In the following year, 1908, his family took the most memorable trip of all; by train they travelled to St. Louis, took in the sights there, and then proceeded by train back to the homeland of the Raders and Childresses in Hart County, Kentucky.[41]

Beckie and Jim's home was something of a social center for kinfolk and neighbors alike. For nearly two decades, local boys and young men gathered there on Sundays to play baseball, either among themselves or against outside foes. "Sundays . . . all the Pummill boys and some of the Perkinses and . . . the Mahans et al., casually dropped in for Sunday dinner," remembered Everett Pummill two decades later. "And lands . . . alive! The amount of 'grub' we put away was a sight." Beckie, he reported, was an incomparable hostess. "How in the world did you manage such mobs?" he asked her.[42]

In February of 1914, the couple threw an elaborate birthday party for Beckie's baby sister, Dona (Pummill) Hogan, and nearly all the young people of Delaware attended. "The evening was spent very pleasantly in games," reported "Blue Eyes," a neighborhood correspondent, to the *Shannon County Democrat*.[43] In the meantime, the Raders sent their oldest daughter, Theodosia, who was to become a basketball and track star, to the Fourth District State Normal School (today Missouri State University in Springfield), from which she obtained a degree in 1914. Theodosia later taught mathematics and agriculture at the Willow Springs, Missouri, high school.[44]

Above all other activities, Jim's construction of a new family home in 1910 offered a visible testimony of how far his family had ascended. Only a couple of decades earlier, both Jim and

Beckie had lived in log houses. With perhaps but two exceptions (the home of U. M. Randolph, completed in 1900, and that of the Pummill brothers, completed in 1907, both of which were wooden structures), the homes in the neighborhood continued to consist of log houses and hastily constructed "sawmill" houses.[45] Not unexpectedly, given his temperament, Jim built a daringly different kind of structure, one made of cast concrete blocks molded to give the appearance of stone. An asymmetrical "central-hall house" of Georgian-style origins (sometimes also described as an I-style house), it was much larger—thirty-two by thirty-eight feet and two stories high, perhaps making it the largest family dwelling in Shannon County—and, with its expensive cabinetry and extraordinarily tall ceilings of pressed tin, it made an incontrovertible statement of not only the family's modernity but also their claims to high social standing.[46]

Few of his neighbors were as generous or as civically engaged as Jim Rader. In 1907, for example, he provided the sons of the newly arrived French family with a free cabin for the winter; later, in 1910, William "Bill" French recorded in his diary that

Jim and Beckie Rader's new home in about 1910. *Courtesy of Nicholas Raper.*

Jim, unlike four of his neighbors, graciously provided Bill with a horse free of charge to carry his belongings from his boarding-house in Pine Hollow to the French household two miles east of Eminence. While, apparently, neither Jim, Beckie, nor any of their children ever joined the local New Harmony Baptist Church, the district repeatedly elected Jim to the Delaware school board. Likewise, Jim frequently served as one of the township's election judges. In 1908, the Shannon County Court, the county's administrative agency, appointed Jim as Delaware's road overseer.[47]

Nothing excited Jim more politically than William Jennings Bryan's campaigns for the presidency. In 1896, as with countless other farmers and traders in the South and the Midwest, Jim was swept up in an enthusiasm for "free silver," which he believed would increase the nation's money supply and the income of upwardly aspiring men such as himself. In 1896, local residents in the township elected him as president of the Delaware Free Silver Club, which enrolled forty-seven "enthusiastic" members. Aided by Jim, Bryan, as the Democratic (free silver) candidate, easily carried Delaware Township. Despite his disappointment with Bryan's defeat nationally in 1896, Jim again campaigned for the Great Commoner in 1900. In this election Jim's support must not have swayed many voters, for Bryan carried the Delaware Township by only seven votes, the lowest margin of any township in the county. In 1912, Delaware elected Jim to the Shannon County Democratic Central Committee, and that year he must have experienced considerable elation to finally see a fellow Democrat, Woodrow Wilson, not only easily carry the Delaware Township but also be elected to the White House.[48]

Jim had a flair for the dramatic. In June of 1912, one of his nieces, "handsome" fifteen-year-old Charlotte Nancy Cheney, from Carthage, Missouri, stayed with the Raders while visiting her kinfolk on Mahans Creek. A few days after Charlotte's arrival, a twenty-year-old visitor showed up at the Jim Rader farm, one Frederick Cowgill, "who had been employed in the moving picture show" in Joplin, Missouri. Cowgill had come to see Charlotte. The young couple declared their mutual intent for matrimony and set about to return to Carthage. Jim was suspicious; he had his doubts about whether Charlotte's parents approved of the proposed union. Jim and Cowgill argued, and "to cap the matter Mr. Rader had the ardent swain arrested on the charge of attempted abduction, or kidnapping, or some such charge," explained the *Current Wave*. "[Cowgill] now resides in the county bastille until the parents are heard from." Jim sent Nancy's parents a telegram, and the parents apparently responded favorably to the proposed union, thereby sending the young couple "on their way rejoicing." Four days later, the couple married in Carthage. But, in the long run, Jim's judgment of the situation appeared to be correct, for the marriage lasted only two years.[49]

Jim also had a knack for arriving at ingenious solutions. A hobo once arrived at his farm asking for aid. Jim said, "Sure," provided that the newcomer was willing to work for his food and lodging. Although Jim was unimpressed by the hobo's work ethic, he allowed him to join his other hired hands living on the farm. About a year later the vagabond presented Jim with a bill for a year's wages. Jim consulted with his attorney, who advised him that a court might find in favor of his "hired" hand. However, Jim, aware that the hobo was fond of drink, plied his lodger with whiskey until the hobo had become so inebriated that he could hardly stand. Jim then purchased the drifter a ticket and put him on a train to a distant city. He never returned.[50]

✦ ✦ ✦

Not all farm families on Mahans Creek responded to the timber boom with as much entrepreneurial enthusiasm and imagination as did Jim and Beckie Rader. Among them was Jim's younger brother, Sam. Sam loved too much the older ways of life handed down to him by his ancestors.

✦ CHAPTER 9 ✦

He Chose His Hounds

SAM RADER WAS a Childress through and through. Not only did his wiry build, his quick movements, and his equanimity remind those who knew him of his mother and her family, but he was also "not overly ambitious," to quote J. Anderson Childress's description of members of the Childress clan.[1] Maximizing his material welfare was never at the forefront of his mind. True, he worked hard when required for planting and harvesting, but he resisted temptations to quit farming and to take a job created by the Shannon County timber boom. He never worked on the railroad or in the lumber mills or hacked ties. His major concession to the sudden expansion of the local economy was to plant a bigger watermelon patch. Once a week beginning in August and continuing into September, he loaded the ripe melons onto his wagon and peddled them in the county seat of Eminence or in the mill town of West Eminence. Once in a while he also sold a wagonload of pork or corn there as well.[2]

But his chosen way of life was *not* simply because he was a Childress. Nothing pleased him more or determined his destiny with greater force than the presence of the fresh-water creek that ran through his farm. Its bottomland offered the possibility of material self-sufficiency, but even more compelling for Sam was its magic. Mahans Creek itself was replete with life and forever changing. And on both sides of it were the steep hillsides, the hollows extending out from creek's waterway like tree branches. Everywhere for the taking of those skilled in their secrets were feral animals: fish, muskrats, mink, raccoons, opossums, wild turkeys, foxes, deer, wolves, squirrels, and rabbits. Nothing pleased Sam more than to awaken before sunrise, saddle and mount his horse, and, accompanied by his hounds, plunge into the woods in quest of prey. Returns from pelt sales at the end of the hunting season usually paid his property taxes. Until as late as 1918, he also regularly hunted wolves; that year he killed two wolves, for which he received bounties from the county totaling twelve dollars.[3]

In a sense, he never grew up. His granddaughter Gloria Dene remembered that in the 1930s he took great pleasure in making her a complete miniature farm from cornstalks and corn ears. His own children addressed him as "Sam" rather than as "daddy," "dad," "pappy," or "pa." "In many ways, he was one of us boys," declared his son Hulbert, "especially w[h]en it came to hunting, fishing, swimming and eating watermelon." When plowing corn or putting up hay in July or August, Hub remembered that Sam as likely as not would call a halt to the sweltering labor and join his sons by stripping off his clothes and jumping into the cold creek.[4] Rather than devoting more toil to the farm, which might, in fact, have produced diminishing returns with each unit of additional work, Sam sought a life that balanced work with play. Rather than hard work, he was known far and wide for his watermelon-eating hounds, his hunting prowess, his good nature, his lack of pretension, and his integrity.

✦   ✦   ✦

Born in 1874 on the Rader farm on Cane Creek near Roseburg in Hart County, Kentucky, the youngest of eleven children, Sam was only six years old when his father, George Washington Rader, died. As with many other Upland South boys, his rearing was indulgent and permissive, but in his case unusually so. He was a family favorite; his older siblings affectionately referred to him as "Granny's Baby." His mother, Nancy, it was said, "diligently prayed and watched over him lest he take to drinking, fighting and gambling."[5] She set aside special treats for him: "punkin [pumpkin], sorghum molasses, butter, blinky [soured] milk and cornbread." His two older sisters—Rose and Keziah—who came next to him in the family's ascending birth order, also doted on him. (In the 1880s his six older brothers left or were shortly leaving the family household). He chose his own nickname. When he was a child, a visitor named Sam had given him a nickel "and a lot of attention." After that, when asked what his name was, he would say 'Sam,'" and the name stuck for his entire lifetime.

Unlike many fellow Upland Southerners, Sam liked school. For an unknown number of years in the 1880s he attended the one-room log school at Delaware, sometimes called the Mahans Creek School or the Catlett School.[6] At the time, the school made no formal distinctions between students in terms of "grades" and remained in session for only four months from September until Christmas. The absence of a father, his enthusiasm for school, and his amiability, it was said, made him a teacher's pet. He returned the affection.

Like many nineteenth-century schoolchildren, he took a special pride in his handwriting (in cursive) and spelling skills. He frequently emerged triumphant in the school's weekly spelling bees, a feat that won him the admiration of both his peers and the neighborhood.[7] In the spelling exercises of the day, the students first pronounced the word, then pronounced and spelled each syllable separately, and finally pronounced the entire word again. He liked to regale his children and later on his grandchildren with his rendition of spelling the word, "incomprehensibility." (I am not quite sure at what age I learned to spell this word, but not wanting to be embarrassed by his queries, I soon learned to spell it correctly.) Upon at least one occasion, he put Carl Herren, one of his visiting school-age grandsons, to a spelling test: How do you spell "gnat," he asked. After thoughtful deliberation, Carl responded, "K-n-a-t." "He had fooled me and was tickled about it," remembered Carl.[8] Sam could recite from memory long passages from *McGuffey's Reader*. Perhaps his favorite was this: "Mother, may I sew today?" "Yes, my child, what do you wish to sew?"

As a young man, Sam gained something of a countywide

reputation for his swiftness afoot. Allegedly, he could run the 100-yard dash in nine seconds flat in bare feet, though the source of this account was his Uncle Mike Rader, who was not always a reliable storyteller. At the Fourth of July celebration of 1895 in Winona, Sam hoped to test his mettle against other Shannon County sprinters. His mother made him a special pair of running trunks. But, alas, the day before the event, a cloudburst, whose dimensions had never been equaled before (or since) flooded both Winona and the Mahans Creek waterway, cancelling the track meet and preventing Sam Rader from becoming a famous runner.[9]

While Sam treasured the solitude of the woods, he also enjoyed conversations, poetry, reading, and music. He gained something of a local reputation for his fiddle playing and loved to render, among other folk favorites, "The Arkansas Traveler," "The Fox Hunt," and "Sally Goodin." As a young man, he performed at local square dances. Inasmuch as some hollers people frowned on square dancing and considered fiddle playing as "especially . . . wicked," one wonders if his mother approved of Sam's avocation.[10] In his later years (in the 1930s) he fiddled and sang at the Pummill family's annual reunions. His pleasure from listening to the recordings of the great Italian tenor Enrico Caruso was such that he named his favorite hound "Caruso."

He encouraged the musical interests of his children. These included Elsie, Velma, and Audrey (all played the piano), Lowell (the fiddle), and Hulbert (the French horn and the banjo). For a time, Hub performed for a local band headed by Edwin Faust. In 1945, Lowell even once played "Old Dan Tucker" on Radio Station KWPM in West Plains, Missouri. Alas, for reasons unknown, nearly all of Sam's grandchildren failed to inherit his talent or enthusiasm for music.[11]

Sam may have received little or no religious instruction from his father, who died when Sam was only six years old. His mother was another matter entirely. Nancy Jane was reared as a Methodist and was buried by a local Holiness exhorter. She was widely known for her exceptional piety and strictness in personal behavior. It could be that both Sam and perhaps his future wife, Ada Pummill, attended a religious revival that swept through Delaware in 1895. What we know with certainty is that the couple joined and became active members in the newly founded New Harmony Baptist Church (Missionary) at Delaware in 1905. Indeed, Sam even took on the responsibility of serving as the church's clerk for several years and in 1906 represented the local church as a delegate to the Shannon County Baptist Association's annual convention.[12]

Yet for his entire life Sam remained something of a religious seeker and skeptic.[13] In particular, he was reluctant to accept the Baptist conversion narrative, one which held that all of mankind, including children, inherited the sins of Adam (original sin) and that in order to obtain entry into heaven one must experience a spiritual rebirth (be "born again"). Rather than understanding conversion as telescoped into a single, dramatic moment, Sam's views were closer to those Christians who believed that leading a morally exemplary life was more likely to gain one the keys to heaven. Consistent with his skepticism regarding the doctrine of spiritual rebirth, it appears that as youngsters none of his children testified to a conversion experience.

On the other hand, he did insist that his children attend and participate in the Sunday school at New Harmony Baptist Church. For example, in 1913, Gilbert, at the age of fifteen, served as treasurer, and Elsie, age sixteen, performed as organist for the local Sunday school, but neither apparently was baptized or joined the local church. Indeed, Gilbert did not join a church until he was fifty-seven years old.[14] While in his later years, he stopped attending church services, Sam himself remained a pious man throughout his life. A habitual Bible reader, he loved to discuss religion, and he was known in the neighborhood for his hospitality to visiting preachers.

Compared to his older brother, Jim, and his Pummill brother-in-laws, Sam's engagement in politics was minimal. As with his ancestors and his brothers Lewis and Jim, he usually voted for the Democratic ticket. On several occasions, he served as a Democratic election judge in Delaware, and in 1922 he ran unopposed as a Democratic candidate for Delaware's constable.

In 1926, he also ran successfully, along with his brother-in-law Arthur Pummill, for justice of the peace.[15] However, he apparently served only one term in each office. He had amicable relations with his Pummill brother-in-laws, who were all Republicans (except Elva, who was at least for a time an active Socialist). He doubtlessly voted for them when they ran for public office. He was especially close to Arthur, who ran for county-wide office twice as a Republican and served in several capacities in Delaware as a Republican officeholder. He probably had few if any qualms about two of his daughters, Elsie and Audrey, marrying publicly declared Republicans. As with his religious beliefs, Sam seems to have retained his personal independence when making political decisions.

While Sam could hold his own with others, peers remembered him as an extraordinarily patient, gentle, and considerate man.[16] He rarely criticized anyone. There is not a single remembrance by family members of Sam—unlike most of his neighbors—ever making a negative remark about African Americans, Catholics, or Jews. Sam was, above all, unpretentious. While he loved to needle his brother-in-law Arthur Pummill with claims about the superiority of his hounds and his watermelons, it was always in good humor.

✦   ✦   ✦

We know little of Sam's courtship and marriage to Ada May Pummill. It seems likely that Ada's older sister, Beckie, and perhaps her husband and Sam's brother, Jim, got the couple together. Ada apparently had a happy childhood. "No modern child had more fun with streamline toys than she [Ada] and others used to have with Old Bob," the family's ox, observed Beckie many years later.[17] Unlike many brides in the upcountry, Ada was no immature youngster when she married Sam on February 25, 1896; she was soon to be twenty-three years old (Sam was twenty-one) and she had lived apart from her primary family for at least a year while teaching school in Osage County. Unlike many hollers women, on more formal occasions she

Ada and Sam Rader, wedding photograph, 1896. *Courtesy of the author.*

dressed in the fashions of the late Victorian age (corseted with flowing skirts nipped in at the waist) and owned a sidesaddle, which allowed her to ride (in proper fashion) aside rather than astride her saddle horse.

Family members contributed to the new couple's welfare. While Granny Nancy was none too happy about her "baby's" marriage to Ada, Sam's brother, Mike, built the new family a house across the creek from the family's original homestead. Though Mike was a builder of some repute within the family, the house was a primitive structure without double walls, but it did permit the Sam Raders to set up a separate household that at first offered ample room for their growing family. The young couple was especially close to the Pummill family. Their oldest daughter, Elsie, remembered fondly seeing "grandma [Lydia] coming on Old Topsy [her saddle horse] with that little white head [Dona] (to me the head of knowledge) bobbing behind her." Sisters Ada and Beckie, the latter who lived a short distance down the creek, spent at least one day a week at each other's homes. These were all-day affairs in which the two women, accompanied by their younger children, sewed, cooked, and visited.[18]

The relationship between Ada and Sam seems to have been a happy one, albeit, one can imagine that Sam's lack of material ambition may have concerned Ada, who, after all, was a member of the more industrious Pummill family. Reflective of Sam's love was his purchase of a beautiful sidesaddle for Ada. Everett Pummill, one of Ada's brothers, remembered that many years earlier he had seen the young couple together, laughing and cavorting, as they pulled one of their youngsters (Gilbert) through the snow on a sled. Ada may have found Sam, who had come from a predominately female household, less hard-edged and more approachable than was typical of the hollers men of the day.

To Sam, no one could contest the keen intelligence and love of his slender, dark-haired Ada, who possessed such striking and unforgettable eyes as well as an abundance of long black hair. Based on her childhood memory of her parents, the couple's oldest daughter, Elsie, many years later composed a short poem:

> Dear Fireplace, What an artist you are!
>> You have chosen your brush with care.
> And painted my mother lovely and young,
>> Combing her beautiful hair.
> And there is my father putting yams
>> In the ashes to roast to his heart's desire
> With the stroke of your brush he seems but a boy,
>> His face very red with your fire.
> Looking at the old fireplace and remembering
>> My childhood this came to me.[19]

That the family purchased a pump organ and later a piano for the daughters suggests that Ada nourished aspirations consistent with nationwide, middle-class Victorian respectability.[20]

✦   ✦   ✦

"A sad thing occurred in our neighborhood last week," reported "Blue Eyes" in her column on Delaware happenings published in the *Current Wave*. From complications arising from the birth of Merle Eddie in August of the previous year, an irregular heartbeat, rheumatism, and pneumonia, Ada died on December 3, 1913. Before expiration, a Bible was placed on her chest and she gathered the family to her bedside and quietly talked to them. Conscious until the moment of death, her last words were "There'll be no Dark Valley," an optimistic expression of her faith in the hereafter. She was deeply loved and respected by family and neighborhood alike. She was buried two days later in the Rader cemetery; a "large crowd" attended her funeral, which was officiated by the Reverend E. C. Bullick, pastor of the New Harmony Baptist Church.[21]

Sam fell into a deep, unshakable "melancholy."[22] Not only was he depressed by her loss, but he (at the age of thirty-nine) was also left with the responsibility of rearing seven children ranging from to sixteen years to fourteen months of age. He always claimed that he had little to do with guiding his children into adulthood, that his children essentially reared themselves. Even if so, he, more than anyone else, bequeathed to each of them a supreme example of a man whose life was guided by moral precepts. Likewise, he was always a caring father. Few children loved their father more than Sam's. They remained devoted to him to the end of his life.

Other women filled some of the lacuna left by Ada's death. There are scattered and brief reports in the *Current Wave* suggesting that Sam, typical of male widowers with children, at one time or another in the first few years after Ada's death courted one or more local widow women, but he did not remarry.[23] Keziah (Rader) Klepzig, Sam's sister who was separated from her husband and lived on a farm across the hollow, helped Sam out and may have lived for a time in the Rader household. Always ready to assist when they could find time from their own family duties were Arthur (Ada's brother) and Mayme Pummill (Sam's niece and sister-in-law); on occasion, Sam and his children appear to have spent entire weekends in the Pummill household. Perhaps in gratitude, Sam exchanged honey—he maintained several hives

—with Mayme for canned goods.[24] After Elsie had married Cordell Rhinehart two years after her mother's death, daughters Velma and later Audrey were said to have taken on many of the household chores earlier assigned to their mother.

To help out, Sam also employed at least one widow from the neighborhood, a Nancy Rose Scott. Nancy had eleven grown children of her own from an earlier marriage to William Rose. Effie, one of her daughters, was married to Sam's nephew, Jacob Perkins. In 1902, Nancy remarried, this time to a local farmer, Ambrose Scott of Delaware. Scott's fondness for drink undid him. One Saturday evening, Scott's brother-in-law helped the drunken man mount his mule in Eminence and headed him up Mahans Creek toward his home. About two miles from town, Scott either fell out of the saddle or the mule threw him off; his foot caught in one of the stirrups and his mule dragged him three miles farther up the creek. The next morning, a neighbor, John Creagar, awoke to find Scott near his front gate dangling from the stirrup—dead. He was buried in the Rader Cemetery. In 1917, Sam brought Scott's seventy-one-year-old widow, who was known locally as a pipe-smoking raconteur, into the household, where she apparently remained for at least a year. (She died in 1920.) The younger children remembered her fondly; indeed, Hub and probably Merle thought of her as their "mother."[25]

✦ ✦ ✦

More so than their own extended family, Sam and his children admired their Pummill kinfolk. Throughout their lives, they looked upon them with awe. Primarily, it was due to their mother, Ada, whom with time all family members idolized. Before her untimely death in 1913, Ada inculcated the older children (especially Elsie, Gilbert, and Velma) with the Pummill family's values. The 1910 census listed her occupation as "school teaching." Whether at the time she had an appointment in one of the county's one-room rural schools is unknown, though a year later the local weekly reported her serving as a substitute teacher in Delaware. All the children except Lowell graduated from high school, and three of them—Gilbert, Velma, and Audrey—did some college work, an especially unusual feat for the offspring of local families of the day.[26] The youngest children were only six years old (Lowell), four years old (Hulbert), and an infant (Merle) when their mother passed away. They did not attend college. That Velma for a time taught school and Elsie, Velma, and Audrey all married ambitious and, for the most part, successful men outside the neighborhood may also have been indicative of the Pummill influence on Sam's family.

✦ CHAPTER 10 ✦

The Neighborhood Awakens

NEVER BEFORE HAD a party in the neighborhood approximated the extravaganza thrown by Mary and Ulysses Madison (known locally as "U. M.") Randolph on the occasion of the seventeenth birthday of their son, Ernest, on June 2, 1909. U. M. and Mary opened the doors of their "Meadowbrook Farm" to more than seventy guests. While no list of attendees survives, everyone in the neighborhood of any consequence came. They found, according to the *Current Wave*, a "most delightful and perfectly arranged social event." Besides offering food delicacies and non-alcoholic drink, the hosts led their guests in playing "games and various [other] mirth-producing diversions." Later, in September of the same year, the Randolphs hosted a somewhat smaller event, a birthday party for their fourteen-year-old daughter, "Miss Gettie," who was reportedly "charming, cultured, and refined." Until reaching high school, Miss Gettie was schooled by her parents.[1]

Everywhere, or so it seemed, social interaction within the neighborhood increased. Visits with neighbors, especially with kinfolk, had long been a feature of creek life, but during the timber boom era the tempo of social life picked up; the number of face-to-face gatherings for parties, box suppers, the literary society on Friday nights, neighborhood dances, and sporting events all proliferated. In 1913 residents could even see motion-picture shows at the schoolhouse and on at least one occasion witness the ascension of a man in a balloon. Insufficient evidence makes it impossible to reconstruct the complete history of baseball on the creek, but scattered newspaper reports suggest that nearly every summer Delaware hosted at least one team of adult men and teenage boys. For at least a year or two the Delaware school sponsored both boys' and girls' interscholastic basketball. The farmers had long gathered at the schoolhouse each campaign season to hear candidates make their case for receiving the nomination of the Democratic Party for countywide offices. In particular, the candidacy of William Jennings Bryan for the presidency in both 1896 and 1900 sparked an unusual enthusiasm for political engagement in the neighborhood. But the most visible and enduring testimony of the neighborhood's civic awakening was the erection of two new church houses and the building of three new schoolhouses in the Delaware Township.

A convergence of circumstances set the stage for the creek's denser social life. One was the economic abundance that accompanied the harvesting of the neighborhood's yellow pine. Although the distribution of wealth among creek families had grown to be more lopsided than ever and a majority of the families remained trapped in poverty, nearly every family experienced some degree of improvement in their standard of living. In particular, additional income flowed into the hands of the favored few, such as the U. M. Randolph, the Pummill family, and the John Creagar, Jim Rader, and Sam Rader families. These creek-bottom families now had the wherewithal to underwrite social innovations while minimizing the risks involved. Of equal importance to the new era was a religious awakening led by the neighborhood's women. Invigorated by a series of spectacular revivals across the county, evangelical Protestants founded two new churches and lent their support to social reform. In particular, the reformers sought to restrain or prohibit drinking, gambling, and other activities long associated with the county's male culture.

✦ ✦ ✦

In earlier times Methodist circuit riders had conducted services in private homes or occasionally in the schoolhouse, but, until 1904, no permanent religious organization existed in the entirety of the Delaware Township. A turning point in the neighborhood's religious history came with the influx of the timber workers. In 1895, in what may have been the first revival ever held in the township, an evangelist whose name has not survived in any sources led an "enthusiastic" meeting at the Delaware log camp in Pine Hollow. Perhaps conducted in a brush arbor, the revival yielded thirteen converts. Four years later, near the same log camp, an "Elder Finly" held another successful set of "protracted" meetings. Perhaps the example of these meetings and a rising concern that the behavior of the timber workers, who were frequently younger, unmarried men, represented a threat to the stability of the neighborhood were the immediate catalyst for the religious awakening among the creek's more permanent residents. In any event, in 1902, U. M. Randolph organized a regularly scheduled Sunday school at the Delaware schoolhouse.[2]

Two years later, in 1904, a Baptist exhorter, E. D. Bullick of Summersville, in nearby Texas County, led a revival that netted twelve baptisms and resulted in the founding of the New Harmony Missionary Baptist Church. The next year the new church proudly reported a total membership of thirty-three and even hosted that year's annual convention of the Shannon County Baptist Association. Initially, the new church was mostly the handiwork of the U. M. Randolph and the Sam Rader families. U. M. donated the land (though neither he nor his family became members of New Harmony) for the building of a new edifice on a picturesque site atop the hill adjacent to the schoolhouse and overlooking the Jim Rader farm. Later, in the 1930s, a Works Progress Administration (WPA) official credited the timber workers rather than the creek-bottom farmers themselves with giving their free time to erect the new balloon-framed church house. Consistent with other Protestant rural churches in the Upland South, it was a simple, plain white structure with a rudimentary steeple, wooden benches, and a woodstove for heating, but no religious icons of any sort could be found either inside or outside of the building.

On August 2, 1906, in all-day services, including a dinner on the church grounds, the members dedicated the new building. Hitherto, the only public cemetery of sorts had been that of the Raders, but the new church also set aside a plot for a new cemetery.[3] Religious enthusiasm continued to run high along the creek, peaking in the fall of 1910 when two exhorters held a revival at New Harmony that stretched over nearly three weeks. "Quite a number . . . principally of the juvenile class" came to the services by train from Eminence, the *Current Wave* reported, and it was "an emotional awakening indeed."[4]

The initial religious fervor was difficult to sustain. New Harmony never had the support of all the neighborhood's leading families; for example, neither U. M. Randolph, Jim Rader, nor members of the Pummill family (with one exception) joined the local church. Partly, it was a matter of declining material fortunes in the wake of the timber boom, but sharp swings in attendance also reflected the quality and popularity of the church's leadership and its pastors. Proponents of congregational government, in which all members theoretically had an equal voice, the members were suspicious of those who volunteered for leadership positions.[5] Lacking adequate resources due in part to the parsimony of its parishioners, New Harmony also found it necessary to share pastors with other small Baptist congregations in the county. On only one weekend per month, "the preacher," as he was called, would exhort, frequently both on a Saturday night and on the following Sunday morning. The neighborhood never seems to have celebrated Decoration Day. Several years frequently elapsed between neighborhood cleanups of either the New Harmony or the Rader cemeteries.

In the meantime, during 1905 and 1906, a religious schism surfaced, one that was to divide the creek's families for more than a half century. The breakdown of religious accord may have erupted mainly over the issue of baptism; the Baptists insisted on the total immersion of the converted before they could become full-fledged members of the church. Such a requirement may have offended the neighborhood's Methodists, which included the Randolphs, the Harpers, and the Klepzigs. Among the Methodists, a Pentecostal influence swept into the neighborhood. The upshot was the formation of a new church, which in 1905 built a modest balloon-framed place of worship, called the "Saints Chapel," in Open Hollow.

Its membership came mainly but not exclusively from the ranks of the branch-water folk. Described by their detractors as "Holy Rollers" and by themselves as "the sanctified people," the worshippers were more expressive in their religious services than were the local Baptists. That they permitted preaching by women, specifically, by Elizabeth "Lizzie" Harper, the neighborhood's midwife, was also seen by the local Baptists as scandalous. Even though its membership was from families of more modest means and was smaller in numbers, the church usually enjoyed more consistent support than the Baptists. Well into the 1930s, the church scheduled weekly prayer meetings on Wednesday night and annual week-long camp meetings in August.[6]

Females supported the great awakening in the creek basin and countywide with far more alacrity than did the males. For example, in 1913, New Harmony reported a membership of twenty-four females but only nine males. In terms of the sheer number of conversions and baptisms, almost equal gender imbalances characterized the revivals across the county. Indeed, a few of the men, especially younger ones, offered visible resistance to the county's growing religiosity. They, according to newspaper reports, might loll in the nearby woods or, their inhibitions unleashed by drink, yell and fire pistols during religious services. Whether embarked in advancing religion or education, it was the waterway's women who were mainly responsible for weaving a stronger neighborhood social fabric.[7]

Regardless of male opposition or the changing fortunes of the two churches, a feminine-dominated evangelical Protestantism represented a powerful new force in both the creek neighborhood and Shannon County. The Eminence-area revival reached a crescendo in 1913, which allegedly resulted in more than 500 new conversions. As a consequence of that revival more than

1,500 persons gathered at the Jacks Fork River on a cool Sunday afternoon to witness a mass baptism.[8] Upon the organization of a women's temperance society in Winona, the young women resolved "that a large part of the carelessness of conduct, drunkenness and crime of men is due to the meager demands made of them by the women."[9] While holding lingering attachments to the traditional free-wheeling, male-centered honor culture, few if any men on the creek outright rejected either the fundamental theological propositions or the behavioral demands of the neighborhood's evangelical Protestants. Indeed, along with the women, the creek men seem to have increasingly embraced a Victorian sensibility of behavioral restraint grounded in evangelical Protestantism.

Accompanying the religious revivals was an inching away from traditional forms of courtship. While tradition continued to demand that unmarried young people extend attentions to one another exclusively within the sheltered contexts of home and neighborhood, the young began to take up courting practices more characteristic of the larger Victorian society of their day. An invaluable source for this change was a detailed diary kept by young William French. While serving as Pine Hollow's first schoolmaster, French reported in some detail the attentions that he extended to Sybil Turner of Delaware. Much of their courtship, which did not culminate in marriage, revolved around meeting together at and after religious services at the New Harmony Baptist Church. The diary indicates that increasingly both young men and women began to take charge of their courtships without reference to their parents or other adults in the neighborhood.[10] Perhaps another manifestation of the growing power of women in the neighborhood was a fall in the township's birth rate; between 1910 and 1920 the average age of the first marriage by the neighborhood's women increased by one year (to 23.2).[11] With artificial means of birth control unavailable or difficult to obtain, women may have been increasingly able to impose prolonged periods of abstinence on their husbands.

But no issue revealed the new feminine power more clearly than prohibition. Aroused in part by fears of unruly behavior by the timber workers, a coalition of evangelical preachers, women, and ambitious, upwardly mobile young men succeeded in 1906 in winning the approval of a county-wide local option law.[12] This measure came fourteen years before the adoption of nation-wide prohibition. Still, by no means did the law stop drinking in Shannon County. On special occasions drink seemed to flow as freely as ever, especially in Eminence. On Christmas Eve 1910, for example, William French scrawled in his diary: "Went to town in the afternoon. All Eminence drunk, so drunk that it staggered."[13] Perhaps even worse, according to the *Current Wave* in 1924, hardly a social gathering could be scheduled in the more remote parts of the county without the disturbances of young men and boys "crazed" with drink.[14]

✦   ✦   ✦

Another sign of the neighborhood's growth in civic vitality was its increased support of schools. Although, as elsewhere in the Upland South, there was a suspicion of the merits of formal learning among the local farm families, suddenly, in the late 1890s the influx of timber workers' children into the area over-whelmed the tiny schoolhouse. In 1899, according to one report, Delaware had sixty-five enrollees, which, if all had been in atten-dance at the same time, would have meant the spectacle of about four students crowded into each two-child desk. But, few of the enrollees regularly attended school.

Sometime in the first two decades of the new century—the exact dates are unknown—the township created two new dis-tricts and built two new schoolhouses. One, called Pine Hollow, was on the side of a ridge about two miles up the hollow from Delaware, while the other, Crescent (or sometimes called Buckhart), was about two miles up Mahans Creek. Neither school was the beneficiary of families with as much wealth as those in the Delaware district, and with the departure of many of the timber workers in the 1910s, their enrollments slowly declined. By 1930 enrollment in Delaware had fallen to seven-teen students, and that year Pine Hollow enrolled only twelve and Crescent only eight students.[15] Both schools closed during the final years of the Great Depression. When I came of age to attend school in 1941, only three school-age children lived in the Crescent district. The district employed the father of two of the children, Lufton Barton, to drive us in his car to the school in Delaware.

Unlike in the instance of religion, the neighborhood's "leading families" took command of the Delaware school. Specifically, this included U. M. Randolph, who was exceptionally literate, John Creagar and his brother James Creagar, and the Pummills, including not only the popular brothers who became school teachers but at least two of their sisters, Ada May (Pummill) Rader, the wife of Sam Rader, and Beckie (Pummill) Rader, the wife of Jim Rader. By extending the term of instruction from four to eight months, hiring teachers who had scored exceptionally well on the county exams, and building a new schoolhouse, this group determined to make the Delaware school one of the best if not the best one-room school in the county. Rather than a balloon-framed structure, the standard for one-room schools throughout the Upland South, Delaware employed Sam Smith, a stone mason from Winona, to build a more permanent structure of prefabricated concrete blocks. Completed in 1910, the new building was the envy of every school district in Shannon County.[16]

Surviving evaluations based on the annual visits of the county superintendent of schools in 1910 and 1911 offer snapshots of Delaware's school.[17] In 1910, the first of the school's sessions in the new building, the superintendent gave Susie Grey, the teacher, "excellent" marks for her knowledge of the subject matter, her instructional methods, and the discipline of her students. As salary, Grey received $40 a month for an eight-month term. The school proudly claimed to have eighty books in its library, located in the back right-hand corner of the classroom. Missouri's State Department of Education proceeded to place Delaware on its "approved" (those primary schools meeting minimum statewide standards) list, at the time the first and only rural school in the county to receive such recognition. With

Delaware schoolhouse (as it looked in 2009). After the closure of the school in 1956, it served for a time as a church house and as a private home. The structure in the front was added after the school's closure. *Courtesy of the author.*

this honor in hand and a recently completed new building, the neighborhood celebrated the end of school in June of 1911 with a big box supper and a program of songs, recitations, and drills.[18]

However, the very next year, when the board decided to cut costs by restoring a six-month term, the school lost its coveted position on the state's approved list. The decision may have reflected a reduction in school revenue occasioned by the creation of Buckhart and Pine Hollow schools within the old Delaware district. At least the district's total assessment fell from $63,552 to $56,674 in 1911. The board paid the teacher, Amy Carr, $45 per month. While Delaware had a "very good school," the superintendent reported after his visit in 1911 that it was "a very hard community to satisfy."[19] He did not specify the nature of the dissatisfaction, but he may have been referencing a gathering dispute between Jim Rader and U. M. Randolph, both members of the neighborhood's leading families. Soon afterward, the district began to once again offer an eight-month term and again became one of only a few schools in the county to be placed on the state's approved list. In 1917, the *Current Wave* observed that "Oak Grove and Delaware have long been known as two of the leading schools in the county."[20]

Disguised in the details of the 1910–1911 visitations is the conclusion that, in terms of educating the entire population of school-aged children in the neighborhood, the district enjoyed limited success. In 1910, the superintendent reported that twenty-nine boys and twenty-one girls of school age resided in the district, but that only twenty-five actually were present at school on November 28, the day of his visit. High rates of absenteeism were also the case in 1911. That year, twenty-three boys and twenty-seven girls of school age lived in the district, only thirty-two of which were actually enrolled, and only twenty-one were at school on October 17, the day of the superintendent's visit. In other words, on any given day half or more of the district's eligible children were not in school.[21] Furthermore, from the 1911 report, it appears that eighteen of the district's fifty children may never have been enrolled in school.

As with the neighborhood's churches, the district's school board might have also posed the question: "Where are the boys?" Though comprehensive data is unavailable, the *Current Wave* reported that Delaware's enrollment in 1912 was eleven boys and thirty girls![22] Similar gender imbalances in the schools, though not quite as pronounced as in 1912, ran throughout the boom era. It may be that many of the boys attended school occasionally, perhaps enough to be counted later on in the census as "literate." In any case, self-reported literacy rates in the censuses of 1910 and 1920 exceeded 90 percent for the Delaware Township. Yet the school data throws in serious doubt whether the majority of adults in the neighborhood were sufficiently literate to do much more than sign their name to a document or do the most elementary of arithmetic problems.

Put another way, attendance at the local one-room school reflected the creek's social structure. Only the children of the ambitious, better-off families regularly attended school while those of the log camp and the branch-water families were more often than not absent. "They came to school only when they felt inclined," observed Elva Pummill, regarding another one-room school in the Jacks Fork–Current River region in which he taught.[23] In the latter cases, parents frequently kept their children, especially the boys, out of school so that they could work to support their families. Feelings of inferiority, arising at least in part from the poorer families being unable to clothe their children in a "respectable" matter, may also have contributed to the high rates of absenteeism. Finally, few of the families at the bottom of the creek neighborhood social structure saw education as a possible means of ensuring their children's futures. From their perspective, early work experience afforded their sons better opportunities for providing for their future economic security or advancement than did schooling.

Reasoning that a prolonged education might be as valuable as the inheritance of a farm, the leading families, on the other hand, began sending their offspring to school even beyond the standard eight years. During the first decade of the twentieth century, all three nearby towns—Eminence, Winona, and Birch Tree—opened high schools. First one of the Pummill boys, followed by children of the Raders, Randolphs, Harpers, Klepzigs, and Bradleys, entered the new schools. Far more surprising was a sudden surge in the number of Delaware youngsters—no fewer than eight—who enrolled in colleges between 1905 and 1915. Inspired by the example of the Pummill boys, nearly all of them became students at the state normal schools at Springfield, Cape Girardeau, or Warrensburg. At least for a time, they all taught in schools scattered across Missouri and even elsewhere. One of them (Lawrence Pummill) eventually obtained a PhD degree, and two of them received master's degrees.

✦ ✦ ✦

Unlike the Civil War and Reconstruction, World War I was not a cataclysmic event for either Shannon County or the Delaware neighborhood. The local newspapers barely took note of the events leading up to the war and, even after American entry in 1917, the hollers people never developed much enthusiasm for the conflict. Only a few young men volunteered their services, and only two appear to have served from the creek neighborhood. At one time Shannon stood at the bottom of Missouri counties in its sales of war bonds. It never reached its "quota." The county did organize a Council of Defense, but it was able to locate only one deserter, and its chair explained to the state committee that the county's residents were too "poor" to buy very many war bonds. A half-hearted effort to get the county council to take action against "slackers" in buying war bonds came to naught. Neither did the local residents mount any public campaigns against their German American neighbors. At the conclusion of the war, the Winona weekly, the *Shannon County Democrat*, did speculate that the war was "good for people" but did not offer reasons why.[24]

✦ CHAPTER 11 ✦

From Down in the Hollows to Ozark Towns

LET US GLANCE back to the final decade of the nineteenth century. Seven of the nine offspring of John and Lydia Pummill lived on the old Billy Mahan farm deep in the hollows of the Missouri Ozarks. There, on Mahans Creek in Shannon County, Joseph, Lawrence, and Everett Pummill, as well as their three brothers (William, Arthur, and Elva), learned how to break ground with a horse-drawn plow, how to mow and put up hay, and how to make handles for axes and hoes. But what they loved most were the lulls in farm work; they then could roam into the woods or traipse along the creek. Accompanied by the family's hounds, they ferreted out raccoons, opossums, wolves, and bobcats, and, when the dogwoods were in bloom in the spring, they gigged the spawning yellow suckers in Mahans Creek. They also liked school. Four months each year they walked two and a half miles each way to attend Delaware's one-room, rural school.

Only two decades or so later, we find three of the Pummill brothers in startlingly different circumstances. While all six of the brothers and the three sisters were married, three of the brothers wore white collars and neckties to work and lived in well-appointed bungalows either in small Missouri towns (Joe and Everett) or eventually in the small city of Springfield, Missouri

(Lawrence). Joe and Everett were school administrators, while Lawrence, who had earlier served in three different towns as a superintendent of schools, accepted in 1920 an appointment as an instructor of mathematics at the normal school in Springfield. Whenever they could, the brothers still liked to hunt and fish, but they also loved to travel—back for extended visits to their old home place on Mahans Creek and, in the instances of Joe and Lawrence, the two most prosperous brothers, to far-off places scattered across the nation. The families of Joe, Lawrence, and Everett Pummill had become Ozarks townspeople. In the towns, they adopted a way of life that was in some respects markedly different from that in the hollows of their childhoods.

✦   ✦   ✦

Their neighbors quickly learned that the Pummills—notwithstanding their origins in the hollows of Osage and Shannon Counties and their love of the hollows—were different from themselves. Not insignificantly, unlike the Raders or neighboring men, only two of the six Pummill boys ever smoked or used tobacco in any form. No other family in the Mahans Creek basin was more esteemed for their integrity and their neighborliness than the Pummills. Reflective of their ancestry, which included influences on their folkways of a blending of regional cultures and a bevy of preachers and teachers, the Pummill boys were dreamers: they aspired "to do great things." They had taken to learning with an enthusiasm quite unlike their peers. As children, they had "studied many nights by the light from the big fireplace fed with pine knots gathered from the hills." They were exceptionally competitive: no family of boys in Shannon County was better known for their enthusiasm for baseball than the Pummills. Except in the wintertime, nearly every Sunday found them playing on various local teams. "The Knott, Perkins, Pummill (mostly Pummill) baseball nine . . . 'whipped' everything in Shannon Co.," reported Everett Pummill many years later.[1] Both Joe and Lawrence lettered on the Springfield normal school nine.

Had the Pummill family enjoyed more success from farming,

James Everett Pummill: Aurora, Clinton, Crane, Eureka, Lebanon, Linn Creek, Mansfield, Mountain View, Sarcoxie, and Winona.

Joseph Gilbert Pummill: Camden Point, Ellisnore, Eminence, Linn Creek, Mount Vernon, Seneca, Seymour, Winona, and in Jefferson City as a statistician and rural school supervisor for the Missouri Department of Education.

Lawrence Edgar Pummill: Cassville, Crane, Greenfield, Seymour, Winona, and in Springfield as a professor and head of the mathematics department at the normal school (today Missouri State University).

High school teaching, college teaching, and administrative positions of the Pummill brothers in southern Missouri. *Map by Katie Nieland.*

the career trajectories of the boys would likely to have taken a different course. In the best of times the family farm offered little more than a bare subsistence. In the worst of times, droughts or floods could threaten the very existence of the family. After the Great Flood of 1895 on Mahans Creek, which destroyed the family's corn crop and much of the farm's fencing, John avoided a total disaster by borrowing $150 from the Shannon County school fund. There was also the matter of the family's long-term future. The family's farming operation failed to offer all six sons a reasonable prospect for inheriting a large enough patrimony in land so that each son could someday succeed in striking out on his own as a farmer. John's untimely death in 1900 and his will further complicated the family's material future. After having provided care for his wife during her lifetime, John's will divided his estate equally among his children. No one person was left in charge of the farm, and the full implications of the will itself were not resolved until 1915, five years after the death of Lydia in 1910.[2]

To supplement the family's cash-strapped position, the boys sought employment apart from the family farm. In the 1890s William, the oldest of the boys, and perhaps one or more of the other boys, began working part time in the region's rapidly expanding timber industry. In 1897, Joe took a teaching position at a nearby one-room, rural school. In the first decade of the twentieth century, his younger brothers—Arthur, Lawrence, Everett, and Elva—soon followed in his footsteps.[3] Teaching offered the young men a source of cash income (some thirty dollars a month) for usually four months of work while leaving them with eight months of each year free to toil on the family's farm. Meeting the minimal qualifications for teaching in one-room schools was also an easy matter, at least for the Pummills. All they had to do was finish eight years of primary education and pass a teacher's examination administered by the county's superintendent of schools.

While continuing to live either at home on Mahans Creek or rooming and boarding with a family in the school district where they taught, teaching, along with baseball, introduced the Pummill brothers to the wider life of Shannon County's small towns. Almost at once, Joe, in particular, began to throw his boundless energy into an effort to "professionalize" the county's rural schoolteachers. No single teacher was more active in the annual countywide "teachers Institutes," gatherings in which the teachers heard speakers offer advice on subjects ranging from dealing with unhappy parents to teaching arithmetic. Likewise, Joe helped to organize, chaired, and led discussions at the county's "reading circles" for teachers.[4] In the spring of 1903, he single-handedly formed and taught a "normal school" in Eminence for rural teachers, and in a 1904 essay published in the *Current Wave* he publicly chastised his fellow teachers for their failure in showing "enough interest in their profession." He went so far as to predict, that in the "not far distant" future, when making hiring decisions, school boards would take into consideration attendance at reading circles and the annual teacher institutes.[5]

The Pummill brothers reached out beyond their rural neighborhood in other respects. Against overwhelming odds, arising from the supremacy of the Democratic Party in the county, and before reaching the age of thirty, Joe, Lawrence, and Arthur permitted their names to be submitted as token candidates of the Republican Party for countywide public offices. (Elva, the youngest son, ran twice for countywide offices as a Socialist Party candidate.) None of the siblings appear to have put much effort or money into their campaigns, but in each of the six local elections in which they were candidates, they carried their home township of Delaware, indicating that they enjoyed a positive reputation among those who knew them best. During the first decade of the new century, Joe also frequently engaged in public debates in Eminence, at which he invariably sided with such "progressive" Republican positions as women's suffrage, immigration restriction, and better treatment of African Americans. Although the full details elude inquiry, it appears that both Joe and Lawrence won a measure of respect and admiration from town boosters regardless of party affiliation. In 1909, for example, when Lawrence submitted his name as the Republican candidate for county school commissioner, the *Current Wave* described him as "an unmarried gentleman . . . [of] high personal character. . . . [W]e heartily recommend him for his high honor and good citizenship."[6]

No single year was more important in the brothers making a transition from farm to town than 1910. In Winona, some ten miles as the crow flies from the family farm on Mahans Creek, the boys found their first jobs as high school teachers.

Joe took a job there in 1907 as a mathematics teacher, and two years later the Winona school board named him the superintendent of the town's schools. Joe at once set about upgrading the school's physical plant, adding new courses, and promoting interscholastic sports for both girls and boys. In 1909, he married Atlanta Ware, a fellow teacher and a town girl, who came from an established Winona family. She too was on the path to becoming a lifelong teacher. As superintendent in 1910, Joe first hired his brother Lawrence, and the next year Everett, to teach in the high school.

In the meantime, Lawrence rented a large house in Winona that accommodated at one time or the other the family's sick mother (Lydia, who died in 1910), younger brothers (Everett and Elva), younger sister (Dona), and niece (Theodosia Rader). Elva, Dona, and Theodosia attended the local high school, where the two girls played on the first women's varsity basketball team. Their aunt, Atlanta Pummill, founded and managed the team. Apparently, Dona graduated at the top of her class, for in 1911 she gave a graduation oration entitled "Back to the Farm" at the Winona City Hall. Lawrence himself helped to organize and played on Winona's first men's basketball team.[7] Another brother, Arthur, who had formerly taught in Shannon County's one-room schools, set up a separate household with his wife, Mayme Perkins, and their three children; Arthur clerked in Winona's Ozark Store. At this point in the family's history, only the oldest brother, William, remained year around on the family farm.

While Winona was a lumber boom town of only 444 people in 1910, moving there was a momentous decision for the Pummills. True, the grunting of pigs in quest of garbage and the pungent smell of horse manure in the town's streets served as a daily reminder of their farm back on Mahans Creek. Still, nature was no longer at the front door; there were nearby neighbors, the voices of others going about their daily tasks, and streets (albeit primitive ones) filled with horses, carriages, wagons, and, later, cars. A family member could board a train bound for almost anywhere in the United States, and the railroad brought with it a plethora of new mass-produced consumer goods that were on display at local stores. Along with the railroad came circuses and travelling vaudeville troupes that performed at the local opera house. In 1911, the Pummills may have heard an oration by Kate O'Hare at a Socialist picnic and barbecue. It is even possible that O'Hare's four speeches in 1911 persuaded Elva to become a Socialist candidate for representative of Shannon County to the state legislature in 1912.[8] Although there were no African Americans permanently residing in Shannon County, in Winona local whites from time to time witnessed the arrival of gangs of black laborers who were assigned the dangerous task of loading heavy ties onto railroad cars. In the evenings the black workers sometimes entertained local white audiences with musical performances.[9] With their residence in Winona, albeit a short one, never again would their rural past be so important in shaping the ways of the Pummill family.

✦   ✦   ✦

Equally if not more important in propelling Joe, Lawrence, and Everett from farm to town were their experiences as career educators. Apart from his 1904 essay, other evidence in the first years of the twentieth century hinted that Joe was inching his way toward becoming a professional educator. At first he considered entering law. While he did not attend law school or serve an apprenticeship with an attorney, in 1905 he obtained entrance into the Missouri bar. But he never practiced law. Apparently influenced by the rapid growth of Missouri high schools and a new statewide compulsory school law, he decided in 1905 to enroll for a summer term at the inelegantly named Missouri Normal School District Two (commonly called the Warrensburg Normal School).[10] As with normal schools elsewhere, the school welcomed both female and male students, students from modest circumstances, and students who were without high school or academy training. Returning from Warrensburg as an enthusiast of college work, Joe continued his formal education after 1905 by attending summer sessions at the Missouri State Normal

School District Four (commonly referred to as the Springfield Normal School).[11] In 1914, perhaps sensing that coursework offered by the teachers' college of the University of Missouri in Columbia might be rewarded more than similar coursework in the normal schools, both Joe and Lawrence began routinely taking summer school courses at the university. Lawrence received a bachelor degree in education from there in 1917 and Joe did the same in 1921. In 1928 Everett earned a degree from the renamed normal school in Springfield—Southwest Missouri State Teachers College.[12]

Attendance at the normal schools and the state university by the Pummill brothers not only aided them in obtaining better jobs but also nourished their intellectual curiosity and appreciation of "high" culture. While approximately a third of their coursework was in pedagogy (including practice teaching), they thrilled with the opportunity to explore advanced work in mathematics, the sciences, the language arts, and history. However, at times they ran up against a scarcity of challenging courses; on one occasion, for example, Lawrence was the only student enrolled in a trigonometry course at Springfield.

All three of the boys enthusiastically participated in the extracurricular activities of the colleges. The caption accompanying Lawrence's photo in the 1911 *Ozarker*, the Springfield normal school's yearbook, acclaimed, "No man can carry so many subjects, think deeper in mathematics, work harder on debate, or play better on the athletic field." Observation and emulation of better-off town people and the formation of a web of personal connections, when combined with coursework, extracurricular activities, and living in town, all prepared the Pummill boys for participation in the region's small-town, middle-class life.[13]

Apart from their normal school and teachers' college training, their mastery of mathematics and their gender eased the way for their career advancement. That the Pummill brothers could and were willing to teach algebra appears to have been an important consideration for their entries into several high school teaching jobs and even ascendency into positions as school superintendents. Although women outnumbered men in the classroom and enjoyed similar academic credentials, Ozarks school boards in the first half of the twentieth century rarely if ever hired them as administrators.[14] In terms of income and the absence of competition from females, of the educators of the day, only male administrators enjoyed the autonomy, the authority to control their own destinies, and the financial means equivalent to such professions as medicine and law.

One by one, Joe, Lawrence, and Everett left Winona in quest of opportunities elsewhere in southern Missouri. In the fall of 1912, Joe became superintendent of schools at Seneca, a small town near Joplin in the southwest corner of Missouri. His wife, Atlanta, also taught in the local high school. Joe quickly made his mark; by hiring superior teachers, raising standards, and expanding offerings of approved work, he obtained a reclassification of the high school from "third class" to "first class," a recognition not shared by the much larger high schools in the nearby towns of Joplin and Carthage, Missouri.[15] His superior performance came to the attention of Missouri's Department of Education in Jefferson City, where in 1919 he took a position as a statistician and later as the state's rural school supervisor. He enhanced his reputation for integrity when he resigned from that post in 1921 over a dispute apparently involving what Joe believed to be false reports; Joe was not given to sacrificing candor on behalf of expediency.[16] That year Joe returned to his old post at Seneca. Few administrators were better known and respected in southern Missouri. In a feature article about Joe and Atlanta, the *Missouri School Journal* of 1922 praised Joe for his "rugged independence," "common sense originality," and "practical idealism." In 1921, fellow teachers elected him president of the Southwest (Missouri) Teacher's Association.[17] In the 1930s and 1940s Joe and Atlanta returned to south central Missouri, where they took posts in Shannon and Texas Counties.

Everett's career was somewhat less illustrious. Upon leaving Winona, Everett, who had married a local woman from a family of some prominence (Lulu Jones in 1911), taught at Aurora before becoming principal of Lebanon High School. Described as a "workaholic" by his nephew, Arch Pummill, he held administrative posts in seven other small Missouri towns. During the final four years of his life, he worked toward a master's degree by taking summer courses at Washington University in St. Louis. Life was not as easy for Everett as for Joe and Lawrence. Though he "went on bravely and uncomplainingly," wrote Lawrence upon the occasion of his premature death in 1939 from a heart attack, "he had more than his share of misfortune." During much of his married life, his wife was bedridden and a son had prolonged attacks of "nervousness."[18]

Lawrence pursued a more varied career. In 1911 he left Winona for Cassville, where he taught mathematics and science. In 1914, he married a former student, Crystal Evans, "a bright redhead who sat in the front row" and who was a town girl and described in a local newspaper as a "charming and refined lady."[19] In 1918 and 1919, he served as superintendent of schools in Greenfield, Missouri, where he taught mathematics, offered a teacher's training course, and jointly coached the high school basketball team.

It was while at Greenfield that a regent was said to have in effect offered him a position to teach either English or mathematics at the Springfield normal school, provided that he obtain a masters degree.[20] He thereupon enrolled in Columbia University's famed teachers college in 1920. The young Ozarks couple had never before experienced anything quite like the glitter and glamour of Manhattan. Lawrence not only obtained instruction from a renowned faculty but also was able to see Babe Ruth play in a major-league baseball game. Crystal took art courses and developed considerable skill as a painter of china. Upon receipt of a master's degree and his return to Springfield in 1921, the college paid him $227.50 per month to teach mathematics.

Before his death in 1963, Lawrence, in the words of his obituary, had become "an Ozark legend." Upon obtaining a doctorate degree in 1938 from George Peabody College for Teachers in Nashville, he served as head of the Mathematics Department at the college for eighteen years.[21] Erasing the blackboard with his left hand while simultaneously writing out the solutions to mathematical problems on the blackboard with his right hand, Lawrence stomped his foot when he sought to emphasize a point. For his keen interest and helpfulness in their welfare, he was beloved by students.[22] In recognition of his longtime service, the renamed Southwest Missouri State College named a campus building (Pummill Hall) after him and set up a mathematics scholarship in honor of him and his wife, Crystal.

✦   ✦   ✦

Their success as educators was only one indication of sharp transition that the Pummill brothers had made in their lives. Their incomes rose sharply, placing all three of them above the average for family incomes in the Ozarks as well as nationally. Everett, the least successful of the three, typically received about $2,500 annually from the late 1920s until his death in 1939. Between 1923 and 1941, Lawrence averaged $3,205, a figure roughly twice the national household average for this period. In the 1920s and into the 1940s, Joe and Atlanta, combined, earned as much as $5,000 annually. These figures do not quite capture the total household incomes of Joe and Lawrence, each of whom received some compensation from rentals and share-cropping revenues of the Pummill farm that they owned on Mahans Creek. Lawrence also earned additional money by sometimes teaching in the summers. While there are no exact figures on income for the siblings of Joe, Lawrence, and Everett, their occupations—two farm housewives, one carpenter's house-wife, one teamster, one farmer, and one machine operator— suggest that they probably earned less than half as much as the educators.[23]

The Pummill brothers married later and had fewer children than their rural siblings or other Americans. Joe did not marry until 1909 when he was thirty-one years of age; he and Atlanta had their first and only child fifteen months later. Everett married in 1911, when he was twenty-five years of age. His wife had their first child six years later and then a set of twins in the following year. Lawrence did not marry until 1914 when he was thirty-one years old. Inasmuch as his wife had had a "female" operation as a teenager, which gave rise to the couple's belief that they would have no children, they were surprised by her pregnancy and birth of a daughter in 1925 and another daughter in 1930. The couple had no other children.[24] In contrast, the other Pummill siblings married earlier and had many more children. The two older sisters, Rebecca (married at the age of twenty-one in 1891) and Ada (married at the age of twenty-three in 1896), wed local farmers and between them had a total of sixteen children, three of whom died at birth or shortly thereafter. While the career-teaching Pummills averaged having two children each, their other siblings (even though one had no children) averaged having nearly twice as many children.[25]

Rather than passing on agricultural land to their offspring, the career teachers in effect sought to prepare the future of their children by ensuring that they received an advanced education. In this regard, Joe and Lawrence succeeded. Of the three career educators, one, Wilda Dorothy "Dot," the daughter of Joe and Atlanta, eventually obtained a doctorate degree and taught physical education at several colleges and universities. Both of the daughters of Lawrence obtained college degrees, for a time taught school, and married successful men. On the other hand, none of Everett's three children attended college. One son, a member of the US Navy, died as a victim of the Japanese bombing of Pearl Harbor in 1941, while another son worked for many years as a barber in Eureka, Missouri. Of the twenty-six children of the non-career educators to reach adulthood, several attended college for short times and taught in one-room schools, but only one appears to have earned a college degree.

The full intimacy of the Pummill marriages eludes inquiry, but available evidence suggests that the marriages of the career educators differed from those of their siblings in respects other than marrying later and having fewer children. Whereas the rural side of the family embraced a model of marriage that valued the institution itself above the individual needs of either partner, the marriages of the career educators appeared to have been more equalitarian and companionate. This included a more "modern" view and practice of sexuality within marriage. For Crystal and Lawrence, sex included more than a mutual obligation to produce children. Many years later Crystal observed in a hand-written memoir prepared for her children and grandchildren that "the young of today didn't invent sex" and concluded that "sex is one of the most important elements in human behavior and blessed is the couple that finds [sexual] fulfillment in each other."[26]

Perhaps influenced by their work environments, which included female teachers, both Joe and Lawrence recognized more fully than most the men of their day the needs of their spouses to experience individual satisfactions apart from their husbands. Apparently, Joe fully supported his wife, Atlanta, in her career as an educator; to aid with the care of their child and their household, the couple hired a series of housekeepers; and Joe, himself, at times babysat and cared for their child. For nine years of their marriage, they had positions in separate towns, though they did manage to see one another on weekends with some regularity. Atlanta, who embodied the "new woman" of her day, added a level of middle-class sophistication to her household. She played the piano and was a skilled ballroom dancer. Likewise, the life of Crystal, Lawrence's wife, entailed more than simple homemaking for a college teacher. With an unusually warm personality, she loved to entertain and threw herself into the social life of the college.[27]

The leisure ways of the career educators distinguished them from their rural relatives as well. While employed in a state that extended only lukewarm support to public education, the Pummill boys did have enough financial resources to purchase and furnish comfortable homes. Sometime in the 1920s Lawrence and Crystal bought a relatively modest three-bedroom bungalow in an upper-middle-class neighborhood within easy walking distance of the college. Later on, they added sleeping quarters in the basement and in an enclosed porch to the back of the house. Little is known about the residences of Joe and Atlanta until they settled permanently onto a beautiful spot two miles south of Eminence. There at a fresh-water, year-round spring, they build an unusual three-bedroom, Cape Cod–style home designed by Atlanta. The house included running water and an indoor toilet, while the grounds had a fishing pool and a tennis court. It was one of the more striking homes in Shannon County; the Pummills combined their first names to call their estate "Jolanta Springs."[28]

Travel was yet another distinctive feature of the educators' urban, middle-class way of life. Comprehensive data on automobiles owned by the boys is unavailable, but Joe was known to have owned one of the first cars, a Ford Model T, in Shannon County.[29] Throughout his long tenure at Seneca, during vacation times he and his family regularly drove back and forth from there to the Pummill home place on Mahans Creek. On at least two occasions the Joe Pummill family took long, extended auto trips to the West Coast and at least three others to the East Coast.[30] Beginning in the 1910s, all of the three boys frequently made the Mahans Creek neighborhood a part of their Christmas season and summer travel destinations.

✦   ✦   ✦

That the Pummill boys lived in urban areas, held white-collar jobs, enjoyed incomes well above the national average, formed "modern" families, and exhibited a particular style of living placed them within the boundaries of what may be described as the era's loosely-defined, national middle class.[31] But, an examination of their family histories indicates that their respective experiences of social class in the early twentieth century were far from uniform. While Everett served as superintendent of schools at the small town of Eureka (population of about 300) for fifteen years, was active in a Masonic lodge, and attended the local Methodist church with some regularity, pressing family problems absorbed much of his time away from his job. Joe Pummill, on the other hand, was extraordinarily active in the life of small-town Winona where he served as superintendent of schools on three separate occasions for a total of twenty-two years. Joe and his energetic wife, Atlanta, hobnobbed with the town's wealthiest residents. Indeed, throughout the 1930s, they regularly invited prominent Winona couples to weekend supper parties on the picturesque old Pummill farm where they ate lavishly and entertained until far into the night. Perhaps not insignificantly, the combined incomes of Joe and Atlanta may have exceeded that of any family in Winona, including one of their friends, the president of the local bank, George C. Rollins.

Residents of the much larger urban area of Springfield (population about 60,000) from 1921 to 1963, Lawrence and Crystal Pummill's social and civic life revolved almost exclusively around the faculty and students of the normal school. While Lawrence himself served at various times as the Sunday school superintendent of the Grace Methodist Church, president of the local University Club, and on both the city's park and airport board, he and Crystal never joined the local country club and rarely socialized with non-academic families. Within the college's social circle, he and Crystal belonged to a bridge group and in their earlier years hosted formal dinners. They attended nearly all of the college's athletic contests. In his later years Lawrence became a golfing aficionado but played exclusively with fellow academics on Springfield's public park course. When queried about her parents' social standing, Virginia (Pummill) Dailey, one of his daughters, emphatically asserted many years later that the family never had enough money to join Springfield's elite.[32]

None of the three Pummills ever completely abandoned their ties to rural Shannon County. They retained to their deaths extraordinarily strong links to their rural place of origin and to their kinfolk. Neither did the transition occasioned by their careers substantially alter the social vision of the Pummill brothers. Throughout their lives, they remained loyal to the principles handed down from their ancestors but which were also consistent with many of those in the nation's newly emerging urban, white-collar middle class. In a sense, they were "radicals," for they dreamed of a middle-class democracy that extended, as they understood it, a "fundamental fairness to all people." They rejected an ideal society that prized cut-throat individualism and unfettered commercialism.[33] In the midst of the Great

Depression, for example, Everett Pummill in the family newsletter expressed regret that the region's tall pine forests "have long since been sacrificed to the slashing crashing wheels of commercialism."[34] "The strong must help the weak," Lawrence bluntly lectured the Winona high-school graduation class in 1959.[35]

Neither Lawrence nor his brothers were very specific in the kind of obligation that this invocation might impose on the strong, but they did unequivocally endorse private charity and appeared with some reluctance to have approved of New Deal work relief projects. Perhaps more startlingly, Lawrence went on record endorsing the national government using its powers to improve farm income and to regulate both "capital and labor." None of the boys protested when New Deal agencies helped construct new school buildings or, in the instance of Lawrence, when the National Youth Administration subsidized students at the Springfield normal school. Neither did they raise objections to the federal relief received by several of their relatives in the 1930s.

More explicit and closer to the heart of the boys' social vision were their ideas of individual success. They shared Lawrence's oft-repeated if unoriginal maxim that "a man's success is measured in usefulness. Not money." Viewing themselves as exemplars of persons who had risen in status from lowly circumstances mainly via education, they of course warmly endorsed public schools as a means of closing the economic and social gap between the poor and the rich. Schools were, however, not an easy sell to a people who saw their children as valuable laborers. Joe Pummill, explained the author of his hyperbolic obituary, spent countless hours in "dark hill cabins . . . sitting in hickory-bark chairs around stone fireplaces, explaining to a suspicious parent. . .how a high school training could be the golden key that unlocks the door of success for a talented youngster."[36] Observing in 1911 that high school work prepared youngsters for becoming successful in either business or teaching, he advertised the merits of attending Winona High School in the local *Shannon County Democrat.*[37]

✦   ✦   ✦

A succession of experiences took the Pummill brothers from their childhoods on the family farm in the Mahans Creek basin to become teachers in one-room schools in Shannon County, to attend Missouri's normal schools and teachers colleges, and to have careers in education. This ushered the brothers and their families into Ozarks' town life and into the nation's fast-growing if amorphous urban middle class. At first glance, the Pummill brothers seem to have been unlikely candidates for such a transition, but upon a closer examination it becomes clear that the experience of their ancestors on the periphery of the Upland South and the existence in their family history of an unusual number of preachers and teachers may have impelled them to seek their fortunes in education and in urban America. Their success in the profession permitted them to acquire the markers that distinguished the emerging middle class of professional white-collar families from others in urban America. Still, while educational careers to some degree reoriented their lives toward impersonal networks based on specialized knowledge and skills, the Pummill boys simultaneously remained steadfast in associations that were based on kinfolk and their pasts.

✦ CHAPTER 12 ✦

Leaving the Homeland

EVEN IN THE final years of her life, Elsie Maude (Rader) Quisenberry, the firstborn of Sam and Ada Rader, remembered a painful experience from her childhood. One evening she had "balked at her chore of doing the dishes," but her protests went for naught. Her mother explained that washing dishes was a lifelong responsibility assigned to women by virtue of their sex. Elsie should learn "how to do it well and get lots of practice while she was still at home," she said. Pondering the implications of her mother's remarks, the full force of them suddenly hit her. Reviewing her life as it stretched out in front of her, all that she could see was "unending stacks and piles of dirty dishes extending out into [her] future ad infinitum." Though perhaps faintly or unconsciously, she may have also associated doing stacks of dirty dishes with other even more negative feelings—with a future marriage to a local hollers boy, with bearing numerous children, and with aging before her time. Finally, she could take it no longer. She "laid her head down on the table and boo-hooed for . . . 10 minutes!"[1]

Elsie was not alone among Sam Rader's children in holding reservations about the goodness of life on Mahans Creek. While each of the three oldest children—Elsie (b. 1897), Gilbert (b. 1898), and Velma (b. 1904)—retained an abiding affection for life in the hollows, each of them also knew firsthand the hardness

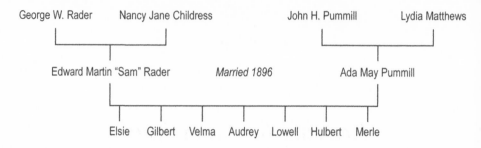

The Sam and Ada Pummill Rader family. *Courtesy of Katie Nieland.*

of life there, especially for a woman, and each of them embraced dreams that would in time take them elsewhere. Partly it was a matter of their mother, Ada, and her family (the Pummills), who pulled, or perhaps a better word would be "pushed," the Rader siblings from the creek. Unlike the four youngest, who were unable or barely able to remember their mother before her death in 1913, Elsie, Gilbert, and Velma—sixteen, fifteen, and nine years of age, respectively—remembered Ada well. Immaculately groomed, fashionably dressed, poised, and, like her school-teaching brothers, infatuated with words, Ada was different from the typical hollers woman. She, more than most, shared the middle-class aspirations of her time. And then there was the timber boom itself, which not only brought more cash into Shannon County but also introduced its residents to the wonders of the outside world. Even the Raders on Mahans Creek were not immune to the lives of those whom they furtively glimpsed in the ads of the Sears and Roebuck catalogs and in the silent movies shown at the Eminence Opera House. There, they witnessed alluring images of modern living, excitement, and perpetual youthfulness.[2]

✦   ✦   ✦

From an early age, Elsie stood out among her peers. Encouraged by her mother, she dressed as stylishly as the family's resources permitted, but it was her hair more than anything else that set her apart. A Delaware School photo taken in 1913 shortly before her mother's death reveals, as one of her granddaughters observed a hundred years later, a fifteen-year-old who was "particularly well groomed [and] with a modern bob haircut." The bob was introduced in the 1910s by Irene Castle of the famed wife and husband ballroom-dancing team, and shearing long locks represented for Elsie and her cohorts a small sign of female rebellion as well as dreams of becoming an entertainer or movie star themselves. All of her life, Elsie "made a production of everything," one of her granddaughters remembered, she even dressed up when joining the family for the evening meal.[3] Not only did Elsie seek to present herself as a glamorous young woman of her day, but, perhaps inspired by her Pummill uncles and her mother as well as the prospect of escaping the destiny traditionally assigned to hollers women, in 1913 Elsie took and passed the county's teaching exam.[4]

But Elsie never taught. That was because Cordell Rhinehart, perhaps the county's most eligible bachelor, came a courting. Cordell was emphatically not just another farm boy from the hollows. Although, typical of many such boys, he had cut short his education (he finished only the fourth grade of school, exclaiming that learning how to spell "cat" and "hen" was enough "useless" knowledge for anyone), Cordell was a flamboyant young man with a commanding presence. In time he became a legendary figure in Shannon County history. To this day, among the county's old timers the very mention of his name brings forth knowing smiles.

"All agreed," recalled his admiring daughter, JoyDell, that Cordell "was Shannon County's authority on law, politics and the stock market, and the wittiest person I have ever known."[5] He was the eldest son and heir-apparent of DeForest Rhinehart, who was the county's biggest livestock dealer, a director of Eminence's Shannon County Bank, and the owner of a two-thousand-acre spread on the Horseshoe Bend of Spring Creek. As a member of the county's inner circle of prominent Republicans, DeForest's political affiliation may have given

Sam Rader some pause.[6] But, if Sam did have misgivings, he laid them aside. Elsie and Cordell were wed on her eighteenth birthday, December 20, 1915, at Sam's farm on Mahans Creek. In order to marry legally, Cordell, who was two years shy of twenty-one, had to obtain his father's permission. It could be that Elsie married for money rather than love. Years later she repeatedly reminded her granddaughters: "Why marry a poor man when you can marry a rich one?"

In retrospect, there is little doubt that from the beginning the marriage did not quite meet Elsie's dreams. Instead of relocating to an exotic place far away from the creek or even to nearby Eminence, she and Cordell moved in with his family at the Rhinehart Ranch. While life on the ranch offered more comfort and luxury than it did back on Mahans Creek, Elsie paid a price. At the ranch she was only one person within a large family consisting of Cordell's parents, his seven siblings, and, depending on the season, a half dozen or more hired hands. The presence of all these people may not have relieved her of boredom and loneliness. But she was at least a two-hour trip by buggy from her family in Delaware, and Cordell was frequently away from home for weeks at a time buying and selling livestock. The ordeal of pregnancies and the burdens of childcare rapidly followed. In the years from 1917 through 1923, she bore four children, three boys and one girl.

Apart from her children, Elsie may have found some comfort in the enduring ties that her marriage established between the Rhinehart and the Rader families. At once the younger siblings of Elsie and Cordell began to form friendships; for a time Elsie's younger brother, Gilbert, dated Cordell's younger sister, Dortha. Ethel Rhinehart became a high school friend of Elsie's sister, Velma; in high school the girls sang duets together at the meetings of the Christian Endeavor Society in Eminence. Cordell hired Gilbert and later Lowell, Elsie's brothers, to, among other chores, drive livestock overland back and forth between the railhead at Winona and the Rhinehart Ranch in Spring Valley. About twice a year the Rhinharts treated Eminence residents to the spectacle of a large cattle drive down the county seat's main street in front of the courthouse. In 1926 the *Current Wave* described Cordell as "the hustling young stock dealer and farmer."[7]

Cordell and Elsie did not remain on the ranch permanently. While continuing to work with his father as a livestock trader, in 1921 he bought a small farm up Pine Hollow only about a mile from Sam Rader's home on Mahans Creek. From there Elsie and her children frequently visited her father and her younger siblings. One can imagine Cordell's characteristic delight in announcing in the same year that he had purchased two jacks: "Big Jim" to serve mares in the neighborhood of his Pine Hollow farm and the other, "Gold Digger," to stand for the mares in Spring Valley and on the Rhinehart Ranch. In 1921, he also invested in an Eminence furniture store. In the mid-1920s, he moved his family back to Spring Valley and then in 1929 rented a farm near Winona. While there, Elsie joined other young women, including her sister, Velma, in their enthusiasm for playing contract bridge, a card game that was then sweeping the country.[8] This could have been one of the happiest periods in Elsie's life.

Lingering in the background and perhaps too often in the foreground was her unpredictable husband. His livestock trading never assured a steady income, especially the way that Cordell did it. He loved the process itself; it was for him a thrilling form of gambling that could entail both substantial losses as well as gains. A man of volcanic passions, it was said that as a boy Cordell nearly killed his pony by riding the exhausted animal without stint up and down the steep hills around Spring Valley. Cordell was also what hollers peoples called "a drinking man." Whether due to his drinking or to his larger-than-life personality or, more than likely, to both, Cordell's escapades in the 1920s were notorious. Arrested at least twice for engaging in brawls—probably while drunk—on the streets of Eminence, he also wrecked at least three new cars on the rough roads around Eminence.[9]

The Great Depression brought an end to Elsie's marriage but not to her allegiance to the nation's glamour culture. After years of conflict arising from Cordell's drinking and the family's economic insecurity, Elsie divorced Cordell in 1939. Even in the midst of hard times, a granddaughter, Nancy Sevy, recalled that Elsie avidly perused mail-order catalogs, for years kept a set of clippings of the King Edward VIII and Mrs. Wallace Simpson romance, and regularly attended the movies.[10] Finally relocating in a city, Springfield, Missouri, she remarried in 1941, took a series of jobs as a clerk in local stores, and made costume jewelry for sale. To the end of her life she continued to groom and dress as fashionably as her means permitted.

✦ ✦ ✦

In the meantime, Elsie's year-younger brother, Gilbert "Gib" Rader, also left home but by a different route. After completing primary school at Delaware, Gib may have then decided to follow in the footsteps of his Pummill kinfolk by becoming a teacher. In any case, in 1914 he enrolled as a sixteen-year-old in Eminence High School, a decision that required a long daily horseback ride of more than ten miles round trip. Handsome, affable, and athletic, he made a favorable impression on all those who knew him. That fall Gib's fellow classmates elected him to the presidency of the Shakespearean Club, an honor suggestive of his lifelong avidity as a reader. The next spring he led the high school basketball team in scoring.[11]

"Pressing farm work" forced Gib to discontinue school for the winter term of 1916. "We are very sorry to see this very splendid student go," reported the Eminence superintendent of schools in the *Current Wave*.[12] But that fall Gib was back in school; indeed, fellow students elected him president of his tenth-grade class. For his final year of high school, in 1917–18, his uncle Lawrence Pummill invited Gib to join his family in Greenfield, Missouri, where Lawrence had just been named as superintendent of schools. As a high-school senior at Greenfield, Gib was something of a sensation; selected as captain of his team and playing center (though barely over six feet tall), his performance on the basketball floor won him "all-state" honors.[13]

Approaching his twentieth birthday, hoping to become a

teacher, and subject to the military draft in World War I, Gib enrolled in October of 1918 as a student in the Missouri State Normal School in Springfield and as a private in the college's Student Army Training Corps (SATC). The SATC subjected him to eleven hours a week of military training plus residence in a tent. For unknown reasons, in the fall term he completed only one of his four courses, a course in trigonometry. In the winter and spring of 1919, he did much better in his schoolwork and starred on the college's basketball team.[14] "Rader plays center and with his wonderful jumping ability and natural aggressiveness, supplemented by a rare ability to cage the ball, he makes a strong addition to any team," reported the school newspaper. "Captain Rader is a quiet, hard working man, whose very quietness drives his team to greater efforts. He is a friend to every man on the squad, and no matter how poor a man's efforts may be, 'Cap' always has a word of encouragement for him."[15] At the same time, he held a part-time job with a local laundry that entailed him picking up dirty clothes from fellow students on Monday and returning the cleaned items on Friday.[16] That fall he even obtained enough playing time to receive a letter in football, a sport that he had never before played.

But in the winter-spring of 1920, the Great Flu Epidemic caught up with him. It was then that he also probably contracted tuberculosis. Somehow he managed to survive the double onslaught, but that spring he was unable to finish a single course.[17] On July 31, 1920, he obtained admission to the State Tuberculosis Sanitarium in Mount Vernon, Missouri, where he convalesced for nearly sixteen months. Treatment by long periods of rest utterly failed. The official diagnosis at the end of his stay was that he had "far adv[anced]" pulmonary tuberculosis "unimproved." While Gib roomed briefly at the Lawrence Pummill home in Springfield, Arch Pummill remembered that Gib was subject to coughing fits that left his bed pillows soaked with blood. Despite the toll of the disease, Gib, according to family remembrances, remained good-humored and optimistic.

Presuming that a higher altitude, cooler weather, lower humidity, and long periods of rest might improve his condition, in 1922 he entered the US Army's Fort Whipple Sanitarium in Prescott, Arizona.[18] He slowly got better, though the disease had permanently damaged his pulmonary capacity. For his disability, he received a small government monthly stipend for the remainder of his life. At some point while in Prescott, he met Eunice Udene "Dene" Young and married her on August 9, 1924. Indicative of his close ties with Mahans Creek, three months after the marriage, Gilbert brought his new bride back for a visit.[19]

To supplement his disability payment, Gib tried a variety of jobs in Prescott. The 1926 Prescott city directory listed his occupation simply as "poultry," that of 1928 as "electrician's helper," and that of 1929 as "salesman." For a year or more he was a traveling salesman for the Fleischmann Yeast Company, a job that took him in a small truck to silver- and copper-mining camps scattered across northwestern Arizona. According to family lore, to abet his work, he learned at least a smattering of Spanish. Sometime in the late 1920s his younger brother, Lowell, arrived in Arizona, and in 1928 his younger sister, Audrey, also made the long trip westward. She served as the family's babysitter.

✦ ✦ ✦

Velma, the third child in the Sam and Ada Rader family and five years younger than Gilbert, left home by yet another route. As with Elsie, Velma was *never* enamored with the prospect of becoming simply a wife and mother in the hollows of Shannon County. Throughout her life, she suffered no nonsense from anyone. Upon her mother's death in 1913 and Elsie's departure to marry Cordell in 1915, Velma not only became the senior female among Sam's children living at home but also learned firsthand the harsh work routines thrust upon the shoulders of hollows females even when they were adolescents. Furthermore, as with Elsie, Velma imbibed deeply in the wider glamour culture of her day. While still at home and a student at Delaware School, she carefully coiffed her blonde hair and dressed fashionably. Attendees at the March 1918 Delaware pie supper chose four-

Velma Rader in about 1922. *Courtesy of Miles Loyd.*

teen-year-old Velma as the supper's "most popular young girl," an election that surely signaled the future direction of her life.[20]

She left home as soon as she could. While living with a family in Eminence, she apparently completed three years of high school and in 1922, as an eighteen-year-old, began teaching at a one-room rural school in Rat in the far northwestern corner of Shannon County. The isolation and loneliness of teaching there did not deter her determination; indeed, Velma enrolled the following summer of 1923 in the Springfield Normal School. That fall she obtained a better teaching position at a two-room school in the tiny village of Low Wassie, located six miles east of Winona. In the meantime, she met J. Talmage "Tal" Loyd, a dashing young man who was teaching at a one-room rural school in nearby Big Spring (also known as Sycamore).

Tal came from an ambitious family of modest means. Exceptionally amiable, Tal's father, J. "Jack" Talmage Loyd, not only worked hard in trying to make a go of a drugstore in the lumber boom town of Winona but also threw himself into the town's civic life. He was involved in nearly everything—the Christian Church, the anti-saloon movement, the local Masonic lodge, the local school system, and Democratic politics.

Neither was Tal a hollers boy. At the age of seven he began working part time in his family's drugstore, where he honed the people skills for which he was later to become well known. As the only boy in a household of four sisters, his mother and three older sisters doted on him. When he graduated from high school in 1921, his mother was so distraught at the prospect of him attending the University of Missouri in "far off" Columbia that Tal decided to seek his fortunes closer to home. After an "off & on affair" that continued for more than a year, Velma consented to marry Tal in June of 1924.[21] In the 1924–25 school year, both taught at Low Wassie, each receiving eighty dollars a month for an eight-month term, a substantial income for their day. In July 1925, Velma birthed Jerry Tim Loyd; suggestive of her and perhaps Tal's "modern" aspirations, she did not again become pregnant until seven years later.

As with her career educator uncles Joe and Lawrence Pummill, the material circumstances of Velma's life were far easier than they were for most of her kinfolk. She did not continue teaching, and Tal resigned a post as a school principal in Missouri's boot heel in 1928, but in the next year he became the publisher and editor of the *Shannon County Democrat*, the Winona weekly purchased by Tal, his father, and some friends. As a supporter of the election of Franklin D. Roosevelt in 1932, he received an appointment as Winona's postmaster in 1933, a post in which he continued to serve until entering the army in 1943. Before mustering out in 1945, he rose to the rank of a captain. During the war years, Velma served as Winona's temporary postmaster.

Throughout her life Velma was something of a "queen bee," to use the apt descriptor of one of her sons. Active in the Eastern Star, hostess to innumerable social gatherings, and deeply engaged in local Democratic politics, no woman in Winona exceeded Velma's public prominence. She seemed to expect that not just her own family but also the lives of her friends would revolve around her. Slim, elegantly dressed, and frequently with a cigarette pressed between her lips, she was a former hollers daughter who at least in minor ways flaunted Victorian proprieties and epitomized the "modern" woman.

✦   ✦   ✦

A memorable trip from Shannon County to Prescott, Arizona, in the summer of 1929 brought into sharp relief the new horizons of Sam Rader's family. At the urging of Lawrence Pummill, who had just purchased a new Buick Touring Car, Sam himself decided to join the Pummills, Elsie and her son Douglas, and Velma and her son Jerry—altogether nine people—on the long trek to Prescott. In Prescott they met up with other members of the family, seven altogether. There was Sam's first son, Gilbert, his wife, and his two children, and Audrey, Sam's third daughter. And there was Lowell, Sam's second son, who had also married a local woman (Rose Contreras) and had been working as an electrician in Prescott since 1927. Everything about the high desert town of Prescott seemed strange to Sam, but he liked it. Lawrence and Gib loved to tell the story of how Sam covered the sandy front yard of the house that Gib rented with brown tobacco spittle. Gib observed afterward that it looked like a pack of mules had tromped through his yard.[22] What neither Sam nor anyone else could foresee in August of 1929 were the frightening trials that lay ahead.

AFTERWORD

"The Celebrated Cow Case"

JIM RADER WAS angry. Perhaps he had never been madder in his life. And this was saying a lot, for Jim always lived "on the edge." He was prone to emotional outbursts, especially when he believed that his honor was at stake. Such was the case when he concluded in 1913 that his well-to-do neighbor, U. M. Randolph, had stolen one of his heifers. Jim did not seek to settle the matter with U. M. in a face-to-face confrontation. Nor did he physically assault U. M. as some hollers men would have done under similar circumstances. Instead, Jim retaliated in 1914 by building a court case against his neighbor. He sought a quid pro quo. He wanted to publicly humiliate U. M. just as he believed U. M. had publicly humiliated him.

Jim's response to what he thought was thievery, but, more importantly, what he believed was an assault on his honor, not only reflected a retributive form of justice common in the Upland South but was a source of his undoing as one of the creek's most prominent agricultural entrepreneurs. Furthermore, in a broader sense, Jim's clash with U. M. marked the end of an era in Mahans Creek history. By 1915, the timber industry was no longer pumping thousands of dollars into the neighborhood economy each year. Never again did the creek farmers experience the same level of general prosperity nor the same level of neighborhood vibrancy that they had enjoyed in the first years of the twentieth century.

✦ ✦ ✦

According to Mahans Creek folklore, "the celebrated cow case," as an out-of-town newspaper headlined the court proceedings involving the creek titans, brought an abrupt end to the career of Jim Rader as one of Shannon County's most successful trader-farmers.[1] The case itself, which entailed multiple law suits, probably cost Jim more than $1,000, but a closer examination of the evidence indicates that Jim was in financial trouble well before 1914. Indeed, hints that Jim might have been overstretching his resources surfaced throughout his entrepreneurial career.[2]

A turning point in his fortunes may have come as early as 1909, when Jim and Beckie borrowed $3,500, to be repaid in 1916; this was the equivalent of at least $70,000 by today's dollars. As collateral, they mortgaged the major part of their farm.[3] Why they took on such a large debt is uncertain. They may have needed the money to pay off earlier debts arising from land and cattle deals that had misfired, or perhaps they borrowed it to pay for construction of their new home. Adding to their difficulties in repaying the debt was a raging forest fire in March of 1910 that destroyed much of their farm's rail fencing. Jim and Beckie may have needed money for yet another reason. In what could have been a gamble by the Raders to recover their precarious financial position, Jim invested $3,000 in a corn planter patent taken out by a Winona farmer-inventor, one Israel Monroe Chrisco.[4] Jim apparently never realized one cent from the invention.

In the meantime, a severe farm depression contributed to the family's growing financial insecurity. Drought struck the Delaware neighborhood in 1913 and 1914. Corn production in Shannon County plunged downward—in 1913 from an average of eighteen bushels an acre to nine bushels in 1914.[5] As if matters were not bad enough, a torrential downpour in late April of 1914 not only destroyed two railroad bridges spanning the creek but also washed out much of the fencing in the neighborhood.[6]

The "deluge" was followed by month after month of abnormally low rainfall. In the meantime, nationally, an economic depression reduced the demand for local railroad ties to virtually nothing.[7]

Not since 1881 had conditions on the creek been so bad. Unable to feed his livestock without purchasing additional grain, Jim sold at least one railroad carload of cattle in July of 1914. Three weeks later, the *Shannon County Democrat* reported that many of the local farmers were "getting rid of their hogs."[8] This may have included Jim. The county's 1914 potato crop was a disaster. Nothing improved much in 1915. In order to relieve the "distress and want [that] are stalking throughout the county," J. Ben Searcy wrote in the *Current Wave*, the county should expend in advance its local road funds. The dire circumstances even caught the attention of a metropolitan daily, the St. Louis *Republic*. In March 1915, the Springfield (Missouri) Manufacturers and Jobbers Association sought to aid the drought-stricken local farmers by distributing to them a railroad car of free seed corn.[9]

✦ ✦ ✦

Yet it was not the farm depression or Jim's risky financial dealings alone that led to his undoing. There was the matter of the heifer. Jim believed that U. M. had removed the evidence by transporting the heifer to a farm near Everton, Missouri, some 160 miles from Delaware. Never in his life had Jim hesitated about moving into the perilous waters of a legal battle. Accompanied by his young brother-in-law, Elva Pummill, whom he believed could identify the heifer, the two men set out by train from Delaware to Everton. Finding what they believed to be the heifer grazing on the farm of Solomon H. Wilson, a local realtor and livestock dealer, Jim in December 1913 filed a 12,685-word deposition in the local justice court in Dade County that would have required the animal's return to Shannon County as evidence. "The cow is going to prove expensive to somebody before the case is solved," wryly observed the *Current Wave*.[10]

More was at stake for Jim than the value of the heifer itself. Before the Dade County justice court had reached a decision, Jim asked the State of Missouri to charge Randolph with grand larceny. The subsequent trial before the circuit court in Eminence excited more public attention than any event in Shannon County since the public hanging of Oscar Baker in 1899. "Both parties are prominent citizens of our county," the *Current Wave* observed.[11] Each side employed a battery of three local attorneys. In a packed room of spectators, more than fifty witnesses appeared before the circuit court in Eminence. After a day and a half spent at trial, on January 14, 1914, the jury acquitted Randolph. In the meantime, the justice court in Dade County rejected Jim's deposition to have the heifer returned to Shannon County as evidence. Jim then appealed that decision to the Dade County Circuit Court. The trial at Greenfield, in which several Mahans Creek residents appeared as witnesses, resulted in a hung jury. With these three adverse rulings, Jim was left with costs "probably aggregating more than $1,500," the *Shannon County Herald* of Birch Tree reported.[12]

To make matters worse from Jim Rader's point of view, "The Celebrated Cow Case" devolved into something of a public farce. The heifer itself was probably worth no more than ten dollars, and, to bystanders, Jim's continuing pursuit of what he considered to be his honor bordered on the ludicrous. Presumably with tongue in cheek, the *Dade County Advocate* of Greenfield reported that "several theories of compromise were suggested. Among others some wag suggested to the court that he would order the heifer put on the butcher block, she would pay all the costs of the case, allow the butcher a reasonable commission and the remainder would probably satisfy both claimants."[13] Jim surely failed to find any humor in the newspaper's recommendation.

For at stake was Jim's conception of honor. As in other more traditional societies where human relationships were or are mostly face to face, no aspect of a man's honor was more important than his good name. Personal reputation was a form of property that rested not only on one's inner conviction of self-worth but upon validation by other men. For someone to have honor, others had to acknowledge its possession. Since honor had to be ratified by the opinions of others, its possession was always tenuous and in jeopardy. Any concession, however small, signified personal weakness and a potential diminution of one's honor.[14]

While neither Jim nor U. M. may have publicly acknowledged it, they had long been neighborhood rivals—rivals in who made the most money, rivals in the way that they made their money (Jim as a livestock dealer and U. M. as a breeder of purebred shorthorn beef cattle), political rivals (U. M. as a Republican who had twice run unsuccessfully for a countywide public office and Jim as an avowed free-silver Democrat), and they were rivals in who owned the most elegant house in the neighborhood (both men had built new, and by the standards of the time, elaborate homes) and who had the most "refined" daughters.[15] Both men were short-tempered. As with Jim, U. M. had the reputation of being "easy to rub the wrong way," as one his descendants put it to me many years later.[16]

U. M.'s efforts at self-promotion surely irritated Jim. In particular, U. M., more than anyone else in the neighborhood with the possible exception of Jim himself, succeeded in planting stories in the local newspapers that offered evidence of his unusual sagacity, his skills in moneymaking, and his cultural refinement. A few examples suffice. In 1893, U. M. let all readers of the *Current Wave* know that he and his wife had attended the World's Fair in Chicago, and six years later the *Wave* reported that U. M. had completed the construction of another large barn, a blacksmith shop, and other buildings, which made him a "very successful farmer in the Delaware Township."[17] After the completion in 1900 of one of the "finest residences" in Shannon County, the following year U. M. and his wife invited the editor, Pleas L. Lyles (and his wife) of the *Current Wave* to his home for a visit. Lyles, who was also Shannon County's representative to the Missouri State Legislature, waxed eloquently about the beauty of the Randolph's new home and of their "Meadowbrook farm." U. M. himself was an able writer; for several years running he reported to *Wave* readers he and his wife's trips to the American Royal Livestock Show in Kansas City, where he frequently purchased purebred shorthorn cattle, particularly young bulls, which he would then offer for sale in Shannon County.[18]

✦   ✦   ✦

While in the midst of the cow case, Jim appears to have been searching for a means of relieving his family's financial situation. Within less than a month after the adverse decision in the state versus Randolph for grand larceny, the *Shannon County Democrat* reported that Jim was building a general store on his property at Delaware Station. Jim also hoped that the newly elected president, Woodrow Wilson, a fellow Democrat, would authorize the establishment of a post office at his store and appoint him as the postmaster. Why this did not happen is unclear. Apparently, neither did the general store succeed, for in July of 1914, Jim sold it.[19]

Over time the legend grew that the costs of pursuing the court case had "bankrupted" both men. But it was Jim who had to pay the court costs, and the subsequent history of the Randolph family suggests that the trials may in the long run have cost U. M.'s family virtually nothing.[20] Even before the expensive heifer case, the Randolphs may have been the most well-to-do family in the Mahans Creek neighborhood, but afterward their supremacy was virtually unchallengeable. For a time U. M. even replaced Jim as a major supplier of pork and beef to the Missouri Mining and Lumber Company store in West Eminence.

In the meantime, Jim found a way out of his financial morass, albeit not without huge and lasting consequences for him and his family. In effect, Jim and Beckie traded their farm to a German American farmer, Julius Lahmeyer, in exchange for an eighty-acre farm in Barton County, Missouri, with the new owner assuming the couple's $3,500 debt.[21] That Beckie, alone, was the legal recipient of the Barton County farm suggests that Jim sought to protect the farm from a potential lawsuit brought by his credi-

Home of U. M. Randolph (built in 1900), 2009. *Courtesy of the author.*

tors. Located near the Kansas border, the new farm was some two hundred miles west of Mahans Creek. Relocation in Barton County did not completely relieve the family's embarrassment in Shannon County. On February 17, 1916, the *Current Wave* carried a large "Notice of Sale under School Fund Mortgage" for the failure of J. P. Rader and Sarah R. Rader to repay to the county $400 plus $75.74 in interest on a school loan that they had received in 1906. Before foreclosure on May 10, 1916, Jim was able to pay off the mortgage, but not before the notice was repeatedly printed in the newspaper.

Except for occasional visits with relatives or for business, neither Jim nor Beckie ever returned to the Mahans Creek neighborhood.[22] Barton County, located on the edge of the Great Plains, had no timber boom, and the Raders were unable to duplicate the life that they had left behind on Mahans Creek. Jim's career as a cattle and hog dealer ended. In order to live in reasonable comfort, Jim became a full-time farmer. Survival on his small farm depended on raising a few acres of corn and truck farming; to make ends meet, he peddled vegetables and eggs to the nearby coal-mining families. As with countless other Americans, the Great Depression of the 1930s treated Jim and his family harshly. In 1932, Jim, probably alone of the Rader-Pummill clan, voted for Norman Thomas, the Socialist candidate for the presidency. Long an agnostic, Jim, in his last years, may have found some solace in his newfound religious faith. In 1939, Jim Rader died at the age of seventy-five. He did not live long enough to enjoy one other possible gratification—to see his youngest son, Delbert, become a successful farmer in the 1940s and 1950s.

Up to the time of Jim's death, Beckie remained as spirited and optimistic as ever. In the 1930s no one in the Pummill-Rader clan supported the annual family reunions and the family's monthly newsletter, *The Passerby*, with more enthusiasm and tenacity than Beckie. "We, Jim and I, have had it rather hard," she wrote to the extended family upon the occasion of Jim's death, "but [we] really got a lot of pleasure along the way." Within a month she had a heart attack and remained invalided until her death twenty-three years later in 1963. Her final years were not easy ones, but she did take some consolation from the frequent visits of kinfolk.[23]

✦ PART IV ✦

WHEN IN PLACES
EVEN THE CREEK
WENT DRY

In November of 1924, one of Mahans Creek's favorite sons, Gilbert "Gib" Rader, decided to bring his new bride, Dene, back to the home place for a visit.[1] After having journeyed more than 1,500 miles by rail from Prescott, Arizona, the young couple finally arrived in Winona, whereupon they boarded the single passenger car bound for West Eminence. As the tiny train slowly curled its way northward down Mahans Creek, concern may have crossed Gib's face; for in the upper reaches of the creek he saw some recently abandoned houses. The couple disembarked at Sam Rader's farm.

Leaving behind a steamer trunk to be picked up later, the young couple walked up a slightly inclined wagon path to Sam's house. Upon their approach, they were greeted by a cacophony of hungry, squealing pigs and "barking and jumping dogs that came from everywhere."[2] Despite Gib's bemused reassurances, Dene was more than a little apprehensive. She had never experienced anything like this before. He introduced her to Sam, his father, to Audrey, his youngest sister, and to his three younger brothers (Lowell, Hulbert, and Merle). The meeting was awkward. At the ages of nineteen, seventeen, fifteen, and twelve, respectively, the siblings were not exactly youngsters, but, to Dene, the boys in particular seemed painfully shy.

An uneasy feeling crept over Gib as well. Nothing was exactly as he had remembered it. Everything seemed smaller and more cramped. The height and steepness of the hills along

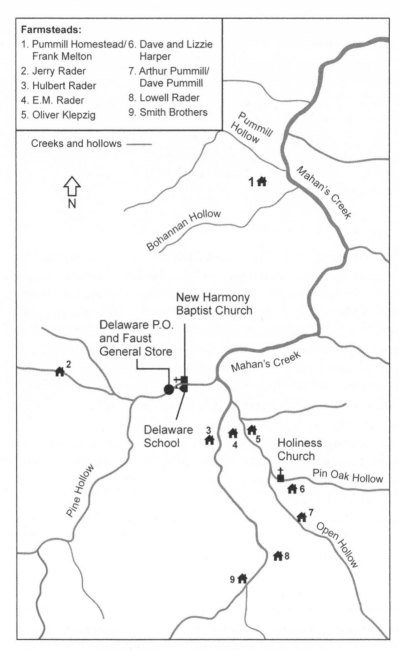

Mahans Creek neighborhood, 1935. *Courtesy of Katie Nieland.*

the creek no longer impressed him; they paled beside the towering mountains around Prescott, Arizona. Neither was the family home as big, warm, or inviting as it had been in the past. Perhaps Gib had forgotten how Sam and his sons "used to go into the kitchen to shoot rats as they poked their heads through cracks in the walls."[3] The house itself had not fared well; it was in the worst shape it had been since it had been built in 1896. Over the years, rain and sun had bleached out its pine sidings, leaving the exterior a dull gray. Strips of the newspapers that had been pasted to the inner walls to keep out the cold now hung loosely or had fallen away. Through a broken windowpane, Gib felt a cool November breeze pushing into the living room.

One of the first tasks that Gib set for himself was to install a new pane in the broken window. Not long afterward, one of the family cats wandered into the living room and rubbed up against Gib's leg. Not an aficionado of cats, Gib yelled, "Scat!" Previously free to enter and exit the house through the broken window, the alarmed animal hurtled itself directly into the newly installed pane and, while fortunately not breaking the glass, fell backward, momentarily stunned. Everyone laughed.[4]

Not so funny was the fact that the shabby condition of Sam Rader's house mirrored a larger, sadder, and not infrequently tragic story, one that may be summed up as the Long Depression in Shannon County. The protracted economic downturn extended from the mid-1910s (with a brief respite in the World War I era) to the beginning of America's participation in World War II (1941). By 1924, when Gib and Dene came back for a visit, Delaware did sport a country store and a post office and a few people owned cars, but the Mahans Creek neighborhood was in the midst of hard times. Its origins went back to the decline of the forest products industry. While the transfusion of outside money into the creek's economy by the timber companies never completely stopped, it shrank from river-size proportions to the mere trickle of a branch-water stream.

Not anticipated by the Rader-Pummill families in 1924, the hard times following the timber boom were only a beginning. With the advent of the nationwide Great Depression of the 1930s, the Long Depression entered its second phase. The latter not only brought with it plummeting farm prices but also closed off a traditional safety valve of the hollers people; no longer could economically desperate farmers or their sons easily find employment by leaving the creek and going elsewhere in the nation. Everywhere, jobs were scarce. This was not the worst of it. With soaring temperatures and abnormally low rainfall in 1930, 1934, and 1936, the Mahans Creek basin experienced some of the most crushing droughts in the neighborhood's history. In places, even the creek went dry.

✦ CHAPTER 13 ✦

"Have We a Moses?"

IN THE SUMMER of 1918, a thunderous roar interrupted their play. In the road leading into the old Pummill place, coming straight at eight-year-old Edna Pummill and her four-year-old brother, Archie, was something they had never heard or seen before—a Model T Ford. At the steering wheel was Cordell Rhinehart, the irrepressible husband of their cousin, Elsie Rader. With one hand, Cordell squeezed the car's air horn and with the other he waved his Stetson, all the while yelling "like a mad man": "Get the hell out of the road!" Edna and Archie scrambled to their feet and ran for their lives. By slamming on the brakes and skidding sideways in a plume of dust, Cordell narrowly averted hitting the children (at least this was the way Arch remembered the incident many years later). Cordell, as was his wont, then greeted the petrified youngsters with gales of laughter.[1]

America's supreme symbol of modernity had finally arrived on Mahans Creek. Even though the price of a new car had fallen sharply since Henry Ford introduced his moving assembly line in 1913, the local farm families had been reluctant to embrace the new technological marvel, partly due to low incomes, partly due to the rough roads that routinely caused tires to blow out and dangerous wrecks, and especially since they saw cars as a rationale for raising their taxes. In 1919, Delaware Township voted twenty-three to five against a countywide road improvement bond. As late as 1921, there were still not many cars in Shannon County; only one car existed for each forty-seven residents (compared to one for each ten persons in Missouri statewide). Even into the mid-1920s, when creek families came to town, they continued to see more horses, buggies, and wagons than they did cars. In Eminence "town hogs" still roamed the streets and, according to the *Current Wave,* had "a good time rooting up the court house yard."[2] But, within a decade, by crowding seven persons into each vehicle, everyone in the county could have been on the road at once.[3]

By 1930, with the possible exception of Arthur, all the senior Pummills owned a car. Even Arthur eventually tried his hand at driving one, but he never learned how. After plowing into his chicken house and killing three hens, he learned that yelling "Whoa" and pulling back on the steering wheel failed to stop the "gal-darned" contraption. To make it easier for the teen-aged children to attend high school in Eminence, Sam Rader bought a car in the early 1920s, but he himself never learned to drive it. Not until the mid-1930s did Lowell, the chief driver of Sam's first car, own a car himself. Indeed, as late as 1936, Joe Pummill marveled at the "drama of different modes of travel" by members of the Pummill-Rader clan. In downtown Eminence, one Saturday trade day, he observed his brother Arthur Pummill afoot, his nephew Lowell Rader on horseback toting a sack of purchases in his saddle bag, and another nephew, Gilbert Rader, driving a brand new Plymouth.[4]

The completion of a state-financed "farm-to-market" road—Missouri Highway E—in 1935 represented a major turning point in the transportation history of the neighborhood. Two contracts let in 1932 provided for a "graded earth road" twenty feet wide running from Bartlett northward atop the ridge separating Pine Hollow and Mahans Creek to Delaware; in 1935, the winding road was completed on to Alley Spring. With help in 1936 provided by the Works Progress Administration, the state Highway Department eventually graveled the surface, but it was not until 1964 that the entire route received an oil aggregate treatment. Not only was the new road of a much higher quality than the existing roads up Pine Hollow and Mahans Creek, but travel on it sharply reduced the time that it took farmers in the township to get back and forth to the nearby towns. The neighborhood understood its significance. Upon completion in 1936 of the one-lane bridge across Delaware Creek near the schoolhouse, Sam Rader directed a huge celebration that included a dance atop the bridge itself. Sam Rader, Hub Rader, Dave Pummill, and Ed Faust provided the music for the occasion.[5]

In the wake of the timber boom, the hollers people, or at least the ones with a little money, continued to buy the latest consumer goods from the Chicago mail-order houses or at the stores of local merchants. As in the past, they went to town not only to shop on Saturdays, but also to see moving-picture shows. In 1918, Julius Lahmeyer, who had acquired the Jim Rader farm in 1914, bought the township's first hay baler, and the following year Sam Rader purchased a cream separator.[6] On the face of it, the civic life in the township changed little. All three schools—Delaware, Pine Hollow, and Crescent—remained open. In the 1927–28 academic year Delaware even hosted a two-year high school, though it apparently enrolled only three students. Local farm families still gathered for Sunday worship services at New Harmony Baptist Church at Delaware or at the Holiness Church in Open Hollow, though not in the numbers that they had during the timber boom. In the 1920s, the neighborhood even witnessed the founding of a new country store with an attached greenhouse, one owned by Edwin and Getty Randolph Faust. In 1924, the Fausts (Edwin was an avowed Democrat though the Randolphs were Republicans) obtained authorization for a post office to be housed in their Delaware store.[7]

✦ ✦ ✦

But not all was well in Shannon County. Careful observers of the local scene recognized that the continuation of organized neighborhood life and the coming of the automobile masked a deep, fundamental contraction of the area's local economy. "Have We a Moses?" queried the distressed editor of the *Current*

Wave in 1927.[8] Even to the normally optimistic newspaper editor, the prospect of a new Moses delivering the region back into the Promised Land of the early twentieth century seemed remote. For a time, a few believed that the promise of a different kind of farming, especially vegetable and fruit growing on the cutover lands abandoned by the timber companies, might restore prosperity. While peach growing and tomato canning in the flatter land around Birch Tree and in nearby Howell County did enjoy some success, they brought virtually no relief to those residing in the hollows of Shannon County. As early as 1914 the Frisco Railroad began publishing a "beautiful folder" touting the area as a paradise for tourists. On occasion, the *Wave* reported that Eminence streets were "full of high-powered cars" from St. Louis and Kansas City "with fishing poles sticking out the windows."[9] The creation of state parks at Alley Spring and Round Spring in the 1920s did bring a few additional visitors. But, in the end, salvation by way of the tourist industry turned out to be a chimera.[10]

The timber boom closed down in fits and starts. Having harvested much of the yellow pine in the southwestern part of Shannon County and on the Mahans Creek watershed, the Cordz-Fisher Lumber and Mining Company discontinued its Birch Tree operation in 1904. By 1919, when it sold its West Eminence holdings to the Forked Leaf White Oak Company, the mammoth Missouri Mining and Lumber Company had cut virtually all of its pine north of the Jacks Fork River. By then, only a few acres of pine stood anywhere in Shannon County. During the depressed lumber market of 1924, the *Current Wave* reported, not a single mill in the county was sawing logs. The next year the lumber industry briefly rebounded, but two years later the Forked Leaf White Oak Lumber Company was unable to meet its payroll of some 350 employees at West Eminence.[11] Shortly thereafter a fire destroyed the company store. West Eminence itself turned into something of a ghost town. By 1928, the most obvious physical reminders of West Eminence's glory days were a few hulking structures of the mill itself. Perhaps ironically appropriate, the county purchased part of the com-

pany's land as a site for the county's new "poor farm." The final
signal of the timber boom era's demise came in 1929 when the
Salem, Winona, and Southern Railroad ripped up its tracks
along Mahans Creek.[12]

Still, albeit on a far smaller scale than the earlier pine harvest, timbering never completely ceased in the Current and Jacks
Fork Rivers' basins. While most of the surviving sawmills were
locally owned, the T. J. Moss Tie and Timber Company head-
quartered in St. Louis became the county's largest holder of
cutover lands upon which stood stands of oak. Into the 1920s,
a few residents on Mahans Creek, as well as elsewhere in the
county, continued hacking ties. A pair of skilled hackers could
hew up to ten ties a day.[13] With a crosscut saw for cutting lengths
of eight feet and six inches and mauls and double bit and broad
axes to square the sides, the ties typically measured six-by-eight-
inches thick.

The work was strenuous, paid poorly, and was dangerous.
My maternal grandfather, Alford Asbury Eddings, sliced off
three of his toes while tie hacking in the fall of 1917. Said to be
fulfilling a ritual of his Native American ancestors, he—perhaps
accompanied by a ceremony—buried his toes near his home, a
sawmill shack that he had built and which he shared with his
wife and children in McHenry Hollow in northern Shannon
County.[14] The Great Depression left "very little market for timber products," but with the repeal of Prohibition in 1933, a few
locals earned precious dollars from the expanded demand for
white oak as staves for the barrels in which bourbon whiskey
was aged.[15]

Though recognized by few at the time, the timber harvest
also contained "hidden" costs. Many years later, in 1977, a local
resident, G. L. Davis, concluded that "the legacy" that "the timber companies left to the people . . . was far more bitter than that
left by the Civil War."[16] Deforestation left behind underbrush
and mounds of pine sash from limbs and treetops. Local farmers sought to increase their grazing acreage in these spaces by
annually burning the woods, an act virtually assuring that the
pine could not reforest itself. In time, more fire-resistant species

of oak, some of which were commercially worthless, such as black jack, replaced much of the acreage laid barren by the disappearance of pine. Likewise, varieties of cheat and broom sedge frequently took over areas of the forest floor once blanketed with the more drought-resistant and nutritious big and little bluestem grasses. Neither were walnuts, hickory nuts, hazelnuts, crabapples, wild grapes, blackberries, and honey from wild bees as plentiful as in the past.

The pine harvest, when combined with the plowing of the hillsides and the hunting and fishing practices of the hollers people, dealt deadly blows to local wildlife. Timbering itself, especially the floating of logs down the Current River in the early years of the twentieth century, damaged the stream as a fish habitat. Laying bare the topsoil by a combination of plowing and deforestation unleashed tons of chert into the creeks and rivers. The quantity of game fish in the Current and Jacks Fork Rivers and Mahans Creek fell, though not due to habitat destruction alone. Residents in Shannon County, as in most other Missouri counties, vigorously resisted enforcement of early twentieth-century state restrictions on hunting and fishing. A few locals even persisted in dynamiting fishing holes and seining the local creeks and rivers.[17] In the 1920s and 1930s the prevailing shortage of cash increased hunting and fishing at the very moment that the feral animal population was declining. In their defense, most of the hollers people saw hunting and fishing as a source of their survival, not simply as sport. In the 1930s record-low rainfalls further set back the wildlife population.

Between 1920 and 1935, according to conservationist advocate Leonard Hall, the quantity of wildlife in the region reached a "low point" in its history.[18] Long before then, the early settlers themselves had wiped out buffalo, elk, bear, and passenger pigeons. By 1914, the *Wave* reported, hunters rarely encountered deer, and in 1920 the state totally closed its season on deer hunting.[19] Early in its history, Shannon County placed a bounty on bobcats and wolves, though it was not until after 1926, when the county paid hunters a whopping eleven-dollar bounty for a wolf, that that animal was finally exterminated. To seize on the opportunities to profit from the munificent bounty, it was "not uncommon," according to the Birch Tree weekly newspaper, "for enterprising farmers to capture a litter of wolf pups, raise them, kill them, and then collect for their scalps."[20] By the 1930s raccoons, at one time found in great abundance, all but disappeared in the Mahans Creek basin. When someone did report having killed one, Donald Pummill remembered, it was "big news."[21] With predators destroyed or dwindling in numbers, rabbit and squirrel populations, on the other hand, may have actually increased. So, apparently, did opossums.[22]

The declining chances of success in hunting and fishing not only deprived the hollers people of food but also dealt a severe blow to one of the most prized leisure activities of men and boys. To be sure, they continued to spend countless hours in the woods and on the creeks and rivers but without bagging as many animals as in the past. No badge of esteem, except perhaps beating someone in a trade, stood higher within their male culture than success in hunting and fishing. I remember that my father (Lowell Rader), a rabid coon hunter, embarrassedly confessed that it was not until the 1940s (and then in another Missouri county) that he had been able to catch and kill his first coon while hunting alone. On the other hand, Lowell, his father (Sam), his uncle (Arthur Pummill), and his first cousin (Dave Pummill) enjoyed more success hunting possums. Indeed, without the earnings from possum pelts in the 1920s and 1930s, they, according to family lore, would have had difficulty in paying their annual property taxes.

✦ ✦ ✦

Neither did farming in the Mahans Creek basin recover the degree of prosperity that it had enjoyed in the early years of the twentieth century. Partly, the decline in returns was due to the collapse of the timber boom; the local demand for foodstuffs fell proportionately to Shannon County's declining population. Corn growing, the single most important index of the basin's economic health, had always been a precarious enterprise. Not only was the creek basin's soil of marginal fertility and highly permeable, but expanding acreage during the timber boom onto the hillsides and up the narrow hollows, along with year after year of planting the same fields, reduced per acre yields from their historic highs. Other threats always lurked in the background. With startling frequency, searing summer temperatures, inadequate rainfall, floods, and armies of chinch bugs destroyed promising crops. A harbinger of the region's declining productivity came as early as 1913 and 1914, when corn yields countywide dipped from a typical average of twenty to thirty bushels to the acre to fifteen and eleven bushels, respectively, for those years. The years of America's participation in the Great War (1917 and 1918) brought a temporary respite, but in the wake of the war, both local yields and prices dropped and remained well below the early twentieth-century figures throughout the 1920s.[23]

Few dreamed that farming on the creek could become even more trying, but it did. Not since the disastrous summer of 1881, old timers remembered, had the weather been worse for corn growing than in 1930. At the very moment that the fledgling stalks needed moisture the most, in June, they received only one inch of rainfall (and that may have been all in one downpour), and in July there was even less than an inch (0.84), both marks a full inch below normal for those months. Countywide yields plummeted to an all-time low of only six bushels per acre, far below that required to meet household needs, let alone those of livestock. Yields for the seasons of 1931, 1932, and 1933 swung back to almost normal, but the next three blistering summers of 1934, 1935, and 1936 saw corn production fall into a trough of only two, fifteen, and six bushels per acre, respectively. Hay yields fared little better.

Despite success in partly offsetting the low rainfall by constructing a primitive irrigation system (including a small dam on the creek), even Sam Rader found himself facing the worst conditions he could ever remember. In one year of the Great Depression, he was almost unable to scrape together enough money to pay his nine dollars of property taxes. Later, simply to make ends meet, he had to borrow money.[24] While it improved, corn and hay productivity continued below normal through the late 1930s and even in the war years of the early 1940s.

✦ ✦ ✦

Not all families on the Mahans Creek waterway suffered equally from the Long Depression. As always, especially vulnerable were the branch-water families who usually lived on forty-acre spreads up the narrow hollows. Many sold out to the Moss Tie and Timber Company, to their better-off neighbors, or, unable to pay their taxes, simply abandoned their farms.[25] In the 1920s more than seven of ten families left Delaware Township. Not since the Civil War decade had there been such a large exodus from the neighborhood. Even though the arrival of new families filled part of the vacuum, the township's total population shrank by 21 percent. During the 1930s, however, with jobs scarce throughout the nation, the township actually gained eight residents. So did the Rader Pummill clan, which by 1940 had added eleven members to the township's rolls. Reflective of the hard times, in the Long Depression young men and women delayed getting married. The birth rate declined, especially in the 1930s, when it plunged from 3.6 to 2.7 children per family.[26]

The leading families who resided mostly along the Mahans Creek bottomland suffered less, albeit none completely escaped the ravages of the Long Depression. During the 1920s and 1930s Ulysses M. and Mary Randolph's extended family continued to hold its place atop or near the top of the neighborhood's social hierarchy; U. M. and his son, Ernest, operated adjacent farms specializing in purebred beef cattle, while U. M.'s daughter, Getty, and son-in-law, Edwin Faust, founded the local store, greenhouse, and post office at Delaware. Together, the value of the families' three houses as self-reported in the 1940 census stood at $3,400, far above that of the Smith brothers ($1,000) and Fred Crider ($800).[27] That the median value of the remaining twenty-four houses in the neighborhood was less than $150 revealed a vivid approximation of the gap in wealth that separated the Randolph family from those at the bottom of the township's social pyramid. That having been said, the Randolphs were not quite as well off as they seemed. Ernest Randolph shared his wealth with a large family of seven members, and by the end of the 1930s the Fausts, finding their greenhouse at Delaware barely if at all profitable, moved it to Willow Springs, Missouri.

During the Long Depression, no family on the creek, including the Randolphs, fared as well as the Smiths, a family comprised of Champ, Champ's wife (Mary), and his older, unmarried brother (Warren). The Smith brothers were related to the Pummill-Rader clan by a common ancestor, Samuel John Matthews of Osage County. The Smith brothers purchased a small farm on the upper reaches of Mahan's Creek in the mid-1910s. Hailed by their neighbors for their exceptional "smartness" and buttressed by an income from Warren, who taught school during the family's early years on the creek at Crescent (Buckhart), the brothers set about acquiring the frequently abandoned forty-acre farms of nearby timber workers and branch-water folk.[28]

Known throughout Shannon County as "progressive" farmers, they eschewed planting large corn crops; indeed, during the drought of 1930, Champ observed that it was cheaper to buy corn from Illinois or northern Missouri than to produce it on the creek. (Perhaps unknown to Champ, this observation offered a key insight into a major cause of the continuation of the declining fortunes in the 1940s and afterwards of the smaller, mostly self-sufficient farms found on Mahans Creek.) They experimented with advice offered by the University of Missouri Extension Service. Accompanied by the local extension agent, farmers from all over the county visited their farm in 1937, observing, in particular, the success of the Smith brothers in rotating Korean lespedeza and oats.[29] Running large herds of cattle and hogs on their own acreage plus hundreds of adjacent acres owned by the Moss Tie Company, the Smiths were, in effect, "open range" farmers. Without children in the household, when needed, they hired extra help. By 1940 they owned 663 acres assessed at $3,885, the highest in the township except for the timberlands owned by the Moss Tie Company.[30]

No family except perhaps Arthur Pummill's was more active in the neighborhood's civic life than the Smiths. They, along with another new family—the Napiers—were bulwarks of the local New Harmony Baptist Church. For many years, Warren served as the chaplain of the Eminence American Legion post, and twice he ran as a candidate in Democratic primaries for Shannon County's representative to the state assembly. On the first occasion he lost by only three votes. Both Champ and Mary repeatedly served as township committeeman and woman on Shannon County's Democratic Central Committee. All three Smiths were equally involved in the movement to promote "scientific" agriculture in the county. For many years, Warren served as chairman of the county's annual soils and crops conference, a meeting at which local farmers were introduced to the latest, most "progressive" developments in farming by agricultural experts.[31]

For elemental survival itself, the remainder of the hollers people relied mostly on their own ingenuity. One ages-old strategy was to hit the migratory trail, sometimes in pursuit of temporary work such as harvesting wheat on the Great Plains or apples in the Pacific Northwest or sometimes in quest of permanent work in equally far-off places. Even with the end of the timber boom, until the 1930s a few locals were lucky enough to find off-the-farm part-time jobs locally, from which, by continuing to produce some of their own foodstuffs, they could survive. Arthur Pummill's family responded to the Long Depression by a complex combination of his wife's hard work, his part-time employment by the county and New Deal farm agencies, and the family's ventures into a more diversified forms of farming. Still others turned to distilling and selling illegal corn whiskey.

✦ CHAPTER 14 ✦

The Folks up in Open Hollow

ON A WINTRY January day in 1926, Brombrey "Bum" Powell, the Shannon County sheriff, finally caught up with James "Uncle Jim" Perkins, who was a son of Lewis and Mary (Rader) Perkins and a bootlegger who lived in a log house up in Open Hollow. Although the specifics are not entirely clear, Bum gave Jim chase down Missouri State Highway 19, a gravel road that ran between Eminence and Winona. Seeking a getaway, Jim suddenly turned his car off the road, came to a quick stop, and scrambled out before Bum arrived on the scene. While reputedly "one of the most fearless officers" in the history of Shannon County, Bum, when he spotted Jim's car, was cautious; after all, he had narrowly escaped death only a few months earlier when trying to arrest another bootlegger. Approaching slowly, Bum spotted Jim climbing a nearby tree.

Bum ordered Jim to come down from the tree and open the trunk of his "jalopy." It was full of moonshine. A few months later a circuit court jury found Jim Perkins guilty of running moonshine. That Jim's young wife had died from influenza three years earlier and had left him with sole care of five young children failed to obtain him any mercy from the court. The circuit court judge sentenced him to three years in the Missouri state penitentiary in Jefferson City. Jim had to make a quick decision

about the care for his five young children. He "farmed" them
out to kinfolk.[1]

As early as July of 1921, in Eminence, according to the
Current Wave, "moonshine whiskey's almost as plentiful as water
around here."[2] Other branch-water folk besides Jim Perkins recognized that the implementation of nationwide prohibition in
1920 opened up new opportunities to earn additional cash from
their meager corn crops. The Bartons became the main moonshining family in Open Hollow. Well regarded by his neighbors,
Milton, the family's patriarch, was active in the Open Hollow
Holiness Church, but his family was desperately poor. The
county sheriff first arrested Milton and two of his sons for operating a still in 1921, but a local jury, sympathetic to the plight
of the Bartons and aware of Milt's good standing among his
neighbors, found them "not guilty."

Almost exactly a year later, the sheriff caught one of Milton's
sons (Verdie) at the site of the family's still; this time the court
fined Milton $100 and Verdie $400. Milt then apparently decided
to stop moonshining, but the arrest may have had the opposite
effect on Verdie, for he subsequently embarked on a lifetime of
crime. With Sheriff Bum Powell and the county attorney, L. N.
"Lem" Searcy, stepping up the enforcement of prohibition in
the county, Verdie seems to have decided that it was safer and
perhaps more profitable to steal than to make and sell moonshine. He soon left the family's Open Hollow farm for other
parts of Shannon County, but he would later serve time in the
state penitentiary for grand larceny, a charge that was brought
against him several times.[3]

The high incidence of moonshining in Open Hollow was not
due solely to the general decline of the local economy or prohibition. Much earlier the families in the hollow had developed a
distinctive subculture.[4] Its very name, "Open," was something
of a misnomer, for, while spacious at its juncture with Mahans
Creek, it was otherwise a long, narrow hollow with steep ridges
on each of its sides. An even narrower hollow, Pin Oak, was a
major tributary. A dry (except with spring rains) creek bed sliced
the hollow floor into tiny patches, only a few of which were big

enough for growing much corn or sorghum. With survival from farming difficult if not impossible, few of the hollow's settlers stayed put for more than a decade or so before they moved on. Still, until the post–World War II era, new settlers frequently took their place.

The branch-water folk living there, especially the men and boys, became known for their "orneriness," a charge that was by no means totally justified. Not only did some of them work as hard as the farmers living on the banks of Mahans Creek, but they also supported their Holiness Church with just as much ardor, indeed perhaps more, than did the creek-bottom folk support their Baptist Church at Delaware. Still, with the conspicuous exception of Arthur Pummill, voters in the township rarely selected a farmer in Open Hollow to serve on the township's school board, as a justice of the peace, as a constable, or as a road overseer. At bottom, both their behavior and their township-wide standing may have been simply a matter of poverty; the Open Hollow farmers lacked the financial resources to command equal respect in the township. But it was also the general reputation of the neighborhood's residents. Too many stories circulated through the township of their male lawlessness, moonshining, drunkenness, proneness to violence, and negligence of family obligations.

✦   ✦   ✦

From the 1880s to the 1940s, two unusually large families, each related in complex ways to the Rader-Pummill clan on Mahans Creek and to each other, not only comprised well over half of Open Hollow's population, but also contributed to the hollow's reputation. The first of these was the Perkins family, headed by Lewis Abraham and Mary (Rader) Perkins. From childhood, Mary, the eldest of Sam Rader's sisters, had been admired for her spunk.

In 1867, at the tender age of fourteen, she defied her family by secretly eloping from her Hart County, Kentucky, home to Illinois with a neighboring man, thirty-year-old Lewis Perkins.

Lewis had a shaky reputation. Having enlisted on the same day and in the same unit as Mary's father, George Washington Rader, during the Civil War, Lewis had subsequently deserted. Captured, rather than shot—the usual punishment for deserters —he was "confined at hard labor with ball & chain attached to [his] leg" for a year.[5] Lewis behaved well enough for the duration of his sentence that he obtained an honorable discharge from the Union army in 1865. He later even received a pension for his Civil War service.

Lewis also seemed to have been considerate of his teenage wife. Upon learning that Mary still liked to play with dolls, he built her a dollhouse. But Mary soon had little time for doll playing. She had her own babies, lots of them. In rapid succession she birthed thirteen children (two of whom died young). Desperately in search of a place where they could at least scrape by, the family moved with unusual frequency: from Kentucky to Illinois, from Illinois to Arkansas, perhaps even from Arkansas to Missouri (before the Raders moved there), back to Kentucky, and finally they accompanied the George Washington Rader family to Missouri in 1878. During the 1880s, they tried to make a go of farming in Wright County, Missouri, but eventually they settled permanently on a sixty-acre farm up Open Hollow.[6]

Sometimes their new farm produced enough corn to feed the family with a little to spare for their hogs and chickens. But cash was always in short supply. To pay for such necessities as salt, condiments, farm machinery, and their taxes, they sold feral animal pelts and some ginseng. By one test, that of reproducing their own kind, they enjoyed an unalloyed success. By 1910, some twenty-five years after their arrival, Lewis and Mary, had thirty-two descendants scattered up and down Open Hollow and into the upper reaches of the Mahans Creek basin. They were mostly offspring of their five daughters, all of whom had married nearby hollers men. All of them, or at least those who remained in the neighborhood, were poor.

So were the seven Perkins sons, though their personal behavior was more suspect than the female side of the family. At least two of them seem to have gotten into trouble as youngsters; on one occasion they were arrested along with two Klepzig boys for damaging a neighbor's watermelon patch. As soon as they reached their late teens or early twenties, at least four of them left the neighborhood—for Kansas, Colorado, Montana, and Louisiana. The boys who remained behind farmed and worked part time in the local timber industry. With the decline in lumbering, Jim Perkins, as we have seen, went into bootlegging; and earlier, in 1913, the state charged another one with felonious assault and later in 1928 with burglary and larceny. One of the grandsons, Harley, had an ear bitten off by an irate husband, who, in a no-holds-barred fight, claimed that Harley had "stolen" his wife. Harley had another dubious distinction; he contributed to the death of former sheriff Bum Powell in 1937. While driving a lumber truck, Harley collided with a pickup driven by Bum's son, Lonnie, east of Eminence. Thrown from the vehicle, Bum died shortly thereafter.[7]

In the meantime, neither did the marriage of Lewis and Mary remain tranquil. Perhaps it had always been tumultuous. In any event, for unknown reasons Lewis successfully sued Mary for divorce in 1903. Presumably, the aging couple soon made up their differences, for they remarried almost precisely a year later. By the time of his death in 1925, "Uncle Lewis," as his neighbors referred to him, had become something of a local institution. The *Current Wave* once hailed him as a splendid representative of the "pioneering spirit" in Shannon County.[8]

Shortly after Lewis's death, "Aunt Mary" shocked the whole county. "MAN 21, MARRIED TO WOMAN, 73," ran a front-page headline in the *Current Wave*'s issue of June 10, 1926. "Elmer Counts," the story continued, while "claiming twenty-one as his age, was married Saturday to Mrs. Mary Perkins of Delaware whose age was given as 73. Mrs. Counts was the widow of Lewis Perkins, late of Delaware, and has many grown children." Because of Lewis's advanced age and ill health, Elmer Counts, a member of a large Shannon County clan of poor hollers people, had for some time served as a hired hand for the day-to-day operations of the Perkins family farm.

Mary's grown children opposed the new union, partly

because they believed that it would require Mary to give up Lewis's Civil War pension. In order to retain the pension but presumably otherwise to live as a married couple, her offspring suggested that she might adopt Elmer as her son! This, she refused to do. She rebutted, "[I] always wanted a young husband [so I] grab[b]ed him." Although the oldest person at her wedding, she afterwards danced away the entire night. "No one," it was reported in family lore, "could keep up with her."[9] Apparently it was a happy union; the couple was later seen "walking down the road all hugged up."[10] Not to be completely outdone by his lively wife, upon the occasion of Mary's death in 1935, Elmer promptly married a fourteen-year-old local girl with whom he eventually had at least two children.

Adding to the Open Hollow Perkins family's negative reputation was the fact that they shared their last name (though they were only distantly related, if at all) with the notorious Perkins gang from nearby Winona and Eminence. Few sessions of the local circuit court went by in the 1920s and 1930s without charges being filed by the state against at least one person with the Perkins surname. As a family enterprise, the gang gained nationwide attention during the Great Depression, when, led by Remus Perkins, they were said to have robbed seven banks in south central Missouri. The gang was finally brought to heel. One of Remus's brothers, Arnett "Web," died in a shootout in a robbery attempt of a tavern in St. Jacobs, Illinois, in 1934; and in a 1935 shootout, the Illinois State Police killed another key member of the gang, William Olin "Bish" Perkins.[11] To this day, many local residents mistakenly presume that the Open Hollow family and the notorious Perkins gang were one and the same family.

✦   ✦   ✦

Although of German rather than Scots Irish origins, the Klepzigs, the second Open Hollow family, acquired a reputation similar to the Perkins family. The family patriarch, Charles Edward Klepzig, born in Leipzig, Germany, in 1839, cut a wide swath through Shannon County's history. From Illinois, he moved to the county in the 1880s and for a time owned the Alley Spring mill and served as postmaster there before he had to sell the mill to pay off creditors during the Panic of 1893. He later built another mill (today a historic landmark) on Rocky Creek, a tributary of Current River near Winona. Perhaps because of the admiration that the hollers people generally extended to German Americans for their industriousness, Charles was said to have been one of the county's most forward-looking farmers—he may have introduced both barbed and woven wire fence to Shannon County. He eventually acquired a substantial farm near Winona, was active in the local Republican Party, and, for his political loyalty, was appointed as Winona's postmaster by President Theodore Roosevelt.[12] Upon his retirement from that position in 1908, the Democratic *Current Wave* generously conceded that, even though "Uncle Charlie" had been a "faithful Republican," he had rendered "good public service."[13]

The positive reputation of the senior Klepzig, however, failed to extend to his offspring, at least not to several of them. A case in point was Thomas, his third son, who in 1888 married one of Sam Rader's sisters, Keziah Rader. Upon the occasion of their marriage, Nancy Jane Rader, Keziah's mother, gifted her daughter twenty acres on the east side of the Open Hollow Creek.[14] While mostly of cultivatable bottomland, the small acreage was not enough to support a rapidly growing family of seven children.

In 1902, apparently unaware of Keziah's latest pregnancy and without prior warning, Thomas deserted his family. "Aunt Kiz," as she was known within the Rader clan, did not seek a divorce, but she was so disgusted with him that she told the 1910 census taker that he was dead. Shortly thereafter she learned that he was, in fact, alive and working as a commercial fisherman in the bayous of southern Louisiana and Texas. Keziah and one of her daughters, Elizabeth, decided to join him. But Keziah did not remain in Thomas's household for long. When she learned that Thomas, who had a fondness for drink, had given Elizabeth a bucket and told her to go to a local bar to have it filled with beer, she was so mad that she and her daughter packed up and backtracked to their Open Hollow farm. Thomas and Keziah apparently never saw one another again.[15] Exactly how Keziah and her large family sustained themselves in the meantime is a matter of conjecture; it is known that her extended Rader family, in particular, her mother, Nancy, who died in 1916, provided her with some aid. From time to time, she also obtained sustenance by joining other households, including her brother Sam's, where upon the death of Ada, she aided him by providing care for his motherless children.

Mysterious circumstances surround the deaths of at least two of the Klepzig brothers. In 1924, Thomas was found dead in Baird's Bayou, Orange County, Texas. According to family lore, he drowned in the bayou with his hands tied behind his back, but an official inquest ruled that he had died from "accidental drownding [sic]."[16] Robert Klepzig, one of Thomas's older brothers, met an equally unusual ending. A bachelor and a one-time justice of the peace, he for many years had lived in a cellar on the "Old Shehee" place up Pin Oak Hollow. He was said to have been "so fat he could hardly keep his eyes open."[17] In 1929 Robert had the dubious distinction of accidentally falling out of his springboard wagon while riding up Open Hollow. A wheel of the vehicle ran over his head, killing him.

Neither did three of the remaining Klepzigs fare well. In 1921, Clarence, the youngest son, was arrested with a fellow resident of Open Hollow (Verdie Barton) for grand larceny. During the Great Depression, Clarence's oldest son, Allan, walked out on his wife and four children—never to be seen again.[18] When the United States entered World War I, according to family lore, Jerry Rader, the uncle of Oliver and Alonzo Klepzig, frightened his nephews with stories about how badly the army mistreated young men. Perhaps they also worried that they would be subjected to abuse because they were the sons of a German immigrant. According to Klepzig family lore, their father, Charles, had come to America in order to avoid the Prussian draft. In any event, shortly after the United States joined the fray in 1917, they fled Shannon County. Oliver renamed himself James Williams and Alonzo adopted the alias of, first, John Roberts and then, later, James Yates.

Under the assumed name of James Yates, Alonzo eventually married and wound up living in a crossroads neighborhood south of Portland, Oregon, where he had five or six children. Not until more than twenty years later did his new family learn of his real name. Sometime after the war, Oliver, who never married and worked in a circus, resumed use of his real name and inherited or purchased Keziah's little farm near the mouth of Open Hollow, adjacent to the farm of Sam Rader. Oliver returned now and then for short visits and regaled kinfolk with tales of outside world. A bachelor, he was generous. He welcomed a series of relatives to live in his small house free of charge, including, briefly, my own family.

None of the Klepzig's had a sadder fate than Thomas and Keziah's youngest daughter, Rose. In 1920, at the age of seventeen, Rose married Frank Melton, also of Open Hollow, and proceeded to birth twelve children over the next twenty-three years. At first in the 1920s the young couple may have tried to scratch out a living on a small Open Hollow farm before moving to a farm in Phelps County near Rolla, Missouri, sometime in the late 1920s. They returned to the Delaware Township in the grim 1930s to farm the "old Shehee" place, once owned by Rose's fat uncle, Robert.

Rose had to contend not only with a dozen children but also with Frank, who had a violent temper and was verbally abusive. In the economic severity of the late 1930s, each Saturday Frank instructed his ragtag children to beg for money on the streets of Eminence. The spectacle so embarrassed Gloria Dene Rader, a sensitive teenager and resident of Eminence (and thereby a "town" girl), that she refused to acknowledge that the Meltons were her cousins. (In 1961, in an argument apparently precipitated by an investigation of forest fires, one of the Melton's sons struck a state conservation agent in the head with the butt of his rifle. Then, in an act later declared by a court to be in self-defense, the agent shot and killed twenty-year-old Melton.)[19]

✦ ✦ ✦

Not all of Keziah's daughters or their children suffered such grim fates. One, Maude, never married, worked her way through college, and taught high school for many years in Enid, Oklahoma. Another, Elizabeth "Lizzie," and her husband, David Harper, became a family of some consequence in the wider Mahans Creek waterway. Lizzie served for many years as Delaware's chief midwife; mounting her horse and riding side saddle, she would "answer the call at any time, night or day," to deliver a baby. Lizzie did far more than assist in delivering babies; she, along with neighboring women, offered emotional support to new mothers.[20] In 1905 Lizzie and David donated three-fourths of an acre of their land to found the local Holiness church, initially called the Church of God of the Evening Light and later the Saints Chapel. It was built on the Open Hollow road across Pin Oak Hollow from the Harper homestead. The church rarely had a settled pastor, but Lizzie frequently preached in the small white hall.[21] In 1913, one of the daughters of David and Elizabeth Harper, Laura Belle, married Raymond "Ray" Perkins, a son of Lewis and Mary Perkins, thus completing another link in Open Hollow's dense and complicated kinship network.

Equally reputable was Mayme Perkins, who married Arthur Pummill. Nobody in the neighborhood worked harder. Referring to her mother's forty-sixth birthday in 1934, her daughter, Thelma, reported to the Pummill-Rader clan: "I declare if she *ain't* a getting younger each day. She walked about 14 miles yesterday before noon."[22] Mayme never seemed to stop working. She birthed and cared for the family's six children, prepared meals, combed the woods for ginseng, planted and harvested the biggest vegetable garden in the neighborhood, sometimes canned up to 150 gallons "of all kinds of grub," transformed feed sacks into colorful smocks and shirts, made soap from scratch, and supervised and did most of the work in tending the family's flock of chickens, guineas, and geese. In the 1910s and 1920s she helped her husband, Arthur, load the wagon and hawk vegetables, roasting ears, and watermelons in West Eminence and Eminence. In the late 1930s, she supplemented the family's income by working part time at Ed Faust's green-

Mayme Perkins and Dona Pummill as teenagers. Notice the "sawmill" house in the background. *Courtesy of Lucille Pummill Orchard.*

house in Delaware.[23] She never complained. A woman of few words, she frequently answered questions with a monosyllable or, on occasion, put everything in proper perspective by saying, "It don't matter none."

Mayme and Arthur were an unlikely pairing. The eleventh child of Lewis and Mary Rader Perkins, Mayme grew up in a huge branch-water family in Open Hollow. Survival rather than ambition was the hallmark of the Perkins family's existence. The fifth child of John and Lydia Pummill, Arthur was, on the other hand, from an ambitious creek-bottom family. In terms of achievement, Arthur himself was no slouch. As a young man, he was said to have been the best baseball pitcher in Shannon County, he was adept at mathematics (as were apparently all of the Pummll siblings), and in the family circle he was credited with having a special knack for "spilling out" the oratory.[24] Having taught when a young man in one-room country schools at Blair's Creek and Delaware, Arthur seemed destined to join his three brothers by becoming a professional educator. But his marriage to Mayme in 1905 at the age of twenty-five and a quick succession of six children born over the next sixteen years set his life on a different course. Unlike all of his brothers, he was to remain in the hollows of Shannon County for the entirety of his life.

In responding to the duress of the Long Depression, the Arthur and Mayme Pummill family embraced both the old and the new. Like other farmers in the hollows, Arthur continued to place a high value on leisure; he never abandoned his love of the traditional male pastimes of hunting and fishing. Neither did his three sons. Simultaneously, except perhaps for the Smith brothers (Warren and Champ), no farmer in the neighborhood was more responsive to new farming strategies than Arthur. He was described by the weekly *Current Wave* as "one of the most progressive farmers in Shannon County."[25] In the 1920s he actively supported Eminence High School's vocational agriculture program and in the following decade was equally committed to the work of the University of Missouri Extension Service. Despite his severely limited financial means, in accordance with their recommendations, he was at the forefront of neighborhood farmers in experimenting with more diversified forms of farming.

✦   ✦   ✦

Even in the midst of the timber boom, Arthur and Mayme teetered on the precipice of abject poverty. For a time early in their marriage, Arthur clerked in the Ozark General Store in Winona, but either he did not earn enough from the job to support a growing family or the family did not like town life. In 1910, Arthur tried his hand at politics. He submitted his name as a Republican candidate for the county clerk, and while he easily carried his home township of Delaware, he fared poorly countywide. Twenty years later he ran as a Republican for the county's recorder of deeds, and again, while crushing his opponent in Delaware Township, he failed countywide.

In the mid-1910s, probably on the occasion of his older brother William's departure for Oklahoma, Arthur and Mayme moved their large family back to the old Pummill farm on Mahans Creek. At this juncture in Arthur's life we have the first concrete hint of the formation of an ad hoc family safety net by the extended Pummill family, one that was to become more pronounced and expansive during the 1930s. Arthur did not own the family's old farmstead. Somehow—the details have not survived—upon the death their mother in 1910, Joe and Lawrence acquired the interests of their siblings in the property. What kind of an arrangement Arthur had with his brothers is uncertain; they probably extended to him some kind of "sweetheart" deal that required a low rental payment, some returns via sharecropping, a combination of these, or, perhaps in especially lean years, no financial obligation at all. At best, they may have hoped, Arthur would generate enough income to pay the farm's property taxes and for its upkeep. In any case, Arthur's family lived in the main house while his younger brother, Elva (who worked in the wagon-hub mill factory in West Eminence until it closed in 1921), and his family lived in the old homestead's log houses.

The survival of the Arthur Pummill family on the creek farm entailed more than the help extended by his brothers—notwithstanding its importance—or Mayme's propensity for hard work. As with other creek families, the Pummills, in one sense, turned to the past; they began to live much as families lived before the advent of the timber boom. They mastered the art of living without—especially without store-bought items. They deferred or denied themselves the purchase of non-necessities and tried to make do by producing more of their own food and clothing.[26] The story is told that in order for one of their sons, Dave, and his first cousin, Lowell Rader, to attend the Fourth of July celebration at Alley Spring in style, the two young men pooled their pennies and bought a new pair of pants to be shared between them. In the morning, Lowell enjoyed the festivities in the new pants, but at noon he went into the nearby woods and exchanged the pants for Dave's tattered overalls. Dressed in new pants, Dave attended the celebration in the afternoon.

While the old Pummill farm was larger and more fertile than

most on the creek, Arthur "was not much of a farmer," remembered James Chilton, his grandson.[27] Indeed, Arthur did not relish spending long hours in the hot, humid weather plowing, putting up hay, or picking corn. Neither did he like milking cows, spreading cow manure, or feeding chickens. His main contribution to the family's welfare came in other ways. His reputation for affability, math skills, and integrity opened up opportunities for non-farm, part-time work not available to his fellow farmers in the creek waterway. One of these was clerking at stores in West Eminence and Eminence, which he did off and on during the Long Depression.

Arthur exhibited a knack for picking up other cash-paying, part-time jobs. For many years, he received about fifty dollars annually from the Shannon County Court to serve as Delaware Township's road overseer. One of his nephews, Jerome Rader, remembers helping him fill potholes with gravel from a horse-drawn wagon.[28] The respect with which he was held countywide (including among Democrats who controlled the county government) was such that when the New Deal arrived in 1933, he received a series of temporary appointments with federal farm agencies. In 1934, he served on the three-man committee that administered the "corn and hog" program of the Agricultural Adjustment Administration (AAA) in Shannon County, and in 1936 he worked part time measuring land for those farmers participating in the programs of the newly created Soil Conservation Service.[29] Well-known as an avowed Republican, his son, Leroy, teased him in the Pummill family newsletter about his employment by New Deal agencies. He let the entire clan know that his dad was "working for Franklin D. [Roosevelt]."[30]

In 1928, by purchasing the rights of heirs, Arthur and Mayme completed the acquisition of the old Perkins family farm up Open Hollow.[31] In terms of bottomland, it was not much of a farm, but, upon moving there in 1930, the couple apparently squeezed out of it about all anyone could have expected and perhaps more. They succeeded in part—or so it appears—from their willingness to abandon the traditional reliance by hollers people on raising corn and hogs. Unlike most of their cohorts, they were receptive to advice tendered by the University of Missouri Extension Service. The service recommended that the local farmers try to become more self-sufficient through greater diversification of their farming operations. This meant putting more acreage into other row crops such as sorghum and growing more chickens and sheep rather than hogs.

Arthur led the neighborhood in planting sorghum, a crop more resistant to drought than corn. To transform sorghum cane into molasses, Arthur purchased and for many years operated a portable mill (powered by a horse or a mule walking in a circle). He converted his own sorghum cane into molasses with the mill, and he did the same for his neighbors. They usually paid him for the service in kind rather than in cash. Moreover, Arthur was at the forefront among neighborhood farmers in planting Korean lespedeza in hayfields and pastures. Though lespedeza was less productive than clovers or alfalfa, it grew better on poor soil and was more resistant to drought. Reflective of perhaps their desperation as well as their respect for modern expertise, the farmers countywide nearly doubled their acreage of lespedeza between 1935 and 1937.[32]

Among the Delaware families, the Pummills pioneered in chicken farming. Resisting the traditional presumption among hollers men that chickens were inferior farm animals and that their care should be relegated to the women folk, as early as 1928 their second son, Howard, raised one hundred white leghorn hens as a vocational agriculture project at Eminence High School. By the mid-1930s the family owned the largest flock (four hundred chicks and forty hens in 1935, for example) and sold the most eggs in the entire county.[33] Arthur apparently took no offense when in 1935 the *Current Wave* described him as a "progressive farmer and a poultryman." Perhaps not incidentally, however, the newspaper on one occasion described the family's flock as "Mayme's hens." Despite her more traditional upbringing, Mayme herself was not averse to the admonitions of those expounding "scientific" agriculture. She was a charter member of the Delaware Homemakers Club, organized in 1935.[34]

In 1935 and 1936, the family participated in a monthly

statewide contest to determine whose flocks produced the most eggs per hen. For the first five months of 1935, the Pummill flock ranked eighth in the state of Missouri. The family, Arthur proudly reported, "cleared $132.48" from egg sales during this five-month period, which was no mean sum for the depression years. Given the drought on the creek in 1936 and the low corn yields, it is unclear how Arthur and Mayme managed to feed their chickens. Still, frequently averaging slightly more than twenty eggs per month, their hens continued to perform near the top of the charts.[35] Apart from eggs, consumption of chickens themselves provided an invaluable food source for the family. They ate the young roosters as fryers, but Mayme was also adept at identifying hens that were falling behind in laying their quota of eggs. Such hens invariably found themselves in the Pummill's Sunday stewpot.

The Pummill family was extraordinarily forward-looking in other respects. Arthur served as the registrar for Shannon County's annual soils and crop conference, beginning with its founding in 1934. It was a meeting in which farmers and agricultural experts met to exchange ideas about the latest advances in agriculture. He was equally active in his support of the county's extension service.[36] Arthur encouraged all three of his daughters—Thela, Thelma, and Maudeline—to attend college in Springfield. His youngest, Maudeline, obtained a degree and became a career primary school teacher. None of his three sons, however, attended college.

Few, if any, of the neighborhood's farm families were as civically engaged as the Arthur Pummill family. Typically like his siblings, Arthur threw himself into neighborhood life at a tender age. He ran (unsuccessfully) for countywide office twice, and Delaware repeatedly elected him to the school board and as a township justice of the peace. Nearly every election year, the county court appointed him as one of the township's two Republican election judges. He promoted better roads; in 1930, he began service on a three-man committee to build a farm-to-market road—State Highway E—from Bartlett through Delaware, a road that eventually connected to improved roads leading to

Alley Spring and Eminence. During World War II, he served on Shannon County's Selective Service Board.[37] Both Arthur and Mayme also fostered a quickening of the associational life of the neighborhood. Apart from their active involvement in the New Harmony Baptist Church, no family hosted more visitors than they did. Rarely a week went by without kinfolk or neighbors visiting their home, especially for Sunday "dinners."

◆　◆　◆

Mayme and Arthur Pummill in about 1940.
Courtesy of Lucille Pummill Orchard.

While Mayme and Arthur were receptive to the advice tendered by modern agricultural experts, few families in the township were more enthusiastic in their support of the old ways of leisure than the Pummills. The family especially enjoyed folk songs and dance. Dave, the oldest son, achieved some local renown for his skills in singing, dancing, square-dance calling, banjo playing, and playing a "washtub base" that he had made himself. In the early 1930s, the county experienced something of a revival in old-time dancing; Arthur himself escorted his youngest daughters to dances, sometimes as far away as Birch Tree.[38]

But, above all else, Arthur and his sons found joy in traipsing through the hills and hollows, hunting and fishing. By the time of his death at the age of ninety in 1997, no single person in Shannon County had spent more time in the woods than Dave, who was also widely acknowledged as the county's most skilled woodsman and thus appropriately went by the nickname of "Crockett." Sharing a skill common to the senior Pummills, Dave, along with his first cousin, Lowell Rader, were also said to be the neighborhood's two best baseball players. They both played on the Delaware Tumblebugs baseball team in the 1930s, a team that competed successfully with nines from the nearby local towns.

And then there was the magic of Mahans Creek. Years later, Thela, the oldest daughter, remembered fondly not only her family regularly catching messes of fish from the creek but also a big swimming hole, at which "the boys built a diving board and also put a rope on a big oak tree that grew on the bank of the creek. We would swing out and dive into the clear, cold water." When the work was done during the summer months, the entire family retreated to the swimming hole. "We'd play follow the leader and other games. My father and mother always entered into our activities."[39]

✦   ✦   ✦

Because deforestation of the yellow pine early in the century and plowing of the hillsides had compromised the capacity of the local area to offer a luscious habitat for swimming, fishing, and hunting, participation by the Pummills in the traditional ways of leisure offered by the creek and the nearby woods was not as easy as it once had been. Still, enthusiasm for one sport, fox hunting (or, perhaps more accurately, chasing), seems to have increased in the wake of the timber boom. For the fox hunter, the greatest joy was found not in killing the fox but in listening to his hounds trail the elusive and cunning animal. Hunters loved to take to the woods in groups, where they regaled one another with commentary on past hunting exploits, the fox's strategy in evading their hounds, and the relative quality (including the voices) of their respective hounds.

In 1929, the local hunters in Delaware formed the Shannon County Foxhunters Association, organized by Arthur Pummill. An estimated crowd of five hundred hunters from several Ozark counties plus one hundred hounds arrived on the weekend of October 17 at the "old Cutts field," also known as the "Sadler farm," a large cleared spot up Open Hollow, about halfway between Eminence and Winona. There, many of the hunters and their families camped in tents. The hounds were put to the test. The first night of the gala affair, Arthur scheduled "three good races," one of which included a pack of his own dogs plus those of his friend Fred Williams.

The second day and night consisted of a medley of races, trials, speeches, and a fiddle-playing contest. The women's horn-blowing contest was so competitive, the *Current Wave* reported, that "the judge of the event, J. W. Miller, just couldn't decide [a single winner] and gave an equal prize to each of the three participants." The first night "a clamor went up for a dancing floor." One was built the next day. Both young and old joined in the frivolities, which extended far into the night. "There was plenty of everything on hand as advertised," the *Current Wave* reported, "and a little more of a certain article, however, no particular unpleasantness was reported." And no foxes perished. While perhaps none quite equaled the excitement of the 1929 meet, the fox hunters continued to hold annual meets through the 1930s and the 1940s.[40]

✦ CHAPTER 15 ✦

Clashing Cultures

SELF-CONFIDENCE CAME SLOWLY for Lowell Leslie Rader. As a youngster, he lacked the derring-do of Elsie, Gilbert, and Velma. Having had the loving care of their mother, Ada, before her untimely death in 1913, the older siblings had developed a confidence and a boldness that eluded Lowell. Shyness nearly paralyzed him. He was so reluctant to face the challenges of school that Sam permitted him to stay home until he was eight years old. Finally, in 1915, he joined his brother, Hub, in the first grade at Delaware. Hub also may have contributed to Lowell's insecurity. Both talking and learning came easily for his younger brother.[1]

Still, while missing many class sessions from sickness, Lowell did well enough at Delaware to obtain admission into Eminence High School in 1922. According to his recollection, high school course work was difficult, though he did exhibit exceptional skills in playing basketball. For example, on December 20, 1923, he emerged as something of a local hero in a game against Birch Tree, a team to which Eminence had lost the previous two games. "The shot that really won the game was a field goal by Lowell Rader from near the center [of the court?]," reported the *Current* Wave. "Rader was everywhere during the last half after having been a little slow in warming up during the first."[2] Yet success on the hardwoods at the Eminence Opera House was not enough to keep Lowell in school. At the end of his freshman year, he quit.[3] Apart from helping Sam on the farm, from time to time he worked for the Rhinehart family on their Spring Valley ranch.

Lowell was always something of a workaholic. Not only did he see work as morally efficacious, but he also seized upon physical toil to compensate for other feelings of inadequacy and in hopes of fulfilling his material ambitions. His work ethic followed more the Pummill-Matthews side of the family than it did his Childress-Rader ancestors. But, of course, a propensity for exhausting work guaranteed him nothing. Lowell came of age in a most unpromising time and place. He could expect little or no assistance from Sam, who was experiencing difficulties of his own in supporting himself and his four youngest children. Gilbert and Dene Rader's visit from Arizona to the home place in 1924 may have been the immediate catalyst for Lowell making a momentous decision. He decided to leave Mahans Creek. In seeking his fortunes outside the Ozarks, he adopted a strategy that was particularly popular among young hollers men in the 1920s.

✦ ✦ ✦

Leaving the familiarity of Mahans Creek for northern Arizona represented a daring move for Lowell. The mountains, the deserts, toiling by the clock, and living in town—all of these were alien to him. But perhaps Lowell gained some confidence from finding himself in a strange place and among strange people; he now had an opportunity to reinvent himself. Somehow, perhaps through the intercession of Gilbert, he obtained a job as an apprentice electrician. He may have for a time worked as an electrician's helper in the silver and copper mines in and around Flagstaff, Arizona. What is known with certainty is that in 1928 he was employed as an "electrician" by the Vyne Brothers Electric Company in Prescott, Arizona.[4]

Perched more than a mile above sea level, Prescott was a wide-open mining town of slightly more than five thousand inhabitants.

Old-stock Americans lived there, but so did recent immigrants from southern and eastern Europe, Native Americans, Chinese Americans, and Mexican Americans. Catholics equaled or outnumbered Protestants, and men outnumbered women. Along notorious Whiskey Row in downtown Prescott, saloons openly flaunted national prohibition. Prostitution flourished. During the 1920s, movie stars Tom Mix, the King of the Cowboys, and Tony, his Wonder Horse, lived in Prescott. When not acting in films, Mix hung out in the Palace Saloon on Whiskey Row.

For a year or two Lowell lived in a room or an apartment in the 100 block of North Granite Street. Nearby, upon the corner of Granite and Gurley, stood a saloon, which included on the second floor accommodations for "ladies of the evening." Many years later, Lowell told me that, while doing electrical work in one of Prescott's brothels, he encountered prostitutes for the first time. To his surprise, he remembered, they did not seem to be as different from other women as he had expected. My guess is that it was somewhere in Prescott that he first sampled alcoholic beverages. But, given his character, I doubt that he sampled the sexual wares of the city's red-light district.[5]

He did, however, meet a dark-haired exotic—from his perspective—beauty, Rose Contreras, who clerked at the local F. W. Woolworth store. Perhaps Lowell simply wandered into the store and began talking to her, or he may have met her at the boardinghouse on North Granite Street, where both of them lived, or perhaps his sister-in-law, Dene, who had earlier been employed in her own sister's nearby photography studio, already knew Rose and introduced her to Lowell. Or it could be that Lowell became acquainted with Rose through her father, Francisco "Frank" Contreras, or an uncle, Jose "Joe" Contreras, both of whom at one time or the other worked in the building trades in Prescott.[6] All three could have been employed simultaneously at the same construction site, for the building of the swanky Hassayampa Inn in downtown Prescott. Lowell, now twenty-one years of age and who, insofar as is known, had never before had a serious relationship with a member of the opposite sex, was probably at once smitten by eighteen-year-old Rose.

The couple was a bundle of opposites: Lowell was fair skinned, blue eyed, with light brown hair, five feet ten, Protestant, and of Northern European ancestry, while Rose was a Mexican American, dark eyed, with coal-black hair, petite, and a Roman Catholic. She was from a far more expressive and celebratory family culture than Lowell. Yet their differences can be exaggerated. The Contreras family had, to a large degree, assimilated into the dominant Anglo culture of Prescott. All members of the family appear to have been fluent in English. Indeed, Rose's older brother, Frank Jr., was employed as an English translator at Prescott's Yavapai County Court House.

On August 9, 1928, Rose and Lowell married in a Catholic ceremony conducted by Father Victor Marin at the rectory of the Sacred Heart Church. Curiously, the official witnesses of the ceremony were Robert and Laura Aitken rather than Gilbert and Dene Rader or any members of the large Contreras family. Robert was a reporter with a local newspaper. One would have expected that the Contreras family would have hosted a huge party with dancing and drinking after the wedding, though there is no evidence that they did so. Perhaps they had reservations about the marriage, or it could be that, given his background, Lowell squelched any such plans. Still, during the first year or so of their marriage, the couple lived on North Granite Street in the same apartment house as Rose's immediate family, an arrangement suggesting Lowell's basic acceptance into the extended Contreras family.

✦   ✦   ✦

Exactly what prompted the Rader brothers, their spouses, and their sister Audrey (who had been caring for Gib's two children), to leave Prescott in January of 1930 is not known with certainty. True, the stock market had crashed in October of 1929, but evidence that it was a precursor to the protracted depression of the 1930s was not yet manifest. Declining silver prices and a depressed local economy might have driven them from Arizona; both brothers could have lost their jobs in late 1929. More likely, however, it was the pull of their homeland. That same year they learned that Arthur and Mayme Pummill had left the family's home place to take up farming on the old Perkins place that they had recently acquired in Open Hollow. Apparently, Joe and Lawrence Pummill then offered Gib and Lowell the opportunity to rent or sharecrop jointly the old Pummill farm vacated by Arthur and Mayme.[7]

Just as Lowell must have been surprised with what he experienced in Prescott, Rose must have been equally shocked by what she encountered on Mahans Creek. Unlike the high mountain area around Prescott, the Mahans Creek waterway was humid and sylvan. Rose was a town girl who was suddenly thrust into the countryside, where people lived apart and were surrounded by the sights and sounds of nature. The men and women spoke slowly, quietly, and with a droll sense of humor. Although invariably courteous, they were extraordinarily suspicious of new arrivals, even those with whom they shared ethnic and religious origins. Except for Rose herself, no other Mexican American or practicing Catholic lived in the Delaware Township or perhaps the entirety of Shannon County.

Nonetheless, on the surface at least, Rose slipped into the mainstream of local society, including that of both Mahans Creek and Eminence, with remarkable ease.[8] Partly, it was a matter of her personality. Friendly and easy-going, she entranced Arch Pummill, a fourteen-year-old cousin of Lowell's who was visiting the creek neighborhood from Pittsburg, Kansas. She was "a nice person and exceptionally good looking," he remembered. While canning fruit, she once sent Arch and Merle to the Faust country store in Delaware to buy additional lids; but on their way back, upon encountering a baseball game in progress at the schoolhouse, the boys forgot their mission. Though embarrassed when they finally arrived at Sam's house with the lids, Arch remembered that Rose smiled and forgave them. She even acquiesced to an incalculably important family and neighborhood convention (along with Lowell) by agreeing to be baptized (by complete immersion) into the New Harmony Baptist Church in Delaware.[9]

But nothing probably contributed as much to Rose's acceptance into the family and the neighborhood as her friendship with her sister-in-law, Dene Rader. Being a "new woman" and a "town" girl, Dene herself was viewed with some suspicion by the local people, but she was extraordinarily gracious and genteel and had a forceful personality. And, in terms of her own acceptance, she enjoyed the advantage of being Gib's wife. Gib had long been an exceptionally popular figure among his kinfolk, in the creek neighborhood, and with people living in and around Eminence. If not at once, shortly after his arrival he' became active in the local Masonic lodge. The young couple must have had some money when they arrived in Missouri—from Gib's World War I disability pension and perhaps some savings they had accumulated in Arizona. In any case, they immediately plunged into the local social scene.

Only a few months after their arrival, on April 25, 1930, on the picturesque old Pummill Farm, they "royally entertained" the junior and senior high school classes of Eminence. To everyone's amazement, they even hired an airplane and a pilot to take those guests willing to risk life and limb up for "thrilling rides" over the creek. Apart from the high school students, those known to be present at the event included Rose and Lowell Rader, Joe and Atlanta Pummill, Audrey Rader, and Rawland Rhinehart (son of Elsie).[10]

At the center of Dene's small, semi-exclusive social network were about ten women who had formed the N.T.W., a literary and social club in Eminence. The club's acronym stood for "nobility, truth, and wisdom"; but for those envious women not invited to join it, according to one source, the acronym more accurately stood for "nasty talking women." Described in the *Current Wave* as a "clever hostess," Dene was soon leading the programs of the N.T.W. She also embraced the local mania for playing contract bridge. She welcomed Rose into her new social circle; indeed, Rose appears to have been a regular member of the N.T.W. and to have attended at least a half dozen of its meetings, though no surviving evidence indicates that Rose herself ever hosted the club (after all, living in Delaware made attendance there by Eminence women difficult) or led a discussion.[11]

✦ ✦ ✦

In the meantime, Lowell and Gib could have hardly chosen a worse time for returning to the farm. In the summer of 1930, the creek bottom received less than two inches of rain in June and July, two months critical to a successful corn crop. In late July, Gib and Lowell joined a neighbor, Al Honeycutt, in damming Mahans Creek.[12] At best, the irrigation project was a limited success. Able to create only a small reservoir for holding water and handicapped by an inadequate pumping system (a pump powered by a car engine), they were able to irrigate only four or five acres of corn as well as a garden and a watermelon patch.

Countywide, corn yields plummeted to an all-time low of only six bushels per acre. That winter the Red Cross reported that there was "dire suffering in Shannon County. Most of the calls for help are from localities where timber works were the order of the day some months ago, but are now down and out, however, there are requests [for assistance] from practically every portion of the county."[13] That summer, two young men from the Pummill-Rader clan, Dave Pummill and Merle Rader, sought to supplement the incomes of their families by finding temporary work in the Kansas wheat harvest. By October 1930, the coffers of the county's Red Cross chapter were almost empty.[14] In desperation, many families turned to kinfolk.

Economic prospects for the neighborhood improved in 1931. It rained and then rained some more. That spring Rose became pregnant. Neighborhood life seemed to quicken; the weekly "Delaware Items" in the *Current Wave* indicated that an unusual number of families visited one another, mostly after services at New Harmony Baptist Church. Particularly active were the family of Arthur and Mayme Pummill and Lowell and Rose Rader. The highlight of the summer came in late August, when Lawrence Pummill and his family from Springfield and Jim and Beckie Rader from Barton County, Missouri, spent a week visiting relatives on the creek; they made their headquarters at the old Pummill farm with Rose and Lowell.[15] Later on, on Saturday, December 6, 1931, Dene and Velma hosted a tea party and shower for Rose in Eminence. "Mrs. Rader received many practical and lovely gifts from friends, some coming from persons not present. . . . A number of games and contests [followed] in which everyone participated."[16] Attendees included women from the leading families in both Winona and Eminence.

Joy and then tragedy soon followed. Rose successfully delivered a baby boy, Lawrence Lowell Jr., on Christmas Eve 1931, but only thirteen days later the infant died from "acute bronchitis." Whether Rose fell into a postpartum depression is unknown; possibly, she then began to consider returning to the more familiar surroundings of northern Arizona. If she did, it was *not* manifested immediately in her behavior. Less than two months after the loss of her baby, she accepted an invitation from Dene to attend a meeting of the N.T.W. club.[17]

Likewise, she appears to have enthusiastically participated in Delaware's Society of Very Common Farmers, founded in the winter-spring of 1932 by Hub Rader. Meeting weekly on Friday nights, this social organization of young men and women in the neighborhood devoted itself to making its membership "less common" and providing "entertainment" for "the community of Delaware." In a "hilarious meeting" on March 11, Lowell and Rose served as medical doctors who took X-rays of Tom Chilton's brain in a mock trial to determine his guilt or innocence on charges of stealing hogs. The X-rays revealed that Tom had a less than fully developed brain; hence, the jury found him innocent. At the same meeting the society elected Rose as its new president![18]

Because the *Current Wave* temporarily stopped carrying its weekly column of Delaware news, the sequence of events that followed is difficult to reconstruct. Between September 8, 1932, and August 31, 1933—nearly a year—references to Rose failed to appear a single time in any of Shannon County's three weekly newspapers. Apparently, in December of 1932, she decided to return for a visit to Arizona, though it could have been that she left sometime after early September.[19] In any case, the January 4, 1933, edition of *The Passerby*, the Pummill family's newsletter, queried: "Lowell, how's batching? Gib tells us your wife is visiting in Arizona." The next month, *The Passerby* reported that Rose was still in Arizona.

Perhaps based on a letter that he received from her, sometime in 1933 Lowell apparently learned that Rose did not intend to return to Shannon County. In late August 1933, he sued her for divorce on the grounds of desertion; the circuit court ruled in his favor.[20] Curiously, in September, after they had purchased a new Plymouth automobile, Gib, Dene, and their two children, along with Hub, toured the Rocky Mountain West and stopped at Prescott. Dene met one-on-one with Rose.[21] No one knows the details of their conversation. The consensus of opinion in the Rader-Pummill family seems to be justified: in the end, the disparity between the couple's respective cultures was a larger burden than their marriage could sustain.

✦ ✦ ✦

Lowell's female kinfolk wasted little time in proposing candidates for Rose's replacement. His sister, Velma Rader Loyd of Winona, had a prospect in mind, one of her friends, Wilma Davis, a no-nonsense schoolteacher. But Wilma squelched the idea. She was reluctant, according to family lore, to marry a divorced man. However, shortly thereafter, in 1935, she did, in fact, marry one of Sam Rader's boys, Hulbert.[22] Another suggestion came from Beulah Powell Rader, who had recently married Merle, the youngest of Sam's sons. She advanced the candidacy of her cousin, Lydia Eddings. Lydia was a soft-spoken, eighteen-year-old farm girl from the Ink neighborhood of northern Shannon County. While attending high school in Eminence, she had been a member of the Bum Powell household, and, upon her graduation in the spring of 1933, she had dreamt of becoming a one-room rural schoolteacher. But a surplus of teachers occasioned by the Great Depression dashed her hopes. She had to settle for a menial job in an Eminence hotel.[23]

Rebounding from his divorce and introduced by his sister-in-law, Lowell at once seized on the opportunity to court the comely lass from the end of the dirt road in McHenry Hollow. As he approached the Eddings farmstead in a shay pulled by a white horse, he cut a dashing figure. The entire hollow, according to the memory of Lydia's sisters, echoed with his yodeling and crooning of a song, "My Lydia," that he had composed for his new sweetheart. According to family lore, possibly fortified by couple of swallows of home brew, he proposed marriage on their first date. In any case, they did marry on May 30, 1934.

✦   ✦   ✦

In some respects, the Eddings family was quite similar to the Rader-Pummill family. Lydia's ancestors were mainly of English and Scots Irish origins. Upon arrival on American shores in the eighteenth century, they had sought to improve their fortunes by frequently moving from one part of the Upland South to another. But, unlike the Raders, Native Americans, according to unverifiable family lore, figured in the paternal side of Lydia's family history.[24] Her great grandfather, William Caswell "Flying Cloud" Eddings, allegedly a Cherokee, married Edna Moody, who was said to have been either a "full-blooded Cherokee" or a Creek. Both Moody and Caswell appear to have been born in North Carolina. According to the 1850 census, neither of them could read nor write.[25]

On their way to Indian Territory, according to family lore, they stopped because of a "serious illness" in the rugged hills and hollows of southern Wright County, Missouri, in a place that resembled their ancestral home. There, according to the census of 1850, Caswell's household of eleven members squatted upon or rented a farm that consisted of thirty "improved" acres and eleven "unimproved" acres. At best, survival of such a large family on the tiny farm must have been an extraordinary feat. The Eddings family had eleven milk cows—an unusually large number for their time and place—the cash value of their livestock in 1850 was $296, and they produced five hundred bushels of corn. In the late 1850s Caswell and part of his family abandoned Wright County for Sevier County, Arkansas. There, according to family lore, a white man beat Caswell to death.[26] Members of his family subsequently drifted into Texas, Oklahoma, Kansas, and back into Missouri.

Among several family members who remained behind in the

Lydia and Lowell Rader, wedding photograph, 1934. *Courtesy of the author.*

Missouri Ozarks was one of Caswell's sons, Alford Asberry
Eddings. He died in 1884, before Lydia's father by the same
name was born in Summersville, Texas County, Missouri.
Without a natural father but with a Euro-American mother,
during childhood, "Raz," as Lydia's father was known, lived
in several households, including those of kinfolk in Wellington,
Kansas, and in Okmulgee, Oklahoma. The latter was a center of the Creek Nation. How long he stayed in these places is
unknown. When about thirteen, Raz quarreled with his mother's
new husband and was thrown out of the household. He then
joined the family of his mother's sister, Martha Ramsey Shelton,

on a farm near Birch Tree, Missouri. From his uncle Charles Shelton, in the early twentieth century, Raz learned the skills of a timber worker. Toiling in the woods north of the Jacks Fork River, he encountered the Burke George family; he may, in fact, have worked seasonally on the George farm. In any case, in 1910 twenty-four-year-old Raz married fifteen-year-old Madie Florence George.

Contrary to the romanticized notions of several of his descendants, Native American ways appear to have had virtually no influence on Raz. Childhood photographs suggest that, despite the modesty of his financial means, Raz lived in the midst of all-Anglo family groupings during his childhood and adolescence; and these families also had middle-class, Euro-American aspirations. Indeed, at no time in his life, insofar as it is known, did Raz exhibit any indisputably Native American traits. He knew no Cherokee words, ate no distinctively native foods, never adopted any aspects of native dress, and never sought to live in Indian Territory, nor was he known to have practiced any forms of native religion. Indeed, according to family lore, he insisted that his own children attend Christian religious services.

He appears to have publicly avoided asserting his claims to native ancestry. While on at least two occasions Eddings family members filed lawsuits in the late nineteenth and early twentieth century to recover money they believed was owed to them from Cherokee land settlements in North Carolina and Georgia, Raz did not join in these endeavors. Confronted with the fact that the Caswell "Flying Cloud" Eddings family had stopped in Missouri rather than proceeding on to Oklahoma and the Eddings family had never officially enrolled in the Cherokee Nation, both of their lawsuits failed.

Still, Raz's children believed that his Native American ancestry deeply influenced his beliefs and behaviors. It was from his Indian heritage, they said, that Raz gained his extensive knowledge of the medicinal value of roots and herbs. His Ink neighbors frequently called on him to minister to their sick. It was from his ancestors that Raz learned how to deliver babies, including his own children. When he was about to aid his wife in a new delivery, he instructed the remainder of their children to leave. He then hung the kitchen table "oil cloth" on the clothesline outside their house. When the birth had been completed, he took down the cloth and the children returned. It was from his Indian forebears, the family believed, that Raz arrived at the conclusion that one of his daughters, Iva, had, in effect, murdered her twin sister by denying her food while in the womb. Iva was therefore a "witch," and hence he refused to let her be baptized. It was from his native ancestors, the family thought, that he accepted a wide set of "superstitions" and adamantly rejected such notions as a heliocentric universe. Yet most of Raz's odd beliefs and behaviors were similar to, if not always identical with, those of many Euro-Americans living in the Ozarks.[27]

Raz Eddings's idiosyncrasies aside, he represented only one influence on Lydia. Her mother, Madie Florence George, who was a hollers woman through and through, was another. At the time of her marriage to Raz, the George family had lived in the hollows of northern Shannon County for more than a half century and were part of a family network that owned farms extending down Spring Valley from Ink to Round Spring on the Current River. While Lydia had an older brother, also named Alford Asberry Eddings, she was the oldest of ten sisters. At a tender age, she assumed adult responsibilities. And then there was poverty. The Eddings family were quintessentially branch-water folk. They resided in a sawmill house designed and built by Raz himself, alongside a hollow fed by a dry-water stream. The house contained only three substantially sized rooms—a bedroom for Raz and Florence, a bedroom for Alford, and a room with bunk beds for the ten girls.

When the Great Depression struck, the Eddings family could no longer make the loan payments on their 160-acre farm. So, in 1935, they allowed the farm to relapse to creditors and sold all their livestock and farm machinery at public auction. The following year, they rented a truck and a driver to move the family and their household belongings to a wheat farm owned by one of Raz's nephews near Wellington, Kansas. Until 1942, they rented this farm.[28]

In a letter to her granddaughter in 1973, Lydia vividly described some of her childhood experiences while living in McHenry Hollow. She aided in rearing her younger siblings, she explained, but she also did "outside work like milking cows—working in the fields & gardens. . . . One farm chore was either riding or walking after milk cows. And really hunting them in the wood pastures. . . . But it was more fun than washing dishes or cooking.—However, I did some of that too." Unlike her siblings and most hollers girls, Lydia "liked to read books."[29] The Eddings family owned no books except perhaps a Bible and an almanac, but Lydia did have access to a better-off neighbor's library. She remembered reading fifteen or twenty of Zane Grey's novels, but her favorite author was Gene Stratton Porter. From Porter, she chose the middle name of her oldest son, "Gene," and her third son, "Stratton." From these romantic writers, she also nurtured a lifelong sense of adventure, one that included travel to exotic places.

✦   ✦   ✦

In terms of economic prospects, conditions in 1934 could not have been worse for Lydia and Lowell. July, the third full month of their marriage, was the hottest on record. For ten consecutive days the temperature soared above 100 degrees, and on July 24 it reached 109, the highest ever recorded for Shannon County.[30] "If you can survive a drowth [sic] like that, you can make a living on a sand rock," Sam Rader wryly observed in the October issue of the Pummill-Rader newsletter.[31] The corn stalks shriveled up and died, leaving behind a countywide average of only two bushels to the acre. It was just as well that Lowell had not planted much corn that year, for he received a small payment in 1934 from the New Deal's Agricultural Adjustment Act (1933) for reducing the size of his corn planting that season from 20 to 3.2 acres.[32]

Desperate for a source of livelihood, that fall Lowell joined the Civilian Conservation Corps while Lydia and Thelma Pummill, Lowell's cousin, were, as the family newsletter put it, "batching or old-maiding [it] in Winona," where Thelma was employed in the local relief office. After working four months on a project south of Winona and with Lydia pregnant, he left the corps in early 1935. Sam, Lowell, and Hub then appear to have concocted a scheme that they hoped would establish their financial solvencies while simultaneously launching both brothers into careers as self-sufficient farmers. In the spring of 1935, Sam applied for and eventually received a $1,500 loan from the St. Louis Federal Land Bank, financed by the New Deal's Farm Credit Administration. Later in 1935, Lowell borrowed $500 to purchase a seventy-eight-acre farm up Mahans Creek that had once been owned by one of the Mahans.[33]

Taking up life on the new farm represented something of a throwback in time and place for both newlyweds. Few farms on the creek were more physically isolated; travel to and from the farm required using a recently abandoned county road that followed the course of the creek or crossing the steep ridge separating the creek hollow from Open Hollow on an equally primitive road. Travel by horseback or wagon or walking to and from the Delaware schoolhouse required nearly two hours. No neighbor's house was within eyesight. The log house itself was one of only a handful of its kind that remained in the Delaware Township. Made of pine logs, it had only two rooms—a small kitchen with storage space and a single room for sleeping and living quarters. At first, it had no well. Lydia had to lug water from a nearby branch that dumped into Mahans Creek.

The isolation was difficult, especially for Lydia, who had come from a large, lively family and had recently resided in the town of Eminence while attending high school. Within three years she found herself the mother of two boys (born in 1935 and 1936), further trapping her into countless hours of loneliness. Lowell may have had little understanding of her plight, for he loved few things more than to while away his time by toiling long hours alone on the farm. But, unlike his new wife, in order to pick up mail and purchase necessities, he made weekly trips by horseback to the general store and post office at Delaware or to Eminence and thereby enjoyed a more active social intercourse with neighbors and kinfolk than she did. After 1935, all of her immediate relatives lived in faraway Kansas, while Lowell's father and one of his brothers lived only a half mile away. Their relationship was for the most part harmonious, but not always. Despite his far more limited experience with child rearing, Lowell insisted on imposing a rigorous regimen of feeding, toilet training, and sleeping on the couple's infants. When crying ensued, Lowell, unlike Lydia, opposed picking up and comforting the infants, and the incessant colic of their firstborn child (me) made early, married life difficult for both parents.[34]

More than Lydia, Lowell engaged in the creek's neighborhood life. In the summertime he continued to exhibit his superior athletic talents with the Delaware Tumblebugs baseball team (as a pitcher and shortstop), which played its games against nearby West Eminence, Eminence, Birch Tree, and Winona nines. When they could, both Lowell and Lydia attended the local Baptist church, though with young children this was not an easy matter for Lydia. In 1934, Lowell served as a delegate to the Shannon County Baptist Convention. Probably at the behest of his nearby neighbors and kinfolk—the Smith family—he twice (in 1936 and 1938) agreed to present himself as a candidate (and was elected) Delaware Township's representative to Shannon County's Democratic Central Committee.[35]

✦ ✦ ✦

The times continued to be hard, incredibly hard. Low rainfall and high temperatures continued to plague the farmers in the hollows. Average corn yields remained in a trough, even until 1944 and 1945, when they reached a modest twenty-one and twenty bushels to the acre, respectively.[36] Lowell desperately sought to grow more corn by putting to the plow a few acres of new ground on the hillside behind the family home, but the backbreaking chore of preparing the soil, planting, and cultivating between the tree stumps and rocks brought only a modest increase in total yields. There was only enough pasture and

Ben Rader and his
cousin Gloria Dene
Rader, about 1938.
Note the log house of
the Lowell and Lydia
Rader family in the
rear of the photograph.
Courtesy of the author.

hay to support a few cows; the few chickens and hogs that they
owned had to scramble for survival mostly on their own from the
mast in the "open range" of the adjacent woods owned by the
T. J. Moss Tie Company. But it was the hogs and the chickens
more than any other part of their farming operation that kept
starvation at bay. Elementary comfort was difficult. In the summers, day after day of sweltering, blisteringly high temperatures
made sleep all but impossible.

The details of how they avoided utter ruin will never be fully
known. Kinfolk provided a large part of the answer. By on occasion paying Lowell a dollar a day to work on their adjacent farm,
the better-off Smith brothers (Warren and Champ, and Champ's
wife, Mary) helped out. Other kinfolk provided temporary work:
Uncle Arthur Pummill, to build a barn, Uncle Joe Pummill, for
work on a new rural estate, and his brother Gib Rader, for work
on a road from the Pummill farm to Highway E. While Lowell and
Lydia rarely produced a surplus, Gib and Dene purchased some
butter and eggs from them. Some aid came from Sam, Lowell's
father. Straitened circumstances drove the family to abandon

the creek in 1939 to live on the Eddings farm near Wellington, Kansas, while Lowell worked as an electrician in nearby Winfield, Kansas. In the fall of 1939, the family moved again—to Carmi, Illinois, where Lowell joined his younger brother, Merle, working in the nearby oil fields. In July of 1940, the family returned to the creek.[37]

Economic conditions for the Lydia and Lowell family improved slightly during the war years of the 1940s. But the drought hung on and Lowell simply did not have enough good acreage or the resources required for purchasing fertilizer to take full advantage of rising farm prices. The birth of two more boys (in 1942 and 1943) finally brought an end to the family's existence in the Mahans Creek basin. To supplement the family's cash-stressed position, Lowell first tried to join the US Navy, even though he was thirty-six years old. Because of a heart murmur, he failed the physical; the murmur led him to believe (mistakenly) thereafter that he would die young.

Even though he had only briefly done electrical work during the previous fifteen years, he decided to again try his hand—first on his own in the nearby small town of Thayer in Oregon County, where he may have concluded that the coming of rural electrification in the region would open up opportunities for additional electrical work. Apparently, the venture in Thayer failed, for in 1944 he found employment as an electrician in the somewhat larger town of West Plains, Missouri.[38] In the late summer of 1944, he moved his entire family to a small farm six miles northeast of West Plains. Working as an electrician for Neathery Radio and Electric, in 1948 he bought a 132-acre farm in the same neighborhood and in 1953 sold his Shannon County farm to his brother Merle.

✦   ✦   ✦

On a personal endnote, for several years—in a sense, permanently—my younger brother Mike and I mourned the family's departure from the creek. There were no springs, no fresh-water creeks, no steep hollows in the red-clay country around West

Plains. Even though we were only some forty miles away, the terrain and (we thought) culture was so different from Mahans Creek that we could not conceive of it as our true homeland. We found few experiences as exciting as returning on weekends to the creek, where we played with our first cousins Jerome and Max Rader. For hours on end we rambled over the steep hills and through the woods and waded and swam in the creek. As the years passed, we returned far less frequently but perhaps idealized the creek even more. Much later, as a senior citizen, I on occasion dreamed, as in the past, of having lived on the creek or, curiously, returning there to live. Upon awakening, I sensed a profound loss.

◆ CHAPTER 16 ◆

When the Tribe Came Together

ON JULY 1–3, 1932, all eight of the offspring of John and Lydia Pummill came together for what they called a "tribal reunion." They did not meet at the old Pummill farm on Mahans Creek, where they had shared their childhoods. Instead, they gathered at Beckie and Jim Rader's farm near the tiny town of Nashville in southwestern Missouri near the Kansas border. Including spouses and children, the "bunking party," as one family wag described it, included some forty Pummill kinfolk. They could hardly have chosen a worse time for a reunion. It was in the midst of the Great Depression. Not everyone came. Conspicuously absent was Sam Rader, the widowed husband of their deceased sister (Ada), and his family. For them it was at least partly a matter of money. "Of course the trip and other expenses cost some [members of the tribe] . . . considerable," Everett Pummill confessed, "but what is the value of a few dollars compared to the lasting good that comes from such an occasion."[1]

While not everyone may have shared Everett's opinion, those attending the reunion did have fun. Jim Rader, the male host, was nothing if not entertaining. Seizing on a break in the drought that had gripped the nation's midlands, he swelled with pride when he showed off his cornfield to his male kinfolk. In the meantime, the womenfolk, led by Jim's wife, Beckie, swatted away pesky flies and prepared meals of homegrown food, which they set out on long tables. Later on, the senior Pummill siblings, assisted by a few of their spouses, challenged the younger generation to a baseball game. Not surprisingly, given their superior playing skills, the oldsters defeated the youngsters. At the end of the three-day festivity, the family voted unanimously to make the reunion an annual affair.[2]

While there had been many earlier gatherings of the Pummill siblings and their families, this reunion triggered a new era in the family's history. Despite or perhaps partly because the depression loomed in the background, the family set about strengthening family bonds. They developed more opportunities for face-to-face encounters, for recollections of the family's shared history, and for family members to re-experience their ties to their ancestral home on Mahans Creek. At the forefront of the movement were Joe, Lawrence, and Everett, the three brothers who had become professional educators. Shortly after the reunion of 1932, Everett took charge of and began editing the family's new monthly newsletter, *The Passerby*, which was published almost continuously until early 1939. Each subsequent year until 1939, Joe and Lawrence, the joint owners of the old Pummill farm, welcomed everybody to gather there in August for the family reunion. The same two brothers did even more to keep the extended family intact. In the trying 1930s, they created, in effect, an ad hoc, informal safety net for their less fortunate kinfolk.

✦ ✦ ✦

In the 1910s and continuing into the 1920s and 1930s, the senior Pummill siblings and their families had scattered—into northeastern Oklahoma, southeastern Kansas, and across southern Missouri. By 1932 Arthur Pummill and Sam Rader were the only family members of their generation who remained in the Mahans Creek neighborhood. In 1932, Joe had returned to Shannon County to become Winona's superintendent of schools, Lawrence continued to teach mathematics at the normal school in Springfield, and Everett served as superintendent of schools in Eureka, Missouri. To the west near the Kansas border was the "Pittsburg Gang," consisting of the Beckie and Jim Rader family at Nashville, Missouri, and, across the border in Pittsburg, Kansas, the Elva Pummill family. Jim farmed, while Elva was employed as a machinist with the McNally Pittsburg Manufacturing Company. Also in Pittsburg was Dona (Pummill) Glaser, the youngest sister. Her husband, Verne, was a carpenter and house painter. Finally, there was William, the oldest sibling, who, when physically able, labored in the oil fields around Kiefer, Oklahoma.

Despite their spatial separation, the senior Pummills kept in touch with one another. As lovers of words, they regularly exchanged letters, though, alas, few copies survive today. During the summers and other holidays, when they enjoyed free time from their teaching schedules, Joe and Lawrence frequently loaded up their families and traveled by car to visit one or more of their siblings. Above all else, the old Pummill place continued to lure kinfolk back to Mahans Creek. Almost every year, twenty or more family members routinely rendezvoused at the ancestral farm for Christmas dinners. For the dinners, Lawrence made his quest for killing a wild turkey an annual rite.[3]

The sustenance of family bonds revolved around Lawrence more than anyone else. He, along with his exceptionally generous wife, Crystal, and (later) their two daughters, regularly spent part of summer and Christmas vacations on the family farm. Lawrence loved returning to the place where he grew up. "I think we should just sell out and move back to Mahans Creek," his wife smiled and said more than once.[4] But it was the Lawrence Pummill family home in Springfield that developed into a remarkable way station for Pummill kinfolk. Lawrence and Crystal always left their doors open to family members. When traveling through or shopping in Springfield, countless relatives stayed overnight. Upon one occasion, the graduation ceremonies for Everett in the summer of 1921, eighteen relatives stayed the night at their small house on Fremont Street. Others lodged for days at a time with the Pummills while receiving advanced medical treatment unavailable in their hometowns.

Still others, mainly about a half-dozen of Lawrence's nieces and nephews, moved in with the Pummills for varying periods of time while they attended the normal school in Springfield.[5]

✦ ✦ ✦

In late 1931 or early 1932, Lawrence and Joe seized on an opportunity to transform a gently sloping hillside on the old Pummill farm into a campground while simultaneously helping Sam Rader's boys, Gib and Lowell—both just back from Arizona—cope with the trials of the Great Depression. They may have commissioned their nephews to do most of the work in exchange for use of the farm. In any event, under the direction of Gib, Lowell, Lawrence, and Arch Pummill (another nephew) began work on the project in the spring of 1932 and finished it that summer. It was located in a grove of oaks above the spring where the Pummills had kept their milk and butter; they cleared the grounds of underbrush, erected a rail fence around the plot, and built "an excellent cabin" and a "two holer *Chick Sales* in the back." The cabin's main room was fifty by thirty-five feet with a fireplace on one side and a long, screened-in porch across the front of the other side. It also included a kitchen and a storage room. Scattered around the grounds were picnic tables, camping sites, and some playground equipment. At the close of each summer term as well as several Thanksgivings and Christmases, Lawrence and his family loaded up their car with supplies and headed for the cabin.[6] Living in nearby Winona, Joe, in particular, used the cabin for entertaining non-family friends on weekends.

During the next six years, the grounds and the cabin became the site of the family's annual reunions. The women and children usually slept on the main floor while the men slept on the porch, nearby outdoors, or, sometimes, in tents. While things were not highly organized, a specific family member was usually put in charge of each major task: food preparation, cleaning up, and entertainment.[7] Typically a large, gala affair with fifty or more kinfolk present, the reunion offered an opportunity to engage in a nostalgic ritual of reconnecting to the singular place in which the senior Pummills had lived as children and numerous occasions for the renewal of personal relationships among relatives otherwise separated by time and space, but it also reinforced among those present the family's oral history. The senior Pummills were nothing if not story tellers. They regaled one another and their juniors with humorous tales of their childhoods.

Apart from eating—especially enjoyed was fried chicken and Sam Rader's watermelons—organized activities included contests in horseshoe pitching, marble playing, bridge, and, more often than not, a baseball game. Everett complained that Jim Rader was the champion "fudger" in marbles, though his brother, Sam, according to Everett, also appeared sometimes to take advantage of the loosely enforced rules. The 1936 reunion even scheduled a contest for the prettiest baby in the family. Judiciously, the selection committee decided to offer first prize to all five of the babies who were present, one of whom happened to be not-so-pretty me.

Jollity reached a crescendo in the evenings, when the family gathered in the great room, pushing aside chairs, tables, and bunk beds. They were treated to an exhibition of Joe Pummill's monumental memory when he recited, in a rolling cadence, William Cullen Bryant's long and mordant poem "Thanatopsis." They sang, together and individually. Everyone went silent when Sam Rader, accompanied by his trusty fiddle, sang a medley of old Kentucky folk ballads. The next generation joined the fun. Dave Pummill played the base tub, a homemade instrument with a single string, and Hub Rader played the French horn or the banjo. And they danced. With Sam at the fiddle, square dancing was a favorite. As a child, Gloria Dene (Rader) Fry fondly remembered years later, her uncles who, especially Lowell, taught her how to square and jig dance.

Perhaps the most unusual and effective means of nurturing family bonds was the monthly newsletter. At the beginning of each month, each member of the family was encouraged to write a letter to "The Gang" or "The Tribe," as they described themselves, in care of Everett Pummill. Rather than transcribing the letters literally, Everett edited and paraphrased their contents and, as often as not, added amusing comments of his own. Trivia, ranging from the health of a family dog to weather, dominated the pages of *The Passerby*. But the newsletter also included "hard" news of family unemployment, sickness, and heartbreak. On a few occasions, family members shared views about the current state of affairs.

Humor occupied a conspicuous place in *The Passerby*. Both sexes engaged in good-natured gender sparring. Wives reported instances of their husbands' idiosyncrasies, while husbands less rarely informed the newsletters of the equally bizarre behavior of their wives. One or more of the Pummill brothers—all Republicans except perhaps Elva—chided the Rader side of the family for their loyalty to the Democratic Party. On one occasion, Sam Rader shot back that, though the Democrats may not have been successful in their efforts to restore prosperity, at least now (in the wake of the election of Democratic candidate Franklin D. Roosevelt in 1932) it was legal to drink beer. Doubtlessly, upon reading this retort, Pummills and Raders alike smiled and chuckled. For Sam was a well-known teetotaler. If Everett was unable to fill the single-spaced two pages of the mimeographed newsletter from the letters of family members, he sometimes added his own recollection of an event in the family's history. That its readers prized these vignettes more than any other content in *The Passerby* suggests the importance of a shared history in promoting family togetherness.

✦   ✦   ✦

In the background of efforts to build a stronger, extended family always lurked the Great Depression. It projected in sharp relief the growing disparities in wealth and income among families within the Pummill tribe. On the one side were those with essentially depression-proof jobs; these included not only Joe, Lawrence, and Everett Pummill, but also Gilbert Rader, who received a federal government disability pension, albeit a small one, and J. Talmage "Tal" Loyd (husband of Velma Rader), who, beginning in 1934, enjoyed a patronage appointment as

Winona's postmaster. With consumer prices falling faster than their incomes in the 1930s, at least two members of this group—Joe and Lawrence—probably experienced an actual improvement in their standard of living. They routinely purchased new cars and took extended travel vacations to both coasts of the United States.[8]

On the other side the income divide was the remainder of the Pummill tribe. They all struggled. This included Everett, who was confronted with the debilitating sickness of his wife, the costs of rearing three children, and even delays on occasion in receiving his paycheck from the Eureka School District.[9] He apparently had to borrow money to survive the depression. Neither did the Pittsburg gang do well. This included Elva, who went without work for weeks on end and was never fully employed as a machinist. Indicative of Elva's hardship and that of the Jim Rader family was the absence of the entire Pittsburg gang except Elva's son, Arch, at the 1936 reunion.[10] In the creek neighborhood, Arthur and his brother-in-law Sam likewise barely managed to withstand the brunt of the depression. As they frequently put it, since nearly everyone else in the neighborhood was "poor," they were not fully conscious of how bad off they were themselves.

The better off helped out the less fortunate tribal members. While the details can never be fully recovered, enough survive to indicate that upon learning of the plight of particular family members, they frequently arranged to offer some kind of assistance. For instance, in 1932 the Loyd family invited JoyDell Rhinehart, their niece from the financially strapped Elsie Rhinehart family, to join their family and attend high school in Winona. Later on, after Elsie's divorce from Cordell in 1939, their son, Sammy, went to live with his grandfather, Sam Rader. In obtaining work, if only temporary and poorly paid, family influence, as Thelma Pummill explained in *The Passerby*, could be of the utmost importance. Receiving an appointment as the chief investigator of poverty in Shannon County in 1934 for the Civil Works Administration, Thelma herself appears to have been the beneficiary of an intercession by her aunt, Atlanta Pummill.[11]

The existence of old Pummill farm itself helped shield several family members from the worst of the depression. Not only did Arthur Pummill and his family live and farm there in the late 1910s and in the 1920s, but both Gib and Lowell Rader and their families did the same in the early 1930s. In 1937 and 1938, so did the most financially strapped family of all, that of Frank and Rosa (Klepzig) Melton. Beginning with the construction of the cabin and campground on the farm, Joe and Lawrence Pummill offered Gib and Lowell Rader other forms of work. In 1941, for example, Gib supervised and helped build Joe and Atlanta their new home south of Eminence, and Lowell worked several months on improving the grounds.[12]

While theoretically opposed to relief from the federal government's New Deal agencies, the Pummill family found it difficult to draw a firm distinction between what it considered legitimate and illegitimate governmental activity. For example, Elva Pummill vetoed a proposal that his son Arch join the Civilian Conservation Corps. On the other hand, Sam Rader, heir of a Jacksonian Democratic tradition, apparently raised no objection when his son Lowell joined the corps. Furthermore, as noted earlier, Arthur Pummill accepted several temporary administrative appointments from New Deal farm agencies. And as hostile as they were in principle to such agencies as the Civil Works Administration and the Works Progress Administration, Everett Pummill welcomed their assistance in the construction of a new high school building in Eureka, and Lawrence Pummill apparently raised no objections to the Federal Emergency Relief Administration and the National Youth Administration providing financial aid to students attending the normal school in Springfield.[13]

Still, the depression and the New Deal brought about almost no changes in the Pummill tribe's political affiliations. Apparently, all of the senior Pummills, with the possible exception of Elva, remained loyal to the Republican Party of their ancestors. (However, in the post–World War II era, Arthur's granddaughter, Lucille (Pummill) Orchard, became a Democrat and, as Shannon County's first female elected official, served thirty years (1968–1998) as the county's circuit clerk and recorder of deeds.) The Raders had never been quite as firm in their commitment to the Democratic Party as the Pummills had been to the Republican Party. Unorthodox as always, Jim Rader voted for Norman Thomas, the Socialist Party's candidate for president in 1932. In the late 1930s and early 1940s, both Lowell and Hub Rader revealed at least their nominal affiliation to the Democratic Party by serving locally as committeemen and election judges.[14]

✦ ✦ ✦

The year of 1939 represented something of a turning point in the Pummill tribe's history. After a long illness, Jim Rader, a family favorite, died. Before the year was out, lightning set fire and burned down both the home of Arthur and Mayme Pummill and the big house built in 1909 on the old Pummill farm. In 1940, fire also consumed the home of Tal and Velma Rader Loyd in Winona.[15] But the key event in unraveling the close ties within the Pummill family was the unexpected death of Everett Pummill on June 5, 1939. Without prior warning, except bouts of high blood pressure, the fifty-two-year-old Eureka, Missouri, school superintendent passed away from a massive heart attack when chasing a cat away from a bird's nest in his front yard. At his funeral, attended by several hundred people in the Eureka High School auditorium, his siblings talked about the extended family's future.

To keep tribal bonds intact, they agreed, they had to find a way to continue publication of *The Passerby*. Lawrence eventually acquiesced to overtures that he try his hand at preparing and distributing the newsletter, but he knew it would be a heavy burden and told family members that, under his direction, it would come out far less frequently than it had when Everett had been in charge. For reasons not entirely clear, Lawrence got out only a single issue (in June of 1939). In the wake of Everett's death, no one felt like calling for a family reunion in 1939. That same summer Joe and Lawrence leased the family farm to a non-family member, thereby reducing the likelihood of scheduling a future reunion there. In 1942, the farm was sold. It had been in the Pummill family for forty-nine years.[16] The sale signaled the end of an era.

There were other indicators of the shrinking presence of the Rader-Pummill clan in the Mahans Creek neighborhood. Jerry Rader, an older brother of Sam, related to the Pummills only by virtue of marriage, passed away from acute indigestion in 1940. The war years opened up jobs elsewhere for the creek's residents. Lowell Rader moved his family to adjacent Howell County in 1944. Sam's youngest son, Merle, and his family had moved first to Illinois in 1938 to work in the oilfields and then to San Francisco in 1941to work in the shipyards. At the end of the war, only Hub, of Sam's children, remained on the creek. During the war years, Arthur and Mayme Pummill moved from their Open Hollow farm to Alley Spring, where Arthur accepted an appointment as caretaker of the state park there. In 1946, Arthur's son, Dave, who had been tending the Open Hollow farm, also purchased and moved to a farm on the Jacks Fork River.

EPILOGUE

"The Creek Has Changed a Lot since Then"

SOME FIFTY YEARS after the epic feat of Sam Rader and Arthur Pummill in gigging fish in Mahans Creek, on an equally warm day in 1975, three of Sam's sons—Gilbert, Hulbert, and Merle—along with Roy Lahmeyer, Dave Pummill, and Oscar Harper, embarked on a walking tour of their boyhood haunts. Only Hub Rader and Roy Lahmeyer still lived on the creek, and they were no longer youngsters. Lahmeyer, the toddler in the group, was fifty-five, and Oscar Harper, the oldest, was eighty-two years old. The creek had "changed a lot since then," remembered Harper. Their inspection brought back childhood memories of swimming and fishing, but the old-timers also noticed that the creek carried far less water than it had in the past. Choked with gravel, the once-deep holes—the Creager, the Blue, the Long, the Pummill, and the Rowlett—were "no longer worthy" of their names, Harper concluded.[1] Many of the springs that had once fed the creek with cold, clear water had shrunk to a mere trickle or dried up altogether. No longer did a huge pilgrimage of spawning yellow suckers annually make its way up the creek. Mahans Creek had lost a measure of its magic.

If the old-timers looked carefully, which they no doubt did, they would have observed other changes in the creek's basin.

Towering sycamores no longer provided a canopy over the creek, nor did saplings and underbrush crowd its banks. Beaver that had been restocked by the Missouri Conservation Service and bulldozers that had been deployed by the nearby farmers not only had removed much of the vegetation along creek's banks but also had, in some cases, altered and straightened its historic course. With perhaps an exception or two, the old-timers in 1975 would *not* have seen any nearby fields of corn stalks peeking through the ground, nor would they have seen family milk cows chewing their cuds. Neither would they have seen any newly planted watermelon patches. When the old-timers gathered at Hub Rader's place for dinner, a noontime meal that Hub himself prepared, perhaps they also talked about how the ages-old sources of livelihood of the neighborhood had given way to new ones. Likewise, they may have discussed how family and neighborhood ways had changed in the years since they had been barefooted boys in their bibbed overalls carrying their fishing poles or their gigs down to the creek.

✦   ✦   ✦

As a firsthand witness to these changes, no one was better equipped than my uncle, Hulbert Rader. Next to the youngest of Sam's children, Hub was exceptionally perceptive and quick-witted; his sister Audrey once exclaimed that he had "the gift of gab" and was "a lot smarter" than she was.[2] Other family members concurred with her assessment. Like his older brother Lowell and younger brother Merle, Hub had no real memories of his mother, Ada (Pummill) Rader. Still, he received motherly affection from one of Sam's live-in housekeepers and, especially, from Audrey. Unlike Lowell, he found schoolwork easy, and it surprised no one that upon graduation from high school in 1927 he taught school for a couple of years at Pine Hollow and one year at Delaware.[3]

But Hub disliked teaching. And, even more startlingly, unlike his ancestors, neither did he like to hunt or fish. He barely found farm chores tolerable. In other key respects, however, he resembled his father and his Childress ancestors. Like them, he loved his physical and cultural habitat, its seasons, its relaxed pace of life, its neighborliness, and its family ways. Unlike his siblings, the lure of good jobs and of new experiences elsewhere never appealed to him much. Audrey once wrote that Hub would be perfectly satisfied to "live in his cave."[4] Except for about a year during World War II, when he temporarily operated a forest fire tower south of Bartlett, he remained on the creek for his entire life.

He stayed on the creek for other reasons. With the arrival of the Great Depression in the 1930s, jobs were scarce everywhere; and after completing high school in 1927, it was less of a hassle for him to remain on the farm and to help his father, Sam. As the sole permanent sibling in Sam's household, Hub may have also felt bound by a filial obligation to remain at home until he married Wilma Davis in 1935. He then reached an agreement with Sam by which he eventually obtained ownership of about half of the original Rader farm, including the house that had been built in 1896. Sam erected himself a small bungalow across the creek about a quarter mile away, near the mouth of Open Hollow.

Hub's wife, Wilma, adapted to creek life easily. While she had attended the Springfield normal school for two years (1928–1929), had taught at Winona and in a one-room school at Bartlett, and had been active in the Winona social circle of Velma (Rader) Loyd, she had grown up on a Shannon County farm near Montier.[5] Upon her marriage to Hub, she took charge of an ad hoc, multipurpose strategy that permitted the Rader family (she gave birth to sons in 1937 and 1938 and twins, a boy and girl, in 1943) to survive the Great Depression, World War II, and the early postwar years. Like the Arthur Pummill family, she and her family mastered the art of doing without, that is, without store-bought items. This meant planting an unusually large garden, canning dozens of quarts of green beans, tomatoes, wild blackberries, and peaches, making clothing from feed sacks, and, above all else, raising chickens. Her family consumed eggs, fryers, and aging hens, and they also regularly exchanged some eggs, along with cream, in Birch Tree for cash. As in the

Hulbert Rader and sons in about 1940. Note the Sam Rader house, built in 1896, in the background. *Courtesy of Jerome Rader.*

past, Max Rader, the second son, remembered many years later, "There was always work to be done when one lived on a little creek bottom farm along Mahans Creek during the 1940s and 1950s."[6]

The Hub Rader family was representative of other, larger changes in the creek waterway's economy. While initially continuing to raise corn and turn a few hogs into the woods to forage on mast, Hub began to speculate in nearby timber land that was being auctioned off by the county in exchange for delinquent taxes. Upon the sale of more than one hundred hogs in 1949 for a sum that "fell short of making us rich," he explained in a family round-robin letter, he turned away from his practice of running hogs on the open range.[7] An even more important turning point in the family's economy came in 1951 when Wilma returned to teaching. The family now had a regular and reliable source of cash income. The following year, Hub sold a substantial amount of timber rights; with the proceeds, he bought additional beef cattle. In his fields he, along with other creek farmers, began to replace Korean lespedeza with fescue.

Unknown to Hub and Wilma at the time, the centuries-long dependence on corn and hogs by the Raders and their neighbors was about to come to an abrupt end. Beginning in the Great Depression and continuing after the war, American farming itself experienced a great transformation. New technology, hybrid seeds, fertilizers, and federal farm policies—while often well intentioned—disproportionately benefitted the larger farmers on better acreages in the Upper Midwest. Soaring productivity on these farms drove down the price of corn and dealt devastating blows to the smaller, more traditionally self-sufficient farmers in the Ozarks. Each year in the 1940s Shannon County's farmers had routinely planted more than 5,000 acres of corn; partly driven by a severe drought (1952–1954), by 1969 the figure had plummeted to 477 acres! Partly because of the closing of the open range in the 1960s, the total number of hogs in the county fell in almost equal numbers. In the same era, Delaware Township's population also began shrinking—from 177 persons in 1940 to 112 in 1960.[8]

Of those who remained in the township, the Hub Rader family was only one of many whose daily routines shifted from their farms to the nearby towns of Birch Tree, Winona, and Eminence. All three hosted small factories that employed mostly local women. With a twinkle in his eye and his ubiquitous pipe in his hand, Hub liked to explain this geographic and gender reorientation of work with a story. When anyone asked him what he did for a living, he responded, "I'm a Go-Getter. When my wife goes to town to work, I go get her."[9] Even Hub toiled briefly—less than a year—as a maintenance man at the Angelica Uniform Factory in Eminence. Along with jobs in town and income from grass-fed cattle, more and more of the creek's residents came to depend on Social Security payments and retirement income that they were likely to have earned elsewhere.

✦   ✦   ✦

At first, these startling changes seemed to have left the neighborhood's social fabric mostly intact. In the immediate years after World War II, the continuing presence on the creek of old-time families—the Raders, the Randolphs, the Pummills, the Harpers, the Smiths, and the Lahmeyers—served as a reminder of Delaware's historic identity. In the wake of the war, the neighborhood scheduled a "big supper" for twelve of its returning veterans. As beneficiaries of subsides and training in scientific agriculture provided by the GI Bill of Rights Act (1944), a few of them, including Roy Lahmeyer, took up farming, married, and began to have children. In the late 1940s the County Extension Service organized a 4-H Club at Delaware, though it had only a handful of members and lasted only a few years.[10]

While the schools at Crescent and Pine Hollow had closed in the late 1930s, Delaware's one-room school remained open after the war, and, as in the past, locals gathered at the schoolhouse to attend pie suppers, to vote, and to watch the children exhibit their academic achievements. In 1956, however, this all-important contributor to a shared neighborhood life ended when countywide consolidation closed the school. With the closure of the school, "we lost the focal and social point of our community," observed Thela (Pummill) Winterbottom, a former student and teacher at Delaware.[11] As in the instance of working wives, thereafter the arrival and departure of the yellow school bus signaled yet another example of the fundamental shift in the neighborhood's life from the countryside to the nearby towns.

In the postwar years, organized religion continued, though in fits of starts and stops. Under the auspices of the Smith family, Sunday school services and occasional preaching resumed at the New Harmony Baptist Church at Delaware, but not for long. With the church house leaning precariously to one side and propped up by oak poles, Sam Rader's funeral in 1950 was the last service held there. The following year, aided by the American Sunday School Union, John J. Allen and his family from Michigan began holding regular services in the schoolhouse. Allen's little group became the nucleus of what officially became the Delaware Baptist Bible Church in 1957.[12] As a fundamentalist sect not affiliated with the more mainstream Southern Baptist Convention, the church failed to recruit most of those families who had formerly been members of the New Harmony Church. Families such as Hub Rader's began attending services in Eminence or Birch Tree. Irregular church services continued in the schoolhouse until the late 1980s, when the church finally expired.

A long-term trend was unmistakable. In the end, efforts to retain and to restore the traditional neighborhood failed. Within two years, in 1949 and 1950, neighborhood pioneers Sam Rader, U. M. Randolph, and Julius Lahmeyer died, while in 1949 Dave and Lizzie Harper retired to Birch Tree, where their son Oscar built them a new house. That fewer farmers spent as much time in their fields or in their barns and that fewer women could be found during the day doing chores in their homes meant that neighbors dropped in on one another less frequently than in the past. They had fewer opportunities to share experiences and discuss matters of common concern. Only ten persons in the township bothered to vote in the off-year election of 1950.[13] Fewer young people than ever before remained in the neighborhood; many went away to college and eventually took jobs elsewhere. For example, all four of Hub and Wilma Rader's offspring did so. As with the nation's population as a whole, television—introduced in the late 1950s—began to occupy more and more of the spare time of the waterway's residents. Neither did the neighborhood remain unaffected by the more recent media revolution. Today, nearly everyone owns a cell phone and desk or laptop computers can be found in a majority of the township's households.

The departure of the timber boom in the 1910s, the Long Depression, and the unraveling of the creek neighborhood's social fabric encouraged tendencies to look backward. Visions of a more purposeful and coherent past grew in popularity.[14] Perhaps nothing more graphically reflected the growing nostalgia for the old days than the publication (irregularly) by the *Current Wave* of the *Shannon County Historical Review* (later renamed the *Ozarker*). In issue after issue, local old-timers offered wistful accounts of life in the hollows during earlier times. Even despite the county's meager population, the journal managed to continue publication from 1964 through 1981. More than a few of the residents began to see the hollows as a "sure nuff" hillbilly haven and to behave accordingly. Hub Rader liked to tell the story of how he "put on" the popular radio comedians Fibber McGhee and Molly at his mailbox in 1946. They stopped their car. "Excuse us," Molly said. "Where can we find a real hillbilly?" Hub responded, "You're lookin' at one right now!" More seriously, a longtime resident of Eminence wrote in 1950 that the locals should take pride in being called hillbillies by "furiners." Hillbillies, he explained, were especially "good people"; they were humble, pious, sociable, and had "plenty of common sense," virtues that he implicitly suggested were lacking among Americans elsewhere.[15]

Insistence on the uniqueness of the local way of life became a standard argument of those opposed (probably a majority) to the establishment of a corridor by the federal government along the Current and Jacks Fork Rivers that became known as the Ozark National Scenic Riverways, though it affected the Mahans Creek neighborhood only indirectly. Exempting the land along the rivers from future private development, the project required that the farmers owning such land sell it to the federal government. "Outsiders don't understand," explained Leroy Lewis, the physical education teacher at Eminence High School, to a *Saturday Evening Post* reporter in 1961. "We have what you might call a special culture here. You can call us hillbillies if you want, but we enjoy it. Put a park in here, and it will tear our way of life to pieces."[16]

Local entertainment entrepreneurs enjoyed some success in capitalizing on the region's physical ruggedness and its allegedly unique folk culture. Fishing and float trips by canoe and kayak in the local rivers remained popular. For a time, each year Eminence hosted two musical festivals and an arts and crafts show. By far the most popular venues of entertainment in the area today are the cross-country trail rides that attract several thousand horseback riders annually. Still, visitors to these events pale beside the mammoth numbers posted by the tourist industry in Branson, Missouri. Indeed, the popularity of camping at Alley Spring and by the nearby rivers has actually declined in recent years. Between 1972 and 2014, park attendance fell in half. Likewise, local music festivals have shrunk in popularity.[17]

✦   ✦   ✦

Still, the creek and its past linger. As of 2015, not a single stop-light, chain motel, or nationally franchised fast-food outlet existed in the entirety of Shannon County. These facts alone helped to buffer the creek's residents, especially the old-timers, from modern America's jolting quest for wealth and conquest. So do memories. Not only do each of the crooks and crannies of the local terrain have their names, but so do each of the long-abandoned farms. The continuing presence of a few flat rocks, perhaps a collapsing hole of a former root cellar or outdoor toilet, and the persistence of day lilies remind the old-timers that a Perkins or a Rader family once lived there. Given the importance of names, it came as something of a shock to old-timers when they encountered signs posted on the local roads by the Missouri Department of Conservation designating much of the Mahans Creek waterway and its surrounding area as the Rocky Creek Conservation Area. "Where is Rocky Creek," they queried? That the Conservation Service named a small picnic area off State Highway 19 between Eminence and Winona as "Mahan" offered the old-timers only a small consolation.[18] But neither were they happy that the state had acquired not only the former T. J. Moss Tie and Timber Company timber lands, but also hundreds of additional acres in the Delaware Township. Even had there been an increase in the numbers of those seeking to live in the waterway, they would have found far fewer acres than in the past available for setting up new households.

The neighborhood continued to serve as a nexus, albeit a tenuous one, for Rader-Pummill clan members who lived elsewhere. In particular, from the late 1940s to the early 1960s the descendants of Mayme and Arthur Pummill liked nothing better than to return for visits at the old Perkins place in Open Hollow. Up to Sam Rader's death in 1950, his offspring also frequented their old home place on Mahans Creek. Gilbert and his family lived only a few miles away in Eminence; and until the 1950s Lowell and his family, while residing in an adjacent county, routinely came back to the creek for visits. Sensing the area's magnetism and its role in preserving family ties, the extended family, led by Wayne and Gerrie Rader, began to schedule an annual reunion in the 1970s at their Railtree Campground on Highway E near Alley Spring. Eventually, Gloria Dene Rader Fry, daughter of Gib and Dene, became the chief instigator and organizer of the affair, which continues to be held at Alley Spring to this day.

For those no longer driven by a desire to reinvent themselves outside the neighborhood, the hills, the creeks, the woods, and the dilatory nature of life in the hollows continue to offer comfort. Nothing confirms the abiding power of the waterway as much as the inclination of former residents to choose the old neighborhood as a place for retirement. Four aging grandchildren, plus a widow of a grandchild of Sam Rader and Arthur Pummill, took up residency there in the second decade of the twenty-first century. Among the retirees was also a non-relative but offspring of an old Shannon County family, Tom Akers. A former school principal, college professor, and astronaut—a veteran of four space flights—today he leads trail rides in the Jacks Fork River area.

That Tom Akers is a quintessential example of a hollers man who has one foot in the modern world and another in the past throws into sharp relief the major conclusions of this book. While the uniqueness of the Mahans Creek physical habitat did shape in ways both small and large the customs, beliefs, and behaviors of its people, the history of the neighborhood is a complicated one. Most of the Rader family tended to hang on as long as they could to the more leisurely ways of their ancestors, while the Pummills embraced a work ethic similar to that attributed to the Yankees of the North. Neither did the Mahans Creek neighborhood ever consist solely or even mainly of autonomous, isolated, individual families. The families always had some connections to the outside world (especially via trade), but they also related to one another within the neighborhood itself. They shared a folk culture, visited one another frequently, nourished kinship ties, socialized at the rural one-room schools, and eventually worshipped together at the New Harmony Baptist Church at Delaware or the Saints Chapel in Open Hollow. Neither did families on Mahans Creek basin fully evade the effects on their lives of the Civil War, the arrival of the railroad and the timber boom, the protracted economic depression of the 1920s and 1930s, or the more recent revolution in information technology.

In sum, the cultural history of the hollers people of Mahans Creek is both exceptional and unexceptional. On the one hand, as Sam Rader explained in a note to his kinfolk in 1933, he and the other hollers residents were a "backwoods" people.[19] Put another way, much of their behavior was the product of a special physical and cultural habitat. On the other hand, remember that Sam named his favorite coon dog Caruso. Even Sam Rader would be the first to acknowledge that, in key respects, the Mahans Creek's neighborhood and its family histories had much in common with the experience of rural people everywhere.

NOTES

Preface ✦ My Journey into Ozarks History

1. *The Passerby*, Jan. 4, 1933, a mimeographed family newsletter, in my possession.

2. *Current Wave* (Eminence, MO), Aug. 27, 1931. For a mostly anecdotal history of an Ozarks family, see Tate C. Page, *The Voices of Moccasin Creek* (Point Lookout, MO: School of the Ozarks Press, 1972).

3. Russell Gerlach, in his *Immigrants in the Ozarks: A Study in Ethnic Geography* (Columbia: University of Missouri Press, 1976), pioneered in mapping the origins and migratory routes of Ozarks immigrants from other parts of the Upland South. Most of them, he found, came from Tennessee and Kentucky. See also Russell Gerlach, "The Ozark Scotch-Irish: The Subconscious Persistence of Ethnic Culture," *P.A.S.T.*, *Pioneer American Society Transactions* 7 (1984): 53–54. For the importance of Scots Irish ethnicity to a specific place, see also Robert Flanders, "The Kith and Kin of Caledonia," *Ozarks Watch* 5 (Spring 1992): 24–31. Grady McWhinney, in his *Cracker Culture: Celtic Ways in the Old South* (Tuscaloosa: University of Alabama Press, 1988), contended that ethnic variants of British culture, in particular, those of Celtic origins, shaped the folkways of the Old South, while David Hackett Fischer, in his *Albion's Seed: Four British Folkways in America* (New York: Oxford University Press, 1989), forcefully argued that the "Borderlands British," especially the Scots Irish, passed on their folkways to the American "backcountry," where they continue to shape beliefs and behaviors to this day. See also a less contentious study, James G. Leyburn, *The Scotch-Irish: A Social History* (Charlotte: University of North Carolina Press, 1989). For a critique (based on the examination of the material culture) of the alleged importance of Scots Irish ethnicity, isolation, and the static quality of hollow neighborhoods in the Upland South, see Audrey J. Horning, "In Search of a 'Hollow Ethnicity': Archeological Explorations of Rural Mountain Settlement," in *Historical Archeology, Identity Formation, and the Interpretation of Ethnicity*, ed. Maria Franklin and Garrett Fesler (Colonial Williamsburg Foundation: Colonial Williamsburg Publications, 1999), 121–37.

4. C. J. Vaughn, comp., *Osage County Business and Individual Directory* (1915), http://www.osagecounty.org/documents/1915index.html (accessed June 8, 2016).

5. For an excellent review of the recent revisionist scholarship, see

Brooks Blevins, *Ghost of the Ozarks: Murder and Memory in the Upland South* (Urbana: University of Illinois Press, 2012), 177–202; and, as examples, Brooks Blevins, *Hill Folks: A History of Arkansas Ozarkers & Their Image* (Chapel Hill: University of North Carolina Press, 2002); and Mary Beth Pudup, Dwight B. Billings, and Altina L. Walker, eds., *Appalachia in the Making: The Mountain South in the Nineteenth Century* (Chapel Hill: University of North Carolina Press, 1995).

6. David C. Hsiung, in his *Two Worlds in the Tennessee Mountains: Exploring the Origins of Appalachian Stereotypes* (Lexington: University Press of Kentucky, 1997), finds the origins of conflicting images of Appalachia arose from among the early settlers themselves. For later history, see also Blevins, *Hill Folks*, and Anthony Harkins, *Hillbilly: A Cultural History of an American Icon* (New York: Oxford University Press, 2005). For an argument not only for the existence of the hillbilly in Shannon County, but for his persistence into the second half of the twentieth century, see Bernard Asbell, "The Vanishing Hillbilly," *Saturday Evening Post* 234 (Sept. 23, 1961): 92–95, and, to a lesser extent, *Shannon County: Hearts of Children*, DVD (2014), Special Collections, Duane G. Meyer Library, Missouri State University, Springfield, Missouri.

7. For a delineation of the boundaries of the region and description of some of its folkways, see Terry G. Jordan-Bychkov, *The Upland South: The Making of an American Folk Region and Landscape* (Santa Fe, NM: Center for American Places in association with the University of Virginia Press, 2003).

8. *The Passerby*, Feb. 8, 1939.

9. For a recent treatment of women in the Ozarks, see especially Janet Allured, "Ozark Women and the Companionate Family in the Arkansas Hills, 1870–1910," *Arkansas Historical Quarterly* 47 (Autumn 1988): 238–39. For reviews of the historiography and essays on women's history in another part of the Upland South, see, for example, Barbara Ellen Smith, "Beyond the Mountains: The Paradox of Women's Place in Appalachian History," *NWSA Journal* (Autumn 1999): 1–17; and the essays in Connie Park Rice and Marie Tedesco, eds., *Women of the Mountain South: Identity, Work, and Activism* (Athens: Ohio University Press, 2015).

10. Quoted in Robert B. Flanders, "Pride and Progress: The Evangelism of Modernity," *OzarksWatch* 5 (Winter 1992): 6. For a specific example of the popular contention that Ozarks culture has been static and premodern, see Vance Randolph, *The Ozarks: An American Survival of Primitive Society* (New York: Vanguard Press, 1931). However, Randolph confessed in the preface that his book was not concerned "with the progressive element in the Ozark towns, nor with the prosperous valley farmers" but rather with the "'hill-billy' or 'ridge-runner' of the more isolated sections" of the Ozarks.

11. In terms of scholarship, apparently, geographer Carl O. Sauer, in his *The Geography of the Ozark Highland of Missouri* (Chicago: Geographic Society of Chicago, Bul. No. 7, 1920), was the first to identify what he called the Courtois Hills as a distinctive region. See also Harbert Leslie Clendenen, "Settlement of the Southern Courtois Hills, Missouri, 1820–1860" (PhD diss. Louisiana State University, 1973); and Cynthia R. Price,

"Frontier Settlement in the Current River Valley: Variation in Organizational Patterning," in _Visions and Revisions: Ethnohistoric Perspectives on Southern Cultures_, ed. George Sabo III and William M. Schneider, Southern Anthropological Society Proceedings, no. 20 (Athens: University of Georgia Press, 1987): 114–31. Price contrasts the settlement patterns of the upper and the lower watersheds of the Current River Valley in Missouri. Mahans Creek is in the upper watershed. Walter Odro Cralle, in "Social Change and Isolation in the Ozark Mountain Region of Missouri" (PhD diss., University of Minnesota, 1934), presented an array of statistical measures (based mostly on a 1930 US census) such as automobile ownership, telephone ownership, and marriage rates, comparing Ozarks counties with non-Ozarks counties in Missouri. He found Shannon County was not only among the most "isolated" but also among the five most distinctive counties in the region. For a summary of his findings, see also Walter Odro Cralle, "Social Change and Isolation in the Ozark Mountain Region of Missouri," _American Journal of Sociology_ 41 (January 1936): 435–46.

12. Margaret E. Bell, "Place Names in the Southwest Border Counties of Missouri" (MA thesis, University of Missouri–Columbia, 1933), 28–29. Though applied to counties farther to the west, Bell's comment is equally appropriate to Shannon County. For the importance of naming places in the Arkansas Ozarks, see E. Joan Wilson Miller, "The Naming of the Land in the Arkansas Ozarks: A Study in Culture Processes," _Annals of the Association of American Geographers_ 59 (June 1969): 240–51. And in another part of the Upland South, see Durwood Dunn, _Cades Cove: The Life and Death of a Southern Appalachian Community, 1818–1937_ (Knoxville: University of Tennessee Press, 1988), 19, 147–48. For the names of hollows in Missouri, see "Missouri, USA Place Names," http://www: placenames. com/us/291 (accessed Oct. 16, 2012). Jordan-Bychkov (_The Upland South_, 7) has observed that, "meaning an elongated, flat-bottomed valley, the term 'hollow' . . . is one good index of the presence both of upland southerners and their preferred habitat." For the physical uniqueness of the area, see James E. Price, "The Preservation of Two Wild and Scenic Ozark Rivers," http://www.nps.gov/ozar/historyculture/establishment.htm (accessed Nov. 2, 2014).

13. On December 14, 1911, the _Current Wave_ observed that "only a few years earlier thousands of acres" of Shannon County land had been in the public domain, but as of that date only forty-eight acres remained open for sale. While not ascribing poverty specifically to living in hollows, Kathleen Blakeny Morrison attributes the protracted poverty in Shannon County primarily to its uniqueness as a "place." See Kathleen Blakeny Morrison, "The Poverty of Place: A Comparative Study of Five Rural Counties in the Missouri Ozarks" (PhD diss., University of Missouri–Columbia, 1999).

14. I subsequently learned that Cratis D. Williams had earlier posited three types of southern mountaineers: "towns and city dwellers," "valley farmers," and "branchwater mountaineers." Cratis D. Williams and Martha H. Pipes, "The Southern Mountaineer in Fact and Fiction Part I," _Appalachian Journal_ 3 (Autumn 1975): 22–23.

15. See _Current Wave_, Nov. 14, 1912. Elva also received more

votes countywide than did Eugene Debs, the Socialist candidate for the presidency.

Prologue ✦ The Magic of Mahans Creek

1. Jerome Rader, telephone interview with author, Feb. 2, 2010; and Arch Pummill, digitally recorded interview with author, Sept. 18, 2010, in my possession. See Oscar Harper, "A Trip into Yesterday," *Ozarker* (Dec. 1975), 11; and Thela (Pummill) Wnterbottom, "The Old Swimming Hole," *Ozarker* (June 1979), 18, for descriptions of the creek. For a recent description of gigging suckers in the Current River, see Jason Jenkins, "Olde Tyme Gigging: Locals Reach into the Past to Honor Ozark Traditions," http://www.ruralmissouri.org/08pages/08DecOldeTymeGiggin.html (accessed June 19, 2016).

2. Jerome Rader, digitally recorded interview with author, Oct. 13, 2009; and Arch Pummill, phone interview with author, Feb. 11, 2010.

I ✦ Their Kentucky Homeland

1. Jayne Rader, "Rader Family" (2002), 21, unpublished manuscript in my possession.

2. J. Anderson Childress, *Beyond the Cross Roads: A Genealogy, History, and Traditional Folkways of Western Hart County, Kentucky* (Utica, KY: McDowell Publications, 1981), 57.

1 ✦ The Childress Clan

1. H. N. Hobbs, untitled, printed obituary of John W. Childress, source and date unknown but perhaps published in a local newspaper on the occasion of John's death on August 8, 1876, in the Hart County Historical Society, Munfordville, Kentucky.

2. J. Anderson Childress, *Beyond the Cross Roads*, 50–66. After the Civil War, several of the descendants of John W. Childress were buried in the Baptist Cemetery (as well as in the Methodist Cemetery) in Cub Run.

3. J. Anderson Childress, quoted in Jayne Rader, "Rader Family," 27.

4. Hulbert Rader to Ben Rader, April 15, 1979, copy in my possession.

5. The 1940 US Census lists eighty-one persons with the Childress surname. See http://1940census.archives.gov (accessed June 28, 2016).

6. J. Anderson Childress, *Beyond the Cross Roads*, 53. A somewhat different version of the courtship and marriage can be found in Lewis S. Childress, "John W. Childress of Virginia and Kentucky," unpublished manuscript, 1970, in Hart County Historical Society, but it reports the wrong year for the marriage and confuses Mary Hare with John's first wife, Sarah Jordan. See http://www.so-ky.com/cem/hartcem/o/oldmaple/church.htm (accessed Nov. 16, 2012) for speculation that Mary Hare may have been at the Bardstown nunnery. However, research in the archives of the Sisters of the Charity of Nazareth and the Sisters of Loretto has not uncovered evi-

dence of her existence. Email from archivist to Benjamin G. Rader, June 26, 2013, in my possession.

7. Hardin County, Kentucky, Marriage Records, No. 185, in Kentucky State Library and Archives; J. Anderson Childress, *Beyond the Cross Roads,* 57.

8. See J. Anderson Childress, *Beyond the Cross Roads,* 55–56.

9. Ibid., 52. According to Vicki Tobias, "Rader Family Tree," www. ancestry.com, (accessed June 28, 2016), Mary's parents, John and Mary Hare, resided in Connaught, a region of western Ireland.

10. Mary Hare might have been a descendant of Jarvis Hare, who, as a felon in Ireland, was sent as punishment to Maryland in 1740. See http:// www.ctaz.com/~firefly/ship.htm (accessed June 4, 2014). In J. Anderson Childress, *Beyond the Cross Roads,* Anderson Childress speculated that Mary could have been the daughter of Ignatius Hare, who allegedly appeared in the Green County, Kentucky, US census in 1810. However, the name in the manuscript census to which Childress apparently referred appears to be Ignatius Hasel, rather than Ignatius Hare. See http://www.usgwcensus.org/cenfiles/ky/green/1810/pg17.txt (accessed Aug. 25, 2012).

11. Undated letter of J. Anderson Childress to Hulbert Rader, Jayne Rader, "Rader Family," 27.

12. No documentation or family lore of the European origins of the family exists, but see http://freepages.genealogy.rootsweb.ancestry.com/~tqpeiffer/Documents/Surnames/MMPS/Childress/CHILDRESS%20Surname%20Webpage.htm (accessed June 28, 2016).

13. Garland K. Childress and Leda Childress, "The Childress Family Tree," unpublished manuscript, in Hart County Historical Society; Phillip Childress Will, Goochland County, VA, 1812 Probate Court, attached to Tobias, "Rader Family Tree." See also J. Anderson Childress, *Beyond the Cross Roads,* 60–64.

14. Terry G. Jordan-Bychkov, *The Upland South: The Making of an American Folk Region and Landscape* (Santa Fe, NM: Center for American Places, in association with the University of Virginia Press, 2003), 15–18.

15. That the nearby Old Maple Church was said to have been built with poplar indicates the possibility that John also built his cabin with poplar. See "A Building Called Maple," *Hart County News,* Nov. 25, 1971, 6, copy, see Vicki Tobias, "John Wesley Childress," www.ancestry.com (accessed June 28, 2016).

16. For the history of various kinds of vernacular log houses in the Upland South, see especially Terry G. Jordan, *American Log Buildings: An Old World Heritage* (Chapel Hill: University of North Carolina Press, 1985).

17. J. Anderson Childress, *Beyond the Cross Roads,* 57; and tax lists, Hart County, Kentucky, 1843, microfilm copy in the Kentucky Department of Libraries and Archives, Frankfort, KY. A thorough examination of the tax lists for Hart County reveals that John Wesley's acreage varied considerably, almost from year to year. I have no explanation for this unless he did not always report the correct acreage—perhaps to escape taxation—or had some kind of option to purchase some of this land but did not actually own it. The poverty of the Childress family can be profitably compared with

the apparently much better off Oliver family in Cades Cove in Tennessee. See Durwood Dunn, *Cades Cove: Life and Death of a Southern Appalachian Community, 1818–1937* (Knoxville: University of Tennessee Press, 1988).

18. Little evidence of hunting and fishing by the Childress family survives. We do know that Bartholomew Hare hunted raccoons in the antebellum era and that a son, Benjamin, of John W. Childress reported that he went to Missouri because the hunting and fishing was allegedly better there. J. Anderson Childress, *Beyond the Cross Roads,* 55; J. Anderson Childress to Hulbert Rader, July 16, 1978, in my possession; and Jayne Rader, "Rader Family," 27.

19. Application of modern agricultural methods to John's land indicate that at least patches of it could have yielded as much as 95 bushels of corn and 2,300 pounds of tobacco per acre. However, without the benefit of fertilizers and hybrid seeds in the nineteenth century, it is unlikely that the land produced more than 30 bushels of corn per acre. See Michael J. Mitchell, *Soil Survey of Hart County, Kentucky* (US Department of Agriculture, Soil Conservation Service, 1993), 127, Hart County, Kentucky, sheet number 11.

20. See US Bureau of the Census, "Non-population Census of Fifteen Southern States, Agricultural" (Hart County, Kentucky, 1850, 1860, 1870, 1880), manuscripts in National Archives, Washington, D.C., microfilm copies in the Department of Libraries and Archives, Frankfort, Kentucky, hereafter cited in this chapter as "Non-Population Census." The farming and dietary lives of the Childress family also conform for the most part to Richard Lyle Power's findings in *Planting Corn Belt Culture: The Impress of the Upland Southerner and Yankee in the Old Northwest* (Westport, CT: Greenwood Press, 1953, 1983), 92–112.

21. For this and other alleged differences between Upland Southerners and Yankees, see also Colin Woodard, *American Nations: A History of the Eleven Rival Regional Cultures in North America* (New York: Viking, 2011), 190–93.

22. See Sam Bowers Hilliard, *Atlas of Antebellum Southern Agriculture* (Baton Rouge: Louisiana State University Press, 1984), 63–67; and Sam Bowers Hilliard, *Hog Meat and Hoecake: Food Supply in the Old South, 1840–1860* (Carbondale: Southern Illinois University Press, 1972), esp. chaps. 5 and 8.

23. John Mack Faragher, *Sugar Creek: Life on the Illinois Prairie* (New Haven, CT: Yale University Press, 1986), 98.

24. "1874 Hart County Tax List (Northside)," in Hart County Historical Society. Copied from the original list in the Kentucky Department of Libraries and Archives.

25. Paul K. Conkin to Benjamin Rader, Oct. 27, 2011, email copy in my possession.

26. "Nonpopulation Census" (1850). Of the three or perhaps four of John's offspring who moved outside of Hart County, all appear to have become small farmers. Two of them moved to the Texas frontier.

27. J. Anderson Childress, *Beyond the Cross Roads,* 125. See also Childress, *Beyond the Cross Roads,* 58.

28. See J. Anderson Childress, *Beyond the Cross Roads*, 108–16; and Rachel Nash Law and Cynthia W. Taylor, *Appalachian White Oak Basketmaking: Handing Down the Basket* (Knoxville: University of Tennessee Press, 1991). The latter book contains several references to the basket-making members of the Childress clan.

29. J. Anderson Childress, *Beyond the Cross Roads*, 43.

30. Copy of letter of Lilly May (Rader) Raper, July 4, 1978, in Jayne Rader, "Sam's Siblings," copy of unpublished manuscript in my possession. Lilly's father, James Rader, also seems to have been surprised by the family's poverty. He invited one of his cousins, a Felix Childress, who was with a wife and two small children, to sharecrop and live in an empty log cabin on his farm on Mahans Creek. Felix and his family accepted the invitation but returned to Hart County sometime in the 1910s.

31. Undated letter of Childress to Hulbert Rader, Jayne Rader, "Rader Family," 27.

32. See, especially, Anthony Harkins, *Hillbilly: A Cultural History of an American Icon* (New York: Oxford University Press, 2005); but also, for the origins and history of the stereotype, see David Hsiung, *Two Worlds in the Tennessee Mountains: Exploring the Origins of Appalachian Stereotypes* (Lexington: University of Kentucky Press, 1997); and Brooks Blevins, *Hill Folks: A History of Ozarkers and Their Image* (Charlotte: University of North Carolina Press, 2002). Since the 1980s there has been a sea change in Upland South historiography, much of which revolves around the hillbilly stereotype. Recent studies have not only deemphasized the region's exceptionalism and emphasized its complexity and diversity, but have also granted the regions inhabitants more agency in shaping their own destinies. For a good summary of recent scholarship, see Brooks Blevins, *Ghost of the Ozarks: Murder and Memory in the Upland South* (Urbana: University of Illinois Press, 2012), 177–202.

33. See chapter 3 regarding an alleged no-holds fight between a grandson of John W. Childress, Mike Rader, and a neighboring man.

34. J. Anderson Childress, *Beyond the Cross Road*, 82. From conversations occasioned from my on-site visits to Hart County, it appears that the family continues in the twenty-first century to enjoy a positive reputation among its neighbors.

35. See description of an Ozark farm family in Donald R. Holliday, "Autobiography of an American Family" (PhD diss., University of Minnesota, 1974), 113. This section also arises from my own experience of living and working on an Ozarks farm.

36. Myrtle Robinson, "Obituary of Grandma Rader," *Current Wave* (Eminence, MO), undated, in my possession

37. For the formulation of these opposing cultures, see especially Ted Ownby, *Subduing Satin: Religion, Recreation, and Manhood in the Rural South, 1865–1920* (Chapel Hill: University of North Carolina Press, 1990).

38. J. Anderson Childress, *Beyond the Cross Roads*, 60.

39. Ibid., 60. For the popularity of bartering in another part of the Upland South (the Ozarks) in the early twentieth century, see Otto Ernest Rayburn, *Ozark Country* (New York: Duell, Sloan & Pearce, 1941), 127–32.

40. The body of scholarship treating middle-class culture is now immense. For a summary see Benjamin G. Rader, *American Ways: A History of American Cultures, 1865–Present,* vol. 2 (Belmont, CA: Thompson Wadsworth, 2006), chaps. 13–14.

41. For the importance of kinship in establishing personal identities in Taney County, Missouri, in the twentieth century, see Elizabeth Hagens Herlinger, "A Historical, Cultural, and Organizational Analysis of Ozark Ethnic Identity" (PhD diss., University of Chicago, 1972).

42. In 1847, James Childress, one of Nancy's older brothers, had married sixteen-year-old Sarah Taylor. Sarah was a younger sister of Ben Taylor. George's sister, Mary Rader, was Ben Taylor's wife. So it seems likely that George Rader's eventual marriage to Nancy Childress resulted from these kinship connections. See Tobias, "The Rader Family."

2 ✦ The German Hat Maker's Family

1. While few Germans migrated to North America in the Revolutionary War era, this date accords with the 1850 US Census, which recorded Charles's age as seventy-two and his birthplace as "Germany." See Vicki Tobias, "The Rader Family Tree," in www.ancestry.com (accessed June 10, 2014). There is another family legend that the family came from Stuttgart, which is a large city in Baden-Wurttemberg, a state in southern Germany, which eventually became a part of Prussia and still later of Germany. Family folklore is the source for most of the specifics found in this and subsequent paragraphs. Part of this folklore is based on the memory of Robert "Mike" Rader as recorded in a letter composed by Nancy Rader Croghan, Mike's daughter, to Melvin Rader, Feb. 3, 1972, copied by Martha Ellen Coffman Porzig Gammons, in my possession.

2. See http://books.google.com/books?id=P04VAAAAYAAJ&pg=PA 26&source=gbs_toc_r&cad=4#v=snippet&q=prices&f=false (accessed June 29, 2016) for the costs of hats in the early nineteenth century in Highland County, Ohio.

3. See ibid.; and http://wc.rootsweb.ancestry.com/cgi-bin/igm.cgi?op= GET&db=mjr6387&id=I186627 (accessed Oct. 2, 2014).

4. See data in Tobias, "The Rader Family Tree." Scots Irish ancestry was also present in the Jeremiah Dawson line. In 1706, Nicholas Dawson married Mary Doyne, whose parents were from Carrickfergus, a town in Northern Ireland.

5. See http://files.usgwarchives.org/ky/hart/cemeteries/dawson.txt (accessed Oct. 3, 2014). This description of Jeremiah Dawson is repeated in several documents, but the author is unknown. It may have been written by a descendant long after Dawson's death. See Charles Carol Dawson, *A Collection of Family Records* (1874), 331–32, http://books.google.com/ books?id=YckUAAAAYAAJ&printsec=frontcover#v=onepage&q=&f=false (accessed June 29, 2015). See also file of Jeremiah Dawson pertaining to "Federal Military Pension Application" of Nancy Dawson (NATF 85A), National Archives, copy in my possession.

6. The conclusion in Tobias, "The Rader Family Tree," that Jeremiah's two oldest sons migrated to Kentucky in about 1817 appears to be incorrect. Beginning with Susan Dawson, born in about 1796, the censuses of 1850, 1860, and 1870 report the remainder of the children as being born in Hart County before 1817. See Susan Dawson in Tobias, "Rader Family Tree." For a discussion of the settlement of Virginia war veterans in the Green River valley, see Helen Bartter Crocker, *The Green River of Kentucky* (Lexington: University Press of Kentucky, 1976), chap. 1. For soil fertility, see Mitchell, *Soil Survey of Hart County, Kentucky,* sheet number 20 (soil map) and 124. The soil on the Dawson farms is mostly Crider silt loam, which today, under high-level management, can be expected to produce between 105 to 125 bushels of corn per acre and 2,900 to 3,200 pounds of tobacco per acre.

7. Jayne Rader, "Rader Family," 21. For data on the farms of the Dawson family, as well as others in this chapter, see the US Bureau of the Census, "Non-Population Census of Fifteen Southern States, Agricultural" (Hart County, Kentucky), manuscripts in National Archives, Washington, D.C., microfilm copies in Kentucky Department of Libraries and Archives, Frankfort, Kentucky, hereafter cited as "Non-Population Census."

8. See "Hart County, Kentucky, Slave Census," 1850 and 1860, http://ancestry.com (accessed March 11, 2015).

9. See Tobias, "Rader Family Tree."

10. See letter of Lillie May Rader Raper (daughter of Jim Rader), July 4, 1978, in Jayne Rader, "Sam's Siblings." Arch Pummill remembered that Jim Rader "had a lot of books." Arch Pummill, digitally recorded interview with author, Sept. 18, 2010, copy in my possession.

11. Based on my own knowledge and discussions with Arch Pummill, Gloria Dene Fry, and Jerome Rader.

12. Nancy Rader Priddy, "The Rader Family," *Shannon County Historical Review* (Summer 1966): 3.

13. On two occasions, Alfred sold goods to the Confederate army. See "Confederate Papers Relating to Citizens and Business Firms, 1861–65," National Archives. Also in Fold3, http://www.fold3.com/ (accessed Sept. 14, 2013). For a description of the Rader home, see Carol Rader, in Arthur Rader, "Rader Legend," July 8, 1979, unpublished manuscript, in my possession. For the statistics in this paragraph, see tax lists, Hart County, 1840, microfilm copy in Kentucky Department of Libraries and Archives; and "Non-Population Census." Alfred Rader was one of a small number of Hart County farmers who paid a tax on "slaughtered animals" in 1865 to the Internal Revenue Service. See Tobias, "Rader Family Tree."

14. For camp meetings in Hart County, see Virginia Davis, *A Glimpse of the Past* (n.p., 1994), 53.

15. See Tobias, "The Rader Family Tree."

16. If he existed, Andrew Jackson Rader left behind no official documentation. He may have died in infancy. The naming ways of the Charles Rader family may be compared with those of colonial New Englanders, who more than 90 percent of the time named their children for biblical persons or their ancestors. In presidential elections, Hart County did give Whigs

William Henry Harrison (1840) and Henry Clay (a favorite son in 1844) and Republican U. S. Grant (1872) the nod, but otherwise in the nineteenth century supported Democratic candidates. For presidential votes by counties, see Jerome M. Clubb, William H. Flanigan, and Nancy H. Zingale, "Electoral Data for Counties in the United States: Presidential and Congressional Races, 1840-1972" (ICPSR 8611), www.icpsr.umich.edu (accessed June 29, 2016).

17. Charles Carol Dawson, *A Collection of Family Records* (1874), 334, http://books.google.com/books?id=YckUAAAAYAAJ&printsec=frontcover#v=onepage&q=&f=false (accessed March 13, 2011).

18. Telephone conversation with Calvin Childress, Feb. 24, 2011.

19. See Hart County tax lists for taxable property and goods, Kentucky Historical Society.

20. Iva Eddings Shumate provided me with anecdotal evidence that additional children could be unwanted. A member of an upcountry family, she remembers as a child during the 1930s that she found her mother crying. She asked, "Why are you crying?" My grandmother, Florence Eddings, replied, "I am going to have another baby." Iva Marie Eddings Shumate, digitized interview with author, October 12, 2009, in my possession. Florence already had seven children.

21. Quoted in Jack E. Weller, *Yesterday's People: Life in Contemporary Appalachia* (Lexington: University of Kentucky Press, 1965), 62. See also John Mack Faragher, *Sugar Creek: Life on the Illinois Prairie* (New Haven: Yale University Press, 1986), chap. 12.

22. See David Hackett Fisher, *Albion's Seed: Four British Folkways in America* (New York: Oxford University Press, 1989), 683–86.

23. See discussion of Brooks Blevins, *Ghost of the Ozarks: Murder and Memory in the Upland South* (Urbana: University of Illinois Press, 2012), 184.

24. A grandson, Hulbert Rader, reported that his grandmother, Nancy, was extraordinarily strict. "She was very much against drinking and gambling." Hulbert "Hub" Rader, "What I Tell My Grandchildren," in Jayne Rader's, "Rader Family," 31–32.

25. Tax lists, Hart County, 1874, microfilmed copy in Kentucky Department of Libraries and Archives. No other couple on the tax lists for the county report husbands and wives owning property separately, but Nancy's independence in this and other regards is evidence supporting the contentions of recent scholarship on women in southern Appalachia. See for example, Connie Park Rice and Marie Tedesco, eds., *Women of the Mountain South: Identity, Work, and Activism* (Athens: Ohio University Press, 2015).

3 ✦ Hard Times in Hart County

1. Quoted in Lowell H. Harrison and James C. Klotter, *A New History of Kentucky* (Lexington: University Press of Kentucky, 1997), 196. See also Susan C. Lafferty, *Civil War in Hart County, Kentucky: A Different Perspective* (Munfordville, KY?: by the author, 2009).

2. *Land Grants in Hart County, Kentucky, 1836–1924*, vol. 1, book 2, 1616, Kentucky Department of Libraries and Archives.

3. The sons could have been living in the John B. and Mary G. Childress Grimes family in Lavaca County, Texas. The Grimes family moved to Texas in about 1852. Mary was a half-sister of Nancy Childress Rader, the mother of the Rader sons. J. Anderson Childress, *Beyond the Cross Roads*, 67.

4. "NARA M323 Compiled service records of Confederate soldiers from Texas units," Roll 0013, National Archives. Also in Fold3, http://www.fold3.com/ (accessed Feb. 6, 2013).

5. Ibid.

6. Jayne Rader, "Rader Family," 29.

7. Nancy Rader Priddy, "The Rader Family," *Shannon County Historical Review* (Summer 1966): 3. The information found in this source should be approached with caution.

8. My uncle Hulbert Rader remembered hearing from descendants yet another reason why George joined the Kentucky Volunteers. George had been conscripted (i.e., drafted), according to this account, but had paid $500 to a black man to serve in his place. Alas, the black man then fled with the money so that "Grandpa had to do his soldiering [anyway], [ironically] fighting for the black man's freedom!" Hulbert "Hub" Rader, "What I Tell My Grandchildren," ca. 1979, in Jayne Rader's "Rader Family," 31, 33. As good as this story is, I reluctantly discount it. Apart from the apparent fact that George could not have possibly raised $500 in 1862, the Union draft did not commence until March of 1863, almost a year after George had joined the Kentucky Volunteers!

9. For a list of Hart County Civil War Union soldiers, see http://www.cenusdiggins.com/civilwarky3.html (accessed Nov. 23, 2013). Here, George Washington Rader is listed as "George Radar." See also http://archives.gov/veterans/military-service-records/pre--ww1-records.html (accessed Nov. 23, 2013).

10. "Confederate Papers Relating to Citizens and Business Firms, 1861–65," National Archives. Also in Fold3, http://www.fold3.com/ (accessed Nov. 16, 2013).

11. Evidence from file of George W. Rader, WC 452–541, 371.920, R. C. Drum, "War Department, Adjutant General's Office," June 27, 1888, National Archives, copy in my possession.

12. Certificate of Disability for Discharge, Army of the United States, Aug. 14, 1862, George W. Rader, in the National Archives, copy in my possession and in George Rader Service Record, in Fold3, http://www.fold3.com/(accessed Nov. 16, 2013).

13. See Lafferty, *Civil War in Hart County*, 96–98.

14. For this conclusion, see note 13 above and file of George W. Rader, Declaration of Original Pension of an Invalid, August 1, 1874, National Archives. Copy in my possession.

15. See Hart County Tax List, 1865, in Kentucky Department of Libraries and Archives.

16. There is a vast literature on southern honor, but see especially the discussion of Nicole Etcheson, *The Emerging Midwest: Upland Southerners and the Political Culture of the Old Northwest, 1787–1861* (Bloomington: Indiana University Press, 1996), chap. 3. Etcheson observes that resorting

to violence may have been a way that the ordinary Upland Southerners could assert their equality in an otherwise unequal world.

17. Nancy Rader Croghan to the editor, *Ozarker* (Sept. 1972), 7.

18. See Mary Lucy Coffman, "Tribute to My Grandfather," in Jayne Rader's " Sam's Siblings." Interestingly, however, this story is not repeated by Mike's daughter; see Nancy Rader Corghan, "Mike Rader, My Father," *Ozarker* (May 1972), 7; nor in Nancy Rader Croghan to the editor, *Ozarker* (Sept. 1972), 7. Furthermore, according to Mary Lucy Coffman's account, the George Rader family had already left Kentucky before Mike's fight!

19. The exact location of the Rader family farm is unknown. However, the Hart County tax list for 1874, in the Kentucky Department of Libraries and Archives, indicates that his nearest neighbor was Thomas D. West, and the list for 1875 shows Samuel Sanders as a neighbor; both farmers were known to live near John W. Childress.

20. J. Anderson Childress, *Beyond the Cross Roads*, 117.

21. Ibid., 43.

22. See Hart County Tax List, 1865, Kentucky Department of Libraries and Archives. Previous tax lists indicate that George Rader owned no land. In 1865 the tax list also reports that he had three horses, thirteen head of cattle, and six hogs and that he produced only 75 bushels of corn.

23. According to J. Anderson Childress, quoted in Jayne Rader, "Rader Family," 30.

24. See W. B. Stephens, *Sources for U.S. History: Nineteenth-Century Communities* (New York: Cambridge University Press, 1991), 202, for criteria used in the agricultural censuses.

25. In letter of Lillie May Rader Raper (daughter of Jim Rader), July 4, 1978, in Jayne Rader, "Sam's Siblings," she reported that her father, James, a son of George and Nancy, received a small inheritance from Alfred Rader's estate.

26. Hambleton Tapp and James C. Klotter, *Kentucky: Decades of Discord, 1865–1900* (Lexington: University of Kentucky Press, 1984), 294.

27. Lydia Florence Eddings Rader, "George Rader Family," undated and unpublished manuscript. Copy in my possession.

28. In the wake of the Civil War, available evidence suggests that Lewis (sometimes spelled "Louis") and Mary Perkins moved several times: first from Kentucky to Illinois, then from Illinois to Arkansas, and then back to Kentucky, before finally joining the Raders for the trip to Shannon County, Missouri, in 1878. While I do not know the source, another intriguing scrap of evidence in my possession asserts that "Robert" (no last name is given but internal evidence indicates that it should be "Rader") "drove a team of mules with a covered wagon from Kentucky to Missouri in 1874." This would logically be, of all persons, "Mike" Rader. But the document goes ahead to say that Robert "rafted logs down the Osage River. [He] also worked in an Iron Foundry in Missour [*sic*] in a Cotton Jin [*sic*] in Arkansas." The iron foundry could have been in Meramec, MO. In any case, it does not appear that "Robert" (Mike) traveled through the area that later became Shannon County at this time.

29. Quoted in J. Anderson Childress to Hulbert Rader, July 16, 1978, in my possession, and Jayne Rader, "Rader Family."

30. Based partly on the observations of Eunice Pennington, *History of the Ozarks*, rev. ed., (n.p.: School of the Ozarks, 1971), 22, who was familiar with the overland trips of settlers from middle Tennessee to Carter County, Missouri. Carter County is adjacent to Shannon County. It took Thomas Lincoln's family two weeks to make a one-hundred-mile overland trip from Kentucky to Indiana. Kenneth J. Winkle, *Abraham and Mary Lincoln* (Carbondale; Southern Illinois University Press, 2011), 7. See also James Walsh, "Overview," in *History of Shannon County Missouri 1986*, Friends of the Shannon County Libraries, Eminence, MO (Dallas, TX: Taylor Publishing Co. 1986), 6. Walsh asserted that it commonly took twenty-five to thirty days for settlers to travel by tar-pole wagons or two-wheeled ox carts from mid-Tennessee to the central Ozark region.

31. Priddy, "The Rader Family," 3.

32. *Current Wave*, March 25, 1885.

33. Oscar Harper, "Birch Prairie," *Shannon County Historical Review* (Winter 1966): 7.

34. US Bureau of the Census, "Nonpopulation Census, Agricultural" (Shannon County, Missouri, 1880), manuscripts in National Archives, Washington, D.C., microfilm copy in State Historical Society of Missouri, Columbia, Missouri. The data for corn productivity is for the crop year of 1879.

II ✦ Settling on Mahans Creek

1. This version of his death is attributed to Jeremiah Rader, one of George's sons, by Hulbert Rader, a grandson. Hulbert "Hub" Rader, "What I Tell My Grandchildren," (1979), in Jayne Rader's, "Rader Family," 32.

2. "Widow's Declaration for Pension or Increase of Pension," April 23, 1888, by Nancy Rader, in my possession. According to http://www.rootsweb. ancestry.com/~moshanno/cemeteries/Rader.htm (accessed June 3, 2013). George Washington Rader was buried in the Rader Cemetery in Delaware, MO, but this cemetery does not include his tombstone or any other evidence that he was buried there. Furthermore, a document prepared by Betty Sue Rader, "1996 Missouri Century Farms," asserts that he "is buried north of Birch Tree, Mo.," manuscript in my possession. Wayne Rader also believed that he was buried on the family farm near Birch Tree. Wayne Rader, telephone interview with author, Feb. 2, 2010.

3. Hulbert Rader, "What I Tell My Grandchildren," 31.

4. Oscar Harper, "Birch Prairie," *Shannon County Historical Review* (Winter 1966): 7; Wayne Rader, interview, Feb. 2, 2010.

5. Harper, "Birch Prairie."

6. Hulbert Rader, "What I Tell My Grandchildren," 31.

4 ✦ Like Coming Home Again

1. For its history, see especially Susan Flader, "A Legacy of Neglect: The Ozark National Scenic Riverways," *George Wright Forum* 28, no. 2 (2011): 114–26; or see http://www.georgewright.org/282flader.pdf (accessed June 29, 2012). For a discussion of the physical environment

and the process of early settlement of the area, see also Harbert Leslie Clendenen, "Settlement Morphology of the Southern Courtois Hills, Missouri, 1820–1860" (PhD diss., Louisiana State University, 1973).

2. *Current Wave*, March 25, 1885.

3. G. R. Kenamore, "The Ozarks Fifty Years Ago," *Current Wave,* Oct. 1, 1925.

4. Quoted in ibid. Luther Rowlett told a somewhat different version of this story. See Luther Rowlett, "Eminence 1876," *Ozarker* (July 1977), 2. High water prevented the delivery of the mail from Salem to Eminence for three weeks in 1896. *Current Wave*, May 29, 1896.

5. *Current Wave*, Dec. 17, 1884. Also quoted in http://www.rootsweb. ancestry.com/~moshanno/memory_lane.htm (accessed June 29, 2012).

6. Oscar Harper, "Delaware of Yesterday," *Shannon County Historical Review* (Autumn 1966): 3.

7. In 1912, Shannon County exported 3,768 pounds of "medicinal products—roots and herbs." *Thirty-Fifth Annual Report of the Bureau of Labor Statistics* [1913], 479, in Missouri Digital Heritage Collection, http://cdm.sos.mo.gov/cdm4/document.php?CISOROOT=/redbk&CISOPTR=17909&REC=5 (accessed June 10, 2012).

8. Quotations in Harper, "Birch Prairie," 7; and in Kenamore, "The Ozarks Fifty Years Ago."

9. Robert Cunningham, interview with author, July 16, 2012; [James Everett Pummill] *Passerby,* May 7, 1934; *Current Wave*, Oct. 22, 1885.

10. James C. Chilton, *Reminiscent History of the Ozark Region* (Chicago: Goodspeed Brothers, Publishers, 1894), and htttp://www.accessgenealogy. com/scripts/data/database.cgi?file=Data&report=SingleArticle&ArticleID (accessed June 24, 2012).

11. Eunice Pennington, *A History of the Ozarks,* rev. ed. (n.p.: School of the Ozarks Press, 1971), 65. See also Pennington's description of other Ozarks animals (ibid., 65–67).

12. Harper, "Delaware of Yesterday." See also Daniel McKinley, "A History of the Passenger Pigeon in Missouri," *Auk* 17 (Oct. 1960): 391–420.

13. *Current Wave*, Nov. 24, 1887.

14. Ibid., Nov. 24, 1887, Aug. 18, 1887.

15. Ibid., Oct 11, 18, Nov. 1, 1928.

16. C. A. Westlager, *The Delaware Indians: A History* (New Brunswick, NJ: Rutgers University Press, 1972), 361; C. A. Weslager, *The Delaware Indian Westward Migration* (Wallingford, PA: Middle Atlantic Press, 1978): 212–13; Alan Banks, "The Delaware Immigrants," *Ozarker* (June 1979): 17–18, and the documents appended to this article; and Lynn Morrow, "Trader William Gillis: Delaware Migration to Southern Missouri," *Missouri Historical Review* 75 (Jan. 1981): 147–67. The government documents reprinted in Banks refer to the group of settlers as "the Delaware Indians on the Currents." There is in addition an extensive though unverifiable folk history of Native Americans either hunting or residing on the creek. According to one of these accounts, in 1849 a group of Cherokees allegedly camped

briefly on the Jacks Fork River before moving on westward. This could have been the party of William Caswell Eddings, my great-great-grandfather on the maternal side, who, along with his family, appears in the 1850 census in southern Wright County, Missouri. See Vicki Tobias, "Rader Family Tree," www.ancestry.com (accessed June 29, 2016). Today there is a county road in the neighborhood labeled "Cherokee." See *Current Wave*, Oct. 21, 1897; and Ruth Eddings Shelton, "Wagon Train," unpublished and undated manuscript in my possession.

17. Cynthia R. Price, "Archaeological Investigations at Old Eminence: An Isolated Political Center in Shannon County, Missouri," *Missouri Archaeological Society Quarterly* 1 (April–June 1984): 8–11, 16–18.

18. For the absence of elections in the county, see Thomas J. Chilton to William Ewing, Sept. 14, 1851, in 1851 Election Returns, box 4, folder 6, Missouri State Archives, Jefferson City, MO, in which Chilton reported that the county court had not met for two years. For the absence of county government, see "George F. Chilton," *Current Wave* (Eminence, MO), Jan. 11, 1900, a special edition of the newspaper; and Eunice Pennington, "Early Shannon History," *Ozarker* (Nov. 1968), 8.

19. See the discussion of Clendenen, "Settlement Morphology," 25–32.

20. Quoted in *History of Shannon County Missouri 2001* (Eminence, MO: Friends of the Library, 2001), 7.

21. While admitting that the sources are sparse, see, for more detail, Clendenen, "Settlement Morphology," chapter 5.

22. See the discussion of Clendenen, "Settlement Morphology," 61–76.

23. The printed edition of the US Bureau of the Census reported 173 residents, but the manuscript census reveals 225 residents. See www.ancestry.com (accessed Sept. 29, 2014) Delaware at this time included the area that in 1909 became the Alley Township. The Mahan's Creek Post Office apparently continued operations throughout the Civil War but was closed in 1867. A new post office at Delaware, called Orchard Point, opened in either 1871 or 1876 and closed in either 1873 or 1878. See *Current Wave*, May 10, 1928. According to the remembrance of William Buffington in 1914, "in about 1855 old man Mayhan [William Mahan] built a small" water-driven mill on Mahans Creek. Quoted in *Shannon Herald* (Birch Tree, MO), March 13, 1914, in Historical Committee, *Birch Tree Bicentennial Project 1776–1976* (Birch Tree, MO?, 1976?), 27. Another source, Luther Rowlett, claimed that Mahan completed the mill "in the early 1840's." Rowlett is also the source for the quotation about the mill's social functions. See *Shannon County Historical Review* (July 1964), 6.

24. See the 1860 "U.S. Population Census" and *Non-Population Census* (1880).

25. For the development of distinctive rural neighborhoods elsewhere in the Upland South, see Ralph Mann, "Diversity in the Antebellum Appalachian South: Four Farm Communities in Tazewell County, Virginia," in *Appalachia in the Making: The Mountain South in the Nineteenth Century*, ed. Mary Beth Pudup, Dwight B. Billings, and Altina L. Waller (Charlotte: University of North Carolina Press, 1995), 132–62.

26. See "The Joys of Camping Out," *Ozarker* (Nov. 1968), 4.

27. Betty Ames to the editor, *Shannon County Historical Review* (Autumn 1965), 2. Ames was a granddaughter of James and Martha Canavit. While it does not treat specifically Shannon County, the standard history of guerilla warfare in the Ozarks is Michael Fellman, *Inside War: The Guerilla Conflict in Missouri during the American Civil War* (New York: Oxford University Press, 1989).

28. The standard history explicitly treating Shannon County during the war is J. J. Chilton et al., *The Civil War in Carter and Shannon County, Missouri* (Van Buren, MO: West Carter County Genealogy Society, n.d.). It contains a large number of articles originally published by John Jay Chilton in the 1930s as well as official documents. A semi-fictional work is "Dark Clouds over Shannon," by Ray H. Weakly, which was originally published in the *Ozarker* (May 1978).

29. The complete county presidential vote in 1860 was as follows: John Breckenridge (123), John Bell (38), Stephen A. Douglas (27), and Abraham Lincoln (2). See Wm. Deatherage to Missouri Secretary of State, Nov. 9, 1860, box 8, folder 20, Missouri State Archives.

30. Robert Lee, "Along the Current," *Ozarker* (Sept. 1975), 4.

31. Luther Rowlett, "Eminence 1876," *Ozarker* (July 1977), 2. For the role of "leading families" in influencing their neighbors with regard to the war elsewhere in the Upland South, see for example Stephen V. Ash, *Middle Tennessee Society Transformed, 1860–1870: War and Peace in the Upper South* (Baton Rouge: Louisiana State University Press, 1988),; and Durwood Dunn, *Cades Cove: The Life and Death of a Southern Appalachian Community, 1818–1937* (Knoxville: University of Tennessee Press, 1988).

32. See Charles Orchard and Marjory Orchard, *The Chiltons—Their Ancestors and Descendants,* 2 vols. (Eminence, MO: pub. by the authors, 1978).

33. See Orchard and Orchard, *The Chiltons;* J. J. Chilton, "History of the Chilton Family," *Shannon County Historical Review* (January 1965), 6–7; and "Election Returns, 1836–," in Missouri State Archives.

34. For a biographical sketch of Chilton, see *Reminiscent History of the Ozark Region* (Chicago: Goodspeed Brothers, 1894). For the most complete discussion of the capture and murder of Chilton, which is based on official Union military records as well as folklore, see John Jay Chilton, "True Ozark Tales from Bygone Days," *The Current* (Van Buren, MO), September 10, 1931.

35. Based on the research of Vicki L. Tobias, in my possession.

36. See esp. John F. Bradbury Jr., "'This War Is Managed Mighty Strange': The Army of Southeastern Missouri, 1862–1863," *Missouri Historical Review* 89 (October 1994): 28–47.

37. See Bruce Nichols, *Guerrilla Warfare in Civil War Missouri, 1862* (Jefferson, NC: McFarland & Co., 2004), 117, 125, 173–74. For the Mans or Mahans Creek skirmish, see US War Dept., *War of the Rebellion: Official Records of the Union and Confederate Armies,* series 1, vol. 22, chap. 34 (Washington, DC: GPO, 1180–1901), 312–13. Those known to have

joined Confederate ranks were Hiram Adair, John Chilton, Thomas Goff, two James Mahans, Samuel Mahan, and William Mahan. I thank Vicki Tobias for uncovering this information.

38. See "George Franklin Chilton, Sr.," in *Biographical Sketches of the Officers and Members of the Twenty-Seventh General Assembly of Missouri Together with State Officers, Etc.,* ed. John W. Pattison (n.p.: Regain & Carter, Printers, 1874); Maida Thomas, "History of Shannon County," unpublished manuscript, prepared for the Works Progress Administration, 3, copy in the Duane Meyer Library, Missouri State University; Marian M. Ohman, "Shannon County Courthouse," http://extension.missouri.edu/p/UED6100 (accessed Aug. 24, 2014); Leland Adair, "A History of Eminence, Mo.," a typewritten manuscript in the Missouri State Archives, Jefferson City, MO. According to David Lewis, a local historian, the county built a log courthouse with a lean-to jail attached for $75. No one lived at the site, even up the time it was destroyed during the Civil War. See *History of Shannon County, Missouri 2001* (Eminence, MO: Friends of the Library, 2001), 7. For the absence of elections in the county during the war, see "Election Returns, 1836–," Missouri State Archives, Jefferson City, MO. Opened in 1848, the Eminence Post Office was probably located at the cabin of the local postmaster, who for many years was Alfred Deatherage. For the absence of county government, see "George F. Chilton," *Current Wave* (Eminence, MO), Jan. 11, 1900, a special edition of the newspaper.

39. See "Alexander Deatherage," *Ozarker* (Sept. 1969): 7; and *Current Wave,* July 16, 1903, and Jan. 26, 1906. In 1903, Deatherage won the prize at the Fourth of July celebration in Eminence for being the oldest settler in the county. According to a different account, the county hid its records in a cave in a ravine at the head of Horse Hollow. Oscar Harper, "Vignette of Life," no place, no date, manuscript in my possession. For a fictional account, see Ray H. Weekly, "Dark Clouds over Shannon," *Ozarker* (Nov.–Dec. 1978), 20.

40. US Bureau of the Census, "Non-Population Census" (Shannon County, Missouri, 1860).

41. John W. Boyd to John Lovell, Nov. 23, 1863, in US War Dept., *War of the Rebellion,* series 1, vol. 22, part 1, 749; and http://ebooks.library.cornell.edu/cgi/t/text/text-idx?c=moawar;cc=moawar;view=toc;subview=short; idno=waro0033 (accessed June 29, 2016).

42. According to the 1860 census, four James Mahans lived in Delaware Township. This appears to be the twenty-two-year-old son of the patriarch of the Mahan clan, William "Billy" Mahan. See www.ancestry.com (accessed Jan. 12, 2012).

43. Quotations in US War Dept., *War of the Rebellion,* series 1, vol. 22, part 1, 746–47; and http://ebooks.library.cornell.edu/cgi/t/text/text-idx?c=moawar;cc=moawar;view=toc;subview=short;idno=waro0033 (accessed June 19, 2014); and reprinted in Robert Flanders, "Regional History," in *Cultural Overview Mark Twain National Forest,* vol. 1, Mary Lou Douthit et al., report to Forest Supervisor, Mark Twain National Forest, Rolla, Missouri, US Forest Service, Department of Agriculture, 1979, 212–13.

Boyd's report is also reprinted in J. J. Chilton et al., *The Civil War in Carter and Shannon County* (Van Buren, MO: West Carter County Genealogy Society, n.d.), 112–14. See also evidence that Boyd mustered out of the militia on July 1, 1865. See http://books.google.com/books?id=SAFA AAAAYAAJ&pg=PA396&lpg=PA396&dq=LT.+John+W.+Boyd+Missouri+ Militia&source=bl&ots=hRIWFaamYl&sig=RoxwVgSQLctLGKPm6l0E87 cUdNY&hl=en&ei=FWC4Tf-AYOUtwfR9PDeBA&sa=X&oi=book_ result&ct=result&resnum=4&sqi=2&ved=0CC0Q6AEwAw#v=onepage& q=LT.%20John%20W.%20Boyd%20Missouri%20Militia&f=false (accessed June 19, 2014).

44. *Current Wave*, Oct. 8, 1925.

45. US Bureau of the Census, *Non-Population Census for the Southern States*, 1860 and 1870.

46. *Current Wave*, Oct. 22, 1885, referring to Eminence in 1868.

47. As quoted in a reminiscence issue of *Current Wave*, June 25, 1914. In 1872, according to *Current Wave* (Winona, MO), Oct. 30, 1890, only one man in Eminence voted for Ulysses S. Grant for the presidency.

48. The invasion could have been part of the Rocky Mountain locust plague that struck Missouri, though locals referred to it as a grasshopper plague.

49. Eunice Pennington, *History of the Ozarks*, rev. ed. (n.p.: School of the Ozarks Press, 1971), 47; *Missouri Yearbook of Agriculture*, annual report, (Jefferson City, MO?, 1874); and *Current Wave*, Aug. 24, 1893, which refers to 1874. The agricultural yearbook also noted that the price of unimproved land in Shannon County was "quite low."

50. John Bradbury and Lou Wehmer, "William Monks: Union Guerilla and Memoirist," in *A History of Southern Missouri and Northern Arkansas*, ed. John F. Bradbury Jr. and Lou Wehmer (Fayetteville: University of Arkansas Press, 2003), xxxv.

51. John M. Daugherty, County Clerk, to Missouri Secretary of State, Nov. 20, 1870, "Abstract of the Poll Books of Shannon County in the Gen. Election held Nov 8, 1870," Election Returns, box 13, Missouri State Archives. Ex-Confederate soldiers elected in 1870 also included Alex Deatherage, treasurer, and A. M. Depriest, school commissioner.

52. *Current Wave*, Dec. 18, 1947.

53. Ibid., May 20, 1897, as reprinted in issue of May 19, 1927.

5 ✦ Granny and Her Family

1. Consistent with the recent literature on women in the history of the Upland South, I emphasize the importance of Nancy's personality and religiosity as a source of her family leadership. See for example Barbara Ellen Smith, "Beyond the Mountains: The Paradox of Women's Place in Appalachian History," *NWSA Journal* (Autumn 1999): 1–17. Earlier observers have suggested that the sheer determination and spiritedness of older Upland South women in the face of years of toil and tribulations won them the admiration of their sons and grandsons. See for example John C.

Campbell, *The Southern Highlander and His Homeland* (New York: Russell Sage Foundation, 1921), 140; and Emma Bell Miles, *The Spirit of the Mountains* (New York: James Pott & Company, 1905), 37.

2. It may be that these figures actually refer to the farm occupied by the Raders in 1879, rather than their farm on Mahans Creek in 1880. See US Bureau of the Census, "Non-Population Census of Fifteen Southern States Agricultural" (Shannon County, Missouri, 1880), manuscripts in National Archives, microfilm copies in State Historical Society of Missouri, Columbia, Missouri.

3. Abstract C 31180, for E. M. Rader, compiled by Security Land and Abstract Co., Eminence, MO, No. 2279, in my possession; and Sheriff's Deed, March 13, 1885, conveying twenty acres of land from Martin Moon, Daniel Leatherman, and William D. Romer to Nancy Rader; copy in my possession.

4. See Delaware assessments, *Current Wave*, Jan. 28, 1886; and *Missouri Yearbook of Agriculture, Annual Report* (Jefferson City, MO: Tribune Printing, 1886).

5. For this era, there are no crop productivity figures for the Mahans Creek bottomland or by counties for Missouri. Missouri statewide saw the average yield for corn drop to 16.5 bushels to the acre in 1881, more than 10 bushels below the state average for the late nineteenth century. In the 1920–1929 era, years that enjoyed above average precipitation and lower than average high temperatures in July, Shannon County as a whole averaged only 19.9 bushels per acre. This is probably somewhat below yields on the creek and other bottomlands for the 1920s (as well as in the late nineteenth century). See State Department of Agriculture, *Missouri Annual Crop and Livestock Production, by Counties for 20-Year Period, 1919–1949* (Jefferson City, MO, 1950?); *The Bulletin* 40, no. 14 (Dec. 31, 1942). It is possible that these figures considerably understate yields on Mahans Creek and its tributaries. For example, U. M. Randolph, who farmed in the Mahan's Creek basin (specifically, Pine Hollow), claimed that he produced a stunning 81 bushels per acre in 1904! This would have been 55 bushels per acre above the state average yield for that year. As reported in Walter Williams, *The State of Missouri: An Autobiography* (Columbia, MO: E. W. Stephens, 1904), 86. Also see http://books.google.com/books?id=xcQCAAAAMAAJ&print sec=frontcover&source=gbs_ge_summary_r&cad=0#v=onepage&q&f=false (accessed Sept. 3, 2010).

6. Oscar Harper, "A Trip into Yesterday," *Ozarker* (Dec. 1975), 10. See also *Fifteenth Annual Report of the State Board of Agriculture of State of Missouri for the Years of 1880 and 1881* (Jefferson City, MO: Tribune Co., 1881).

7. Hulbert "Hub" Rader, "What I Tell My Grandchildren," in Jayne Rader's "Rader Family," 32.

8. *Current Wave*, Dec. 17, 1884. *The Eighteenth Annual Report of the State Board of Agriculture, Missouri, 1885* (Jefferson City, MO: Tribune Printing, 1885), 215–16, vividly described the symptoms and treatment of hog cholera. The newspaper reported complaints of "hard times" throughout the county. Teacher Ulysses Randolph, for example, had to close down the

"Klepzig" school before Christmas, apparently because the parents were unable to pay their subscriptions.

9. *Current Wave*, Sept. 9, 1886.

10. Ibid., Aug. 26, 1886, Nov. 14, 1887. The issue of April 1, 1886, reported that Jesse Laxton of Delaware lost nearly all of his fencing from a forest fire.

11. *Current Wave*, March 31, 1887. For corn yields, see *Current Wave*, Nov. 24, 1887.

12. *Current Wave*, April 7, 1892. The issue of Jan. 26, 1893, claimed that the average yields for Shannon County were 40 bushels of corn, 30 bushels of oats, 18 bushels of wheat, two tons of hay, and 200 gallons of sorghum per acre for 1892.

13. *Current Wave*, July 11, 1895; Gertrude Dorow, *Shannon County Historical Review* (Spring 1967): 6. The flood in Winona captured the attention of the entire nation. See "Winona's Great Disaster," *New York Times*, July 9, 1895; also see http://boards.ancestry.com/localities.northam. usa.states.missouri.counties.shannon/1623/mb.ashx (accessed Feb. 19, 2012).

14. Hulbert Rader, "What I Tell My Grandchildren," 31.

15. Oscar Harper, "Birch Prairie," *Shannon County Historical Review* (Winter 1966): 7.

16. Hulbert Rader, "What I Tell My Grandchildren," 31.

17. Quoted from her obituary, *Current Wave*, April 6, 1916.

18. Proceedings of the Shannon County Board of Equalization, in *Current Wave*, April 21, 1892.

19. General Affidavit in support of Claim # 3711920 of Nancy Rader by John H. Pummill, July 30, 1897, National Archives. Copy in my possession. The other data for Nancy's holdings in this paragraph also come from statements supporting her claims for a Civil War pension.

20. *Current Wave*, April 7, 1898. See also the recollections of Jon Maxwell Rader to Benjamin Rader, Aug. 2013, in my possession, regarding payments in kind from Sam Rader to Nancy Rader.

21. Examining Surgeon's Certificate in the Case of an Original Applicant, No. of Application 195.023, George W. Raider [*sic*], April, ?, 1875, National Archives. Copy in my possession.

22. Widow's Pension, 371, 920, Nancy Rader, Aug. 28, 1897, National Archives. Copy in my possession. According to an unofficial document apparently copied from an official one, Nancy filed for a pension in 1888. "Widow's Declaration for Pension or Increase of Pension," April 23, 1888, filed in Shannon County. See Jim L. Kiser, "The Family and Descendants of George Washington Rader and Nancy Childress from 1830 to 1973 A.D.," unpublished manuscript in my possession; but there is no evidence in the National Archives that this petition succeeded.

23. See Steven Lee Stepp, "'The Old Reliable': The History of the Springfield Wagon Company, 1872–1952" (MA thesis, Southwest Missouri State College, 1972).

24. Hulbert Rader, "What I Tell My Grandchildren," 32.

25. See Tobias, "Rader Family Tree"; and Jayne Rader, "Sam's Siblings," unpublished manuscript in my possession.

26. *Current Wave*, Oct. 22, 1884.

27. See Jayne Rader, "Sam's Siblings." It could be that in 1899 John considered returning to Shannon County, for Lewis Perkins, his brother-in-law, purchased forty acres of township school lands on behalf of John for $50. Likely, however, John put up the money for this property so that Lewis and his family could use it. See "Township Land Patents," Vol. 4, page 249, Reel # s00203, Record Group: Office of the Secretary of State, in Missouri State Archives.

28. Danny Searcy, telephone interview with author, Nov. 15, 2012; Luther Rowlett, "The Carrs of Shannon County," *Shannon County Historical Review* (Winter 1968): 3; *Current Wave*, Dec. 24, 1884, Jan. 14, 1886.

29. "Court and Legal Documents, James Orchard," Center for Ozark Studies, RG8-11, Series VIII: Shannon County Projects, box 12, file 32, Special Collections and Archives, Missouri State University; *Current Wave*, Sept. 10 and 17, 1896.

30. *Current Wave*, Oct. 22, 1884.

31. Ibid., Jan. 13, 1899.

32. Ibid., Nov. 25, 1920.

33. Ibid., Sept. 16, 1886. See also *Current Wave*, July 1, 1897, which reported that a number of years ago Louis [Lewis] Rader was shot in the leg above the thigh. The bullet had begun to cause him pain. Dr. Frank Hyde, the local doctor, made an incision in Lewis's leg, but could not find the bullet.

34. In his remembrance, "What I Tell My Grandchildren," Hulbert Rader reported that Nancy Jane Childress Rader "was very much against drinking and gambling."

35. See obituary, appended to "Lewis A. Rader," Tobias, "Rader Family Tree." One of his daughters, Myrtle Rader Robinson, taught school for several years in Eminence. Many more of the details of the life of Lewis Rader and his family can be found in the *Current Wave*.

36. *Current Wave*, Oct. 29, 1884, reported the death of Kate Bailey, the wife of Dr. Samuel M. Bailey. Upon the death of his wife, Bailey apparently moved to Elsberry, Missouri, where he continued the practice of medicine. See http://home.comcast.net/~neal4/moelsbe3.htm (accessed July 25, 2012). I thank Vicki Tobias for her research on this subject.

37. See letter of Lillie May Rader Raper (daughter of Jim Rader), July 4, 1978, in Jayne Rader, " Sam's Siblings."

6 ✦ That Old Red Should Be Killed

1. *The Passerby*, October 8, 1932. A monthly mimeographed newsletter of the extended "Pummill Tribe," a copy in my possession.

2. *The Passerby*, March 7, 1933. In a later issue of *The Passerby*, Oct. 5, 1935, James Everett Pummill described Old Red as "the best coon dog that ever sent his voice bounding from the echoing peaks of 'Grape Ridge.'"

3. Arch Pummill, digitally recorded interview with author, Oct. 13, 2009, in my possession.

4. *The Passerby*, February 10, 1933.

5. For family genealogy and family lore see Vicki L. Tobias, "Rader Family Tree," http://www.ancestry.com (accessed July 29, 2014); and an untitled 84-page manuscript apparently put together by Troy F. Pummill in 1996, copy attached to letter, Betty Bresnick to Benjamin Rader, March 21, 2015. Copy in my possession.

6. "Hezekiah Pummell," in Tobias, "Rader Family Tree."

7. The 1830 census reports both a John Pummel and a Sampson Pummel as heads of household living in Paint Township. Notice, however, the different spellings. Sometimes the family's surname was also spelled Pumell. For a Pummell Cemetery, spelled in some sources as Pumell, in which Hezekiah and Barbara Knisley Pummill were apparently buried on their farm in unmarked graves, see http://ohio.hometownlocator.com/maps/feature-map,ftc,2,fid,1044794,n,pumill%20cemetery.cfm (accessed Oct. 12, 2014); and TGPS Coordinates: Latitude: 39.14170, Longitude: -83.40170. The cemetery is said to be on a farm once owned by Hezekiah Pummill.

8. See Andrew R. L. Cayton, "The Ohio Valley," in *Encyclopedia of American Social History*, ed. Mary Kupiec Cayton, Elliott J. Gorn, and Peter W. Williams (New York: Charles Scribner's Sons, 1993), 962–63; Nicole Etcheson, *The Emerging Midwest: Upland Southerners and the Political Culture of the Old Northwest, 1787–1861* (Bloomington: Indiana University Press, 1996). Etcheson sees the Upland Southerners in the area as gradually taking on a new identity as "Westerners."

9. Quoted in Perry McCandless, *A History of Missouri*, vol. 2, 1820–1860 (Columbia: University of Missouri Press, 1972), 229.

10. In Lucy Wortham James Collection, State Historical Society of Missouri, Columbia, Missouri.

11. Obituary in *Current Wave*, Feb. 8, 1900.

12. Based on U S Bureau of the Census, "Non-Population Census Agricultural" (Osage County, Missouri, 1870), manuscript in the National Archives, microfilm copy in the State Historical Society of Missouri, Columbia, Missouri.

13. John H. Pummill file, "Soldiers' Records: War of 1812–World War I," Missouri State Archives, Jefferson City, MO, http:/osagecounty.org/civilwar/emm/28emm.html (accessed July 12, 2013). John's brother, Joseph, saw fifty-two days of active duty. Attached to Vicki L. Tobias, "Joseph M. Pummill," in her "Rader Family" See also Mark A. Lause, "Enrolled Missouri Militia," in *Encyclopedia of the American Civil War: A Political, Social, and Military History*, vol. 2, ed. David S. Heidler and Jeanne T. Heidler (Santa Barbara, CA: ABC-Clio, 2000), 655–56.

14. See attachments to Vicki Tobias, "John Matthews" and "Sampson Matthews," in her "Rader Family"; and J. Houston Harrison, *Settlers by the Long Grey Trail: Some Pioneers in Old Augusta County, Virginia, and Their Descendants, of the family of HARRISON and Allied Lines* (Baltimore: Genealogical Pub. Co., 1975), 149, 151, 248.

15. Diana Franken, telephone interview with author, November 23, 2010.

16. See http://www.glorecords.blm.gov/PatentSearch/Results.asp?QryId=38171.53 (accessed Oct. 2, 2011).

17. See www.placenames.com/us/29/(accessed Oct. 16, 2011).

18. C. J. Vaughan, comp., *Osage County Business and Individual Directory,* 1915, http://www.osagecounty.org/documents/1915busdir/1915 index.html (accessed June 29, 2016).

19. *The Passerby,* June 4, 1933?, 2. The agricultural censuses of 1870 and 1880 reveal the size of her farming operations. US Bureau of the Census, "Nonpopulation Census, Agricultural" (Osage County, MO, 1870 and 1880).

20. Hattie Mantle, "History of Osage County," *Osage County Observer* (Linn, MO), Nov. 10, 1966.

21. Quoted in http://www.findagrave.com/cgi-bin/fg.cgi?page=gr&GS cid=29164&GRid=34583085& (accessed July 24, 2011).

22. Arch Pummill and Jerome Rader, digitally recorded interview with author, Sept. 18, 2010, in my possession.

23. According to the 1880 census, there were twenty-four blacks living in the Mint Hill (more specifically, Crawford Township) neighborhood. For this paragraph see "Family by Hon. Frank Stoner," undated and unidentified newspaper clipping referring specifically to Delbert Matthews, a long-time county judge in Osage County and grandson of Alexander and Beditha Matthews. Copy in Osage County Historical Society, Linn, Missouri, and in my possession.

24. See, for example, the references to members of the extended Matthews family in *The Passerby.*

25. Both the population and agricultural censuses, taken by the same person (J. K. Kidd) appear to spell John Pummill's surname as "Pommell." The 1870 census also lists John and Lydia as having a one-year-old daughter, "Lydia." This must have been, in fact, Sarah Rebecca Pummill. Because the censuses are handwritten in cursive, it is impossible to be absolutely sure how the census taker intended to spell the surnames. Of course, the census taker could also have been given incorrect information. However, evidence supporting the conclusion that the entries of "John Pommell" were in fact for John Pummill is strong. The ages reported in the population census are the same as the known ages of all three of John Pummill's family members. Supporting the supposition that the John Matthews reported in the agricultural census as owning a farm next to Beditha Boyse Matthews is the fact that the only adult John Matthews in Osage County is reported elsewhere in the census. For the population censuses, see www.ancestry.com (June 29, 2015), and for the agricultural census, see "Non-Population Census Agricultural" (Osage County, MO, 1880).

26. Handwritten commentary at the bottom of the page of Matthews Family Group Sheet in the Osage County Historical Society, Linn, Missouri. Copy in my possession. This document also provides a legal description of the farm.

27. US Dept. of Agriculture, Soil Conservation Service, *Soil Survey of Osage County, Missouri* (no place, no date), sheet number 7 (soil map) and 123, 124.

28. Quit claim deed, John H. and Lydia Pummill to Gilbert D. Matthews, Oct. 15, 1881, and warranty deed, John H. and Lydia Pummill to

H. G. Matthews, Oct. 15, 1884, Osage County Recorder of Deeds. Copies in my possession.

29. "Deed from Samuel Jerome Matthews . . . John P.[H?] Pummill, and wife Lydia Pummill . . . transfer and convey unto C[laiborne] L. Matthews of Osage County Missouri the property consisting of all our right title interest or real estate of every kind and consideration that Burgess Matthews deceased who died in Marion Co, Tn 19 January, 1882," Marion County, Tennessee, Recorder of Deeds; copy in my possession. The family lore is that Burgess Matthews owned a huge acreage, but I have been unable to verify this contention. No acreage is given in the above-cited document.

30. "Register of Teachers," Records of the Liberty School, Osage County [Missouri] Historical Society and the Missouri State Archives. Copies in my possession. The stone foundations of the school were still present when Dianne Franken and I visited the school's site on November 3, 2011.

31. See http://www.mindspring.com/~mgentges/ (accessed March 19, 2011).

32. Quit claim deed, John H. Pummill and wife to G. D. Matthews, Sept. 15, 1881, and warranty deed, John H. Pummill and Lydia Pummill to H. G. Matthews, Oct. 4, 1884, in Osage County Recorder's Office. Copy in my possession. The relevant School Tax Rolls, Osage County, are in the State Historical Society of Missouri, Columbia, MO.

33. The family could have moved to Shannon County in 1889, as indicated in the obituaries of both Joseph and Everett Pummill; however, in "The Need for Forest Conservation," *Current Wave*, March 14, 1946, Joseph Pummill reported that the family first arrived and rented the farm then owned (in 1946) by Julius Lahmeyer in the spring of 1890. The same claim is also made in the obituary of John Pummill, *Current Wave*, Feb. 8, 1900. According to this source, the Pummills lived in Dent County for one year.

34. Mrs. Lawrence Pummill (Crystal Pummill), "The Pummill Family," *Ozarker* (November–December 1978): 1.

35. As quoted in Thela Winterbottom, "Remember When," *Ozarker* (July 1979): 5.

36. Pummill, "The Pummill Family," 1. That the Pummills chose to move specifically to the Mahan's Creek watershed may have been due to a relative by marriage, one Samuel W. Agee, who had been a schoolteacher in Osage County but later apparently took up farming near Birch Tree in Shannon County. As a Republican, he ran unsuccessfully several times for countywide office.

37. *Current Wave*, Aug. 18, 1892. Also see *Current Wave*, March 3, 1910.

7 ✦ The Neighborhood

1. See Vicki L. Tobias, "Rader Family Tree," www.ancestry.com (accessed June 30, 2015); and Jayne Rader "Sam's Siblings," unpublished manuscript in my possession.

2. See Hal S. Barron, *Those Who Stayed Behind: Rural Society in*

Nineteenth-Century New England (Cambridge, Eng.: Cambridge University Press, 1984). Rather than New England, the decennial persistence rate of Delaware families came closer to families elsewhere in the American West. See, for example, John Mack Faragher, *Sugar Creek: Life on the Illinois Prairie* (New Haven: Yale University Press, 1986), 50–51. Yet, while about two-thirds of those living in Sangamon County, Illinois, moved each decade, up to three-fourths of those in Delaware Township left each decade.

3. *Statistics of Churches*, Eleventh Census of the United States (Washington, DC: GPO, 1894). With 261 communicants, the Baptists had the largest membership in the county. The Methodists followed with 81 members. According to the census, not a single active Catholic lived in the county. However, this may have been incorrect because at the turn of the century a priest from White Church in Howell County, Missouri, irregularly heard confessions and celebrated masses in a private home in Birch Tree.

4. The Birch Tree *Herald*, June 23, 1899, sneeringly observed that evangelist D. R. Walker "even had enough nerve" to try to hold a revival in Eminence in 1897.

5. See *Current Wave*, Dec. 17, 1884, June 9, 1887, and July 15, 1886. For a report of the first quarterly meeting of the Eminence circuit of the Methodist Episcopal Church, a meeting in which "Miss Keziah Rader" participated, see the *Current Wave*, May 12, 1887. The Klepzig family, into which Keziah married, were also active Methodists. For a description of such meetings in the Arkansas Ozarks, see Tate C. Page, *The Voices of Moccasin Creek* (Point Lookout, MO: School of the Ozarks Press, 1972), 43–44.

6. Reported in *Current Wave*, Aug. 27, 1888, Oct. 20, 1891, as reprinted in *Current Wave*, Oct. 20, 1927. There are numerous other reports of public disturbances in Eminence, Winona, and Birch Tree during the 1880s.

7. *Current Wave*, Feb. 26, 1891.

8. Ibid., July 1, 1886.

9. For 1882, see *Current Wave*, Aug. 27, 1884, and for opinion of Sholar, see *Current Wave*, April 6, 1893.

10. *Shannon County Democrat* (Winona, MO), Aug. 29, 1913; *Shannon Herald* (Birch Tree, MO), Jan. 2, 1914.

11. See the observations about the small town newspaper editors and publishers by Lynn Morrow, "Modernity and the *Current Wave* in Shannon County, 1884–1896," *Missouri Historical Society Bulletin* 35 (January 1979): 92–98; and Robert B. Flanders, "Pride and Progress: The Evangelism of Modernity," *Ozarks Watch* 5 (Winter 1992): 5–8.

12. *Current Wave*, Nov. 23, 1911.

13. Quoted in G. R. Kenamore, "The Ozarks Fifty Years Ago," *Current Wave*, Oct. 1, 1925. However, the Aug. 26, 1888, issue of the *Current Wave* reported an outbreak of thieves butchering hogs in the woods. This is the only report of this kind that I encountered in the county's newspapers. On the other hand, reports of unidentified missing cows, horses, and hogs appeared in numerous issues of the weekly newspapers.

14. See, for example, Page, *Voices of Moccasin Creek*, 75.

15. Ruby Cloe Langley, "James 'Bear Huntin'' 'Jim' Russell Hill," http://familytreemaker.genealogy.com/users/e/v/a/Jane-M-Evans-MISSOURI/WEBSITE-0001/UHP-0521.html (accessed Sept. 16, 2012); obituary in *Current Wave*, July 11, 1895.

16. The *Current Wave*, May 9, 1918, reported that Sam Rader, Alex Hill, and Mac Stubblefield "went wolf hunting last week."

17. *Current Wave*, Dec. 24, 1884. For a dance at a Mr. Piatt's cabin on Mahan's Creek, see *Current Wave*, Jan. 7, 1887. See also the recollections of Oscar Harper, "Delaware of Yesterday," *Shannon County Historical Review* (Autumn 1966): 1. Copy in my possession.

18. See "Court and Legal Documents, James Orchard," Center for Ozark Studies, RG8-11, Series VIII: Shannon County Projects, box 12, file 32, Missouri State University Archives, Springfield, Missouri; *Current Wave*, Oct. 28, 1897, and July 23, 1891; and, for parallel instances elsewhere in the Ozarks, see Page, *Voices of Moccasin Creek*, 211–18; and, for a somewhat later date, Robert K. Gilmore, *Ozark Baptizings, Hangings, and Other Diversions: Theatrical Folkways of Rural Missouri, 1895–1910* (Norman: University of Oklahoma Press, 1984).

19. *Current Wave*, Dec. 3, 1884.

20. Sept. 30, 1886, reprinted in *Current Wave*, Sept. 30, 1926.

21. July 29, 1886, reprinted in *Current Wave*, July 29, 1926.

22. Controlled by Radical Republicans, in 1866 the Missouri legislature passed a battery of laws establishing a statewide public school system. See William E. Parrish, *Missouri under Radical Rule, 1865–1870* (Columbia: University of Missouri Press, 1965), chap. 7. Since courthouse fires destroyed Shannon County's early school records, it is impossible to reconstruct fully how these laws may have been implemented there. Available evidence comes from scattered and brief reports in the surviving issues of the *Current Wave*. It appears that the first schools in the county were financed by "subscriptions," in other words, the parents paid the teacher with cash or in kind.

23. From a description by an old-timer, Dough Casey, in Oscar Harper, "Delaware of Yesterday," *Shannon County Historical Review* (Autumn 1966): 1, copy in my possession. The *Current Wave*, July 15, 1886, referred to the school as the "Catlett School." The school was located on what was then called the Catlett farm, once owned by Henry Catlett, a pioneer Delaware settler. For typical attendance, see David Lewis, "The Schools of Shannon County," *Ozarker* (Sept.–Oct. 1978): 10.

24. *Current Wave*, Dec. 17, 1884, July 15, 1886.

25. Oscar Harper, "Delaware of Yesterday," *Shannon County Historical Review* (Autumn 1966): 1.

26. See *Current Wave*, Oct. 29, 1884, for a report of the countywide candidates speaking at Lloyd's mill.

27. Arch Pummill, interview by author and Jerome Rader, Oct. 16, 2010. Digital recording in my possession.

28. For a parallel instance in the development of an indigenous folk culture, see Dunn's discussion: Durwood Dunn, *Cades Cove: The Life and Death of a Southern Appalachian Community, 1818–1937* (Knoxville: University of Tennessee Press, 1988), chap. 6.

Afterword ✦ "The Colored Lunatic of Jackson Township"

1. See http://www.nps.gov/civilwar/search-soldiers.htm?submitted=
1&SDkeyword=&SDOriginState_count=None+Selected&SDlName=
Jackson&SDRankIn_count=None+Selected&SDfName=Cyrus&SDRank
Out_count=None+Selected&SDsideName=U&SDfunction_count=
None+Selected (accessed Nov. 23, 2013). The Missouri State Archives
online death certificates list Jackson's full name as "William Camp
Jackson," his father as "Silas Jackson," and his mother as "Caroline."
See http://www.sos.mo.gov/archives/resources/deathcertificates/Results.
asp?type=basic&tLName=Jackson&tFName=William&sCounty=St.%20
Louis&tYear=1952#null (accessed Nov. 23, 2013). Kimberly D. Harper has
rendered me invaluable assistance in unraveling the personal history of the
Jackson family.

2. *Current Wave*, Feb. 8, 1900.

3. See Kimberly D. Harper, *White Man's Heaven: The Lynching
and Expulsion of Blacks in the Southern Ozarks, 1894–1909* (Fayetteville:
University of Arkansas Press, 2012).

4. *Current Wave*, March 27, 1902.

5. Missouri State Board of Health, Certificate of Death, Cyrus Jackson,
May 22, 1918, Missouri State Archives, Jefferson City, Missouri.

6. Missouri State Archives online death certificates, http://www.sos.mo.
gov/archives/resources/deathcertificates/Results.asp?type=basic&tLName=-
Jackson&tFName=William&sCounty=St.%20Louis&tYear=1952#null
(accessed Nov. 25, 2013). For burial site of Jackson and the Dennis family,
see http://archstl.org/app/cemeteries/burial (accessed Nov. 25, 2013).

7. See http://genforum.genealogy.com/lowder/messages/228.html
(accessed Sept. 12, 2013). Vicki Tobias rendered invaluable assistance in
unraveling the history of "Fannie." While the ages correspond, the 1870 census lists her as "Fannie Smith"; the 1880 census, as "Fannie Janes"; and the
1900 census, as "Fanny J. Garrison." Curiously, the 1880 census labeled her
as "white." See www.ancestry.com (accessed June 29, 2025) for the specific
data in these years.

8. *Current Wave*, Nov. 10, 1887, reprinted in issue of Nov. 11, 1926.

9. *Current Wave*, Dec. 9, 1897. The identity of the African American is
unknown.

10. See *Current Wave*, Oct. 17, 1901, for a detailed report.

11. *Current Wave*, Oct. 22, 1902. The original intent of the cartoon may
have been the opposite of that of the editor of the *Wave*. The illustrator may
have been suggesting that African Americans should question their continuing support of the Republican Party. I thank Gary Kremer and Barbara
Huddleston for their aid in interpreting the meaning of the cartoon.

12. *Current Wave*, June 30, 1904.

13. Ibid., April 19, 1906. For details see Harper, *White Man's Heaven*.
From 1907 to 1914, Lyles, as a Democrat, represented Shannon County in
the Missouri General Assembly.

14. *Current Wave*, April 19, 1903.

15. Prior to 1911, I found no references to blacks in the *Birch Tree*

Record or the Winona *Shannon County Democrat.* But for the tie loaders and
the baseball references in Winona, see *Shannon County Democrat,* Aug. 4,
1911, Feb. 14, 1919, Aug. 1, 1919, and March 5, 1920. For black tie loaders
in Grandin in nearby Carter County, see David Benac, *Conflict in the Ozarks:
Hill Folk, Industrialists, and Government in Missouri's Courtois Hills* (Kirksville,
MO: Truman State University Press, 2010), 30–32; and for the performance
of "Uncle Tom's Cabin," see *Birch Tree Record,* Oct. 17, 1902.

16. *Current Wave,* Oct. 27, 1921. For repetitions of this theme, see
issues of Dec. 25, 1924, reprint of item for Sept. 23, 1886, in issue of
Sept. 9, 1926, and Sept. 8, 1927.

17. *Current Wave,* Nov. 23, 1922; *Shannon County Democrat,* Oct. 12,
1923.

18. *Current Wave,* Nov. 8, 1928. In the 1932 presidential election
Franklin D. Roosevelt, a Democrat, defeated Herbert Hoover, a Republican,
2,935 to 873. *Current Wave,* Nov. 10, 1932. In the *Shannon County Democrat,*
Dec. 11, 1903, a Winona resident, Robert Borah, queried: "How is it the
Irish, Sweeds [*sic*] and Germans (who are coming into this country daily)
don't stop in Shannon County? Let a man come here and say he is a Baptist
or Methodist and he is welcomed with open arms, but should he be a
Catholic, Lutheran, etc., he gets the 'marble hand' right away and this is
no way to build a community." Borah suggested that "our big men and landowners get together and donate land, lumber, etc., for church purposes . . .
and the country will blossom like a flower. . . . To realize that these advantages really exist [i.e., good weather and agricultural opportunity], and our
cut-off timber lands and forest oak will soon disappear, to be replaced by
orchards, vineyards, and fertile fields of grain, owned by prosperous, healthy,
hard-working frugal foreigners who would be a financial aid to any community—if they are well treated and made to feel at home. I hope all our
neighboring own[er]s will vie with each other in at [*sic*] spirit of love to make
the 'newcomer' feel welcome and know we are glad he is with us and that
we wish to help him all we can and try to make him happy amid his [new]
surroundings." The Jew was Isaac "Ike" Epstein, a long-time resident of
Eminence, where he was a businessman and a justice of the peace. He
converted to Christianity and married Mary Carr, and, upon her death,
Zenia Lewis.

19. *Current Wave,* March 2, 1922; *Shannon County Democrat,* Jan. 19,
1923. The opera house in Eminence also hosted a "colored minstrel troupe"
from Poplar Bluff, Missouri, in 1924 (*Current Wave,* May 22, 1924).

20. *Current Wave,* Oct. 24, 1923.

21. Ibid., Sept. 8, 1927, June 20, 1929, July 9, 1931, July 7, 1932,
July 7, 1938; *Shannon County Democrat,* July 5, 1934.

22. *Current Wave,* March 11, 1943. Her remarks were apparently based
on a play written in early 1943 by Hecht, entitled "We Will Never Die,"
which helped to raise awareness in the United States of the Holocaust. See
http://www.ushmm.org/wlc/en/article.php?ModuleId=10007036 (accessed
Nov. 14, 2013).

III ✦ "The Scream of the Saw Mill"

1. *The Passerby*, Jan. 7, 1939. See also *The Passerby*, Jan. 4, 1936. Copies in my possession. *The Passerby* is a mimeographed monthly newsletter of the extended Pummill family sent to family members during the 1930s.

2. *Current Wave*, June 17, 1897.

3. For parallel circumstances in Appalachia, see, for example, Ronald L. Lewis, "Railroads, Deforestation, and the Transformation of Agriculture in the West Virginia Back Counties, 1880–1920," in *Appalachia in the Making: The Mountain South in the Nineteenth Century*, ed. May Beth Pudup, Dwight B. Billings, and Altina L. Waller (Chapel Hill: University of North Carolina Press, 1995), 297–320. While the impact of extractive industries on Appalachia has been the subject of numerous monographs, the timber boom in the Ozarks had been less thoroughly studied, but see David Benac, *Conflict in the Ozarks: Hill Folk, Industrialists, and Government in Missouri's Courtois Hills* (Kirksville, MO: Truman State University, 2010); Judy Ferguson, *The Boom Town of West Eminence and Its Lumbering Days* (Rolla, MO: Rolla Printing Co., 1969); David Lewis, "The Logging Era," *Ozarker* (May 1979), 19–20, and (June 1979), 12–13; Donald L. Stevens Jr., *A Homeland and a Hinterland: The Current and Jacks Fork Riverways* (Omaha, NE: National Park Service, Midwest Region, 1991); James Lee Murphy, "A History of the Southeastern Ozark Region of Missouri" (PhD diss., Saint Louis University, 1982); and Leslie G. Hill, "History of the Missouri Lumber and Mining Company, 1880–1909" (PhD diss., University of Missouri, 1949).

8 ✦ The Coming of *Euphemia*

1. J. V. Cooper, "Then, and Now," *Shannon County Democrat* (Winona, MO), Sept. 15, 1938.

2. Oscar Harper, "Early Days of Lumbering," *Shannon County Historical Review* (Winter 1967): 3. See also *Current Wave*, June 23, 1893, Sept. 7, 1893, Nov. 9, 1893; and for the locomotive works, see Raymond F. Shuck, *A Brief History of the Lima Locomotive Works* (Lima, OH: Lima Historical Society, 1983).

3. *Birch Tree Record*, May 5, 1899; http://www.ttarchive.com/Library/Biographies/Fisher_OW_AL.html (accessed Oct. 16, 2013); "The Cordz-Fisher Lumber Company," *Current Wave*, New Year's Edition, Jan. 11, 1900. I would also like to thank Douglas Dowden, the retired owner of the Birch Tree Bank, for providing me with information on the impact of the timber boom as well as a guided historical tour of Birch Tree and the surrounding area on May 13, 2012.

4. For workers living in tents, see *Current Wave*, Nov. 9, 1893. See also Gertrude (Rader) Dorow, "Gertrude Dorow," *Shannon County Historical Review* (Spring 1967): 6.

5. *Current Wave*, Jan. 21, 1897. In 1909, the county produced 365,500 railroad ties and 36 million feet of lumber. *Missouri Red Book*, Thirty-Second

Annual Report of the Bureau of Labor Statistics (Jefferson City, MO: Bureau of Labor Statistics, [1910]), 182.

6. Rav Von Harrison, telephone interview with author, Dec. 10, 2012; *Current Wave,* Jan. 13, 1898; *Shannon County Democrat,* May 3, 1912; www. ruralmissouri.org109pages/090ctTieRafters.htm/ (accessed Dec. 2, 2012).

7. See especially "Tap Line Case Summary of Salem, Winona & Southern Railroad," published in decisions of the Interstate Commerce Commission, http://www.ttarchive.com/library/Articles/TapLineCase_ SalemWinona&Southern.html (accessed Dec. 14, 2012).

8. C. C. Sheppard to J. B. White, Aug. 17, 1907, folder #554, Missouri Lumber and Mining Company Collection, State Historical Society of Missouri, Columbia, Missouri. See also the vivid recollection of J. V. Cooper, "Leaves from Paul Bunyan's Notebook," *Shannon County Democrat,* Sept. 15, 1938.

9. *Current Wave,* July 18, 1907. For a general treatment of the timber boom but without documentation, see David Lewis, "The Logging Era," *Ozarker,* May 1979, 17–18, and June 1979, 12. For a scholarly study focusing on adjacent Carter rather than Shannon County, see David Benac, *Conflict in the Ozarks: Hill Folks, Industrialists, and Government in Missouri's Courtois Hills* (Kirksville, MO: Truman State University, 2010).

10. Apparently there was only one effort—an abortive one—to organize mill workers in the region. That was at the Cordz-Fisher mill in Birch Tree. See *Birch Tree Record,* June 6, June 19, 1903.

11. Judy Ferguson, *The Boom Town of West Eminence and Its Lumbering Days* (Rolla, MO: Rolla Printing Co., 1969); *Current Wave,* Nov. 20, 1919; Jerry Ponder, *Grandin, Hunter, West Eminence, and the Missouri Lumber and Mining Company* (Doniphan, MO: Ponder Books, 1989).

12. C. C. Sheppard to James P. Rader, Sept. 26, 1908, Nov. 17, 1908, Center for Ozark Studies, RG8-11, Series VIII: Shannon County Projects, box 12, file 32, Missouri State University Archives. Originals in J. B. White Correspondence, Missouri Mining and Lumber Company Collection, State Historical Society of Missouri.

13. Birch Tree *Record,* Jan. 13, 1899.

14. Ibid., Sept 15, 1910; *Current Wave,* Oct. 3, 1912.

15. Arch Pummill and Jerome Rader, digitally recorded interview with author, Sept. 18, 2010, in my possession.

16. *Current Wave,* Oct. 14, 1909; "Statement of Salem, Winona and Southern Railroad Co. for Fiscal Year Ending June 30, 1913," Center for Ozark Studies, RG8-11, Series VIII: Shannon County Projects, box 12, file 32, Missouri State University Archives. Original in the Missouri Mining and Lumber Company Collection, State Historical Society of Missouri.

17. William French, in the *Shannon County Historical Review* (May 1968): 1.

18. *Current Wave,* Aug. 29, 1907, April 25, 1907, July 25, 1907; *Shannon County Democrat,* Jan. 22, 1904. For Jim Rader's difficulties with the railroad see C. C. Sheppard to J. P. Rader, June 8, 1907; J. B. White to C. C. Sheppard, June 13, 1907; C. C. Sheppard to J. P. Rader, June 14,

1907; C. C. Sheppard to L. A. Rader, June 26, 1907, all in J. B. White Correspondence, Missouri Mining and Lumber Company Collection, State Historical Society of Missouri.

19. See Ferguson, *The Boom Town of West Eminence*. The State Historical Society of Missouri holds a huge collection of the papers of the Missouri Lumber and Mining Company.

20. C. C. Shephard to J. B. White, June 27, 1906, f. 78, in J. B. White Correspondence, Missouri Lumber and Mining Company Papers.

21. See Gertrude (Rader) Dorow, "Gertrude Dorow," in *Shannon County Historical Review* (Spring 1967): 6, for the Randolph story; and Mabel L. Cooper, *3-R's in the Ozarks* (Eminence, MO: Chilton Printing Co., 1980), 56–57, for the Pummill story.

22. See the agricultural censuses of the decadal US censuses from 1880 through 1920 for Shannon County, Missouri.

23. This is based in part on comparing photographs from the era with the models presented in JoAnne Olian, ed., *Everyday Fashions: 1909–1920 As Pictured in Sears Catalogs* (Mineola, NY: Dover Pubs., 1995). For Randolph, see *Shannon Herald*, April 17, 1914.

24. Arch Pummill, digitally recorded interview with author, April 22, 2010. Copy in my possession.

25. For quote, see *Shannon County Democrat*, Aug. 25, 1911. In 1899 alone Rader filed two suits. See *Birch Tree Record*, Sept. 3, 1899.

26. J. E. Pummill, in *The Passerby*, Sept. 1932. For a more detailed description of the kind of marble game played by Jim and his brother-in-laws, see "Traditional Games," http://missourifolkloresociety.truman.edu/traditionalgames.html (accessed June 30, 2014).

27. *The Passerby*, Jan. 4, 1936.

28. Nancy Rader Corghan, "Mike Rader, My Father," *Ozarker* (July 1972), 7. See "Obituary of Lawrence E. Pummill," in Vicki L. Tobias, "Rader Family."

29. For a biographical sketch and a photo of William Marion Freeman, see *History of Shannon County Missouri 2001* (Eminence, MO: Friends of the Library, 2001), 172. See also the photo and sketch of his father on the same page. For Jim's purchase of the Catlett farm and the re-evaluation of his property, see *Current Wave*, Feb. 10, 1898, and Jan. 25, 1900. For the lawsuit against Cordz-Fisher, see "TIMBER DEED," Misc Record "A" (Nov. 6, 1898), 531, Recorded Misc. Record "A", 459, re Shannon County Court, Sept. Term, 1898, Cordz-Fisher Lumber Co. vs. James P. Rader and W. M. Freeman, copy in my possession; "TIMBER and RIGHT-OF-WAY DEED," Recorded: Book 36, Page 223, Dec. 27, 1898, Abstract of the Title No. 211A, in the possession of James Chilton; *Current Wave*, Feb. 10, 1898, Feb. 17, 1898; March 10, 1898, April 28, 1898. The issue involved a right-of-way agreement apparently made between Freeman and Cordz-Fisher. Subsequently, Jim acquired the land from Freeman and sought unsuccessfully to bar Cordz-Fisher from using it. Curiously, while Cordz-Fisher won the case, they agreed to pay the court costs for the trial. This may have been because the company was at the same time seeking to purchase the pine on

Jim Rader's farm. For later sales of timber by Jim to the "Dunn Brothers," perhaps for railroad ties, see *Shannon County Democrat*, Feb. 27, 1914.

30. The bottomland of Jim's farm has been classified by modern soil scientists as mostly "Relfe-Sandbur Complex." For a more detailed description of this complex, see Melvin Simmons and J. Daniel Childress, *Soil Survey of Shannon County, Missouri, North and West Parts* (Washington, DC: National Cooperative Soil Survey, 1999), 53. The soil's permeability is 2 to 6 inches per hour and available water capacity ranges from "very low" to "moderate."

31. For later sales of timber by Jim to the "Dunn Brothers," perhaps for railroad ties, see *Shannon County Democrat*, Feb. 27, 1914. For his acquisition of township school lands, see Township School Land Patents, Missouri Digital Heritage, http://www.sos.mo.gov/archives/land/details.asp?rid=91512, 91513, and 91515 (accessed June 30, 2014).

32. Exactly how and when they acquired the Catlett place is unknown. It appears that they may have initially purchased it jointly with a William A. Freeman in 1898. See *Current Wave*, Feb. 10, 1898.

33. See *Current Wave*, May 7, 1892, regarding the relocation of the county seat to Delaware. Of Rader's dreams, see C. C. Shephard to James P. Rader, Nov. 17, 1908, Center for Ozark Studies, RG8-11, Series VIII: Shannon County Projects, box 12, file 32, Missouri State University Archives. Original in Missouri Mining and Lumber Company Collection, Missouri State Historical Society.

34. *Current Wave*, Jan. 19, Oct. 5, Oct. 12, 1893.

35. Ibid., Nov. 17, 1895.

36. Ibid., Nov. 25, 1897.

37. Ibid., Nov. 27, 1903. Joseph W. Folk, St. Louis reformer, was to be elected Democratic governor of Missouri in 1904.

38. For a time, one of the occupants was the recently arrived young William Aden French, along with his brother from Tennessee. William later became the longtime owner and editor of the *Current Wave*. Diary of William Aden French, Sept. 24, 1906, folder 12, Nov. 16, 1907, folder 13, microfilm, vol. 1, William Aden French Papers, State Historical Society of Missouri, Rolla. From time to time French and his brother did farm work for Jim.

39. It is possible that Jim borrowed some money from local banks, especially for land purchases, but there is no evidence of his having done so. In 1912 the county had four banks: Birch Tree State Bank, Citizens State Bank of Birch Tree, Shannon County Bank (Eminence), and the Winona Savings Bank. The sellers of land also frequently financed purchasers.

40. See Claude Anderson Phillips, *A History of Education in Missouri* (Warrensburg, MO: Hugh Stevens Pub. Co., 1911), 44–45.

41. *Current Wave*, Aug. 8, 1907; letter of Lillie May Rader Raper (daughter of Jim Rader), July 4, 1978, in Jayne Rader, "Sam's Siblings," unpublished manuscript in my possession. From the newspaper reports, it is not always clear why Jim took some of his trips. It may have been that he was purchasing livestock or scouting out possibilities for moving elsewhere. See, for example, the *Current Wave*, Aug. 21, 1913, for a report that he traveled

"through Illinois," returning by way of Osage County, where he visited his wife's relatives.

42. *The Passerby*, June 9, 1935, Jan. 1938.

43. *Shannon County Democrat*, Feb. 20, 1914.

44. See document attached to "Theodosia Rader," in Tobias' "Rader Family Tree."

45. *Current Wave*, Sept. 21, 1900, and April 18, 1907.

46. Ibid., Sept. 30, 1909. See Henry Glassie, "The Impact of the Georgian Form on American Folk Housing," in *Forms upon the Frontier: Folklife and Folk Arts in the United States*, ed. Austin Fife and Henry Glassie (Logan: Utah State University Press, 1969), 23–25. Dale Gibbs, professor emeritus of architecture, University of Nebraska–Lincoln, also aided me in understanding this home and its significance. The principal builder was likely to have been Sam Smith of Winona. Perhaps the county's leading stone mason, he also built and probably designed the new Delaware school house in 1910.

47. See French Diary, Nov. 24, 1910, William Aden Elmer French Papers, Missouri State Historical Society, Rolla, MO, and also in Archives of Missouri State University, Springfield; *Current Wave*, Feb. 6, 1908.

48. *Current Wave*, Oct. 1, 1896, April 12, 1900, Feb. 1, 1912. In 1896, Jim's brother, Lewis, was elected chairman of the Eminence Free Silver Club. *Current Wave*, Sept. 10, 1896. For 1900 returns see *Shannon County Record*, Nov. 9, 1900.

49. *Current Wave*, June 20, 1912. For their marriage, see "Missouri Marriage Records, 1805–1902," attached to "Nancy Charlotte Cheney," in Tobias' "Rader Family Tree."

50. Jon Maxwell Rader (a great nephew of Jim Rader), telephone interview with author, March 12, 2012.

9 ✦ He Chose His Hounds

1. For similarities among the descendants today of Nancy Hare and John Wesley Childress, see Vicki L. Tobias, email to Benjamin Rader, Dec. 2, 2012. In this email, Tobias, referring to Calvin Childress and me, observed, "The physical similarities were obvious to me immediately. Similar body type, stance and mannerisms, especially when walking and talking. . . . [T]here was certainly a similar tone and pattern to your voices and speech." My wife, Barbara K. Rader, who also observed us together, shares this conclusion.

2. For a wagonload of pork, see *Current Wave*, Nov. 28, 1918, and corn, Jan. 16, 1919.

3. *Current Wave*, Aug. 22 and 29, 1918. Ten years later he received a five-dollar bounty from the county court for killing a bobcat. *Current Wave*, Dec. 6, 1928.

4. Hulbert "Hub" Rader, "Edward Martin 'Sam' Rader," in Jayne Rader, "Rader Family 2002," 78, unpublished manuscript in my possession; Arch Pummill, telephone interview with author, Feb. 11, 2010. Sam's

children were not alone among the Rader-Pummill clan in addressing their parents by their first name. For example, when Donny Pummill was late for school as a student at Delaware, the teacher threatened to punish him if he were late again. Donny responded, "Yes, and Alta won't like it either." "Who is Alta?" asked the teacher. "Oh, that is Dave's wife," Donny explained. Alta and Dave were Donny's parents. *The Passerby,* Feb. 3, 1938.

5. Hulbert Rader, "Edward Martin 'Sam' Rader," 78. Much of the information in this and the next paragraph is based on this account.

6. See, for example, *Current Wave,* July 15, 1886, reprinted in *Current Wave,* July 15, 1926; and *Current Wave,* Aug. 23, 1888, reprinted in *Current Wave,* Aug. 4, 1927.

7. For the high value placed on winning spelling bees in the Ozarks, see Robert K. Gilmore, *Ozark Baptizings, Hangings, and Other Diversions: Theatrical Folkways of Rural Missouri, 1885–1910* (Norman: University of Oklahoma Press, 1984), 41–43.

8. Carl Herren to Benjamin Rader, email, Sept. 19, 2013. In my possession.

9. Inasmuch as the current world's record (2010) for the 100-yard dash is 9.3 seconds, Sam's alleged time in the 100-dash would have constituted a world's record. For descriptions of the great flood, see "Winona's Great Disaster," *New York Times,* July 9, 1895; and *Current Wave,* July 11, 1895.

10. Quotation from Melissa Akers in the *Ozarker,* 1968, 4. For this negative view toward the fiddle and suspicion of square dancing among Ozarkers, see also Otto Ernest Rayburn, *Ozark Country* (New York: Duell, Sloan & Pearce, 1941), 110–11.

11. There was at least one exception, a grandchild, Joy Dell Rhinehart, had a "beautiful soprano voice and played the piano beautifully." Shelia Fay Allen to Benjamin Rader, Sept. 14, 2013, email in my possession.

12. Obituary of Ada May Pummill Rader, attached to Vicki L. Tobias, "Rader Family Tree" www.ancestry.com (June 30, 2016); "Minutes of the Shannon County Baptist Convention, 1906," microfilmed copy in Southern Baptist Seminary Library, Nashville, TN.

13. The conclusions in this paragraph are based in part on my own memories of discussion between Sam and his son, Lowell Rader, as well as the religious history of Sam's children. For a brief description of his faith, see letter of Sam Rader "to all my dear children," Dec. 19, 1948, copy in my possession, in which he emphasized the importance of "universal love."

14. *Current Wave,* Jan. 23, 1913; obituary of Gilbert Rader, attached to Vicki L. Tobias, "Gilbert Lenox Rader," in her "Rader Family."

15. *Current Wave,* Sept. 21, 1916, Sept. 7, 1922, Oct. 9, 1924, Nov. 11, 1926. Township constables in Missouri had the same duties as county sheriffs. See http://books.google.com/books?id=nS9GAQAAIAAJ&pg=PA865 &lpg=PA865&dq=township+constables+Missouri&source=bl&ots=w MyFP9G2pz&sig=FE6Uw2ZROVRjs-KfIkqZWenN-u0&hl=en&sa= X&ei=05QHUqz8CuHg2AX384DYDQ&ved=0CFoQ6AEwCQ#v=onepage &q=township%20constables%20Missouri&f=false (accessed Jan. 16, 2013). In addition, the *Current Wave,* Oct. 26, 1922, reported that Sam served as a Democratic election judge in Delaware Township.

16. See, specifically, Tal Loyd to Hub Rader, Aug. 3, 1980, copy in my possession.

17. *The Passerby*, May 5, 1937.

18. Ibid., Dec. 6, 1932. The description of the relationship between the two sisters is based on the remembrances of Lillie May Rader, July 4, 1978, in Jayne Rader, "Sam's Siblings," copy of manuscript in my possession. Lillie May was a daughter of Jim and Beckie Rader.

19. My thanks to Nancy Rhinehart Sevy, Elsie Rader's granddaughter, for a copy of this poem.

20. Hulbert Rader to Pages, Feb. 9, 1974, in my possession. In the 1910s Elsie, and perhaps Velma as well, took piano lessons in Eminence. For similar instances elsewhere in the Ozarks, see Janet Allured, "Ozark Women and the Companionate Family in the Arkansas Hills, 1870–1910," *Arkansas Historical Quarterly* 47 (Autumn 1988): 230–56.

21. Obituary and death certificate attached to Vicki Tobias, "Ada May Pummill," in her "Rader Family"; Jerome Rader, digitally recorded interview with author April 22, 2010, in my possession.

22. According to his daughter, Elsie. Phone conversation of Benjamin Rader with Shelia Fay Allen, Sept. 19, 2013.

23. For example, a "Mrs. Matthews and her children spent Saturday night at E. M. Raders." *Current Wave*, Aug. 10, 1916.

24. For example, see *Current Wave*, Feb. 5, May 21, 1914. Regarding the exchange of honey, Gloria Dene (Rader) Fry, telephone interview with author, Oct. 13, 2013.

25. *Birch Tree Record*, Sept. 9, 1904; *Current Wave*, Oct. 18, 1917, and Jan. 10, March, 28, June 13 and 21, 1918; Jerome Rader, digitally recorded interview with author, April 22, 2010. It appears that Sam also employed for shorter times other neighborhood women, for example, a "Mrs. Blackledge." *Current Wave*, Feb. 24, 1916.

26. The oldest daughter, Elsie, also passed the county teaching exam but apparently never taught. *Shannon County Democrat*, Jan. 30, 1914.

10 ✦ The Neighborhood Awakens

1. *Current Wave*, June 17, 1909, Sept. 23, 1909; *Birch Tree Herald*, June 29, 1917. For a study of "theatrical" diversions based on the lives of rural people in adjacent counties west of Shannon in approximately the same time period, see Robert K. Gilmore, *Ozark Baptizings, Hangings, and Other Diversions: Theatrical Folkways of Rural Missouri, 1895–1910* (Norman: University of Oklahoma Press, 1984).

2. *Birch Tree Record*, Feb. 24, 1899. According to Vance Randolph, brush-arbor revivals were also sometimes referred to as "branch-water revivals." See Vance Randolph, *The Ozarks: An American Survival of Primitive Society* (New York: Vanguard, 1931), 49.

3. See "Church Buildings, Shannon County," US Works Progress Administration Historical Records, 1935–1942, f 2055, State Historical Society of Missouri, Columbia, MO; *Minutes of the Organization: Shannon County Baptist Convention* (1904 and 1905), microfilm copy at Southern

Baptist Seminary, Nashville, TN; *Current Wave*, Aug. 5, 1906; and *Shannon Herald*, May 22, 1914. My conclusion that Nancy Jane Rader did not join the local Baptist church is based on her obituary, which reports her as being a lifelong member of the Methodist South Church and that her funeral was conducted by the Reverend William Barton, a Holiness minister. See attachment of Nancy Jane Childress Rader, Vicki L. Tobias, "Rader Family," www.ancestry.com (accessed June 30, 2016).

4. *Current Wave*, Sept. 15, 22, Dec. 1, 1910.

5. While sources fail to permit extensive documentation of the cyclical variations in Sunday school attendance, it is noteworthy that the *Shannon County Democrat*, on March 15, 1912, reported a low attendance. Also in several years in the late 1910s the church failed to send in reports of any activities to the annual Baptist convention. The persistent and continuing leadership problem in Upland Southern churches is discussed in Elmora Messer Matthews, *Neighbor and Kin: Life in a Tennessee Ridge Community* (Nashville, TN: Vanderbilt University Press, 1965), 80–82.

6. See *Current Wave*, Aug. 15, 1907, Sept. 10, 17, 1908; *Shannon County Democrat*, Jan. 30, 1914; and *Current Wave*, Aug. 15, 1918, May 21, 1931.

7. *Minutes of the Organization: Shannon County Baptist Convention, 1913*. The ratio of female to male converts at an Eminence revival in 1912 was five to one. *Current Wave*, Feb. 22, 1912.

8. *Current Wave*, Oct. 16, 1913.

9. "A Resolution Passed by the Young Ladies of Winona, Missouri," Nov. 22, 1903, copy in Center for Ozark Studies, RG8-11, Series VIII: Shannon County Projects, box 15, file 115, Missouri State University Archives, Springfield.

10. Benjamin G. Rader, "'My Girl': Bill French Goes a Courtin'—The Old and the New in Missouri Ozarks Courtships, 1908–1913," *Missouri Historical Review* 109 (July 2015): 254–67.

11. Complete demographic data is unavailable. I deduced an approximation of the township's fertility rate from the number of children in each household recorded for mothers from the ages of thirty-five through forty-nine from the decadal censuses of 1880 (4.7), 1890 (no surviving manuscript census), 1900 (4.6), 1910 (4.6), 1920 (3.5), 1930 (3.6), 1940 (2.7). Of course, the actual fertility rate is somewhat higher than this. For the age of marriage, I subtracted a year from her age at the time her first child was born. For a similar methodology applied to a rural Arkansas county, see Janet Allured, "Ozark Women and the Companionate Family in the Arkansas Hills, 1870–1910," *Arkansas Historical Quarterly* 47 (Autumn 1988): 238–39.

12. Winona was said to have been the victim of a "Whiskey riot" on Christmas Eve, 1903. Winona *Shannon County Democrat*, April 1, 1904. For the passage of the countywide local option law, see *Current Wave*, June 21, 1906.

13. William Aden French Diary, Dec. 24, 1910, vol. 1, microfilm, William Aden French Collection, 1877–1934, State Historical Society of Missouri, Rolla.

14. *Current Wave*, Oct. 16, 1924. See also incident at Cedar Grove, in *Current Wave*, May 5, 1925.

15. *An Administrative Survey of the Schools of Shannon County* [1931], 1450, in copy in Center for Ozark Studies, RG8-11, Series VIII: Shannon County Projects, box 14, file 19, Missouri State University Archives. For additional statistics on the Delaware School for the 1920s and 1930s, also see ibid, box 14, file 19.

16. *Current Wave*, Oct. 27, 1910, Dec. 29, 1910; Tania Grey, *Reflections at Alley Springs* (Eminence, MO: Tania Grey, 1980), At the same time, the Pine Hollow School, which had more timber-worker children than Delaware, met for only four months. William Aden French Diary, Dec. 9, 1910.

17. Annual visitation of the County Superintendent of Schools, Shannon County, Nov. 28, 1910, in the County Clerk's Office, Shannon County, MO.

18. *Current Wave*, Dec. 29, 1910, which announced that Delaware was "the first and only approved school in the county so far." Unless my memory fails me, when I attended Delaware School in the 1940s, the library had added few if any books since 1910.

19. Annual visitation of the County Superintendent of Schools, 1911, in Office of the Clerk of the Circuit Court, Shannon County, MO.

20. *Current Wave*, March 22, 1917.

21. "Rural School Teacher's Term Reports for Delaware," in 1915 and 1917 in County Clerk's Office, reported that average attendance as almost exactly 50 percent of enrollment. Average attendance at Owl Bend, another Shannon County rural school, was even lower. In the 1912–13 school year, of 20 enrolled students, the average daily attendance was only 6.2. William Aden French, "Term Report for Owl Bend School (7 ½ months)," Aug. 5, 1912–March 7, 1913, Vol. 1, microfilm, in William Aden French Collection, 1877–1934, State Historical Society of Missouri, Rolla.

22. *Current Wave*, Oct. 14, 1912.

23. Quoted in Mabel L. Cooper, *3-Rs in the Ozarks* (Eminence, MO: Chilton Printing Co., 1980), 60.

24. See Missouri Council of Defense Papers, Shannon County, f 1138-1140, State Historical Society of Missouri; *Shannon County Democrat*, Feb. 15 and May 10, 1918, Jan. 17 and Feb. 15, 1919.

11 ✦ From Down in the Hollows to Ozark Towns

1. *The Passerby*, June 8, 1938. See for example the report in *The Passerby*, Feb. 4, 1939, of Arthur's dramatic homerun while playing with a Fishertown team against a Rogersville nine. While the county's weekly newspapers frequently reported the results of games and sometimes the box scores, they rarely provided details of individual performances.

2. *Current Wave*, May 19, 1897, May 19, 1899. While John and Lydia Pummill were only marginally successful in farming, the assessed valuation of their farm in 1913 was fourth or fifth highest among some thirty-two

farms in Delaware Township. For 1913 assessments, see Shannon County, "Proceedings of the Board of Equalization," *Current Wave,* April 17, 1913. On the disposition of the farm after the deaths of John and Lydia Pummill, see A. L. Pummill, "Affidavit of Heirship" [John Pummill Family], Oct. 10, 1915, Office of the Shannon County Clerk.

3. *Current Wave,* Aug. 12, 1897. "Teacher's Reissued Certificate," First Renewal, Public Schools of Missouri, April 6, 1905, to J. G. Pummill, reprinted in Cooper, *3-R's in the Ozarks,* 48; Arch Pummill and Jerome Rader, digitally recorded interview with author, Sept. 18, 2010, in my possession. If the examination resembled the study questions available in advance, the test was by no means simple. For the study question in 1903, see the *Birch Tree Record,* July 3, 1903. Perhaps the test for 1911 was unusually difficult. Of thirty-one applicants, only two received certificates. The test takers, the newspaper reported, were especially weak in language, arithmetic, grammar (average was only 39 percent), literature, and US history. *Shannon County Democrat,* April 28, 1911.

4. See for example *Current Wave,* June 20, June 27, 1901, March 13, Sept. 6, Sept. 25, 1902, April 30, May 28, 1903; *Birch Tree Record,* March 28, 1902.

5. *Current Wave,* Dec. 15, 1904.

6. See *Current Wave,* June 5, 1902, Aug. 9, Nov. 15, 1906, March 4, 1907, March 4, June 19, 1909, May 30, 1912. *Shannon County Record,* June 28, 1901, Oct. 23, 1914. While none the other brothers ever sought election to a countywide office again, in 1930 the Republican Party nominated Arthur for recorder of deeds, an election that he lost. See *Shannon County Democrat,* Oct. 30, 1930.

7. See Arch Pummill and Jerome Rader, interview, Sept. 18, 2010. On high school graduation oration, see *Shannon County Democrat,* May 3, 1912.

8. *Shannon County Democrat,* May 15, Aug. 25, 1911. In 1913, Winona banned hogs from town streets. *Shannon County Democrat,* June 11, 1913.

9. See for example *Shannon County Democrat,* Aug. 4, 1911.

10. He prepared a substantial essay for the *Current Wave,* July 6, 1905, about his experience in Warrensburg.

11. Transcript, J. G. Pummill, Missouri State University Archives; copy in my possession. The Springfield school remained Southwest Missouri State Teachers College until 1946, when it was renamed Southwest Missouri State College. In 1972 it was renamed Southwest Missouri State University and in 2005 became Missouri State University.

12. See transcripts of J. G., L. E., and Everett Pummill, Missouri State University Archives; and transcripts of Lawrence Pummill, Peabody College of Education and Human Development, Vanderbilt University. Copies in my possession.

13. See especially Christine A. Ogren, *The American Normal School: "An Instrument of Great Good"* (New York: Palgrave Macmillan 2005), 5, 151, 186.

14. Missouri School Directory, 1915–Present," in Department of Elementary and Secondary Education, Documents, Box 19, Missouri State

Archives, Jefferson City, Missouri. While these are incomplete, of the more than one hundred names found in the directory from the forenames provided before 1940, there appears not to be a single woman superintendent of schools in the state of Missouri.

15. *Shannon County Democrat,* May 15, 1914; Current *Wave,* June 12, 1914. Also reflective of Joe's success was the evaluation of Seneca High School in 1917 by the state high school inspector, D. W. Clayton. He commended the school for its "strong teachers" and concluded that there was "no question about [the] school deserving classification as first class this year," a designation not extended to either of the large high schools in nearby Joplin and Carthage or to any of the Shannon County high schools. "Report of High School Inspector," State Department of Education, *Missouri High School Reports for SchoolYear 1916–1917(Incomplete),* for Seneca Public Schools, in Missouri State Archives.

16. For evidence of Joe's candor, see his evaluation of Ellisnore High School in 1920, in which he concluded, "The school has a disorganized run-down appearance. The building is exceedingly dirty. The outbuildings are filthy. If the school-board does not meet [the] suggestions offered [herein], the school should be dropped from the list of approved schools." "Report of High School Inspector," State Department of Education, *Missouri High School Reports for SchoolYear, 1919–1920(Incomplete),* for Ellisnore High School, in Missouri State Archives.

17. "Mr. & Mrs. Joseph G. Pummill," *Missouri School Journal* 39 (1922): 236–37.

18. See obituary in *St. Louis Post-Dispatch,* June 7, 1939. Lawrence Pummill, "MESSAGE TO THE FAMILY" [1939?], copy in my possession.

19. *Current Wave,* Aug. 27, 1914.

20. See John K. Hulston, *A Bakers Dozen of Leading Dade Countians: The First One-HundredYears, 1841–1941(* Greenfield, MO: Citizens Home Bank, 1985), 212–16; *GreenfieldVedette,* March 21, 1918. I thank Betty Nelson and the Dade County Genealogical Society for assistance in locating sources on Lawrence Pummill while he was in Greenfield.

21. Transcript of Lawrence E. Pummill, Peabody College of Education, Vanderbilt University, Nashville, TN. Copy in my possession. The transcript includes his record as a graduate student at the University of Missouri and Columbia Teachers College. For his doctorate degree, he passed both a French and German examination and wrote a dissertation, "The Future of Mathematics in Adult Education." During his long career, he apparently published no scholarly articles on mathematics or education.

22. See the description by E. Rebecca Matthews in a newsletter of the Department of Mathematics, Southwest Missouri State University, *Ad Infinitum* 4 (Spring–Summer 2000): 3.

23. While not comprehensive, the "Missouri School Directory, 1915–Present," in Department of Elementary and Secondary Education, Documents, Box 19, Missouri State Archives, provides scattered reports of the annual incomes and positions of each of the boys, as well as Atlanta Pummill. For the salary of Lawrence while at the teachers college between

1923 and 1941, see the attachment "Lawrence E. Pummill salary-2.xls," Archives (Missouri) Reference to Benjamin G. Rader, Oct. 29, 2013, email in my possession.

24. For data in this paragraph, see Tobias, "Rader Family."

25. See "Median Age at First Marriage, 1890–2010," nationally, www.infoplease.com/1pa/A00561.html (accessed July 24, 2014); and Michael R. Haines, "American Fertility in Transition: New Estimates of Birth Rates in the United States, 1900–1910," *Demography* 26 (Feb. 1989): 137–48.

26. [Crystal Pummill], "This Is the Story of Lawrence and Criss—Told Simply without Sham—And What over Fifty Years of Togetherness, Brought Them, 1912–1963" 25, undated, unpublished, handwritten manuscript, copy in my possession.

27. See Arch Pummill and Jerome Rader, interview, Sept. 18, 2010.

28. Gloria Dene Rader Fry, telephone interview with author, Jan. 17, 2013.

29. His arrival in the county caught the attention of two of the county weeklies. For example, the *Shannon County Democrat*, Aug. 25, 1916, and the *Current Wave*, Aug. 31, 1916, reported that Joe Pummill drove his car from Seneca to Delaware, where he visited with family for a week.

30. See *The Passerby*, Aug. 7, 1934, Sept. 1934, Aug. 8, 1938; *Current Wave*, July 18, Aug. 15, 1929; and Arch Pummill, digitally recorded interview with author, Sept. 18, 2010. One of Joe and Atlanta Pummill's trips to the West Coast that in 1938, entailed 8,200 miles of driving. Apart from two flat tires during the trip, Joe reported, they had a "whale of a good time."

31. While there is no specific scholarship concerning either the growth of the professions or the middle class in the Missouri Ozarks or the Upland South, for the national scene there is Robert H. Wiebe, who first identified a "new middle class" as well as the importance of the professions in its emergence in his seminal classic: Robert H. Wiebe, *The Search for Order, 1877–1920* (New York: Hill and Wang, 1966). For more recent works, see Burton J. Bledstein, *The Culture of Professionalism: The Middle Class and the Development of Higher Education in America* (New York: Norton, 1976); Oliver Zunz, *Making America Corporate, 1890–1920* (Chicago: University of Chicago Press, 1990); Burton J. Bledstein and Robert D. Johnston, eds., *The Middling Sorts: Explorations in the History of the American Middle Class* (New York: Routledge, 2001); and Robert D. Johnston, *The Radical Middle Class: Populist Democracy and the Question of Capitalism in Progressive Era Portland, Oregon* (Princeton: Princeton University Press, 2003). For the development of education as a profession, see Jurgen Herbst, *And Sadly Teach: Teacher Education and Professionalization in American Culture* (Madison: University of Wisconsin Press, 1991); Ogren, *The American Normal School;* and Dana Goldstein, *The Teachers Wars: A History of America's Most Embattled Profession* (New York: Doubleday, 2014).

32. Phone conversation of Virginia Pummill Dailey with author, Feb. 13, 2015.

33. For this variety of radicalism, see Johnston, *The Radical Middle Class.*

34. *The Passerby,* May 7, 1934.

35. Untitled manuscript of a high school graduation speech by Lawrence Pummill, in Winona, Missouri, by inference dated in 1959. Copy in my possession.

36. Forrest E. Wolverton, "Mission Accomplished," *Missouri Schools,* March 1951, 8, reprinted in Cooper, *3-Rs in the Ozarks,* 43–44.

37. *Shannon County Democrat,* Sept. 29, 1911. Through the high school, Joe offered a course specifically in pedagogy.

12 ✦ Leaving the Homeland

1. Nancy Sevy to Benjamin Rader and Sheila Allen, email, Oct. 16, 2013. For assistance in reconstructing the history of the Elsie Rader-Cordell Rhinehart family, I am especially indebted to their granddaughters, Nancy Sevy and Sheila Allen.

2. *Current Wave,* July 3, 1913, reported the showing of a silent movie in Delaware itself. In addition, the Eminence opera house showed movies and hosted dances and roller-skating parties, which Elsie probably attended. See *Current Wave,* Aug. 19 and Sept. 9, 1915.

3. Shelia Allen, telephone interview with author, Sept. 19, 2013; Arch Pummill, telephone interview with author, Feb. 11, 2010, wherein Arch declared, "Elsie thought she might become an entertainer or movie star."

4. *Shannon County Democrat,* Oct. 3, 1913.

5. [Joy Dell Rhinehart], untitled, handwritten manuscript treating the history of the Rhinehart family, no date. Copy in my possession.

6. See National Register of Historic Places Inventory—Nomination form for "Rhinehart Ranch," by Lynn Morrow, http://www.dnr.mo.gov/shpo/nps-nr/80002395.pdf (accessed Oct. 10, 2013). See also a slightly different version, Lynn Morrow, "The Preservation Corner," *Ozarks Watch* 1 (Winter 1988), http://thelibrary.org/lochist/periodicals/ozarkswatch/ow103d.htm (accessed Oct. 10, 2013). Active as well in the Masonic order, Deforest appears to have been well connected in Eminence. Apart from membership on the board of directors of the Shannon County Bank, his daughter, Ruby, married the son of Eminence physician Dr. Frank Hyde. See *Current Wave,* Oct. 21, 1920. Hyde's son, Franklin, became the longtime owner of the Eminence Drug Store. Cordell served as a Republican primary election judge in 1916 for Jasper Township but was apparently never actively involved in politics thereafter. *Current Wave,* June 8, 1916.

7. See *Current Wave,* July 26, 1917, Sept. 12, 1918, Feb. 4, 1926. Cordell's brother, Amos, may have also dated Elsie's sister, Audrey. See *Current Wave,* May 22, 1924.

8. *Current Wave,* April 7, 1921.

9. Ibid., April 7, Sept. 15, Oct. 6, 1921, Feb. 19, 1920, Oct. 2, 1924.

10. Nancy Sevy to Benjamin Rader, email, Oct. 7, 2013.

11. *Current Wave,* Sept. 24, 1914, Feb. 11, Oct. 28, 1915.

12. Ibid., Jan. 6, 1915.

13. Ibid., Nov. 30, 1916, Jan. 10, 1918; "Year Round Athletic

Outlook," newspaper fragment, Oct. 15, 1918?, in author's possession; Gloria Dene Rader Fry, telephone interview with author, January 10, 2010. Gloria Dene has been helpful in reconstructing the lives of her father and mother.

14. Gilbert L. Rader, "Record of Resident Class Work—Collegiate," Missouri Normal School, Springfield; [Gilbert Lenox Rader], "Soldiers' Records," Missouri Digital Heritage, http:www.sos.mo.gov/archive/soldiers/details.asp?id=A104645 (accessed July 26, 2012); Gloria Dene Rader Fry, telephone interview with author, Dec. 8, 2013.

15. *Southwest Standard,* Jan. 30, 1919. See also the *Southwest Standard,* March 6, 1919, for a summary of his play.

16. Advertisement in *Southwest Standard,* Jan. 30, 1919.

17. *Southwest Standard,* May 28, 1920, reported that "Rader [was] scoring right along until he got the Flu."

18. Lorrie Shorney, Medical Records, Missouri Rehabilitation Center, to Benjamin Rader, Oct. 14, 2010, email, in my possession; Arch Pummill, recorded interview with author, Oct. 16, 2009. The *Current Wave,* Dec. 15, 1921, reported that Gilbert was home visiting kinfolk after having received treatment at Mt. Vernon and was to leave for Arizona after Christmas. See also letter from Gilbert Rader to Maude Klepzig, Sept. 10, 1922, from Whipple Barracks, Prescott, Arizona, in possession of Gloria Dean Fry.

19. *Current Wave,* Nov. 27, 1924. For assistance with the Loyd family, I thank especially Miles "Lad" and Philip Roger Loyd, sons of Velma and Tal, as well as their granddaughter, Kelly Loyd.

20. *Current Wave,* March 28, 1918.

21. J. Talmage Loyd to Kathy Collins, Jan. 20, 1980. Copy in my possession. This is a multipage letter in which Tal describes his teaching experiences. For their marriage, see also *Current Wave,* June 12, 1924.

22. *Current Wave,* July 18, Aug. 8, 1929; *Shannon County Democrat,* Aug. 15, 1929; Arch Pummill, interview, Oct. 16, 2009; and Arch Pummill, telephone interview with author, Feb. 11, 2010.

Afterword ✦ "The Celebrated Cow Case"

1. *Dade County Advocate* (Greenfield, MO), June 25, 1914.

2. For example, in 1899 the county sued Jim twice in circuit court for failure to repay school fund loans. *Record* (Birch Tree, MO), Sept. 8, 1899. As a consequence of the suits, Jim apparently paid the loans, though perhaps not in a timely fashion.

3. James P. Rader and Sarah R. Rader to Charles B. Linville, Trustee for, James E. Adams, "Trust Deed," Book K, p. 368, June 19, 1908, Shannon County Deed Records, Shannon County Courthouse, Eminence, MO. Copy in my possession.

4. *Current Wave,* March 31, 1910; "General Warranty Deed," Oct. 12, 1914, between Israel Monroe Chrisco and James P. Rader, Circuit Court and Recorders Office, Shannon County Courthouse. Copy in my possession. Jim purchased a one-fourth interest in the patent.

5. For a report by Ben Perkins, a local farmer, on the drought in Delaware in 1913, see *Shannon County Democrat*, Sept. 5, 1913. For corn yields in Shannon County, see *Missouri Year Book of Agriculture, 51st Annual Report, 1919* (Jefferson City, MO: State Board of Agriculture, 1919), 169. For the effects of drought on corn yields in Missouri, see Qu Hui and Gregory Buyanovsky, "Climate Effects on Corn Yields in Missouri," *Journal of Applied Meteorology* 42, http://snr.unl.edu/climate_change/ research/climate_corn.pdf (accessed June 16, 2012). For precipitation and temperatures in these years for nearby Birch Tree, Missouri, see High Plains Regional Climate Center, http://www.hprcc.unl.edu/cgi-bin/cli_perl_ lib/cliMAIN.pl?mo0668 (accessed June 30, 2016). For newspaper discussion of the hard times, see *Shannon County Democrat*, July 31, 1914, March 26, 1915; and *Current Wave*, Sept. 17, 1914.

6. *Current Wave*, April 30, May 21, 1914; *Shannon County Herald*, May 1, 1914.

7. "Conditions in the Ozarks," *Shannon County Democrat*, May 26, 1915.

8. *Shannon County Democrat*, July 10 and 31, 1914.

9. *Current Wave*, Sept. 24, 1914; *Shannon County Herald*, March 18 and 25, 1915.

10. *Current Wave*, Dec. 11, 1913. On Nov. 20, 1913, the *Wave* had reported without elaboration that Jim Rader had left for Everton and that he was "doing much traveling of late."

11. *Current Wave*, Jan. 15, 1914.

12. *Shannon County Herald*, March 6, June 19, June 26, 1914; *Dade County Advocate* (Greenfield, MO), June 25, 1914. See also J. P. Rader vs. S. H. Wilson, Judge's Term Docket Book, Circuit Court Record Book, June Term, 1914?, Volume 19, 507, Case #6535, in Dade County Courthouse, Greenfield, MO. There is no other documentary evidence of the trial. I thank Jennifer Snider, deputy clerk, Dade County Circuit Court, for locating this document. After this adverse decision, Jim filed yet another suit seeking a change of venue from Dade to Shannon County to decide whether damage should be paid to him for the stolen heifer. Jim lost this suit as well. *Current Wave*, Sept. 24, 1914.

13. *Dade County Advocate*, June 25, 1914.

14. There is a large body of literature on southern honor. For the southern upcountry, see Elliot J. Gorn's pioneering essay, "'Gouge and Bite, Pull Hair and Scratch': The Social Significance of Fighting in the Southern Backcountry," *American Historical Review* 90 (February 1985): 18–43; and Benjamin G. Rader, "'Matters Involving Honor': Region, Race, and Rank in the Violent Life of Tyrus Raymond Cobb," in *Baseball in America and America in Baseball*, ed. Donald G. Kyle and Robert B. Fairbanks (College Station: Texas A&M University Press, 2008), 189–222.

15. Arch Pummill remembers sitting down to supper at the Raders during the 1930s and that, much to his surprise, Beckie said, "Let's say the blessing," which Jim did. Sometime after he left Mahans Creek, Jim apparently "got" religion as a result of Bible reading, rather than under the auspices of a church. Arch Pummill, interview with author, May 16, 2012.

16. Gerald Randolph, telephone interview with author, March 3, 2012; and Nancy Brewer, telephone interview with author March 3 and April 7, 2012. On at least one other occasion, UM encountered a legal difficulty. In 1899 some of his neighbors, including possibly Jim Rader, filed a suit against him for "obstructing a public highway," presumably the road from Delaware to Birch Tree that ran through his farm. He was acquitted of the charge. See *Current Wave*, March 2 and 16, 1899.

17. *Current Wave*, Sept. 7, 1893; Feb. 9, 1899; *Birch Tree Herald*, April 15, 1904.

18. *Current Wave*, April 11, 1901. In 1902, at the American Royal, for example, he purchased a carload of registered short horns that included ten male calves. See *Current Wave*, Nov. 13, 1902.

19. *Shannon County Democrat*, Feb. 13, 1914; *Current Wave*, July 23, 1914.

20. According to Ray Von Harrison, Hulbert Rader, Jim's nephew, told him that Jim lost $10,000 (about $225,000 in 2012 dollars). If Jim's investment in the corn planter patent, the costs of his house, his legal costs, and money that he may have lost when he swapped farms with J.F.A. Lahmeyer in 1914 are included, this figure does not appear to be an exaggeration. Ray Von Harrison, telephone interview with author, Dec. 12, 2011. Harrison was a longtime resident of Pine Hollow.

21. There is a possibility that the family was considering a move from Shannon County before the heifer controversy. In its issue of Aug. 13, 1913, the *Current Wave* reported that Jim had made a trip through Illinois and returned by way of Osage County, Missouri, where he had visited Elna and Marcus Matthews, relatives of his wife. The paper does not indicate the purpose of the trip or whether Beckie accompanied Jim on the trip. For the land transactions, see the indenture between James P. Rader and Sarah R. Rader, parties of the first part, and J.F.A. Lahmeyer, party of the second part, Nov. 11, 1914, copy in Circuit Court and Recorder's Office, Shannon County, MO, copy in my possession; and indenture between J.F.A. Lahmeyer and Augusta Lahmeyer, parties of the first part, and Sarah R. Rader, parties of the second part, Nov. 14, 1914, Book 170, 22, in Recorder of Deeds Office of Barton County, Lamar, MO. Copy in my possession. This transaction did not include all of Jim's property in Shannon County.

22. Apparently, Jim continued for a time to own a lot and a house in Eminence. See *Current Wave*, March 6, 1919.

23. *The Passerby*, Feb. 10, 1933, Oct. 10, 1934; April 7, May 6, 1939; Arch Pummill, telephone interview with author, May 26, 2012. On the Delbert Rader family, see "The Raders of Magnolia, Missouri," an undated video. Copy in my possession.

IV ✦ When in Places Even the Creek Went Dry

1. *Current Wave*, Nov. 27, 1924.

2. Arch Pummill, telephone interview by author, Feb. 11, 2010.

3. *The Passerby*, [Nov. 3, 1935].

4. Arch Pummill, interview, Feb. 11, 2010.

13 ✦ "Have We a Moses?"

1. For the incident, see Arch Pummill, digitally recorded interview with author, Feb. 11, 2010; and Arch Pummill, phone conversation with author, March 8, 2014.

2. *Current Wave*, Sept. 18, 1919, Sept. 12, 1918.

3. State Highway Commission of Missouri, *Tenth Biennial Report for the Period Ending December First 1936* (Jefferson City, MO, 1936), 74–76.

4. *The Passerby*, [Nov. 3, 1935].

5. Missouri Department of Transportation, *Shannon County Project History Map*, n.d., as held by Transportation Planning, Missouri Department of Transportation, Jefferson City, Missouri; Missouri Highway Commission, "Minutes of the State Highway Commission Meeting, held in Jefferson City, Missouri, Tuesday, February 14, 1933," p. 86, May 9, 1933, pp. 103–6, July 10, 1934, p. 30; *Current Wave*, April 2, 1936. I thank Karen Daniels, who provided me with access to the files of the Missouri Department of Transportation.

6. *Current Wave*, Dec. 2, 1918, Aug. 21, 1919.

7. Ibid., April 26, July 12, 1928, Jan. 10, 1924.

8. Ibid., April 21, 1927.

9. *Shannon Herald*, Dec. 18, 1914; *Current Wave*, June 30, 1927.

10. For more detailed accounts of the efforts to attract tourists to the area, see Donald L. Stevens Jr., *A Homeland and a Hinterland: The Current and Jacks Fork Riverways* (Omaha, NE: National Park Service, Midwest Region, 1991), chap. 10; Susan Flader, "A Legacy of Neglect: The Ozarks National Scenic Riverways," *George Wright Forum* 28, no. 2 (2011): 114–26, and http://www.georgewright.org/282flader.pdf (accessed March 9, 3014); and Will Sarvis, "A Difficult Legacy: Creation of the Ozarks Scenic Riverways," *Public Historian* 24 (Winter 2002): 31–52.

11. *Current Wave*, July 17, 1924, March 11, 18, 1926.

12. See *Current Wave*, June 7, 1928, March 7, 1929; Jerry Ponder, *Grandin, Hunter, West Eminence, and the Missouri Lumber and Mining Company* (Doniphan, MO: Ponder Books, 1989). Four years later, the Frisco Railroad also discontinued passenger service to Birch Tree and Winona. See *Current Wave*, Jan. 28, 1932.

13. For a vivid description by a tie hacker, see Virgil Murray, "Tie Hacking," *Ozarker*, May 21, 1973, 16.

14. See http://www.foresthistory.org/publications/FHT/FHT1997/Barnickol.pdf#page=1&zoom=auto,0,778 (accessed May 9, 2013); *Current Wave*, Sept. 13, 1917. Apparently, in the following week, despite his accident, Eddings went about making sorghum molasses. See *Current Wave*, Feb. 2, 1928, for a report of a group of Delaware men loading ties for the Potosi Tie Company in Willow Springs, MO.

15. James Orchard, "Court and Legal Documents, James Orchard," Center for Ozark Studies, RG8-11, Series VIII: Shannon County Projects, box 12, file 32, Special Collections and Archives, Missouri State University, Springfield.

16. G. L. Davis, "Preserving the Scenic Riverways," *Ozarker*, June 1977, 7.

17. For resistance to state efforts to regulate hunting and fishing, see especially David Benac, "Whose Forest Is This? Hill Folk, Industrialists, and Government in the Ozarks," in *The Ozarks in Missouri History: Discoveries in an American Region,* ed. Lynn Morrow (Columbia: University of Missouri Press, 2013), 164–87. No exact figures for the decline of the fish population exist. However, the records of the nearby Carter County Fishing and Shooting Club indicate a sharp decline in average catches on the Current River beginning at the turn of the century. Yields reached an all-time low in the 1930s. See Charles Callison, "How Good Were the Good Old Days— And What Happened to Them?," *Missouri Conservationist,* August 1946, 2–4, 11. In addition to the state, from time to time the local people also organized efforts to halt the dynamiting of fishing holes, though the practice continued at least into the late 1930s. See, for example, *Current Wave,* June 1, 1922, July 15, 1937.

18. Leonard Hall, *Stars Upstream: Life along an Ozark River* (Chicago: University of Chicago Press, 1958), 233.

19. *Shannon County Democrat,* Nov. 19, 1925; Donald Pummill, telephone interview with author, April 15, 2014. For the decline in wildlife along Bryant Creek in nearby Douglas County, see Tommy Medlock, "An Old-Timer Remembers Bryant Creek's Cashless Economy," http://www.watersheds.org/history/oldtimer.htm (accessed May 17, 2013).

20. *Shannon Herald* (Birch Tree), Jan. 11, 1922.

21. *Current Wave,* Dec. 10, 1914, Feb. 11, 1921, Dec. 6, 1928.

22. For example, in the fall and winter of 1935, LeRoy Pummill (son of Arthur and Mayme), who lived in Open Hollow, caught twenty-two opossums. *The Passerby,* Dec. 7, 1935.

23. For corn yields countywide, see *Missouri Yearbook of Agriculture, 51st Annual Report, 1919* (Jefferson City, MO: State Board of Agriculture, 1919); "Missouri Annual Crop and Livestock Production by Counties for 20-Year Period, 1919–1940," *The Bulletin* 40 (Dec. 1942). For monthly total precipitation (in inches) and monthly average maximum temperature as recorded at Birch Tree, MO, since 1893, see http://www.hprcc.unl.edu/cgi-bin/cli_perl_lib/clMONtavt.pl?mo0668 (accessed June 30, 2015).

24. *Current Wave,* June 17, 1937.

25. The *Current Wave,* March 13, 1924, observed that many farmers were leaving the county. More than one hundred farmers, it reported, had been delinquent in paying their 1922 property taxes. Tax delinquencies were also high in 1925, and the 1926 spring "was said to be one of the most unfavorable to farming in memory." Quote is from *Current Wave,* June 7, 1926. See *Current Wave,* Jan. 7, June 2, 1926. In 1921, Shannon County per acre land values were the lowest in the state of Missouri. See *Missouri Yearbook of Agriculture, 1921* (Jefferson City, MO: State Board of Agriculture, 1921).

26. Based on US census data of 1920, 1930, and 1940, as reported in www.ancestry.com (accessed June 30, 2016) and www.1940census.archive.gov (accessed June 30, 2016). I deduced an approximation of the township's fertility rate from the number of children in each household recorded for mothers from the ages of thirty-five through forty-nine from the decadal

censuses. Of course, the actual fertility rate is somewhat higher than this. For the age of marriage, I subtracted a year from her age at the time her first child was born. For a similar methodology applied to a rural Arkansas county, see Janet Allured, "Ozark Women and the Companionate Family in the Arkansas Hills, 1870–1910," *Arkansas Historical Quarterly* 47 (Autumn 1988): 238–39.

27. Delaware Township, manuscript census, "U.S. Census, 1940," and "Land Assessment, Shannon County, Township 28, 1940," County Assessor's Office, Eminence, Shannon County, Missouri.

28. Hulbert Rader to Pages, Feb. 9, 1974, copy in my possession; *Current Wave*, Aug. 21, 1919.

29. "Shannon County Farmers Visit Smith Bros.," *Shannon County Democrat*, July 8, 1937; *Current Wave*, Jan 12, 1939.

30. Shannon County Assessment Book, 1940, in Office of County Treasurer of Shannon County, Eminence, MO.

31. For their involvement in the New Harmony Baptist Church, see the "Minutes of the Missouri Baptist Association of Shannon County," Southern Baptist Seminary Library, Nashville, TN. Dates vary, but the meetings were held annually.

14 ✦ The Folk up in Open Hollow

1. *Current Wave*, Jan. 21, 1926; Registry of Inmates, Missouri State Penitentiary, microfilm reel 5236, p. 102, Missouri State Archives, Jefferson City, MO. On the attempt to kill Sheriff Powell, see *Current Wave*, Aug. 27, 1925. Neither was prison life easy for Jim Perkins, at least according to a story that he allegedly passed on to his kinfolk. For his first supper, he received a bowl of soup. At the bottom of the bowl, he found half of a mouse. Upon complaining to a guard, the guard asked him how long he had been imprisoned. "This is my first day," Jim responded. "Well, you got to be here six months before you get a whole mouse," the guard explained. Jon Maxwell Rader, phone conversation with author, Nov. 12, 2014.

2. *Current Wave*, July 14, 1921. For a general description of the industry in Shannon County, see Eunice Pennington, "Moonshining in the Hills," *Ozarker*, June 1968, 1.

3. *Current Wave*, March 3, 24, 1921; *Shannon County Herald*, March 24, 1922. Verdie may have learned his whiskey-making skills from a cousin, Pete Barton, who lived in nearby Texas County. Pete was arrested twice in 1917 for violating Shannon County's local option law. See *Shannon County Democrat*, Jan. 26, and *Shannon Herald*, Aug. 31, 1917. For evidence of Verdie's later criminal career, see State v. Barton, http://www.leagle.com/decision/19531007255SW2d752_1980 (accessed April 4, 2014). That the county paid the sheriff only from successful convictions encouraged a vigorous enforcement of prohibition. Danny Searcy, telephone interview with author, April 27, 2014.

4. For a roughly parallel discussion of a "separate subcommunity" with a dubious reputation in Appalachia, see Durwood Dunn, *Cades Cove: The*

Life and Death of a Southern Appalachian Community, 1818–1937 (Knoxville: University of Tennessee Press, 1988), 195–200.

5. File of Lewis Perkins, National Archives, Washington, DC, copy in my possession.

6. In 1911, their 60-acre farm's assessed valuation was only $300, compared with the John H. Pummill estate's valuation of $1,240 on 121 acres and James P. Rader's valuation of $1,650 on 258 acres. Shannon County Board of Equalization, 1911, copy in my possession.

7. *Shannon County Democrat*, May 23, 1913; *Current Wave*, Dec. 27, 1928, May 9, 1928; Danny Searcy, interview, April 27, 2014; *Shannon County Democrat*, Aug. 5, 1937.

8. A. L. Perkins v. Mary S. Perkins decree for the plaintiff for divorce granted in *Current Wave*, March 26, 1903; marriage license of A. L. Perkins and Mary S. Perkins (nee Rader), March 9, 1904, copy in my possession; *Current Wave*, July 10, 1924, April 2, 1925.

9. *Current Wave*, June 10, 1926; marriage license, Elmer Counts to Mrs. Mary Perkins, June 5, 1926, copy in my possession; Jayne Rader, "Rader Family," 34, copy of manuscript in my possession.

10. Jenifer (Balz) George, in untitled 84-page manuscript apparently put together by Troy F. Pummill in 1996, copy attached to letter, Betty Bresnick to Benjamin Rader, March 21, 2015. Copy in my possession.

11. For example, four men with the Perkins surname were charged with various crimes in the circuit court session for the spring of 1932. See *Shannon County Democrat*, May 19, 1932. For the history of the Perkins gang, see "Troop G History—Missouri Highway Patrol," https://www.mshp. dps.missouri.gov/MSHPWeb/PatrolDivisions/TroopHeadquarters/TroopG/ documents/TroopGHistory_005.pdf (accessed April 12, 2015); and *Current Wave*, Oct. 4, Nov. 22, 1934, Sept. 26, 1935.

12. See E. A. McCaskill, "History of Alley Spring," *Current Wave*, May 9, 1968.

13. *Current Wave*, April 9, 1908.

14. Judy Melton Scharps, telephone interview with author, April 26, 2014. Apparently, the land transfer was not formally completed until 1901. See warranty deed from E. M. Rader and A. M. Rader to Keziah Klepzig, Oct. 23, 1901, for one dollar. Copy in my possession.

15. Scharps, interview, April 26, 2014; Gloria Dene Rader Fry, telephone interview with author, April 17, 2014.

16. Fry, interview, April 17, 2014, Scharps, interview, April 26, 2014; and attachment to "Thomas Archibald Klepzig," in Vicki L. Tobias, "Rader Family," www.ancestry.com (accessed April 30, 2015). Thomas's youngest brother, Willis Luther Klepzig, lived in nearby Lake Charles, Louisiana, and witnessed Thomas's death certificate.

17. Arch Pummill, telephone interview with author, April 22, 2014.

18. *Shannon Herald*, Sept. 9, 1921; Gloria Dene Rader Fry, telephone interview with author, April 22, 2014. Apparently, Sam Rader sought to assist Clarence by allowing him to use his farm as the site for a farm sale. See *Current Wave*, Aug. 19, 1920. Before the Great Depression and the aban-

donment of his family, Allan Klepzig was apparently respected by his neighbors, for in 1930 he was elected constable of Delaware. See *Current Wave*, Nov. 20, 1930.

19. Sharpes, interview, April 26, 2014; and Fry, interview, April 22, 2014. For a description of Melton's death, see Bernard Asbell, "The Vanishing Hillbilly," *Saturday Evening Post* 234 (Sept. 31, 1961): 92.

20. For a discussion of Ozarks midwifery, see Janet Allured, "In Defense of Granny Women," *Ozarks Watch* 8 (1995): 9–12.

21. *Current Wave*, Sept. 21, 1939, Aug. 8, 1929; "Grandpa & Grandma" [Hulbert Rader] to grandchildren, undated, copy in my possession; Oscar Harper, "Delaware Community," US Works Progress Administration Historical Records Survey, Missouri, 1935–1942 (C3551), folder 2055, State Historical Society of Missouri, Columbia.

22. Quoted in *The Passerby*, June 4, 1934. At least one other member of her family appeared to be equally energetic. Reportedly, her daughter, Maudaline, walked 960 total miles back and forth to Delaware School from the Pummill farm in the 1934–35 school year and was never once tardy or absent. *Current Wave*, March 21, 1935.

23. The figure on canning comes from a letter by Arthur in *The Passerby*, Oct. 1933. Even after Faust moved his greenhouse to Willow Springs, Mayme, then fifty-five years old, on at least one occasion left Delaware and worked for him for a time. See *Current* Wave, April 1, 1943. For several weeks, she also moved to West Plains, Missouri, and helped care for my mother and her family while my mother was recovering from childbirth in 1948.

24. James Everett Pummill, *The Passerby*, March 7, 1933.

25. *Current Wave*, Jan. 13, 1938.

26. For a description of the persistence of traditional agricultural methods and means of survival in the Ozarks, see W. A. Browne, "Some Frontier Conditions in the Hilly Portion of the Ozarks," *Journal of Geography* 28 (May 1929): 181–88. This is based on Ozark, Taney, and Douglas Counties, all three of which were similar to Shannon County.

27. James Chilton, telephone interview with author, Aug. 4, 2014.

28. See, for example, *Current Wave*, July 7, 1927, and Dec. 15, 1928, in which he was paid by the county court, $39.50 and $47.75, respectively. See also Jerome Rader, (his nephew), interview with author, Aug. 16, 2011, notes in my possession.

29. *Current Wave*, April 5, 1934, Nov. 26, 1936.

30. In *The Passerby*, Oct. 5, 1936. While the Pummills were publicly known Republicans, most of the Raders probably voted for Roosevelt in 1932 and 1936. One of Arthur's daughters, Thelma, also benefitted from New Deal programs. See, for example, the *Shannon County Democrat*, March 22, Nov. 22, 1934, July 4, 1935, for her employment as a collector of data for the Civil Works Administration (CWA). For a time, Atlanta Pummill, Joe Pummill's wife, was in charge of the women's projects of the CWA in Birch Tree. See *Current Wave*, Dec. 21, 1933.

31. Warranty deed, from Ed and Bessie Perkins, Jake Perkins and Effie

Perkins, J. W. Perkins to A. L. Pummill, Oct. 5, 1928, copy in my possession; *Current Wave*, March 13, 1930.

32. Thela Winterbottom, "Remember When: Molasses Making Long Ago in the Ozarks," *Ozarker*, Oct. 1977–March 1978, 4. Within the past two years, the *Current Wave*, Jan. 27, 1938, reported that 22,230 acres of Shannon County farmland had been put into lespedeza.

33. *Current Wave*, Oct 4, 1928. Carl Ross, the popular vocational agriculture instructor at Eminence High School, may have been influential in convincing the Pummills to make chickens a major part of their farm program. In December of 1929 he taught an evening class on raising poultry at the Delaware schoolhouse. *Current Wave*, Dec. 19, 1929. For the 1936 figures, see *The Passerby*, April 15, 1936.

34. *Current Wave*, July 18, 1935.

35. Ibid., May 19, 1935; *The Passerby*, May 21, 1935; *Current Wave*, May 19, July 11, Aug. 13, 1936.

36. For several years, he served as secretary of the county extension service's annual convention, and in 1936 he contributed to a campaign to keep the local extension office open. See *Current Wave*, March 5 and 19, 1936.

37. *Current Wave*, Feb. 10, 1944.

38. See, for example, *Current Wave*, Dec. 11, 1930, May 28, 1931.

39. Winterbottom, "Remember When," 18.

40. *Current Wave*, Oct. 24, 1929. For later meetings, see *Current Wave*, Sept. 11, Oct. 9, 1930, Nov. 23, 1950; and Danny Searcy and James Chilton, phone conversations with author, Oct. 7, 2013.

15 ✦ Clashing Cultures

1. Based on information that Lowell passed on to Benjamin Rader.

2. *Current Wave*, Dec. 20, 1923.

3. "Lowell L. Rader," Individual Record, Civilian Conservation Corps, National Personnel Records Center, St. Louis, MO. Copy in my possession.

4. Much of the reconstruction of this paragraph and the ones that follow are based on the city directories for Prescott, Arizona, for the 1920s. These are located in the Sharlot Hall Archives, Prescott, Arizona.

5. While in later years Lowell was, in principle, a strict "teetotaler," he admitted to me having consumed alcoholic beverages as a younger man. To steel his nerves, he even told me that he had a drink of moonshine before his first date or perhaps it was the day he proposed to my mother, Lydia Eddings Rader. Many years later, I think in the early 1950s, he admitted that he had shared a glass of wine with the priest of the local Episcopal Church while doing some electrical work for the church in West Plains, Missouri. After his marriage to my mother in 1934, I know of no other times that he drank any kind of alcoholic beverage. Moreover, he repeatedly warned—directly or indirectly—his own children of the dangers of imbibing alcoholic beverages.

6. See the obituary of Joe R. Conteras, *Prescott Evening Courier*, March 29, 1948.

7. Lawrence Pummill and a family contingent visited the Rader brothers in Prescott in late August of 1929; it may have been then that they proposed that the brothers return to Shannon County and "cultivate the old Pummill farm" together. See *Current Wave,* Aug. 15, 1929; *Shannon County Democrat,* Feb. 5, 1930; *Current Wave,* Feb. 20, March 13, 1930.

8. See Elizabeth Hagens Herlinger, "A Historical, Cultural, and Organizational Analysis of Ozark Ethnic Identity" (PhD diss., University of Chicago, 1972), concerning acceptance of "outsiders" in Taney County, Missouri. The creek neighborhood also seemed to accept equally the family of Julius Lahmeyer. Julius was a first-generation German American.

9. Arch Pummill, notes from interview with author, Jan. 17, 2010. The date that they joined the church is unknown. It might have been on the occasion of one of two revivals in Delaware. See *Current Wave,* Aug. 14, 28, 1930, Nov. 19, 1931.

10. *Current Wave,* May 1, 1930.

11. See Milda "Biddy" Sconce, telephone interview with author, Dec. 21, 2011; and *Current Wave,* Dec. 24, 1931, Feb. 25, Aug. 25, 1932. The N.T.W. club apparently grew out of the national Delphian Society, an organization that published a set of books specifically designed for reading and discussion by women's groups.

12. "Missouri's Annual Crop and Livestock Production by Counties for 20-Year Period, 1919–1940," *Bulletin* [State Department of Agriculture] 40 (Dec. 31, 1942); *Current Wave,* Aug. 7, 1930.

13. *Current Wave,* Sept. 11, 1930.

14. Ibid., June 26, Oct. 9, 1930.

15. Ibid., Sept. 3, 1931.

16. Ibid., Dec. 10, 1931; *Shannon County Democrat,* Dec. 7, 1931.

17. Death certificate of Lawrence Lowell Rader Jr., attached to Vicki Tobias, "Rader Family," www.ancestry.com (accessed June 30, 2015); *Current Wave,* May 19, 1932.

18. *Current Wave,* March 3, 24, 31, 1932.

19. The last newspaper report of her presence in Missouri is a visit made by Mr. and Mrs. Lowell Rader to Winona in September 1932. *Shannon County Democrat,* Sept. 8, 1932.

20. *Current Wave,* Aug. 31, Sept. 21, 1933.

21. For purchase of the new car, see *Current Wave,* Aug. 10, 1933; for a reference to the trip by Hub, see *The Passerby,* Oct. 1933; Gloria Dene Rader Fry, telephone interview with author, June 4, 2014. Lowell's sister, Audrey Rader Herren, when touring the West with her family, also visited Rose briefly at least once after the divorce. Carl Herren, telephone interview with author, July 11, 2013. The Prescott city directory for 1935–36 listed a "Mrs. Rose Contreras, widow, [occupation] Spanish dishes, r. [residence] 125a North Granite Street." This is the last time that she appeared in the directory, at least under the name of Rose Contreras. At that time, she apparently lived in the same apartment house in which she and Lowell lived in 1929.

22. See *The Passerby,* Oct. 1933. Joe Pummill employed Wilma Davis to teach the third and fourth grades at Winona. Wilma also became a

good friend of Velma (Rader) Loyd and active in her social circle. See, for example, *Shannon County Democrat*, Sept. 1, 22, 1932; March 16, 1933.

23. *Current Wave*, Nov. 23, 1933; *Shannon County Democrat*, Nov. 30, 1933.

24. See Tobias, "Rader Family Tree"; but also indispensable is Family, "Eddings/George Family History," an unpublished manuscript of 207 pages in my possession that includes genealogy and reminiscences of family members. Especially important is that of Ruth Eddings Shelton, entitled "Alford's Story."

25. The most reliable research on the Eddings's Native American ancestry is that of Robert T. Eddings. See his communication of Oct. 14, 2000, http://freepages.genealogy.rootsweb.ancestry.com/everyoneged (/filessent/robert_t_eddings/daveweavernotes.html (accessed April 12, 2013).

26. See US Bureau of the Census, "Nonpopulation Census of Fifteen Southern States, Agricultural" (Wright County, Missouri, 1850), manuscripts in National Archives, microfilm copies in State Historical Society of Missouri, Columbia; "Descendants of John C. Eddings," http://family treemaker.genealogy.com/users/m/o/r/Jim-Albert-Morgan/PDFGENE1.pdf (accessed April 16, 2013).

27. Raz's folk medical practices closely resembled those found in the Ozarks in the 1930s by sociologist Walter Odro Cralle in "Social Change and Isolation in the Ozark Mountain Region of Missouri" (PhD diss., University of Minnesota, 1934), 179–87.

28. Sale advertisement of their farm equipment and livestock, *Current Wave*, Sept. 5, 1935; Ivy Eddings Shumate, notes from telephone interview with author, Aug. 13, 2012.

29. Lydia Rader to Anne Rader, Oct. 16, 1973, copy in my possession. See also Lydia Eddings Rader, "Trivia of the late 20's and early 30's from the Eddings farm on McHenry Holler near Ink, Missouri," no date, typewritten copy in my possession.

30. *Current Wave*, Aug. 2, 1934; "Monthly Average Temperatures, BIRCH TREE, MO," http://hprcc.unl.edu/cgi-bin/cliMAIN.pl?mo0688 (accessed April 20, 2015).

31. *The Passerby*, Oct. 10, 1934.

32. *Current Wave*, May 3, 1934.

33. "E. M. Rader Loan Requirements NO. 12, 14, 16, 17, 18, and 19, March 15, 1935"; "The Land Bank Commissioner, at St. Louis, Mo., Abstractor's Extension Service, E. M. Rader [June 1, 1935]"; "Requirement: No.141694 Shannon County, Missouri, 4332, Edward Martin Rader, [July 9, 1935]," copies in my possession; *The Passerby*, Dec. 15, 1934, Nov. 3, 1935. For a school bond loan to E. M. Rader, see *Current Wave*, June 17, 1937, and *Shannon County Democrat*, March 10, 1938.

34. For Lowell shopping alone via horseback in Eminence, see, for example, *The Passerby*, April 15, 1936. For their conflict over childrearing, see Shumate, interview. Iva remembered that Lowell would not permit their first child, me (the author), from sleeping on my stomach, that he insisted on a rigid toilet training, and that, when they were trying to get me to sleep

(even though I was crying), he refused to allow Lydia to pick me up. I also remember reports by my parents of me being an exceptionally irritable and sleepless child.

35. *The Passerby*, Oct. 10, 1934; *Current Wave*, Aug. 13, 1936, July 28, Aug. 18, 1938.

36. "Missouri's Annual Crop and Livestock Production by Counties for 20-Year Period, 1919–1940"; "Monthly Average Temperatures, BIRCH TREE, MO."

37. *Current Wave*, July 25, 1940.

38. Ibid,. Aug. 17, 1944.

16 ✦ When the Tribe Came Together

1. J. E. P[ummill], *The Passerby*, [August, 1932?].

2. *Current Wave*, July 14, 1932; and untitled and undated newspaper account attached to Vicki Tobias, "Rader Family Tree."

3. For example, *Shannon County Democrat*, March 17, 1911, reported that "about 50 people" attended an "excellent dinner" at the Delaware farm in honor of William Pummill's birthday. For Lawrence and turkey hunting, see *The Passerby*, Jan. 10, 1934.

4. Virginia "Ginny" Pummill (daughter of Lawrence and Crystal Pummill), phone interview with author, Oct. 14, 2012.

5. [Crystal Evans Pummill], "This Is the Story of Lawrence and Criss— Told Simply without Sham—And What Over Fifty Years of Togetherness, Brought to Them, 1912–1963," 52, unpublished manuscript, 1969, copy in my possession. Known to have stayed in their home for varying times in order to attend the normal school were Gilbert Rader, Audrey Rader, Dona Pummill, Arch Pummill, Thela Pummill, and Thelma Pummill.

6. See [Pummill], "This Is the Story of Lawrence and Criss," 63.

7. For descriptions of the reunion I rely mainly on the memories of Arch Pummill, digitally recorded interview with Jerome Rader, Sept. 18, 2010, and conversations with Gloria Dene Rader Fry; but also see appropriate copies of *The Passerby*, Sept. 2, 1937; and *Shannon County Democrat*, Aug. 25, 1938.

8. As a consequence of a steady income from his pension and sporadic jobs as a carpenter and a bookkeeper for a local store, as well as falling prices, Gilbert Rader and his family may have also experienced an improvement in their standard of living. The family regularly purchased new cars, and, for example, Gib was able to take a five-day fishing trip on the White River in the summer of 1939. See *Current Wave*, July 27, 1939.

9. *The Passerby*, Feb. 4, 1939.

10. Ibid., Dec. 6, 1932, Sept. 3, 1936.

11. Ibid., July 10, 1935. Thelma served in a variety of federal government posts, including the Social Security Administration and the Office of Price Administration. See *Current Wave*, July 31, 1941, Jan. 15, June 4, 1942, June 3, 1943.

12. *The Passerby*, Aug. 10, 1937; *Shannon County Democrat*, July 21,

1941, June 4, 1942. In [March? 1939], *The Passerby* reported that "Gib, Lowell, and our own W.P.A. worker have been putting the hill road [into the old Pummill farm] into shape." This was apparently the road connecting the farm to State Highway E. While living there, Gib also made other improvements on the "old farmstead" in the spring of 1939. See *The Passerby*, [Dec, 1939 or Jan. 1940?].

13. See *The Passerby*, Jan. 10, 1934, Oct. 6, 1935.

14. See *Current Wave*, Oct. 31, 1946. Hub's wife, Wilma, was elected and reelected as Delaware's Democratic committeewoman from 1940 through 1952. *Current Wave*, Aug. 22, 1940, July 15, 1948, and July 13, 1950.

15. *Current Wave*, Dec. 21, 1939; *Shannon County Democrat*, Jan. 18, 1940.

16. *The Passerby*, [Dec. 1939 or Jan. 1940]; *Current Wave*, Feb. 4, 1943. Apparently, sometime in the late 1930s, Joe Pummill obtained complete ownership of the farm. Then, in 1938, he swapped half of it to Gilbert and Dene Rader for land that they owned south of Eminence. See "Warranty Deed," Joseph G. Pummill and Lucy Atlanta Pummill to Gilbert and Udene Young Rader, March 5, 1938. It was on this land that the Joe Pummill's built their new home. See "Warranty Deed," Joseph G. Pummill and Lucy Atlanta Pummill, his wife, and Gilbert L. Rader and Udene Young Rader, his wife, transferring the property to D. D. Baxter in exchange for a mortgage of $2,600, Nov. 28, 1942. Copies in my possession. I would like to thank Lucille (Pummill) Orchard and Gloria Dene (Rader) Fry for assistance in untangling this matter.

Epilogue + "The Creek Has Changed a Lot since Then"

1. Oscar Harper, "A Trip into Yesterday," *Ozarker*, Spring 1975, 12. See also Joseph G. Pummill's description of changes in the creek in the *Current Wave*, March 14, 1946. For information in this chapter, I am especially indebted to Lucille (Pummill) Orchard, James Chilton, and Tom Akers, as well as to Jerome, Jon Maxwell, and Jayne Rader. The latter three are offspring of Hulbert and Wilma Rader.

2. Audrey (Rader) Herren to folks (a family round-robin letter), June 12, 1949, copy of letter in my possession.

3. *Current Wave*, April 18, 1929.

4. Audrey (Rader) Herren to folks, June 12, 1949. For evidence of his love of the "wilderness" but simultaneously his desire to see it "used," see Hulbert Rader, "Wilderness Land Should Be Used, But Wisely," *Springfield Leader and Press*, Jan. 16, 1983.

5. See "Wilma Marie Davis," in Vicki Tobias, "Rader Family"

6. Jon Maxwell Rader to Ben Rader, [Aug., 2015], copy of letter in my possession.

7. Hub Rader to folks, May 8, 1949, copy of letter in my possession. He retained twenty-seven head of mature hogs plus twenty-one small pigs.

8. See Paul K. Conkin, *A Revolution Down on the Farm: The Transformation of American Agriculture since 1929* (Lexington: University Press

of Kentucky, 2010); *Current Wave,* June 26, 1952; data from the decennial *USDA Census of Agriculture,* www.agcensus.usda.gov/ (accessed Oct. 16, 2014). In earlier decades, it was not unusual for Shannon County farmers to plant in excess of 15,000 acres of corn. Historically, the county had more open range acreage than any other Missouri county. See Allen Brown and Thomas S. Baskett, "Free Livestock Range in Missouri," *University of Missouri Agricultural Experiment Station* (Jan. 1961); and *Current Wave,* Jan. 16, 1969.

9. Since Wilma never learned to drive, this was literally true, but Hub apparently borrowed the joke from Dolly Parton's song "He Is a Go Get Her," in her 1969 album, *In the Good Old Days.* Conscious of a general trend throughout the Upland South of rural women taking jobs in nearby towns, Parton went ahead to sing, "His wife holds down a steady job, he don't turn his hand all day."

10. See *Current Wave,* Jan. 24, 1946, May 15, 1947, Sept. 2, 1948, March 31, 1949. Sixty-two persons attended a neighborhood supper at Alley Spring in 1945. See *Current Wave,* July 12, 1945.

11. Thela (Pummill) Winterbottom, "Delaware School," *Ozarker,* Aug. 1978, 9. See also the conclusion of another one-room schoolteacher, C. J. Sizemore, in *Current Wave,* Aug. 26, 1948. Thela Winterbottom, "The New Harmony Church," *Ozarker,* April 1978, 4, wrote in similar terms about the New Harmony Baptist Church.

12. Friends of the Shannon County Libraries, Eminence, Missouri, *History of Shannon County Missouri 1986* (Dallas, TX: Taylor Pub. Co., 1986), 19.

13. *Current Wave,* Nov. 23, 1950.

14. In 2000 Shannon County was the most impoverished in the state of Missouri. Nationwide, it ranked forty-sixth on the list of counties with the lowest household median income. See http://quickfacts.census.gov/qfd/states/29/29203.html and https://www.census.gov/hhes/www/poverty/data/census/1960/(accessed Oct. 20, 2014). While not ascribing poverty specifically to hollows, Kathleen Blakeny Morrison attributes the protracted poverty in Shannon County primarily to its remoteness. See Kathleen Blakeny Morrison, "The Poverty of Place: A Comparative Study of Five Rural Counties in the Missouri Ozarks" (PhD diss., University of Missouri–Columbia, 1999).

15. *Current Wave,* Jan. 13, 1950. See nearly all of issues of the *Shannon County Historical Review* as well as the *Ozarker.*

16. Quoted in Bernard Asbell, "The Vanishing Hillbilly," *Saturday Evening Post* 234 (Sept. 23, 1961): 94. See also Susan Flader, "The Legacy of Neglect: The Ozark National Scenic Riverways," *George Wright Forum* 28 (2011): 114–26; and http://www.georgewright.org/282flader.pdf (accessed Oct. 21, 2014); and Will Sarvis, "A Difficult Legacy: Creation of the Ozarks Scenic Riverways," *Public Historian* 24 (Winter 2002): 31–52. Sarvis observes that the creation of the protected riverways entails contradictory objectives inasmuch as it seeks to accommodate, on the one hand, thousands of tourists but, on the other hand, to protect the area's sensitive physical habitat.

17. See *Current Wave*, June 26, 1946, Jan. 13, 1950; Friends of the Library, *History of Shannon County Missouri 2001* (Eminence, MO: Friends of the Library, 2001), 68–74; *Current Wave*, June 26, 1946; Tom Akers, phone interview with author, April 18, 2015. For statistics on park use, see https://irma.nps.gov/Stats/SSRSReports/Park%20Specific%20Reports/Annual%20Park%20Recreation%20Visitation%20%281904%20-%20Last%20Calendar%20Year%29?Park=OZAR (accessed July 1, 2015).

18. There is, in fact, a historic "Rocky Creek" in Shannon County, but it is south and east of Mahans Creek. "Shannon County Place Names," http://shs.umsystem.edu/manuscripts/ramsay/ramsay_shannon.html (accessed July 1, 2015).

19. *The Passerby*, Jan. 4, 1933.

INDEX

BENJAMIN RADER is James L. Sellers Professor of History, emeritus, at the University of Nebraska–Lincoln and the author of five books, including *Baseball: A History of America's Game.* He was born and raised in the Mahans Creek neighborhood and today lives in Lincoln, Nebraska.